Ambassador to a Small World

MEMOIRS AND OCCASIONAL PAPERS
ASSOCIATION FOR DIPLOMATIC STUDIES
AND TRAINING

Series Editor: MARGERY BOICHEL THOMPSON

In 2003, the Association for Diplomatic Studies and Training (ADST) created the Memoirs and Occasional Papers Series to preserve firsthand accounts and other informed observations on foreign affairs for scholars, journalists, and the general public. Sponsoring publication of book series is one of numerous ways in which ADST, a nonprofit organization founded in 1986, seeks to promote understanding of American diplomacy and those who conduct it. Together with the Foreign Affairs Oral History program and ADST's support for the training of foreign affairs personnel at the State Department's Foreign Service Institute, these efforts constitute the Association's fundamental purposes. Christopher E. Goldthwait's *Ambassador to a Small World* is the twenty-seventh volume in the series.

OTHER SERIES TITLES

Claudia Anyaso, ed., *Fifty Years of US Africa Policy*
Diego and Nancy Asencio, *The Joys and Perils of Serving Abroad: Memoirs of a US Foreign Service Family*
Janet C. Ballantyne and Maureen Dugan, eds., *Fifty Years in USAID: Stories from the Front Lines*
Thompson Buchanan, *Mossy Memoir of a Rolling Stone*
John Gunther Dean, *Danger Zones: A Diplomat's Fight for America's Interests*
Robert E. Gribbin, *In the Aftermath of Genocide: The US Role in Rwanda*
Allen C. Hansen, *Nine Lives: A Foreign Service Odyssey*
Robert Kemp, *Counterinsurgency in Eastern Afghanistan 2004–2008: A Civilian Perspectve*
John G. Kormann, *Echoes of a Distant Clarion: Recollections of a Diplomat and Soldier*
Nicole Prévost Logan, *Forever on the Road: A Franco-American Family's Thirty Years in the Foreign Service*
Armin Meyer, *Quiet Diplomacy: From Cairo to Tokyo in the Twilight of Imperialism*
William Morgan and Charles Stuart Kennedy, eds., *American Diplomats: The Foreign Service at Work*
Ludwig Rudel, *Memoirs of an Agent for Change in International Development*
Howard Steele, *Bushels and Bales: A Food Soldier in the Cold War*
Theresa Tull, *A Long Way from Runnemede: One Woman's Foreign Service Journey*
Daniel Whitman, *A Haiti Chronicle: The Undoing of a Latent Democracy, 1999–2001*
Susan Wyatt, *Arabian Nights and Daze: Living in Yemen with the Foreign Service*
Virginia Carson Young, *Peregrina: Unexpected Adventures of an American Consul*

For a complete list of series titles, visit *adst.org/publications/*.

Ambassador to a Small World

Letters from Chad

Christopher E. Goldthwait

MEMOIRS AND OCCASIONAL PAPERS SERIES
ASSOCIATION FOR DIPLOMATIC STUDIES AND TRAINING

Washington, DC

New Academia Publishing/Vellum Books 2015

The opinions and characterizations in this book are those of the author and do not necessarily represent official positions of the Government of the United States or the Association for Diplomatic Studies and Training. Unless otherwise indicated, the photographs in this book were taken by the author or by Les McBride for the Department of State.

Printed in the United States of America

Library of Congress Control Number: 2015942055
ISBN 978-0-9864353-6-2 paperback (alk. paper)
ISBN 978-0-9864353-7-9 hardcover (alk. paper)

 An imprint of New Academia Publishing

 New Academia Publishing
P.O. Box 24720, Washington, DC 20038-7420
info@newacademia.com - www.newacademia.com

For Les McBride,
who was my geographic and cultural guide to Chad,
as he was for so many other American ambassadors there.

Contents

Preface

In the Guéra, in central Chad, sprout many odd rock formations. Out of the dry, pancake-flat land, hills and mountains rise abruptly, reddish-brown and gray piles that contrast as sharply with the beige soil of the wide Sahel as they do with the bluebird sky. As you roll along the rough dirt roads, you are tempted to stop and climb the lower escarpments, chimney-like formations that would warrant a national monument back home. Here, and again in a few miles, you will see one that seems to defy gravity itself, a huge flat boulder perched upon a slender spindle of stones, and you wonder that it does not fall. We might call them teeterstones.

Stark, barren, and windswept, the chimneys give nothing easily. The top-heavy superstructure thirty or forty feet up is built on a poor base and seems liable to tumble at any moment. There is no clue to what may, or may not, ensue. But somehow the rocks don't fall. We may climb among them and still our disturbance doesn't send them careening down. Whatever it is that holds them up is masked from us by the dark shadows the stones cast over their roots. It is hard to correct what nature has done half well, and perhaps we shouldn't try.

After four and a half years in Chad, these natural phenomena became for me a metaphor for the country itself. Riven by faults Chad itself endures, seeming also to defy gravity. The fissures are mainly North-South: Muslim-Christian, poorly and better educated, herder-farmer, Arab-Bantu ethnicity, Sahara/Sahel and moist climatic zones. The country almost always has an insurgency brewing. Factions fight over it, but no one wants to break it up. In over fifty years of tumultuous, conflict-ridden independence, a sense of the Chadian has emerged and grown; yet like the chimneys, it remains precarious. Chad teeters precariously, but it doesn't break apart. Its pith is of hard stone.

The Letters

Ambassador to a Small World is my reflection upon nearly four and a half years spent as the US ambassador to Chad, a country in the heart of Central Africa, little known in the United States before the Darfur crisis. The book is a series of forty-five letters that I sent to a dozen close friends, roughly monthly, and one written a week or two after returning Stateside. They are not in any sense a history of the country's major political, economic, and social events during this period (1999 to 2004), though I touch on these frequently. Nor do the letters constitute a traditional memoir.

I'm not quite sure what I had in mind when I began these letters to friends. They started as travelogue mostly, an effort to recount my interesting experiences. Thumbing back through the early ones, I see that they try to convey some sense of the country, its sights, sounds, smells, and so on. But before long, the work began to take on a life of its own. The letters became more analytical, dwelling on a problem facing the country or on an aspect of life here. Ultimately, they became more introspective. Even before the last three or four wrap-up letters, I sensed that I was trying to convey to my readers what my experience here has meant to me, what I take away from Chad. They are my effort to understand and draw a word picture of the country and its people. Moreover, they encompass what the people of this indigent nation taught me during that time.

Thematically, the most obvious thread is what I've said above: The country holds together. Second, I became intensely fascinated by the contrasts I saw everywhere around me in Chad: the sophisticated elite, graduates of the best French universities, versus subsistence farmers and herders whose lives are little different from those of their ancestors three or four thousand years ago; the Mercedes dodging potholes on an unpaved street of N'Djamena, swerving to avoid a camel.

My third theme grew with time as well: how people with so little made so rich a life for themselves. My admiration for them deepened as I traveled and received their meager, intensely warm hospitality in remote villages. We talked about their lives and needs as we ate from the common pot. I visited their strained and undersupplied schools, orphanages, and hospitals, and attended their wakes and public ceremonies in villages, towns, and the capital.

Last, everything is starker in Chad. The little that one really needs to exist, food and shelter, is all that most Chadians have. Death comes swiftly and unexpectedly. The gulf between rich and poor, ease and misery, is wide. In America, *Les Miserables* was a hit because it portrayed these things with empathy. In Chad, you live them.

I say in one letter toward the end that I began to feel like a voyeur as I studied these people. But more important, I began to see how much I had learned from them, and how much the West has to learn from poorer countries. To paraphrase the rite of Communion, we who are many are one when we share the same bread. I hope you will see through these letters what I came to value and respect in this country, small in population but large in geography and heart.

Even to those of whom I'm critical, I render a certain respect for coping with adversity. It didn't take long for me to see that all aspects of life are more barefaced here than at home—greed, poverty, hatred, disease, death, honor, friendship, and love. And more and more as time passed, beneath all my conclusions about political and economic development, I realized that the real fascination and lesson of life in Chad arose from that miraculous combination of good and evil that we call human nature. If these epistles convey to you a fraction of what I have seen and felt, they have been worth my effort.

I would ask the reader also to remember the original audience for the letters, my ten closest friends and relatives—hence the tongue-in-cheek signature "Ambassador Chris" and hence my directness. I speak frankly of my frustrations as an ambassador in a "presence post" and of the lack of aid resources that would have given me a stronger voice with the Chadians. I discuss as well the ways in which the ambassadorial lifestyle was not always the best fit for someone who deeply values privacy, and my decision not to seek a second ambassadorship. I suspect that many ambassadors share my views of the often tedious nature of protocol, necessary as it is. I offer no comment on my critique of US policy toward Africa, and Western development policy in general. I believe that I was on target then, and adjustments in policy, especially development policy, in the decade after I left Chad support my views.

The letters are organized into thematic chapters. For anyone who may care to read the letters in the order in which they were written, a chronological listing follows this preface.

Chad in the Shadow of History

What should I tell you of Chad by way of introduction, for it is unlikely you know more than a quick glance at the map will tell? I could begin by saying that both nature and history have dealt Yarboroughs to Chad.

Nature's blow is easily seen. The country is isolated, poor in natural resources, harsh of climate. It is mostly desert and Sahelian scrub. The colonial French dismissed 90 percent of it backhandedly by referring to the southern tip as *"le Tchad utile,"* or the useful Chad. But the balance isn't quite so lopsided, for Chad does have ample water in the rainy season, and now another precious liquid, oil, will flow as well. Neither attribute may be an ace, but both are face cards.

History's curse is less leavened. Here too we must begin with geography, for Chad's vast, flat plains, dead center in the continent, have made the country a crossroads, a land through which men moved and traded and raided slaves, but where the environment enticed few to settle. Those that did were remnants of many peoples, and only in the nineteenth century did population pressures push more people to try to make a life here. By then different parts of Chad were incorporated into three of Africa's great Sahelian empires: Kanem-Bornu, Ouaddai, and Bagirmi. It was not enough that these states were often at war, but slavers and raiders swept through periodically. Chad's nine million people today reflect all this diversity of origin. Among them are more than 120 languages from four of Africa's five language families. Sadly, the differences in origin and the long history of conflict imply tremendous ethnic tensions within the country's artificial borders.

The colonial era that limned those borders was also born in blood. One of three French columns of *tirailleurs* sent to secure Chad, this one led from Senegal by the sadistic French captains Voulet and Chanoine, was responsible for one of the most reprehensible episodes in African colonialism: The troops murdered, burned, and raped their way across West Africa until the exhausted native troops turned on their French officers and killed them in what is now central Niger. When the Lamy column, coming down from Algeria, finally reached the Chad basin, its first stroke was the defeat of the upstart local chief Rabah, in the Battle of Koussérie. The violence and bloodshed continued with the suppression of various revolts in the north and the forcible resettlement and introduction of cotton farming in the south, during the first decades of French rule.

Nor did Chad's independence in 1960 bring relief, for within five years revolt was brewing, and the country dissolved into civil war that continued off and on for nearly thirty years, until the current regime consolidated its power in the early 1990s. And yet, upon this wicked past the Chadians are beginning now to construct a nation.

What Chad Taught Me

A person learns so much from spending four and a half years in a foreign culture that it is nearly impossible to extract in a few lines the essence of those lessons. I will try, however, to highlight a few themes that may echo as you read through the letters.

At the most basic, I saw the stark contrasts in life more sharply here than at home. Poverty, hunger, violence, death—all are omnipresent and visible. There is not even a television screen between you and the suffering.

On the other hand, I was enormously impressed by how dynamic a life the Chadians made on their narrow resource base. Most still live in mud-brick homes that are hovels by American standards. But they have an amazingly diverse and dynamic culture, with rich religious beliefs, customs, and ceremonies that are like the teeter stones perched upon a narrow base. They also have leisure to rest in the torpid afternoon and time for social interchange, a comforting routinized pace of life that eludes those of us married to cell phones and constant access.

On a more professional note, I saw how misguided much of the Western approach to economic and political development has been. Multiparty democracy, for example, cannot succeed if there is not enough of an economic base to support multiple, competing national parties. After a year in Chad, I was aghast when a senior State Department official (higher ranked now in the second Obama administration) told me with a straight face that we could expect functioning multiparty democracies in African countries within a decade without this economic foundation.

On the contrary, I believe we forget our own history. In America, democracy grew to its present strength over two centuries. We began with a narrow republican base that expanded gradually, with major blocs of people—women, people of color—winning the vote a century or more later. In fact, only with the enforcement of the Civil Rights Act of 1964 did we have real democracy. Africa can move more quickly, but not overnight. We do it no service to push it faster than our own experience suggests is prudent.

Last, turning to economic development, I saw enormous waste and a bloated, expensive, top-heavy development industry. Most effective are those small projects, the self-help projects I saw and described in letters, that have grassroots commitment and contributions. These, to my mind, have more impact than all of the studies, capacity-building exercises, and expensive implementation schemes of most development projects. There are serious issues of scalability here, of course, but how much more effective the $20,000 self-help efforts are than those dependent on $250,000-per-year expat staff. The great exception may be road construction.

This only scratches the surface of what Chad and the Chadians taught me. Much more, I hope, will be evident as you peruse the letters.

THE CHAD LETTERS IN THEIR ORIGINAL CHRONOLOGY

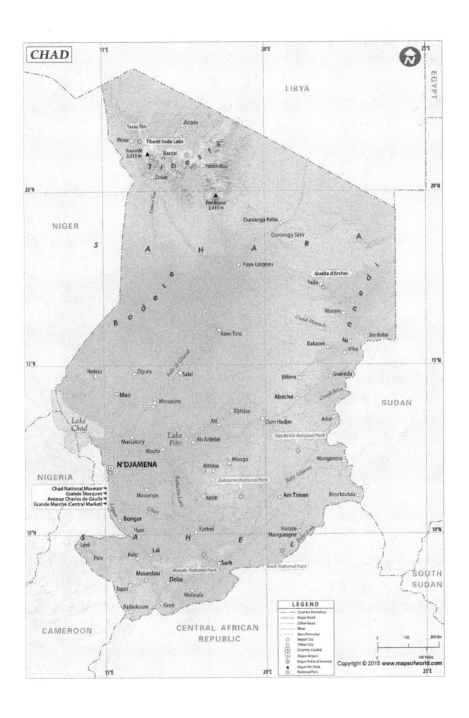

CHAD

15°E   20°E   25°E

LIBYA

EGYPT

Terso Tôh   Aozou

Wour   Tibesti Soda Lake

Toussidé   Bardaï
3.315 m

T i b e s t i   Yebbi-Bou

Zouar

20°N   20°N

NIGER

S   A   H   Emi Koussi   A
3.415 m

Ounianga Kébir

Ounianga Sérir   R

Faya-Largeau

Guelta d'Archeï

Fada

B   Monou
o
d   Ouadi Howach   e
e   Berdoba
l   Koro Toro   Bakaoré
e   Iriba   n
n   i

15°N   Nokou   Biltine   Guéréda   15°N
Ziguey   Salal
Mao   Abéché   Ouadi Bitea
Moussoro   Djédaa
Ati   Oum Hadjer   Adré

Lake   Djédaa   Goz Beïda National Park
Chad
Massakory   Lake   Ati Ardébé
Fitri
Moyto   Mongo   Mongororo

N'DJAMENA   Bitkine   Baly Salamat

Chad National Museum   Zakouma National Park
Grande Mosquee   Massenya   Melfi   Am Timan   Bourtoutou
Avenue Charles de Gaulle
Grande Marche (Central Market)

Bongor   Korbol   Haraze
Ham   Mangueigne   L

10°N   Léré   S   A   H   E   10°N
Pala   Kelo   Laï
Sarh   Aouk National Park   SOUTH
Moundou   SUDAN
Tapol   Doba   Manda National Park

Baïbokoum   Goré   Moissala

CAMEROON   CENTRAL AFRICAN
REPUBLIC

SUDAN

NIGERIA

LEGEND
- - - Country Boundary
—— Major Road
----- Other Road
----- River
----- Non-Perennial
o Major City
○ Other City
☐ Country Capital
⊕ Major Airport
◉ Major Point of Interest
▲ Major Mt. Peak
◉ National Park

0   100   200 Km

0   100 Miles

15°E   20°E   25°E

Ambassador to a Small World

Letters from Chad

1

Living the Life as Ambassador
to a Small World

My book title calls Chad a small world. It is anything but a small country; it is one of the largest in Africa, the size of California, Nevada, Oregon, and Washington. But the country is landlocked, isolated, and 80 percent of its people lead life at the subsistence level in their own self-contained world. They are subsistence farmers and herders, their village and its vicinity or their annual trek limiting their horizons. Cell phones are opening things up a little, but during my years in Chad the linkages of most of these folks to the outside were limited to purchases of a little tea and sugar, and perhaps RFI, the French radio broadcasts. Their world is small geographically, although not culturally.

At the beginning of my tour in Chad I faced a choice in how to approach my assignment. I could focus mainly on official life in the capital, or I could try to be an ambassador to that small world beyond, to bring a touch of the United States to people in the hinterland through travel and outreach. The latter was, of course, my choice, and my efforts and trips are much of what I relate in these letters.

In this chapter, I have grouped the letters that tell more about my daily life in N'Djamena. What is life like for an ambassador heading a small embassy? Private life? Professional life? Who do you spend time with, business and personal? How is a small "presence post" different from a larger one? This first, and maybe most amorphous, group of letters comprises the ones that don't fit neatly elsewhere, the ones that shed light on questions that, like the ones above, are rarely posed until after the fact.

Let's start with the obvious: Ambassador or not, life for an American in Chad is very, very different from life at home. The hardship is not danger; for the most part, the streets were safe for daylight walking. Nor is it a lack of creature comforts, for the embassy expends an enormous amount of energy to maintain our houses and ensure that we have water and generator power to drive the air conditioning and VCR. The hardship is lack of diversions: no movie theater, only half a dozen restaurants, only rarely any Western live music. It was hard to befriend Chadians. For my colleagues who spoke no French, circles were further constrained to embassy folk, a handful of anglophone missionaries, and some Exxon oilmen. Even for the francophone, you can attend only so many formal dinner parties and afternoon cookouts with the same small group before they too become boring.

The answer was for us to find inventive ways of making our own entertainment. Our marines one year went all out with a horror house at Halloween. We did Christmas up big, and Saturday morning softball became a tradition. I hosted a "Decades Party" featuring forty years of hit music, from my generation to that of the junior officers. Some people kept to themselves, and therefore they don't appear often in these pages. They had their videos and eventually satellite TV, secluded dinners, and drinking bouts.

You will see in the letters that I participated actively in the American community events, hosting many at the residence at personal expense, and trying as well to mix Americans with other expats and Chadians. That was business—morale boosting—as well as social life. But the people I called "almost friends" (a careful term) were from outside the embassy: a couple of missionary families, some German diplomats, and some expat business people. I tried to husband a few weekday evenings and Sundays after church for personal time, along with exercise time—tennis or my weight bench—right after work. This was a mixed success.

One thing I learned, reluctantly, was that the American ambassador could never remain anonymous in the small world of Chad. "Jogging in N'Djamena and Giving Blood" tells it all. During my

o-dark-hundred-hour jogs, I was still "Excellence" and under surveillance. When I gave blood for Chadians, it was front-page news.

These letters also introduce you to the wide range of my business contacts. In this small world, the American ambassador has
access to everyone who is anyone, and to anyone else who interests
him, as well. The first letters quickly reveal the standard range of
contacts: government ministers, national leaders in education and
health, opposition politicians, and so on. But I also found myself to
be the only non-Moslem guest at Ramadan Iftars, and I made a special effort to reach out to business leaders, both Chadian and expat.

Here and there in this first group of letters, you may sense that I
didn't think I had enough to do. This was the dilemma of the "presence post," a term that I, a non–State Department type, heard for
the first time when I returned to DC on consultation after my first
full year in Chad. After I'd been at post about three months, I dug
out my predecessor's schedule for his last year and found that he
had not been out and about as much as I. The problem was how to
be active and do outreach without exciting expectations for aid that
you knew you couldn't fulfill. My solution was to attend events
around N'Djamena that most ambassadors would delegate to others, to reach out to nontraditional contacts such as business people
and senior clergy, and to carry the American flag to the hinterland.
Occasionally, however, a day would come when I really felt like an
ambassador performing the full role—see "A Day in the Life ..."

"Being the Ambassador: Three Sides of a Coin" is my reflection on life as ambassador to Chad. Written a few months before
my anticipated departure, its conclusions remained unaltered by
the additional year plus that I ended up remaining in country. I
complain first of all the paltry stuff, such as lack of privacy and the
like. More important are the frustrations of managing a so-called
presence post. The State Department freely admitted that it had no
agenda in Chad, but I was supposed to make first-term junior officers think we did. On the other hand, I had an intimate knowledge of Chad and all its workings, something unachievable in even
slightly larger posts where the United States does field an agenda.
The experience was unparalleled, but you will read why I didn't
seek to repeat it.

Letters from Chad...
Or, More Than You Ever Wanted to Hear

November 1, 1999 (All Saints Day)

As I begin this letter, I hear the muezzin's call to midday prayer, barely perceptible across the city. I'm seated comfortably by the pool with the verdant garden as background. The large tree I see above the embassy wall is tall and scraggly, and will be covered with hundreds of nesting egrets at dusk. Behind the wall that separates my compound from the Chari River the family of the local guard are squatting, making their rude home in the open now that the rains have passed. Such is Chad. I will essay to write a chronicle of observations monthly. This initial one is likely to be one of the longer ones.

First Impressions

My Air France flight left Paris more than an hour late, the delay apparently to allow the party of a Chadian minister to board at their convenience. Welcome back to Africa. The flight was comfortable enough, business class about half full. Upon arriving at Chad's international airport it seemed like I was back in northern Nigeria — an old facility to receive the half-dozen or so scheduled weekly flights; a modern VIP lounge to which the Foreign Ministry's director of protocol whisked me after a cordial greeting at the foot of the gangway. There were tea and soft drinks, a few cordial remarks to allow me to begin using my French, and an introduction to not one but two ministers who had flown in on my flight with me. The minister of transport, it seemed, was the tardy one, returning from Secretary Slater's conference for African transportation ministers in Atlanta.

N'Djamena struck me at once as a nothing city. Old Nigeria hands will know what I mean if I say that it made Kaduna look like London. Now, three weeks later, that all seems so distant and I am noticing the cleaner structures behind the rundown compound walls and can contrast the urban squalor favorably with the even more destitute country villages a few miles away. But the city is largely built of mud adobe; the bricks are formed and sun-dried, and survive perhaps a decade of the annual rains before needing to be restored. I've still seen only a tiny portion of the conurbation of 700,000, and in the less densely inhabited administrative zone where I travel, it is hard to believe that so large a population exists here.

A Cyclical Climate

Despite the somewhat uniform temperatures (very warm to very hot), the year here has a definite pattern. More so, perhaps, than Lagos, where I lived for four years. The demarcations are not just in weather but also in fauna, and more than anything else the presence of water. And the water does spread over vast areas of the countryside. I could see it standing in huge pools from the air. The river behind the house is a mile wide; months from now, I'm told, it will contract to a trickle. The egrets are fond of certain types of trees, a couple of which are in the front of the embassy and my own compounds. They return at night by the hundreds, and in the dusk they dot the mass of the trees like the Milky Way. Their calls are obnoxious for an hour or two until they sleep, but not nearly so obnoxious as the guano they leave beneath. I'm told I missed the worst of it, but the sweepers who clean it up daily wear face masks.

And why do the egrets come? To eat insects, which undergo a population explosion when the fields and riverbanks flood. Flies, dragonflies, mosquitoes, crickets, grasshoppers, and a hundred unknown varieties thrive. They make the extremely pleasant gardens uninhabitable during certain parts of the day. But they too are a season, and there are remarkably fewer of them today than when I arrived.

Now I'm told the pleasant season is beginning. For a sun lover, it is indeed delightful—clear skies broken by only a few wispy clouds, highs in the mid-80s (Fahrenheit). I'm told it will become a bit cooler over the next couple of months (we are, after all, in the northern latitudes by a degree or two), and then after January or February begin to warm again. For now it seems like spring or early summer in my childhood northern California. And when it warms? It will become very hot—highs of 115 F are not unusual from May through June until it rains again and the heat breaks.

Birds and Lizards

I'm looking across the lawn at yet another species of bird I hadn't noticed before. Black head, white throat and forequarters, robin-orange breast, and black wings and back. Bigger than a robin, but hopping across the grass not unlike one. Earlier this morning I saw a blue-headed, greenish bird just a little bigger and less fluttery than a hummingbird in the lime trees by the pool. There are hundreds of unfamiliar varieties here. No wonder the former ambassador became a bird watcher and tried to catalogue the species he saw. Among the standards here at the house are some pigeon-like birds that sit at the edge of the roof. They have brownish wings but a soft blue head and undercarriage. Because of the way they sit looking out onto the yard, I call them my sentinels. Yesterday, up at Lake Chad, I saw the marvelous weaverbirds—shockingly bright yellow with black heads. They build bulbous nests about four inches in diameter and hang them from the stalks of the tall reeds that cover most of the lake.

And lizards and geckos! Life in Africa wouldn't be complete without them. They inhabit the yard by the hundreds, again drawn by the insects, undoubtedly. There are numerous varieties. I'm told that two huge ones, two feet long before counting the tail, inhabit the embassy grounds and were under the special protection of the former ambassador (and now, by default, me). I haven't seen them yet. Occasionally the little critters find their way indoors. But they haven't been bothersome.

House and Staff

The residence is comfortable of course. It isn't all that big, as ambassadors' houses go, but is bigger than it seems. It consists of a huge living room, a good-sized dining room, five bedrooms, a kitchen, and numerous bathrooms. I've been trying to compare it in total square feet to my house on Porter Street. It has fewer rooms, but the rooms are very large, and to match the square footage I need to count both the finished attic and unfinished basement at Porter Street. The house is equipped with everything anyone could ever want, from sheets and towels right through to gourmet kitchenware.

It is difficult getting used to the servants, never having had them in my house before. In addition to the two gardeners, there are three household staff plus a cook. I can't begin to keep them busy. It is also a little disconcerting to have them around all the time, except on Sundays. When I get up in the morning, one of them has breakfast ready to serve. When I get home in the evening, the cook is there with dinner. I have to remember to tell him if I'm not going to come home at lunch or if I'm going out in the evening. And it seems odd to be served dinner at table with several courses, on gold-leaf plate, when I'm eating alone and reading at the table. But that seems to be the only way they know, so I "tolerate" it. The cook is brand new—he was waiting to be interviewed for the job as soon as I walked off the plane and got to the house. He is great, a first-class French chef for about $150 per month. But I will need to work with him to emphasize *la cuisine minceur*. In a combination of European and African tastes, all the cooking here is heavy with cream, cheese, and oil. Especially oil. Indeed, between the week in Europe en route and my first two weeks here, I found I'd regained five of the pounds I'd lost and I'm struggling to get it back off again.

The Embassy

I am fortunate to have a top-flight American staff at the embassy, and numerous experienced Chadians and third-country nationals as well. On the American side, it is basically a new group—only a couple of folks have been here as long as a year. These are notably disenchanted with the Chadians, in contrast to the rest of us. It is important in a small embassy to keep up morale, and I'm devoting great amounts of time to attending all the events of the American community (i.e., the twenty-five embassy staff plus a couple dozen missionaries around town), which means mainly going to events at the Marine House and the American Club. At the Marine House on Saturday evening, for example, we had a haunted house for Halloween. It was about the best I've ever seen. One of the marines led all the kids through in groups of three or four, and each of the other marines, plus a couple of other American staff, were dressed as Frankenstein, Dracula, etc. It would have been genuinely frightening to anyone not expecting it. And as an added touch, on the way out we were shown several graves that had been dug in the garden—for me, the DCM [deputy chief of mission], the gunny, and the regional security officer! On a more professional note, I've been having each of the American staff over for a get-acquainted lunch, and it really is a talented group of people with a broad range of interests.

The embassy structure is a converted two-story house immediately adjacent to my residence. It has a slightly larger compound in which there are several outbuildings. Maintenance offices and warehouses are at a remote location. All in all, the place is in amazingly good condition, considering the supply line. The communications side has been a problem, but we have three top-notch specialists, all just arrived, who are moving mountains to get that in shape. (One of the great tests will come later this afternoon when I see if, after four visits from Poste et Telegraphe du Tchad and two by these American staff, my email at home is finally up and running!)

Seeing Something of Chad

I've made two trips so far, on the theory that getting out into the country is important right off the bat. My first trip was to Doba to the petroleum project that everyone thinks will be Chad's salvation. We had Washington visitors who needed to see it to help folks back there decide if the United States will indeed support the World Bank loans for the project. Never mind that this is the only thing Chad has going for it, and that Exxon is taking the lead, and that the project has the best plan for ecological impact and revenue management ever put together—the folks in our beloved bureaucracy are still in doubt about it right down to the wire! We used my need to go on this trip as leverage to get me in to present my credentials on the first business day I was here (Columbus Day). There wasn't much to see yet from the oil side, but from the air (we flew at 12,000 feet), one got a fascinating panorama of the southern half of the country: huge tracks of land covered with water from the rainy season floods; the major rivers that drain into Lake Chad; a countryside of scrub plains, greener than I had expected, but with solid ground cover only over about the southern third of the land.

On Saturday, I went up to Lake Chad by road. I can now say

that I have driven approximately one-quarter of the paved highway in the country (120 kilometers). I had opined early in the week to the deputy chief of mission, my number two, that it might be interesting to see the lake at its rainy-season best, for purposes of comparison. He said he and his wife would come, and before I knew it we had a four-car caravan of about seventeen, including children. The lake itself is very shallow. We visited the deeper, southern end. It is almost more of a marsh. The paved road took us as far as the village at lake bank, or rather a mile from lake bank, since over the past twenty years the lake has receded that much. We all piled into a plank boat, a scow, one person noted. The regional security officer who was along muttered something about no life jackets, but this is Africa, after all. It took us an hour of alternately motoring and poling through the reeds to get to deep water. Most of the lake is covered by false islands of reeds—they float and mat, and someday will probably form actual islands and cover over the lake itself. The wind carries them and piles them over what were open passageways earlier in the day, so it is hard to know how to best reach the open water. The bird life is again fantastic. People try to snare the birds with nets that catch their feet when they are startled and try to fly away.

We did eventually reach the sea, and there is a huge expanse of open water. We motored out into it for about fifteen minutes before turning back. Many of the boats we saw were Nigerian, with names like "The Young Will Grow." There seems to be a flourishing small-scale smuggling, er, um, informal commerce operation on the lake. En route home we stopped at the "resort" of Dougia, a little hotel and restaurant on the banks of the Chari a few miles inland from the lake. People from N'Djamena go there for the weekend for a change of scenery. There we saw monkeys (wild) and captive tortoises, an ostrich, and gazelles.

I have also been across the river into Cameroon to shop in Koussérie. It is just like N'Djamena, but smaller. But for whatever reason French wine is about half the cost it is here. A decent Côtes du Rhône was $5, and a bottle of Martel cognac, $20. Not much different from Washington. We wandered through the market as well, where I bought an alarm clock for $1.50; Chinese. The rice was from Pakistan, and the other grains local.

The Pace of Life

I will reserve judgment to some degree, but my initial impression is that I will be a little less busy than in Washington. Of course, the distinction between work and play is less obvious. The main difference seems to be that I have no household or garden chores, so that big block of time is freed up for whatever. I spend lots of my free time so far reading French or watching French TV. But the pace in the office seems less intense. I could just delegate everything to others, but that wouldn't be any fun.

The Chadians

I am impressed so far. My official interlocutors seem to be very sophisticated. And reading the official press, it is clear that they have learned to "talk the talk" that we want to hear regarding development priorities, corruption, democracy, and a whole host of other subjects. But as one of the other ambassadors put it to me last evening, they speak perfect French, but there isn't anything behind it in the way of knowing what to do to solve problems. Perhaps he is right, or maybe it is simply the lack of resources in this desperately poor country. The German ambassador observed that there is a culture of dependency here, with the Chadians looking to the Western donors and international financial institutions for everything—or, I might add, to their own government. The government and parastatals—their annual deficits made whole by the donors and IFIs [international financial institutions]—seem to account for some two-thirds of the cash economy. There is virtually no private sector aside from import/export traders and a few construction companies. These issues notwithstanding, I find the people friendly and open.

Business

The big issue is the petroleum project, the fate of which will be decided in a few weeks, and which will in turn decide the fate of the country for the next many years. The issue is playing out like a soap opera. While the United States is taking its time in deciding a position, various other events are swirling around us. It seems the French are trying to stake out a larger share for themselves, and that some of the private sector players are about to take their marbles and go home. As a newcomer, it is very difficult for me to offer serious advice to my hosts as to what steps they could take to help nail down US support. It will all play out, hopefully with US support.

I will stop here for this first missive. I'll shoot for a monthly pace for these, and try to keep them shorter.

Best regards to all!

Ambassador Chris

Odds and Ends

June 5–19, 2000

The past few weeks have been a time of watching and waiting. We have been waiting for the World Bank vote on the oil project, scheduled for tomorrow back in Washington. We have been watching for developments on the northern front of the low-grade insurgency, but there have been none. Ironically, the entire vote tomorrow depends on the US position; if we vote for the loan, it will surely pass; a vote against might kill it. Here, on the eve of the vote, on this, the most important bilateral issue to arise with Chad in a generation, I do not know with certainty what our position is. Such is the arteriosclerosis of the Washington policy process, all too familiar to me before my assignment here. Our process is perhaps the world's most democratic—letting all views be aired, and enormously hesitant to move in the absence of consensus—but for this we pay heavily in the erosion of the influence we could have if we took decisions early and decisively.

So for the past several weeks I've been biding my time, and life in N'Djamena has progressed apace. It has rained a few times, at least a month early by most accounts; this is good or bad depending on whom you speak with. But in the city, perhaps the most important event has been its centennial celebration.

N'Djamena was founded on May 29, 1900, as Fort Lamy, a month after Commander Lamy lost his life in defeating the forces of upstart chief Rabah across the river in what is now Koussérie, Cameroon. From a military outpost a century ago, N'Djamena has grown to a bustling expanse of 700,000 souls.

N'Djamena's centennial celebration was trumpeted for months before the founding date, May 29. The government-leaning daily *Le Progres* ran a countdown beginning 100 or so days before the event. Chad itself originated as an artificial colonial construct, and in many ways the country's founding is entwined with that of its capital. Other papers ran sporadic articles on the town's history that I found illuminating. The mayor's office sent a letter around the beginning of March, soliciting help with the celebration.

The planning committee called on me after I responded that we'd do what we could. We offered several things—a reception or dinner, a joint announcement of some small development assistance or "self-help" projects, a book donation to the municipal library, and construction help for exhibit booths at a commemorative fair to be held on the grounds of the Foreign Ministry. Several weeks went by and we heard nothing. Then another letter arrived: the press of time had eclipsed the possibility of a representation event; the mayor courteously declined the announcement of assistance projects since the donations had been planned anyway (no American politician would have had such a qualm); the book donation and construction assistance were gratefully accepted. The only problem was that the books didn't arrive on time. And the construction foreman at the fair knew nothing about any help from us. So to make a long story short, we did nothing to help commemorate the city's centennial.

And it may have been just as well, for the celebration itself was poorly organized. In contrast to the centennial of Sarh, where we had invitations and phone calls two weeks in advance, it was never clear what the role of the diplomatic corps was to be in N'Djamena's fete. On a Friday evening, ten days before the great day, a sort of invitation-*cum*-schedule of events showed up. It announced a week-long celebration beginning the next morning with the opening of a photo display at City Hall. At first I thought that, perhaps, it was just that N'Djamena's celebration was intended more for its own citizens—hence the parades, the dance of the canoes on the river, and the dusk-to-dawn concert at the National Stadium on the eve of the anniversary date. But soon the news spread of openings delayed by hours when officials failed to show. The city's massive cleanup effort had faltered after a few piles of trash had been removed from the drainage canals and piled in the street. And worst of all, the centennial fell in the middle of a (now) six-week power crisis, which has left most of the city without electricity or water for days at a time.

In any case, I attended two events and visited the fair as well. The first was the opening of N'Djamena's first commercial art gallery. I'd been forewarned to expect an invitation to this, because its promoters include the UNICEF representative here and her husband. I went to the opening ceremony around quitting time, and returned for the celebration/dinner a little later in the evening. The gallery was nicely appointed, with paintings suspended on wires from the ceiling and sculptures in the various niches and corners of the five rooms. It was a good selection of works by Chad's half-dozen professional painters, and a number of capable artisans. There was a brief ceremony at which one of the officials of the Ministry of Culture spoke, along with my UNICEF friends. Moments afterward, I was accosted by a woodcarver who had just completed two chairs for me according to my specifications (solid wood, intricately carved to my design, $90 the pair). He proudly escorted me back to see his sole work on exhibit—a Chadian version of the *Manneken Pis* ["Little Man Pee" in Flemish]. Suffice it to say that my chairs have a very different motif.

When I returned for dinner and the show later, I could tell that it was to be a long evening. Called for 7:00 p.m., only a few folks were around when I arrived at 7:15. I joined the UNICEF table, and various acquaintances filtered in over the next half hour. By 8:00 things seemed ready to roll. The setting—a courtyard under large trees in front of the gallery—was charming. In a few weeks an African restaurant will be ensconced here. The gallery and restaurant are run by a local entrepreneur who has a jewelry store next door, but who is in partnership with a chain of Zebra Art Galleries, scattered around the continent and with an outlet in Miami as well. The program began with a presentation of three dances by the Ballet National. The first was a traditional dance of the Logone Oriental, basically a belly dance. Then came an initiation dance for young warriors, and last, a dance replete with throat yodeling from the Bagirmi tribe, which inhabits the area east of N'Djamena. The second act was a skit performed by the Félix Éboué Drama Company—its punch line was the crash of a twelve-person minibus on the paved road south of town, among whose passengers thirty were killed and fifteen injured (ironic humor must always be believable). And then came the famous Chadian songstress Eldjima, whose husky chanting demanded an acquired taste. And, after 10:00 p.m. as it was, with only the most rudimentary signs of the advertised meal in sight, I excused myself and snuck off between acts. It was just my luck to have a 7:00 a.m. breakfast with my marines the next morning, or perhaps I would have lingered longer into the night.

The other anniversary event was the state dinner hosted by the mayor on the evening of the anniversary itself, May 29. Never mind that this was Memorial Day for Americans, I decided that I should attend. The Foreign Ministry's protocol office had phoned during the day to confirm that the dinner would be held at 7:00 p.m. promptly. The evening saw a rainstorm, and it was with difficulty that Chaibo, my driver, threaded the way through the pitch-black city (no electricity, you will recall) and standing water to reach the Palais 15 Janvier (the National Assembly Building), where the dinner was to be held. No one. Hardly a soul in sight. Come back at 8:00 p.m., we were told. So off we went, back to the house, and duly reappeared at about 8:20. A few folks were around by then, and there was an honor guard to salute as I entered the hall. But the strange thing was that only a third of the guests of honor came. I greeted the French chargé and his wife, and the Algerian and Egyptian ambassadors, and the chargé of the Central African Republic. But around us was the void of nonattendance. Finally, around 9:30 p.m., the president and his party trooped in and the evening began. The food was more ample this time, compared with the last state dinner—perhaps because of all the no-shows. As we ate, a roster of entertainers appeared, one after the other. They weren't quite to my taste, but the Chadians loved them. The minister of defense was the life of the party—seated at the head table, he would descend as each act climaxed, grab a few friends, and in Arabic fashion surround the performers while saluting with right fist clenched and held high, the black-power salute (like I'd seen up at Mao). I won't bore you with the details of the song composed in honor of the president. By 11:00 p.m. he withdrew, and we could all go home.

When I was a tot in the era of the Beats, someone gave my parents an LP entitled *Songs of Couch and Consolation.* It was a collection of songs with a psychiatric bent, one of which was entitled *The Will to Fail.* In Africa, some forty years later, one must fight hard against the will to fail. When we see around us so much warfare, civil strife, simple crime and graft, there is a strong subconscious urge to expect—if not wish for—the worst, that things will go from bad to worse to the point that intervention is hopeless, and we can only gloat over how horrible things are here. There is an excellent reporting officer on my staff who has succumbed to the point that she will write only what is critical of the government, without any perspective as to difficulties in administering this country or sins of the opposition. When I read of the latest acts of Mugabe in Zimbabwe, I am horrified, but entranced—it would be so much simpler if he would continue down the precipice, eschew any shred of legitimacy, and allow us to write him and his country off as a totally lost cause. The natural yen of mankind for simplicity, to see things in black and white, makes you almost to want it, to hope for it: the will to fail, or to see failure. But life is not so simple, for the Mugabes are clever enough to retain just a hint of salvageability. And in Africa as much as, or more than anywhere, nothing is black and white, but all is shades of gray. Still, in Chad one must fight hard against simply accepting fate, stopping from struggling for what is possible and instead letting yourself embrace the will to fail.

The seventeen-year-old daughter of the French chargé didn't make it. She committed suicide on June 1. It was a week to the day after I'd learned that one of my most esteemed colleagues in the Foreign Agricultural Service had done the same thing. It is no longer easy for me to understand the mindset of the teenager, where rumor has it that a conflict with the parents ensued over her Chadian boyfriend. It is easier for me to comprehend the accumulation of pressures over years and years, which must have oppressed my colleague. But even so something is missing. What makes the will to fail triumph over our instinct to cling to life, and over the things a person still wants to accomplish in his allotted years?

I see all the squalor—the failure of development to make a dent in the poverty of this country. The venality and corruption of Chadians unwilling to forgo small personal gain for the greater progress of their country is a big part of the problem. And life in N'Djamena can be stiflingly boring and oppressive, especially if you believe the constant stream of bad news from the opposition press. But this isn't all there is here. I think of citizens' associations that work to create reforestation projects and workshops to employ women, and health clinics in remote villages. Just ask Les, who directs our small Ambassador's Self-Help Fund. And this doesn't even touch the objectives that most of us expats have on our post-Chad agendas. So how to explain the collapse of that seventeen-year-old girl?

If you had told me before coming here that I would play softball every Saturday morning in a game where no one really keeps score and enjoy it, I'd have said you were crazy. Several weeks ago our general services officer (i.e., the guy in charge of every kind of maintenance) put out the word that he was going to organize a game. I felt duty bound to show up for the first game and, despite falling down twice and skinning both knees, I enjoyed it, and I keep going back. It's a very motley group. Lex, at seven, is our youngest player. Nigel, who confuses us with his Canadian rules, brings a third of his dozen adopted Chadian children, ages ten to fifteen. A couple of our marines usually turn up, and a dozen other parents, children, and single folk. We play in a big field by the river, the parade ground of the national police academy. There is often a contingent marching over to the side of the grounds we stake out. A handful of embassy folk come just to watch, and by the time we are half an hour into our game, there are inevitably twenty to thirty Chadians watching as well—children and youth and a few of the police cadets. What I get the biggest kick out of is seeing the marines and other nonparents teaching and encouraging the kids. Last week we nearly came to grief as a Chadian couple strolled slowly through the outfield, completely oblivious to the pop fly descending only a few feet away.

One of the things I enjoy about the game is the drive through the *quartier* [quarter, or neighborhood] to get there. To Chaibo's chagrin, I drive myself out the road vaingloriously called the Corniche, which snakes through an average neighborhood of dwellings along the river. I pass a small field where children are always playing soccer. I see the leisurely pace of the residents who sit in front of their houses, stroll, stop with friends to exchange a word of news or gossip. Invariably a small band of children is running somewhere in the street, playing their favorite game—pushing a pot lid or some other flat, round object with a stick, keeping it rolling as fast as they can run. Along the side of the road there are always vendors of cigarettes and soft drinks, people who I'm told clear perhaps CFA 1,000 or 1,500 a day ($1.50 to $2.25).

As life goes along, I continue to find new and interesting things to do and see here beneath the drab. Last Saturday, after softball, I went to visit a women's weaving cooperative I'd heard about north of town. The fabrics on sale were finely done, of high quality if rather ordinary designs. But the fascinating thing was to see the women working on the old-fashioned handlooms, which they powered with foot pedals. Most interesting was the combination of frames holding the warp threads so as to form the pattern in the finished cloth. I had a professional interest in this as well—since I hope to eventually attract some interest in investment in a textile industry here, I wanted to know if the cotton yarn was of Chadian origin. Alas, one of the women told me that it came from Maroa, a town in the Cameroon, near the center of that neighboring country's cotton production.

If the lifestyle of an ambassador in a presence post is sometimes a letdown, it brings unique opportunities as well. Earlier this week I was invited to the Grand Mosque for the ceremony commemorating the birth of the prophet Mohammed. I'd hoped that the ceremony would be in the mosque proper, but it turned out to be in the auditorium of an outbuilding. When I arrived, exactly at the called time, the hall was already two-thirds filled, men only of course. I was welcomed by smiles, escorted along a line of dignitaries with whom I shook hands, and seated near the front of the room. I saw only one or two faces I recognized; after a few moments, the Nigerian ambassador came in and was escorted to a seat near me. I saw no other European-looking Caucasians in the room, and was immediately glad I'd come.

I had never before been to a Muslim service or religious ceremony. Surprise, surprise—it bore a lot of resemblance to Sundays out at the SIL [originally known as the Summer Institute of Linguistics] chapel. The president never showed, but eventually I recognized the minister of transportation, who came and took the chair of honor. After a quarter hour of waiting, there was a welcome—Arabic, translated after into French. This was followed by brief responses, a chant akin to the call to prayer you hear in any Muslim city, and a chorus by an octet of singers in a similar vein. The atmosphere was casual, with people coming in and wandering out in a way more acceptable in Orthodox Christianity than in Catholicism or Protestantism. Then the octet retreated and a clearly older gentleman took its place and sang a hymn, to which the audience enunciated low responses at points. All this, of course, was in Arabic, so I understood nothing of the substance, but tried to note down the form on the back of the program. Next, a still older gentleman rose and ascended to the dais. There had been some mention of the sultan of Kousséri being present, so I wasn't clear if this was he, or the chief imam (the latter I later learned). He delivered a discourse or sermon of sorts (Arabic, so I have no idea what it was, but presumed it turned on the significance of this day, honoring the birth of the prophet). Another cleric came forth as the chief imam retreated, spoke in thanks (this time translated into French), and, after a last chant, the forty-five-minute ceremony was at an end. The chants? Not all that different from the Gregorian. And the styles are of an age, after all, even if Christianity has evolved a more recent form of fervent, participatory hymns as well.

Another thing I've been trying to do is to get out and meet Chad's business community. The merchants and factory managers are uniformly flattered that I've come. Apparently in this neck of the woods, I'm the first ambassador who has done this. But for me it is just as interesting as the often hollow maneuvering of the political parties. Marx was right about one thing—it's economics that often makes things happen, not just politics.

So last week I called on the managing director of the slaughterhouse that serves N'Djamena—and exports about a quarter of its production by air to neighboring countries! No one knew that. Regrettably, no tour of the plant was offered. But in N'Djamena's still 100-degree heat, I would give the plant good marks based on the external odors, in contrast to all the meat plants I've toured in Russia in recent years. So I believed the director when he told me that there are three veterinary inspections (the live animal, the carcass after slaughter, and the dressed carcass prior to leaving the plant), and that Chadian beef is regarded as top quality by regional markets. Chad's *enclavement* [isolation] interferes again, and because of the enormous cost and unreliability of air transportation, only a couple of hundred tons of meat a month is exported. Enormous quantities that should be slaughtered and dressed here, move abroad on the hoof—the animals I saw at the bridge over to Cameroon. The abattoir has recently been privatized after running up enormous losses as a state enterprise over the years. The manager described his work to eliminate a third of the workforce, and to gradually modernize equipment as profits allowed. And, after all this, the plant only operates at between a quarter and a third of capacity.

Very different was my visit to Tchadipeint, the paint factory which is one of the country's handful of true manufacturing enterprises. When at first I wanted to accompany Ace, our newly hired commercial officer, there, the managing director balked. Young Ace (only thirty-one despite the recent arrival of his fifth child) is like Les, a locally hired American married to a Chadian woman. Ace went to meet with him and reported back that we could both call again in a week's time. The director would have had time to prepare for my august presence. In the event, that turned out to mean ordering in pastries and coffee. But go we did. We received a good briefing, first on the structure of the business—a third French, two-thirds Chadian, but Chadian managed. And the business climate? Difficult because legitimate firms compete not only with smuggled merchandise but also with the output of the gray economy, and because of the problems incorporated businesses here face, ranging from problems in importing inputs to the tax regime to the competition of the informal sector. But Tchadipeint survives. When we toured the factory, I saw a simple operation that basically blends imported dyes and bases into finished paints. But there are some dyes that are beginning to be sourced locally, out east near Abéché. And that is already something.

I also made my second visit to a Chadian hospital during the days that spanned the writing of this letter. This time, I was checking out a minor softball injury. Yes, the sport can be dangerous for those who haven't played for a while. Our political/military officer broke an arm in our first game nearly two months ago. Myself, I took a fall each time I made a base hit in the game, but thought nothing of it. One knee, skinned up a bit, healed nicely; the other was merely bruised and seemed to be on the mend for a while, but then swelled up and over a couple of weeks became very bloated and tender. So, reluctantly, I showed it to our nurse. She prescribed immobility and ibuprofen, but just to rule out the unlikely, an x-ray to be taken at the Hôpital Garnison, the best Chadian military facility, a few doors down from the embassy.

Located at the back of Place de l'Independence, the parade grounds I'd driven by the hospital countless times. My adventure began at the front gate, where the normal procedure of opening only one side wouldn't admit my disgustingly large vehicle, and there was a brief standoff until the gate guard so realized and opened both portals. We drove around the main three-story hospital building to a couple of low buildings in the rear, but I had no idea where we were or where to go. I alit and asked a man who approached where radiology was. He kindly led me there. We tracked through the unpaved yard between buildings, muddy from rain the night before. My guide pointed to an office to the side of what was clearly the x-ray room. I was indeed expected and in a trice was escorted into the x-ray room. All was dingy—there was no suggestion that one should remove muddy street shoes. The radiologist and his assistant, bright young men both, were in street clothes. There were absolutely no indications of sterility, although the room appeared to be generally tidy—at least above ankle level.

At this point Haouoa, our embassy nurse, rushed in and spread a thick paper across the x-ray table beneath my knee, now exposed below the rolled-up pant's leg. It wasn't very clean she opined—

no kidding! Snap, snap. Haouoa led me back to the doctor's office to wait while the x-ray was developed. Despite my protests, his current patient was hurriedly evicted and I was ushered in. A little earlier I'd met the Chadian doctor, a military colonel, but this was a French *cooperant*, or assistance officer, Dr. Fabien. He part apologized, part complained about the conditions under which he worked. While waiting he examined my swollen knee. Fluid, yes. But he wouldn't recommend lancing it—here in Africa the danger of infection is always too great. When I'm back in the States in six weeks? Yes, perhaps. The x-rays arrived. One showed nothing abnormal; the other was half obliterated. "Bad film," claimed the technician. Dr. Fabien asked that I have the x-rays retaken. He would finish a quick surgical procedure that he'd interrupted, examine the retakes, and advise us. So back I went for two more shots. By the way, in Chad there are no protective coverings of the body parts not to be x-rayed.

After this round, I was asked to wait at my car where I'd be comfortable. In five to ten minutes, Haouoa would bring word of the results. Hanging by the car, I began to study my surroundings. There were lots of injured soldiers milling about, a fair number of amputees, and most of the rest with arm or leg injuries. All were dressed, suggesting that the wounds were at least days, likelier weeks, old. Most patients seemed ambulatory, some on crutches.

In the middle of the courtyard, between the main hospital and the outbuilding that housed both the radiology and operating rooms, there was a jumble of people who seemed to be living there, in the open under a vast tentlike cover. At first I assumed it was mainly relatives, camped out, here to care for and feed their relatives. But then I noticed the hospital beds and the men lolling around. So here in the yard live the overflow of wounded for whom there is no room indoors. Later in the day, my defense attaché advised me that the amputees were inevitably mine victims.

And me? Oh, yes, I'm fine. Water on the knee, but I'll wait it out. In two or three months it'll be gone. And I need to avoid aggravating it in the meantime.

I'll close this Chad letter with a non sequitur, a Les story. Les recently traveled to Ghana to a training course. Since there's no

Ghanaian embassy here, he had no visa. He'd been told to seek out the immigration police in the airport upon arrival in Accra; our embassy would have given them the particulars about his business in Ghana to permit his smooth entry. Those of you familiar with Africa will see here a hundred opportunities for graft and gratuities. But it worked! Les approached the officials designated, found that they had his documentation waiting, and they then issued him an airport visa without further ado. Proof patent that this continent can work with the efficiency and honesty we expect elsewhere, if only. ... If only what? If only we or someone else knew the catalyst. I don't only eight months after returning here. Perhaps I'll have a good guess in another six?

Oh, yes. In the end, the US did indeed vote in support of the great oil pipeline loan by the World Bank. Made my life a lot easier, but through what agony!

Best regards,

Ambassador Chris

A Day in the Life . . .

July 14, 2000

Today really felt the way I thought being an ambassador would be. Such days have been rare for me, given the low level of official US activity in Chad. So let me give a shot at describing for you a typical day in the life of an ambassador—along with bursts of energy and moments of fatigue, the emotional highs and lows, that such a day encompasses.

A Friday. I awoke tired after barely six hours' sleep. I'd given a dinner the night before, and it had been nearly midnight before the servants were done cleaning up and I could relax for a few minutes and head for bed. Yet I looked forward to a busy day of official calls, meetings, and ceremonial events. After breakfast and coffee, I am in fact less tired than I'd feared. I head across the compound to the office at 7:40 a.m., about the normal time, after having given the household staff their instructions for the day. We start work at 7:30 a.m. here, and for the incidental reason that Alphonse, who serves me breakfast, shows up at 6:50 a.m. and puts it on the table at exactly 7:00 a.m., I am normally a few minutes "late" walking into the embassy. But this also has the beneficial effect of avoiding the perception of being a clock-watcher, so I compromise my passion for being on time and tolerate it. Walking in, I have in mind the order of the day: at 9:00 a.m., the most difficult meeting—a *tour d'horizon* with the foreign minister, which I will do alone, in French, and for which I've allowed the first hour in the office for preparation. Then a break for in-house meetings. After lunch will be a series of events for which I've had little opportunity for preparation, one after another: an interview with a local newspaper, presentation of awards to embassy employees who have completed a training course, an important phone conversation with my desk officer back in Washington, and a brief speech and certificate presentation to English language students graduating from our instruction program. Last, Bastille Day—the French national celebration hosted by the new French ambassador at his residence. I'm focused nervously on being prepared for the first event, comfortable that the breaks in my schedule will give me opportunity to prepare in turn for each of the subsequent meetings as the day rolls along.

For the meeting with the foreign minister I have prepared a list of five or six topics, mixing the "representational," i.e., subjects where I want to be heard, with subjects where I want to hear his views. I know the topics well enough by now, and in English it would be a breeze to whip through them with credibility if not finesse. But I will have to do it in French, and somehow I manage. I'm understood, even if not eloquent. By now I can understand pretty much everything that the minister says in response. I make a note or two, and thank him for his time. He will not be the action person on much of what I have to say, but will push here and there to be sure that our issues get focus. Back at the office I go immediately into an internal "political–economic" meeting, and relate to my coworkers the results of the meeting with the minister. And I hear what they have picked up regarding the rebellion in the north, the legislative proposal for an independent electoral commission, and so on. When we break, I draft a cable on the foreign minister's meeting—half intended to provide new information, and half to assure folks back home that their messages have been delivered.

After lunch my first event is my first interview with a member of the local press. It is with *Le Temps*, generally recognized as the weakest of the three opposition weeklies, but the reporter who comes is bright and seems to be well motivated. He goes through a series of questions which he'd hinted at when arranging the interview with our public affairs officer: US assistance in the areas of education, agriculture, and more generally. I begin with the defense that we put most of our aid through the UN organizations which are, roughly, one-third US funded. And I talk some about what bilateral assistance we do have here: our self-help programs, demining, and the odds and ends that we get, largely from the Defense Department, believe it or not. The reporter asks a few questions about the commercial side of things, using the petroleum project as his point of departure, and I speculate about future developments in this area. Again, this is all in French, but I'm less worried about it, since with the press here one can always get away with more generalities.

Only a few minutes after the interview is completed I need to be off to our large public conference room to hand out certificates to members of our surveillance detection team, recognizing their successfully completed training. These folks are our first line of security and defense—they move around outside the perimeters of the American real estate here, trying to look into whether anyone is looking at us. A training team from Washington has just completed its work, and I've been asked to preside at a mini-graduation ceremony. Our regional security officer opens with a few remarks, followed by one of the instructors. I add a few comments off the cuff (in French again), and hand out certificates to the roughly thirty participants. These men are genuinely appreciative of the recognition, and I warm to the occasion. Even the more menial jobs at the embassy are among the best in town here. I admire the dedication and self-respect with which these guys approach their duties. They in turn are flattered that the ambassador has bothered to show up for their event. I hope it comes through to them that I respect the pride they seem to take in their efforts to improve their skills. And it is somehow typically Chadian that the American instructors are wearing Chadian dress—undoubtedly a gift of their students along the way.

The highlight of the day is the graduation ceremony for the American Language Center. It is a George Simon/Daniele Brady event. George heads our English language instruction program (one of only a dozen or so run by US embassies worldwide), and Daniele, his wife, is the local UNICEF resident representative (which is akin to an ambassador). These two are utterly devoted to young people. It is they who are the promoters of our nascent Chadian artists' colony, and the local band H'Sao, which has developed a unique blend of traditional Sarh and rock music. H'Sao is playing as I arrive for the ceremony. Although only seventy-seven students were graduating, the hall of CEFOD (Centre de Formation au Development, N'Djamena's best public meeting room) was packed to its full three-hundred-person-plus capacity.

H'Sao's lilty airs and slinky chanteuses continue through a second number and then the ceremony kicks off—all in English, of course. George gives some opening remarks, and then calls H'Sao back up. The group has about a dozen members (it varies by performance) ranging from young teenagers to young adults in their late twenties. Today they are joined by a young boy and a middle-aged (yes, my age) Caucasian woman whom I haven't seen with them before. Instrumentation is limited to several percussion instruments and a keyboard synthesizer played by one of the younger members, who always disguises his youth with a northern-style headdress.

Then it is my turn to utter the "Ambassador's Address." It consists of ten minutes of remarks which I improvise on the themes of the growing usefulness of English worldwide, the way learning a foreign language is also a cultural learning experience, and the need to practice a foreign language in order to retain it.

What comes next is the pièce de résistance, "Poems by American Language Center Members." This group of kids, teens through thirties, is really talented. Some recite straightforward poems they've penned, some sing, and there are a couple of elaborate skits—all original, all in what is for the performers a foreign language, and all imaginative to the hilt. Then we hand out the certificates, after which there is a vote of thanks, my exit (heaven forbid I should have to crowd through the narrow doorway with the audience!), and then soft drinks in the pleasant dusk of the CEFOD courtyard.

But there was yet another event to close what has been a very agreeable day—the Bastille Day reception at the French embassy. It is probably one of only two annual events in N'Djamena bigger than our Fourth of July fete, the other being the president's New Year's reception. It was a lovely, balmy evening, threatening rain clouds having cleared just as they had for our event ten days earlier. The gardens behind the French ambassador's house, somewhat pompously termed "La Résidence de France," are lovely and spacious enough for the throng of several hundred. The new French ambassador made an appropriately brief statement, leaving us to enjoy the evening a little longer in conversation subdued by the lingering clouds. Now that the rainy season has come, it is cooler. On those days when it isn't overcast, but has just a hint of humidity in the air, the weather is again delightful. And after an hour, finding few folks I knew whom I hadn't greeted, I wandered off home.

As Chaibo dropped me off, I saw it was 7:45 p.m. I noticed a couple of cars still in the embassy courtyard and heard a happy shriek of a child's voice. Should I also stop in at the happy hour at the American Club? No, I decided, enough is enough. And it would be winding down by now, and I could safely let one event pass.

And the morning after? Saturdays are also popular for ceremonial events here. Chadians, like diplomats, are less chary of their weekend and evening time than most Americans—perhaps it again goes back to the fact that major events or even work projects are few and far between, so there's less distinction between idle work hours and private time. But this Saturday, July 15, was to be special for it would at last see the formal opening of N'Djamena's new Central Market. I, too, had been wondering when this would occur, and was looking forward to attending.

Typical for such events, the program that came with the invitation gave a long list of arrivals by precedence—the most important, the president, coming last. Experienced by now, I picked a time slot some twenty minutes after diplomats were asked to appear and arranged for Chaibo to pick me up. As we drove the short distance, it was clear that the president would actually attend—there were gendarmes at all the intersections between the palace and the market, deflecting anyone without a flag or an invitation.

Arriving, one of the Foreign Ministry protocol people, Mr. Daoud, whom I'd already seen six times this week, escorted me up to an attendant, who in turn led me to my chair. I greeted other ambassadors and a few government folk who were already there, and settled in to wait for a while. It was a beautiful morning. A plush, Turkish baroque armchair had been put out for the president, facing the main entrance to the market and the main mosque beyond. A tall courtyard fountain, actually working, hid the portal from view. A small crowd, undoubtedly carefully assembled, blocked the view of the lower reaches of the mosque across the street. A machine-made oriental carpet was spread before the cathedra and a long red carpet led from it, around the fountain, to the main entrance gate. A band was playing in the style of contemporary Middle Eastern music. After fifteen minutes they desisted and a second band struck up more of a highlife air. I rose and sat again and again to greet a steady stream of arriving acquaintances, the mayor, the director of protocol at the presidency. Nine a.m. rolled around, and by now the entire crescent-shaped shade structure we were under was filled with several hundred people. A handful of people from the crowd yonder had clamored up into trees to see better. And lo and behold, arriving only five minutes behind schedule, there was the president. We rose; he strode up the red carpet; he sat; we sat.

It was only then that we had our first inkling of the substantive program. It would be mercifully short, with welcomes by the mayor, the Saudi Arabian chargé d'affaires, and a representative of the merchants who would soon move into the market. Then the president would cut the blue ribbon and there would be a brief walkthrough of the facility followed by a refreshment. As I listened to the glittering generalities, it occurred to me that N'Djamena is starting to have a real downtown center, all financed with Saudi money: the Grand Mosque, the Islamic University named for one of the kings Faisal, and now the market. I was a little surprised to hear that the other structures dated back twenty years. Progress is slow here.

The market, when we saw it, was quite attractive and seemed to be well built with pinkish concrete walls and an aluminum roof. It is to house nearly 800 stalls and shops, some only 2 x 2 meters. People are pleased but already anticipate two problems: (1) more vendors than stalls, and (2) power interruptions that limit the electricity for refrigerating meat and pumping running water. With the looming question of who gets left out, no one seems to really know when the merchants will be moving in from the temporary market behind the stadium. But the citizenry is anxious—we saw the real crowds pressing around the fence that has been protecting the worksite, trying to get a look at what the market really looks like. And after brief refreshments, we were off—even the arrangement for getting the cars in to pick us up seemed well organized!

Yours truly,

Ambassador Chris

A Quiet August

September 4, 2000

It is a peaceful evening at the end of a long Labor Day weekend. As I look out over the pool I see the restful green umbrella of the big mango tree off to the right, and the bank of bougainvillea behind. A moment ago I caught sight of the gazelle gamboling on the upper lawn beyond.

For once I was able to take all three days of the long weekend (never mind that I had to put up with the servants, who don't get American holidays, around the house this morning). And a relaxing weekend it was—tennis Saturday morning and a dinner of raclette that evening with some people I'm beginning to think of as real friends. Sunday—a day all to myself, spent reading and (yes!) watching a movie classic on the VCR. Today, softball in the morning, a dip in the pool, and a leisurely cookout for the embassy Americans in the afternoon.

And now the last blue sky of summer fades. The wispy white clouds wax to a deep rose and then disappear. The first evening bat dives low over the pool to drink. Suddenly the security lights come on, and in that flash another season has passed.

Raaaht! The doorbell. My reverie is broken. I shout "hello" through the double wooden panels, grab a robe to pull on over my swimsuit, and fish for the key to open the house. I silently curse this life of so little privacy, picturing in my mind one of the guards there with a letter or an invitation he feared would need immediate attention.

But no one is there when after sixty seconds I push back the door. I look about and there, at my feet, is a small loaf of fruit bread. With it a note from one of the embassy couples saying "Happy Labor Day—we appreciate your work on behalf of the Embassy!" I sigh. Reverie restored. …

And so, perhaps, should all of August have been once I was back from the States. For Chad follows its French model in vacations. The French all evacuate, of course, and senior government folk and Chadian business people make this their time of holidays as well. The National Assembly, like our Congress, is in recess, and all of the opposition newspapers close for a month. So in a normal year, August would have been deadly still. But perhaps, again, there is no such thing as a normal year on this least predictable of continents.

Coming back on August 9, the first thing I found was that the National Assembly was still in special session. It was enacting a series of bills to set procedures for next year's presidential and legislative elections. The first measure, creating an independent elections commission, had been passed while I was away. The government's draft had been enacted unamended, allowing it to name sixteen of the board's thirty-one members. The opposition was livid, claiming that this rigs the process from the very beginning.

The week I returned saw a major debate in the National Assembly over the Electoral Code, governing polling procedures and the like. The debate raged from 10:00 a.m. on Wednesday, with breaks, until 3:00 a.m. Thursday morning. The second largest party, a nominal government ally, broke ranks and voted against, as did others, but the ruling party's majority assures passage by a large margin. On Thursday even the pro-government daily *Le Progres* (N'Djamena's only daily), reported that once again the government had stonewalled and accepted no compromises—hence the anger of even its allied parties. But, when I got a copy of the law as enacted a few days later, the truth proved otherwise. In committee, changes had been made in two key areas to limit the potential for vote fraud. The next day, Friday, the last bill was enacted, mainly setting the boundaries of legislative electoral districts. The government's proposal was for an approach like that of our Senate—one administrative district, one representative, population notwithstanding. Only a handful of large population districts would have two or more representatives. And here, quietly now, another compromise was accepted to add ten more seats for the large-population districts, not enough to offset the heavy rural/northern tilt, but still something.

So I spent the following two weeks talking to all the political party leaders and trying to assess how much improvement to expect over Chad's last, very flawed, elections in 1996–1997. My conclusion? No predictions. The growth of democracy from this rocky soil is sprig by sprig. A government dead set on maintaining its hold on power has accepted just enough additional transparency to keep a skeptical opposition (and foreign observers) from walking out on the process.

Yet somehow, I can't help but feel that something has sprouted in Chad's nearly barren earth. In America, we have the world's freest and most democratic society—but only since 1964 with the passage of the Civil Rights Act. Yet we hope for and expect so much faster progress on this less-hospitable continent. It took us nearly 200 years to perfect our process, constantly breeding and replanting improved seeds in rich humus. Yet here, in the thin tropical soils, we expect everything in a generation. This won't happen in Chad. But I believe that the democratic plants that are adapting slowly to this soil, roots struggling to find nurture in the stones and hardpan, will endure longer and thrive more than the attractive "democratic revolutions" elsewhere on the continent. We've seen how, in the Ivory Coast, Kenya, Zimbabwe, and Uganda, democracy's roots were yanked like weeds. Here, after struggling for years to root deep enough into the clay to ensure its survival, the tree will garner what it needs to grow slowly, eventually to bloom and bear fruit. Or is this again my infernal optimism?

And there is much to do professionally to follow up on my meetings in Washington. Take, for instance, my effort to convince the Nature Conservancy to come in and help revive one of Chad's defunct nature reserves in a lake sheltering Africa's only surviving freshwater manatees. So I met with representatives of the country's main wildlife preservation association. This group has had signal successes—for example, a ban on flying visits to Chad's wilderness regions by Middle Eastern emirs who were decimating the bird population through falconing. The organization is headed by a brother of the foreign minister, but it doesn't hesitate to stand up to the government when necessary. It would be a respectable partner for the Nature Conservancy or another American conservation organization.

August has had its share of more typical activities. It is to the conservation group, for example, that I owe my acquaintance with the "Lion of Farcha." The sole remnant of a somewhat larger collection of animals, the lion sits in a cage in a part of the Farcha neighborhood that is euphemistically identified on my map as *Jardin Zoologique*. Earlier in the year it reached the attention of the association that the lion was slowly starving, as no one was any longer responsible for his care and feeding. They raised some money, there was an article in the paper—but the problem doesn't seem to have been really solved.

Saturday mornings, after softball, are becoming my time to go out with Chaibo and tool around seeing things on my own, shopping, running errands, etc. So a couple of Saturdays ago we went to see the Lion of Farcha. There, across a couple of patches of mud, was his rather dilapidated cage, measuring perhaps 10' x 40'. Inside, the lion, slightly mangy, paced. There was straw, a pile of "food"—mainly bones with more protein in the blanket of flies covering it, it seemed, than in the few shreds of meat adhering to them. The keeper appeared, a short, stout man in a white robe who spoke only Arabic. Chaibo translated into French for me.

The lion was captured down in Zakouma, during the reign of President Habré some seventeen years ago, and has been here ever since. Originally there were a pair, along with a few other critters — ostriches, antelope, etc. Then the government provided a goat a day for the lion's upkeep. Now he gets only the cheapest refuse of the neighboring abattoirs — bones and the fetuses from pregnant female animals brought to slaughter. The keeper reaches inside the cage through a waist-high opening and rubs the lion affectionately on the head. Purr. I give the keeper a thousand CFA for his food and trek back to the car with Chaibo. A visit to the lion will be added to my city tour of N'Djamena.

A couple of days later our nurse (actually a physician's assistant), Denise, mentioned to me that one of Chad's leading doctors would be going to the United States to receive an award. "Dr. Grace" is well known to the embassy. She is Chad's only female gynecologist, out of perhaps half a dozen such specialists in the country. The award, presented by an American/international gynecology association, recognizes one outstanding individual per continent each year. Dr. Grace Kodindo is the African recipient this year. Denise and I agreed to invite Dr. Grace to lunch before she left for the States. Les tells me of some old history in which she was denied a previous honor when the government refused to let her travel.

As she came into the slightly tawdry American Club for lunch, Dr. Grace immediately impressed me as belonging to the category of Chadians whom I admire. She was alert and witty, appreciative of our interest in a way that didn't erode her own gritty self-respect. Here was a woman who had been through a lot in trying to serve the women of her country. She had studied mainly in Quebec, as have many francophone Africans, but had done brief course work in a Harvard public medicine program as well. Dr. Grace immediately asked our advice about subjects to cover in the remarks she would be asked to give in accepting her award. Denise and I, as one, suggested she focus on those challenges of practicing medicine in Africa that are most different from in a developed country — with a healthy footnote on the AIDS situation.

This got Dr. Grace to talking about her frustrations in her practice. She is one of three gynecologists in N'Djamena's central hospital. But here in town as in the countryside, most people come to hospital only after they have tried traditional medicine—the *marabous*—and seen it fail. Western medicine is a last resort, viewed as a sort of long shot to risk if all else fails. And of course, after long delays, it is much more of a long shot than it otherwise would be. So education and trust rank high in Dr. Grace's goals for Chadian women. And AIDS? Yes, it is getting worse fast. Studies she'd participated in suggested an infection rate among pregnant women of 15 percent—double the official estimates of 6–8 percent for the population at large. She also spoke about female genital mutilation, which she believes was imported from Egypt and Sudan only about a century ago, and may therefore be easier to combat here. And she gave us a statistic of one doctor to 36,000 inhabitants in Chad. This would imply a total of 200 to 210 physicians in the country of 7.5 million as a whole, in line with other estimates I've heard. And now that I think about it, in my year here, I've probably met at least a third of these professionals.

August deserves a little comic relief, so let me briefly mention the duel of the head gardener and the gazelle. The gazelle, you may recall, came down from Massakoury some two months ago. By and large, she has thrived—she loves the verdant yard with its variety of succulent vegetation. She is a little tamer, even if she recoils if I try to get closer than two or three feet. But now, with the prime growing season approaching in the wake of the rains, I seem to have a little farmer-herder conflict right here in my own backyard. It seems that Moussa's (the gazelle's) favorite food is the lettuce seedlings that the gardener (Kainan) has planted for my luncheon salads. She also does a good job on the squash vines. Never mind that I wouldn't care if Moussa helped herself to all of it. When I found at my door a very politely intoned note from Kainan requesting an audience to discuss the garden, I guessed the subject. I would have to bring myself to be Solomonic.

So noontime two days later found Kainan and myself strolling the lawn, regarding the flowers and shrubs. Quickly the topic of the gazelle arose—indeed, there she was before us. Kainan outlined his suggestion, that we build a big pen for her outside our yard, behind the embassy, which is adjacent to the house. This had some appeal—it would be by the American Club pool, so the kids could see the gazelle. I withheld final judgment but promised to speak with our maintenance officer. His idea, fencing the vegetable garden and leaving Moussa to roam free, I liked much better.

But there needed to be another meeting. This time with me, Kainan, and Bobby, the construction foreman. We paced back and forth in the rearmost garden. And I expressed my desire that we fence the vegetables, not Moussa. Kainan, the picture of respect, acquiesced. (And indeed, the fence is nearly finished as I edit this in late September.)

An interesting historical footnote: Among my stack of papers upon my return were newspapers—one with a fascinating reference to the town of Bardaï, where the latest northern fighting took place, as having been founded as an Ottoman Turkish outpost. Had the Turks truly penetrated so far south into the Sahara? I'd never thought so from the maps in my historical atlases. And Les nodded that yes, it was true, and not so long ago—in the last half of the nineteenth century. It would make a certain sense as the southernmost base for guarding camel caravans. It would also explain the extreme interest of the regional Turkish ambassador when he passed through, as well as references to Turkish influence I had heard during my one day in Abéché. But nowhere could I seem to find written confirmation. Another typically Chadian enigma.

A couple of incidents have focused my attention on law and order in N'Djamena. Let me tell all, at both the macro and micro levels.

First, a major brouhaha at the criminal court. It began when a young man was put on trial for the murder of a Zaghawa tribesman. Numerous soldiers, reputedly of that clan, the president's clan, showed up in court with noisy, intimidating swagger. According to *Le Progres*, during a break the defendant left the building to *se soulager*, or relieve himself, since the toilets were outside (a certain wall at the back of the compound, Les corrected). At that point the defendant fell under aggressive stoning from half a dozen of the spectator soldiers.

The minister of justice reacted strongly and publicly, decrying the fact that soldiers, supposed protectors of the citizenry, had

acted as criminal aggressors. Even so there was widespread speculation that, since the suspected culprits were from the President's
tribe, nothing would be done.

To general surprise, the very next day the minister of defense
apprehended the suspects and, with fanfare, marched them down
and turned them over to the minister of justice. Several days later
they were tried in a military court, found guilty, and sentenced to
pay a sizable fine and do four years' time *sans* parole. And in the
meantime, to prevent the suspects' escape, the rules at the prison
were tightened—the wardens stopped letting the prisoners out
during the day to go to work, visit friends and family, etc.—and
there were angry riots in protest. Justice had been served in an unprecedented way and the security situation enhanced as well—a
real success story.

Almost. About a week later there was a cabinet shuffle. And
guess who lost his job? Right—the minister of justice, who was
moved to a less prominent portfolio! Is there a connection? Perhaps
not, but this is Chad, and people speculate.

Some also think that a weak judicial system is one reason crime
is bad and worsening in N'Djamena. I'm not (yet) convinced it's all
that much worse than in a major American city, but expats make
obvious targets, and it can be violent when it hits.

Take the case of Duncan C., who heads the local operations of
World Vision—a Christian-oriented developmental organization.
It was he and his wife who gave the raclette dinner Saturday last.
And we guests were the first to hear of Duncan's misadventure.

The fashion for jogging in our little Anglo-expat circle of late
has been to park the cars at the compound of Mary and Alan B.,
both of the World Bank, right where the main road to the north
and east splits from the road to Farcha, northwest of the city. The
northern road is paved, open, and runs along the back side of the
French military base. A safe place for a run? All thought so, and
on Saturday afternoon Duncan was out with his friend Hans for a
quick jog before cleaning up for dinner. They had the B.'s dog with
them, the quid pro quo for parking in the compound.

Duncan and Hans had turned around and were heading back
when they were jumped—five big guys with knives. Duncan is
big himself, 6'4", as is Hans, who is shorter but stockier. Wisely,

though, they gave no thought to resisting. The thieves demanded Duncan's and Hans's shoes and socks. Socks? Perhaps they were high on drugs as Duncan suspected. To show they meant business, one of them stabbed the dog, killing it with one thrust. Shoeless (and sockless), Duncan and Hans hiked back to the house, fetched the car, and brought the dog back and buried it. They left an explanatory note for the B.'s, who wouldn't return from leave until the following day—with their children, who of course, spent a good part of the flight back talking about seeing their dog again. Life's lessons are learned early here, even by expats.

In one important way, August was too quiet here—no thunder, since it didn't rain. I wrote before of the atmosphere of rain I felt getting off the plane. That quickly dissipated, and I can count on one hand the number of good drenchers during the past month. Already folks are worried about the poor harvest they foresee in the Sahelian zone.

And so it always seems to be here, for two steps forward, there are at least one and a half backward. If the soldiers' conviction and the modest election reform are on the plus side, the loss of a good minister of justice and the robbery and death of the dog nearly offset them. Having had two good rain years in a row, 2000 now looks mediocre or worse. Yet beneath it all, even in "quiet" August, I sense some movement in the country.

Regards,

Ambassador Chris

Méchoui

November 1, 2000

There's an old gag among diplomats which says that what the whole profession comes down to is "drinking for one's country." Why? Because in the West, receptions—i.e., cocktail parties—are a principal venue for the diplomatic interaction that breeds information exchange, a degree of personal trust among interlocutors, a chance to whisper what you can't quite say officially, etc.

In Chad, the better phrase might be "eating for one's country." Reasons abound. Many in this heavily Muslim country don't drink. And for the expats, without the local social life of the extended family or clan, eating is what there is to do, one of the major social outlets. And what does one eat in Chad? Chadians eat *boule* or *méchoui*. Boule, you have heard me refer to as the national dish. It is a doughy, soccer-ball-sized globe made from the flour of any grain or tuber, most often sorghum. It is served with sauce in a side dish—you break off a chunk with your fingers, scoop up the sauce and a chunk of meat (if there is any) and chow down. Méchoui is reserved for special occasions. It is a roasted whole animal, most often a sheep or goat, stuffed with couscous or rice with vegetables. The carver serves up a chunk of meat for you, placing it and a scoop of the couscous on your plate. A fork or perhaps a spoon is usually provided, but the meat will still be most conveniently dispatched with fingers and teeth.

With this much background, let me lead you through a recent week of eating for my country. And since these were feasting occasions, méchoui was the keynote rather than boule. More to the point, it is only a little unusual that there should be an event each day of the week! I'm describing the eventful week of the oil project launch; perhaps an average week would see four or five feasts, not eight.

Monday: No, Virginia, the French Don't Do Méchoui

The week led off with a "family dinner" hosted by a French couple, the husband of which is the chief Esso rep, i.e., head of the oil project. Family in this case meant a couple of the local Esso folks, the senior-most Houston Exxon/Mobil people here for the launch, the French ambassador and wife, me—and the prime minister. The idea was to recognize the PM's contribution to the project since he would not be going south to the project launch (which by now we all knew he would be, even though it would denude the capital of authority for the day).

The dinner was called for 8:00 p.m.; mercifully, when I arrived right on time, my hostess Christine hinted that she planned to serve right at 8:30 p.m., so it wouldn't be a late evening. But by 8:30 p.m., still no PM. At 8:45 p.m., a messenger arrived to say he was delayed; he'd be there within a half hour at the outside. But of course he wasn't. A little past 9:30 p.m., just as Christine was about to override Jean-Pierre, her husband, and usher us to table, in came the PM, who of course had to be given a drink (a southerner, he does drink). So allowing him a scant quarter hour to scarf it down, we sat to dine a few minutes before 10:00 p.m.

French meals here are served in courses, à *la métropole.* We began with a seafood salad with large, tasty, imported shrimp surrounding a dab of fish on a bed of greens. Typical of the service in any house but my own (I take no credit — it all goes to my predecessor's wife), I was overlooked in the provisioning of white wine until the plates were just about to be whisked away. The main course followed — beef Wellington, which would have been less dry and tastier if the meal hadn't been delayed an hour and a half. But it's a matter of degree — meat is always overcooked here — which does have the advantage of guarding against the anthrax that occasionally infects Chadian herds. Vegetables accompanied, some fresh, some canned. Next came a course combining salad and cheese: this seems to be a concession of the local French community, to serve salad or cheese, or supply them together as here, rather than in two courses. The dessert was a tasty fruit tart with ice cream, of which I ate enough to be polite. Christine bragged on her Americanism of serving ice cream with the tart — something her years resident in Houston convinced her is quite a good combination. We rose from the table at midnight for coffee back in the living room, and cognac for the two or three who wanted it (including, of course, the PM). At last, the PM rose around 12:30 a.m. to leave, and the rest of us, having ignored Christine's hints to defy protocol and depart ahead of him, fled a moment after.

So there you have a typical French meal in N'Djamena. The food is good, but falls short of what you'd get in France, and with time shows its uniformity. The atmosphere? Always on the formal side, with official overtones — even when billed as a "family" event and hosted by Americanized French. An agreeable evening in all, marred only by the late hour of feeding and departure.

Tuesday: What's an N'Djamena Reception without Méchoui?

On Tuesday, Esso hosted its main event in connection with the petroleum project launch—a reception in the Esso compound under the *boukourou,* or thatched hut, by their pool. All of N'Djamena's "society" was invited: the entire diplomatic corps, all ministers and numerous others in the government, the principal business people, and anyone remotely connected with the project, perhaps 300 in all.

The appetizers at N'Djamena receptions tend to be somewhat uniform, just like the French (or pseudo-French) cuisine. Catered by or imitated after either the Novotel or Hotel Chari, they are divided into *les choses de sel* and *les choses de sucré*—canapes with salt or sugar. The salted items will include red caviar, salmon, smoked ham, and half a dozen lesser things, which I resist. The sweets include cookies, fruit tarts, etc., that I also avoid. Hot foods include little meatballs, fried fish, tiny imported shrimp, and of course méchoui. And there is pizza, for which I'm a sucker. But as I said, it is always the same. I only take the méchoui if I intend to make a meal at the event—for inevitably Dogo, my cook, has left dinner for me at the house.

Such large events—under which rubric I might count our Fourth of July event and a few large receptions we do each year—accomplish their official purposes, but do something else as well. Boringly de rigueur in Washington, here they are a diversion for us expats in the absence of TV, cultural events or what ever else one might do of an evening at home. A chance to chat pleasurably with business acquaintances, even though they are not quite friends.

Wednesday: The Plans of Mice and Men and the Méchoui That Wasn't

Wednesday, October 18, 2000, was the long-awaited date for the inauguration of the petroleum project, the laying of the "first stone" in local parlance. In fact, I had planned my vacation in the Mediterranean so as to be back in Chad for this event. It was also rumored that President Biya of the Cameroon might actually come—making his first visit to Chad after eighteen years in power in the adjacent country.

Esso folk had warned me of the impending chaos. There would

be some 450 people traveling to Kome, in southern Chad, for the ceremony. They'd had to beg the French for two additional planes to convoy us hence. The program would entail transport to Kome, the inaugural ceremony, a celebratory meal, and return to N'Djamena. My printed invitation wasn't specific on the details, but by word of mouth I understood I should arrive at the airport for an 8:00 a.m. departure.

Duly arriving at that hour, the first thing I heard was that I should leave and return in an hour. President Biya was delayed, and that would put all the day's activities behind. So I went and, an hour later, came back.

Returning, I joined the small crowd milling around. My diplomatic colleagues eventually made their way out to the tarmac for a welcoming ceremony for President Biya and I joined them. I enjoyed the honor of shaking hands with him and President Déby. And then there was a polite rush to our plane, a French military aircraft. It was uncomfortable both for its lack of cool airflow when aground, and because of the sling seats without any firm support. But it got us to Kome after an hour's flight, landing just before noon.

At Kome, we were bussed to the Esso base camp, which since my last visit had been transformed into a fortified encampment. We were given a light refreshment and ushered to a review stand. Comic relief: Protocol relegated most western ambassadors, including me, to the shady second row of our section in the stand. The recently arrived French and Sudanese ambassadors decided to crash the front row and moved up. The director of protocol, offended, moved me into position between them and the doyen—i.e., also in the first row now, but closer to the president. We waited and waited. And sweated, the review stand having been positioned with a morning ceremony in mind. The French and Sudanese ambassadors regretted their fervor and retreated into vacant seats in the rear rows of the stand. To show them up, I stuck it out in the sweltering sun.

At last, two hours late, the presidents arrived, the hour-long ceremony transpired, and we were done. We were then escorted to a pavilion arrayed with tables for a meal. Chaos as we found our seats. After half an hour, it was clear that we should proceed to serve ourselves from a distant buffet. It took me perhaps another ten minutes to find my way and wait my turn to take salads, sliced fish, vegetables, and, yes, méchoui. A delectable combination of Western and local dishes collected here, in remote rural Chad. A true accomplishment.

Just as I returned to my place, the director of protocol appeared, yelling: Diplomats, *membres du gouvernement*—you need to go immediately to the plane. So no lunch. Not a bite of the delicious méchoui that I had put on my little plate. But as I went out to the airport and waited yet again in the uncooled French aircraft for an hour and a half before takeoff, I thought to myself that, yes, I would make it back to N'Djamena that evening. I pitied those that I later heard had been left behind—reduced to disorder and fisticuffs, but remaining at Kome for the next day or two for lack of air transport. Even one minister was among them. Méchoui, however succulent, isn't worth a night away from home.

Thursday: Back to Me

For all new arrivals I try to organize a welcome lunch. This day my guests were the new public diplomacy officer, our assistant political/military affairs officer, and a new member of our marine security detachment.

Dogo, my cook, had prepared a typical meal, cooking up a *poulet de chair*, a fattened chicken. My staff serves meals in the French mode: appetizer, main course, salad, dessert. Coffee follows, and liqueurs at evening functions. They are perfect at this, proud of their work, even if I have to speed them along a little.

Honoring my guests with a meal a little special, these lunches serve the purposes of a méchoui. They let me get acquainted with the newcomers in a less formal setting than an office meeting. I hope they also demonstrate my interest in the people who work for me, and thus build morale.

Friday: Awards and Flies (with Méchoui)

Nearly all organizations recognize superior performance with some kind of awards program. This Friday was the day for ours. I presided, delivering comments mainly in French, but retreating to English for the American recipients. And afterward—méchoui of course, served in the back yard of my residence adjacent to the embassy. I love presiding at awards ceremonies and I think the recipients felt my enthusiasm as I shook their hands, presented certificates and checks, and posed with them for pictures.

Tables were laid out in the upper yard behind my house—both for serving and sitting. There were two stuffed animals, condiments, soft drinks galore, etc., intended for just over a hundred guests. The Americans did the serving, showing infinitely more concern for the swarming flies than the Chadians. I mingled with the awardees after the ceremony, going from table to table as they chowed down. Within a half hour both sheep were reduced to bones and the only remaining food was a little rice. There were jokes to the effect that my gazelle would have made even better méchoui than what was served. My guests rose one by one and began to filter off.

Across all cultures, eating together is a communion. Thus it was after our awards ceremony with our Americans sitting down with our Chadian employees. Awkward at first, after a few minutes the mixing works. For the Chadian employees especially, it is a sign of how much we value them and their contribution to our work. And in this incredibly poor country, it is hardly surprising that they left behind nothing on the carcasses of the animals we served up.

Saturday: Méchoui American Style

If the awards event was aimed chiefly at our Chadian employees, the cookout I hosted the next day was for my American colleagues. To my chagrin, I even forgot to invite the Canadian couple we employ because the e-mail address reading "All N'Djamena Americans" excludes them. The pretext for the cookout was a contest to name our embassy boat—"*N'Djaboat*" being the winning sobriquet. But for me it was a chance to have all the Americans in, which I try to do once or twice a year at my own expense. The boat, by the way, is a ten- to twelve-seater, a motorboat, justified as an escape craft to ferry us across the river to Cameroon in the event of serious trouble. We use it mainly to cruise the river on weekends, remarking on birds, hippos, and on very rare occasions elephants.

And what is méchoui "American style?" Why, grilled hamburgers of course. Some might argue for the addition of hot dogs, but I think hamburgers with potato and green salads, and brownies for dessert, hit the mark. My fifty guests (including children) agreed.

Almost every weekend we have some community event like this for our embassy Americans. We make our entertainment here. The definition of "American" often is expanded to members of the American International Club, our American School, or other hangers-on at the American Club or Marine House events. Socially this is what there is to do here, especially for those that don't speak French or have much occasion to interact with the French or diplomatic community.

My party wound down around 4:00 p.m., but most of the guests were also invited to Dyone's twenty-second birthday party later in the evening. Dyone is the daughter of my deputy chief of mission, just graduated from college with a teaching certificate, and here for a year to work at our American School.

But there was nothing at Dyone's party that I can make into méchoui, only a host of delicacies reflecting the New Orleans origins of the family. We all contribute our own specialties in entertaining here, and refined but spicy Creole cuisine made a great counterpart to the hamburgers at my place earlier in the day, and to méchoui or to the old-style French cuisine that is the norm around town.

Sunday: Sports Day at the Marine House

Twice a month on Sunday afternoons our marine detachment opens its compound to a motley crew of expats and a few Chadians for volleyball, swimming, drinks, and fast food. That's Sports Day.

While I often forgo Sunday events in favor of one time during the week when I can have a little quiet privacy, this time I had to go. I was to be "murdered"! It was a Halloween exercise for a class at our school.

So while I was awaiting death, I munched a hot dog—our marines benefit from special military "support flights." In one of those crazy non sequiturs possible only in the US government, DOD [Department of Defense] personnel abroad can order American foods, etc., on these support flights, but I, their boss and the president's representative here, cannot, except for the Fourth of July and Christmas.

So the marine house fetes its guests biweekly with hamburgers, hot dogs, or some other American "méchoui." Usually a treat for all of us who go there.

So what is méchoui, or more broadly, the meaning of all these meals for an expat in Chad? Most authentically, it is the sort of event we hosted for the awards ceremony—a special meal marking an occasion and featuring meat, which, despite Chad's wealth of livestock, shows up only in tiny amounts to flavor the daily boule. For us expats—the Americans, at least—eating is at the center of most all our social events. It brings us together in this rather harsh environment and provides an agreeable way to consume sustenance and our off-duty hours.

Most formally, we have the méchoui of business occasions. But here too, something of the Chadian spirit rubs off, for these people are incredibly hospitable despite their poverty. There is a touch of warmth in the reception or business dinner you wouldn't find back in Washington.

So that's méchoui! It is more than bread for the body, or simply eating for one's country. Here it is the staff of life.

Best,

Ambassador Chris

Happy Holidays from N'Djamena!

Twelfth Night, January 6, 2001

The holiday season here is a curious blend of Western tradition and local exoticisms. This year the mix was unusually rich in as much as Ramadan and Christmas overlapped.

Move over Rudolph, Santa Really Rides a Camel

Christmas festivities in N'Djamena began this year with an afternoon/evening at the Whitehouse's farm. They are a Canadian couple, twenty-five years in the embassy's employ one way or another. They are Bahai, having come to Chad chiefly as evangelists. They raised their own family, founded a local school, and a few years ago took on a second family when close Chadian friends were killed leaving behind eight or nine kids. Their exploits rival those of Les's family; they were recently featured in a story in *State Magazine*. Their farm is on the outskirts of town, on the Logone River. They keep horses, donkeys, dogs, and poultry; visiting nomads bring camels.

Almost as soon as the children had gushed out of their parents' cars, Santa arrived riding on the back of a camel! He was accompanied by one of his elves astride a donkey, and carried both a goody bag and one filled with stones and switches. Some claim that Santa bore an uncanny resemblance to a certain ambassador known to you all, but that cannot be. After all, I haven't gained *that* much weight since getting here. Mercifully, Santa remained atop his high camel perch until the beast approached his cathedra, and then alit with at least a remnant of grace. I have it on good authority that this was only Santa's third camel ride! Enthroned in his chair, Santa greeted the perhaps twenty children and their friends and elders. The elf had candy canes for those that had been good, and, mysteriously, none ended up with switches. The scene slowly devolved into camel and donkey rides for all, and Santa faded quietly away. Just my luck to arrive minutes after he disappeared, and miss all the fun!

But things were only beginning. Next there was food. Everyone had brought a dish to share, and some sort of meat to roast on two huge barbecue grills. There is always a surfeit of food at these events, and this time it was unusually varied because families of several nationalities were represented.

As we chatted and twilight began to descend, I became aware of a huge bonfire that had been lit in a nearby horse paddock. I followed the crowd in that direction. The dark orange fire rose high as various people piled crooked log on top of crooked log. In the deepening evening of this coolest season in Chad, the flame's warmth felt good, almost necessary, to me in my short sleeve shirt. It couldn't have been above eighty degrees Fahrenheit. When everyone had had enough marshmallows, there were Christmas carols. Led by

Shannon, a soprano spouse who is virtually a professional singer and director, we went through all the standard favorites. On the "Twelve Days of Christmas," I suspect we mixed up lords-a-leaping and maids-a-milking, but no harm done. And then, as the fire burned low, it was time to go.

Arriving home at 6:55 p.m., I recalled that Chaibo had passed a message to me just as we were leaving—the minister of economic promotion had invited me to a dinner yet that night. But he had been told of the conflict, and I didn't feel duty-bound to change clothes and rush right out again, since I would have been very late and the invitation had come only a few hours earlier.

A Warm and Genteel Custom

As Ramadan began I found myself receiving invitations to Fatar or Iftar—the ceremonial breaking of the fast at the end of the day. It is a delightful custom.

Moslems in Chad take their fasting seriously, unlike some in West Africa who will allow themselves water during the day. To give myself some sense of the importance of breaking the fast, I limited myself to liquids during the day of my first invitation, i.e., soup for lunch (well, at our club it comes with just a little piece of baguette).

The invitations are for 5:30 p.m. or so, and people come promptly. At the Saudi ambassador's, we were ushered into his capacious living room. Each new arrival made his way slowly around the room, shaking hands and eventually finding a seat in the chairs and couches that line the exterior walls. Small tables were already set with water and juices, and plates of little pastries. Servants entered. The official schedule for breaking fast each day of the month had been printed in the paper. A couple of minutes after the official moment, the servants began to serve drinks as quickly as they could to the three dozen or so guests. They passed the little plates of Middle Eastern sweets as well, and served Saudi coffee—a delicious concoction, clear and pale yellow like *citronelle*, tasting overwhelmingly of cardamom and not at all like coffee.

The guests were mostly Islamic ambassadors, ministers, a handful of other government officials, and a couple of businessmen.

After about ten minutes, at a sign from our host, all rose and began to file through the door to the courtyard. The host approached me, excused himself for the necessity of leaving for evening prayers, but told me that his house was my house while everyone else was outside. The only non-Moslem, I was left to watch a huge, muted TV in the corner that broadcast a Saudi feed, showing evening Ramadan festivities live from Mecca.

It was not more than ten minutes before the crowd began to filter back in. Without ado we proceeded to two large tables set for the main meal in the dining area. The servants had already placed soup, slightly cool at this point for they had had to pray, too, at each place. I was seated between the minister of livestock and a former minister who had been retired in the last cabinet shuffle (never mind; he'll be back). Across from me was my friend the Egyptian ambassador. The host laughed gleefully when I told him I'd taken only liquids during the day.

When soup was done we were invited to a lavish buffet that was waiting just behind us. It was an ample feed, but what struck me most was that people took modest helpings despite their day of fasting. Shrunken stomachs, or anticipation that they would eat again in a couple of hours with their families? After a little while, the servants cleared and we filed past the buffet table again; this time it held an array of Western and Middle Eastern desserts.

Food finished, the majority of guests rose, shook hands with the host, and slid out. I hesitated, wondering if courtesy didn't demand that one linger at least a few minutes. My Egyptian colleague apparently concurred, whispering to me something about the rudeness of running off while still chewing. The half-dozen of us who were left accompanied our host back to a corner of the living room, where we sat and chatted for a quarter hour. Then someone rose, the rest of us followed, and I was home by 7:30 p.m.

The following day, the same festivity was hosted by the Sudanese ambassador, a recent arrival. Seeing me at the Saudi ambassador's, he had asked me if I'd received his invitation, which of course I hadn't. But it came the next morning, and I was glad to relive this welcoming custom.

I arrived in fact a couple of minutes late. Relations being what they are, I hadn't been to the Sudanese ambassador's before, and hadn't realized that it was a bit off the beaten path, in one of the real *quartiers*: two or three turns off the paved road, past a couple of wrecked carcasses of cars or trucks, as well as some heaps of trash. I do love getting into the real city!

I knew my arrival was a moment past sunset for folks were already into the ceremonial soup. But I wasn't really late, for the Algerian ambassador was immediately in front of me. The tables, this time for a larger group of guests, were spread in the courtyard beneath the two-story house of white stucco. On the side were mats covering a large area for prayers. I paused to remove my shoes — my host demurred that I didn't have to, but he was pleased that I insisted. He escorted me to a waiting place at the end of the highest table. Again I found myself next to the livestock minister and we joked about it. He served me dates, and I dispatched my soup.

Then prayer time. My host asked my patience, but indicated that I could of course tucker into my meal. I demurred again. Once more the only non-Moslem, I sat in respectful silence as the others prayed before me. I silently said a prayer in my own ritual — what better occasion?

The meal was again served in two buffet courses. This time there was Chadian boule along with the Middle Eastern dishes, and I sampled some. Again, with only a little more leisure about them, the guests began to slip away shortly after the eating was over. After about fifteen minutes, the Egyptian and I found ourselves this time too to be the last to leave.

As Chaibo drove me home each evening I found myself lost in contemplation of this mildly religious experience. It is a charming custom, at once symbolic and hospitable. It brings people together to share something significant, but is simple and straightforward. The guest list is largely business-driven, but the warmth transcends that. And the brevity is appreciated since families wait at home.

Public Services

At the other end of the spectrum from these intimate celebrations were the massive public celebrations here of both Christmas and the Eid-al-Fitir, the end of Ramadan. I was invited to the first by the

Catholic archbishop whom I've gotten to know a bit, but was not among the members of the diplomatic corps invited to the second. Not liking big crowds, I attended neither but followed both on the radio.

On Christmas morning, the public mass was held in the national stadium (Stade Idriss Mahamat Ouya). Radio Chad gave live coverage, if through amateurish technique. The broadcast house and onsite reporters kept calling back and forth, trying to contact each other. "Stade? Stade? Dominique?" And there were the usual delays getting started. The first lady was expected, but didn't show. Finally, the ceremony kicked off. There were welcoming comments and an invocation, then prayers and hymns followed by a statement from the archbishop. Recognition of the congregations that had gathered from all over the country followed—the women giving their throat yodels as their districts were called. The prayers and mass communion were next, followed by an additional statement or two, followed by songs that eventually devolved into enthusiastic dancing and singing that continued for some time. The overflowing crowd then swept from the bleachers onto the field, and eventually out into the streets. The ultimate chaos was clear from the noisy, unfocused radio reporting. Anne-Nichole, my French instructor, attended, and confirmed to me the joyous confusion in which she had reveled.

For the Eid, I rely on the official news agency report, since the radio coverage was in Arabic and my TV wouldn't pick up TV Chad that night for whatever reason. This celebration of year 1441 of the Hegira was marked in Chad at the Grand Mosque. The chief imam led the crowd in prayer, and again there were delegations from all parts of the city and some districts of the country beyond. The imam's message of encouragement for toleration among faiths, peace, and solidarity was hauntingly similar to the message of the pope for 2001, cited by the archbishop two days earlier. After the formal prayers at the mosque, the president returned to the presidential palace, where he received in closed session the Islamic Committee of Chad. After a quarter hour, the session ended and the president went on to receive a host of dignitaries, including press and Islamic ambassadors, in the gardens of the palace. The event closed with a "cocktail," according to the official statement. I'd give my eyeteeth to know if alcohol was really served.

If you will permit me an aside, the juxtaposition of these two great religious ceremonies suggests a brief commentary on freedom of religion in Chad. Constitutionally, the republic is laic; freedom of practice is protected. And indeed, both faiths had complete freedom to organize their festivities as they wished—the Christians, with 35 to 40 percent of the population compared to the 55 percent of the Moslems, nevertheless had access to the national stadium. But Islam is clearly the first among equals, with the unofficial nod of the state. One need look no further than the fact that the Moslem president used his presence and palace to commemorate the Eid-al-Fitir, whereas his wife, scheduled to do the courtesy of appearing at the Christian commemoration of their holiday, didn't show. The Eid and the president's activities were written up in the daily official news publication; the Christian celebration was ignored. The implications are subtle but feed one of the divides in this disjointed nation, which I have noted before.

Somber Notes

Whether Christmas or Ramadan or not, the precariousness of life in Africa asserts itself at will, blind to the sacred days. (It is not just Africa, of course, given church bombings in Pakistan and Indonesia, and a mass murder in Massachusetts.) Around 2:00 p.m. on the afternoon of December 23, the Saturday two days before Christmas, I was relaxing by my pool, penning Christmas cards and sipping a glass of wine. It was my only afternoon and evening off in two weeks of Christmas events that were crowding my days and evenings, where my attendance was, if not obligatory, highly desired.

My radio blared. I heard the defense attaché (or DATT) ask the marine guard at the embassy if he knew whether I was at home. I chimed in "yes," and the DATT asked if he could come to see me in ten minutes with an important report. Of course.

I threw on a shirt and shorts over my swimsuit, and in no time Chris, the DATT, was at the front door. He declined my invitation to sit—his report would take only a moment.

Chris had just received a report from neighboring Niger, which he also covered for the Department of Defense as regional DATT. The civilian DOD employee there, engaged in setting things up for a full-scale defense attaché's office, had been murdered in the wee hours of that morning coming out of a Niamey restaurant. It was a carjacking of a brand new Toyota 4x4. The marine detachment commander, among the dozen or so Americans in the party, had been shot and wounded as well. The thieves, it seemed, were driving the car hell-for-leather to Mali, where they might sell it to Mauritanians.

I assured Chris that he had my support for whatever he might need to do, including going over to Niger to attend to things. (The Nigeriens and Malians were contrite, efficient, and helpful; only a few days later the vehicle was recovered along with a passel of suspects).

And here in Chad? We are a little safer, but only a little. On New Year's Eve, around 7:00 p.m., I was sitting in my study. I had been unwell that day and that, plus my inveterate dislike of New Year's celebrations, had given me cause to beg off from the parties of that night. Again the radio blared. I heard Denise, our nurse, respond. It seemed that her assistant, a local employee, had been assaulted near her home and had suffered a serious hand injury in trying to deflect a knife that had been pointed at her. Denise was off to meet and treat her, and take her to the French military hospital for whatever additional care she might need.

Again, as it turned out, it was a simple robbery. Haoua had defended herself, resisting what might have become a sexual assault. She had been beaten around the face and stabbed in the hand, but was now safe and her injuries didn't seem to be permanently debilitating.

Haoua is a dedicated, loyal, and very efficient employee. She is charming, with her little diamond nose stud, and warm and comforting to those in our community who need her care. Both events were a shock to us, even more so in this holy season of two religions.

Rekindling the Homefires — Even Here!

But what of American or Western Christmas traditions? Cards and the traditional tree and pageants and our own service for Christmas? We have them all, in one form or another. Let me start with the cards. As at home, the office sends and receives a huge number of seasonal cards. We inscribed ours for the new year, but those we receive run the gamut. Most are very ordinary, with few diverging from the UNICEF or similar models. But one was most intriguing and worthy of mention: that of MASACOT, the local group that is promoting AIDS awareness and the use of condoms. Their card portrayed their signature couple embracing, obviously in a certain degree of excitement barely hidden by their scant clothing, all enclosed in the outline of a transparent condom. The message inside? Something along the lines of "Season's Greetings" and "Happy New Year"—who would recall precisely?

More wholesome were our Christmas pageants. We had two, one by the kids of our school and one by a broader group as part of our Christmas Eve service at church. Both were directed by the indomitable Shannon, who also teaches at the school. The children were marvelous. The first portion was in French, directed by Anne-Nichole, who is also the French teacher at the school. She had done an excellent job of getting them to sing some French carols and act out a little skit. The second act was more of the same, but in English. The third act was the gem: a revue in the mode of a TV variety show, with all thirty of the kids incorporated in one or another of the numbers. A rock group did a "Cool Yule" number, while the Mistletoes were a teenage-girl group in perfect harmony. Even Scrooge made the scene, acted by shy Lex, a diminutive seven-year-old. I attended a "cast party" for the kids a couple of days later. As I walked in, they were dancing up a storm to my favorite seventies' disco music. Later in the evening, Shannon gave out certificates for the child performer who was the most this or the most that; she found a way to recognize each of them, and I'd find it hard to argue with any of her commendations.

Five days later, the adult pageant comprised the main part of our Christmas Eve church service. Entitled "The Good News," the musical may be familiar to some of you. It is the story of a grandfather's first Christmas as a widower, and how he finally finds solace in the day despite his recent loss. Some of the singing approached the professional level, mainly Shannon's. It was clearly as enjoyable for the cast as for the overflowing audience. With carols and readings from Isaiah preceding, and the briefest of sermonettes to wrap up, it was the perfect service for our very mixed congregation.

From this narrative you should get a sense of how well and appropriately we celebrated Christmas in one of the most remote of the world's capital cities. But as I think back, two more serious chords strike home. First, that the temporal coincidence of Ramadan and Christmas enabled me to sense in a very personal way the overlap of so much of their core beliefs, and how sad it is that the fundamentalists of both great faiths are often at odds, violently so. And sadder still, in a fatalistic way, that greed and violence exert themselves even in this holy season.

But I can't close by letting dark thoughts obscure the memory of a lovely Christmas, or deter me from wishing you all the best for the New Year!

Cheers,

Ambassador Chris

It's a Good Thing I Showed Up

March 24, 2001

The invitation was from the president, but he didn't show. The prime minister represented him and muttered something about a conflict with the launching of the national polio vaccination campaign. I learned a couple of hours later, when visiting the orphanage where the launch was held, that the president didn't show there, either. No matter. What I attended was the graduation of the tenth class of the National School of Administration and Magistracy [École Nationale d'Administration et de Magistrature, or ENAM]. It was held on a Saturday morning in the newly refurbished grand hall of the Ministry of Foreign Affairs.

I've mentioned these ceremonies before. They are common here and the Chadians love to hold them. I get invited to at least three a week. I skip most of them, and there are always plenty of extra seats in the diplomatic seating area whenever I do go. I was invited to three on this Saturday alone, and chose to attend the graduation. I'm glad I did, not only because I unexpectedly had a role to play but also because it helped me see something of the nascent sense of national unity which is struggling through its childhood here. And, as you'll see, the entire affair had a sort of comic air to it, one that, despite the laughter, didn't detract from the seriousness with which the participants took their advancement.

The invitations are sort of an art in themselves. A good third of them anticipate the participation of the president or prime minister, but they rarely attend. Yet it was the printed invitation from the president that suckered me into going to this one (along with the French ambassador, who let the senior foreign affairs official present know that bait and switch wasn't really an appropriate practice).

Along with the invitation came a printed program for the ceremony. In a way somewhat reminiscent of the elaborate levée of Louis XIV, about half the time is consumed by the precedence of arrivals. At 7:00 a.m., the installation of students and families was to finish. At 7:30 a.m., guests were to begin arriving. The diplomatic corps was scheduled for 8:30 a.m., followed by the most senior government officials, culminating with the prime minister at 9:00 a.m. and the president at 9:10 a.m. And of course these things never start on time. After a few months I learned never to come at the indicated time. Today I arrived about 8:45 a.m., earlier than usual because I hadn't watched carefully enough the time that my secretary told Chaibo to show up, and I didn't want to keep him and the car idling forever out in front of the house.

When I arrived, the hall was jam-packed with family members, and I saw a good number of cabinet ministers were already there. I filed in between two rows of women in uniform who saluted as I went by. There was someone there, as always, who politely escorted me to my front row seat. Several of the chargés from other embassies were already seated in the second row, and I was joined in the following minutes by the director general (number two) of the Foreign Ministry, and the French and Sudanese ambassadors. I asked the DG [director general] who the women in uniform were. The students from ENAM, he informed me. He joked about the uniforms being a holdover from French colonial days, but noted that the students all did a three-month stint of military service. The DG asked me in turn if the Libyan ambassador was still the doyen of the corps, and speculated that it would fall to the Taiwanese if, as expected, both the Libyan and Egyptian ambassadors were to leave soon. I'm next in line after the Taiwanese. The DG would certainly know who was doyen, and I think he was trying to tease me a little about our, shall I say, "careful" relations with a high proportion of the handful of countries represented here. Meanwhile, the French ambassador also asked about why the students wore uniforms, thinking it odd for civilian authorities. The DG said that of course they were civilian and not military uniforms, and again noted the French influence. We went on to talk about such weighty subjects as globalization and the trial of a former Chadian dictator on torture charges, and generally killed a half hour until, at 9:20 a.m., the prime minister entered and the show kicked off.

I might digress to note that this was only my second time in this grand room. Chad just hosted a ministerial conference of the Francophonie, a French-led association of all the countries that have French as an official language or respect French culture as having had some historical influence on them. The little flags with the symbol of that organization were still aloft the walls of the room in a place or two. The French had paid for the room, which decades ago housed the national assembly, to be renovated and re-equipped in preparation for the conference. But for Chad, it was important to be able to host such a meeting of sixty or eighty countries at the ministerial level. This was a boost for national pride, a status symbol of sorts, and a sign of the country's recently achieved political stability. And now the city has one more large venue for meetings. I noted the tasteful assemblage on the floor composed of local products: huge storage jars from Gaoui, calabashes, and sprigs of ripened sorghum—local, not subject to wilting or spoilage, and inexpensive. I complimented the arrangement to the DG, who told me something of the woman who put it all together.

It was the secretary general of the government who presided, and he opened with brief comments. He could not avoid a reference to a national tragedy that occurred here about a month ago, since it involved a past graduate of the school. One night, around 11:00 p.m., there was a plane crash. Two of Chad's best leaders were killed, along with the pilot of the little craft. The pilot, whether due to the blowing harmattan or simple error, approached the airport too low. His landing gear snagged in a tree, and the two Chadians I most respected and felt the closest to were dead. Minister of Economic Cooperation Hamed Lamine Ali was a polished, talented, dedicated counterpart on all aid issues, most importantly, our demining program here. Abderahman Dadi was the number-two person in the presidency (equivalent of our White House staff and the Office of the President combined). He was the closest thing Chad had to a true statesman, having successfully argued Chad's case for the return of the Aouzou Strip in the International Court of Justice in The Hague. Most recently, he had handled all the negotiations for the oil project. He was the author of a book on national reconciliation, among others. For Chad, it was like losing President Kennedy and Martin Luther King on the same day.

Ironically, Dadi's death, much more than his book, has helped Chadians to realize that they are indeed a nation, or at least a nation-state, however diverse and divided. There has been a real outpouring of sorrow and national feeling at the death of these two remarkable men. The shame is that it takes a great loss to remind people of what they have in common. In Chad, as in the United States.

On the day following the horrendous accident, I had gone to join the wakes at the houses of the deceased. The men were both northerners, Muslims, and the arrangements were a little different from those for my servant Alphonse's daughter, or for a southern minister whose wake I'd attended. There were no chairs, but large mats were spread beneath the makeshift awnings. Senior family members sat against one wall, Indian fashion, with the dead man's father central-most. You shed your shoes on approaching the mats, and if you were a notable or known to the family, you knelt before the patriarch to extend condolences. Muslims said a brief prayer. I don't know that either parent understood my French, but I felt and shared their grief and I believe they understood that. There were literally hundreds of mourners squatting under the shelter at each wake, but a greater canopy of dignified silence shadowed the event, muffling the murmurs and prayers of the mourners. Despite the northern twist, it was the Chadian rite I'd seen before: format, mood, and humble surroundings were the same. The essence of biding some time with the family of the departed is universal.

It was with genuine emotion that I had gone to both the homes of these leaders, spending some time at each wake. And it was again with emotion that all of us in the hall rose for a moment of silence.

The meat of the ceremony was, as in all graduations, the presentation of the certificates. This is where it got funny. The master of ceremonies would read a name, and then announce who would present that person's certificate or diploma as the student approached the dais. The presenter would hasten to catch up. When the DG's name was read and he looked at me quizzically and said "Me?" I realized that the presenters hadn't been forewarned, but instead were being selected from the notables who had shown up as things flowed along.

The nervous students took their uniforms seriously. Each stopped a great distance from the panting presenter and saluted, some stomping the right foot or clicking heels at the same time. No two salutes were alike. One student drew laughter by saluting with the left hand. The students would then approach the presenter and stop at the furthest distance they could still span, lean very far forward, and in awkward elongation shake hands with the presenter, grab the certificate, and swing back upright just in time not to lose balance and fall down. I guess that the maintenance of distance connoted respect to the senior official who was condescending to hand down the diploma.

For a long time I thought that the one thing that all the students did the same way was to retreat from the lofty mien of the presenter. Each would take three huge backwards steps away from the eminence, salute again, take half a step forward with the left foot, pivot, and march sharply away. Some at this point would smile, wave their certificate, and relax to a normal walk. After a while, however, a couple neglected the elaborate backwards move, restoring my confidence in the ultimate triumph of individual interpretation over instruction. The whole thing was taken so seriously by the participants, but carried off with a lack of aplomb that lent irony to the intense formality of the occasion—all in a way that is possible only on this continent. And this was further underscored by the contrast of the nervous, misstepping students with the suave senior Chadian officials who were handing out the documents.

And the uniforms: Not a one seemed to fit. They were obviously European made, with no adjustment for the little differences in the African physique. The female students were mostly chunky, and the jackets bulged and their tails just wouldn't stay pulled down over the rather ample rumps. The skirts were of low-ankle length, the longest I've seen in some time. The men, in contrast, seemed to all be reed thin and tall. The coats hung as on hangers, and the pant cuffs were all high-water. I finally concluded that it wasn't just the idea of the uniforms that were a holdover from colonial days. No, the uniforms themselves must have come directly from France in the fifties, made in only a handful of sizes, and have been reused for each of graduation ceremonies of the ten classes since! Like the gowns back home at college. I tried not to chuckle, but it was hard not to when my French colleague was grinning so broadly. When the DG on my left guffawed, I did as well, no longer fearing that it would be taken as rude.

If we were amused, the students and their families were tremendously moved by this rite of passage. Think for a minute of how it was in the United States back in the fifties or sixties when the first member of many families went to college. That's what this meant to these folks. There were wild cheers and throat yodeling when each name was read—sometimes so loud the emcee had to repeat who he was summoning up to present the diploma. As each student retreated back to his or her seat, he or she would be enveloped by spouses, family, or friends and hugged and kissed. There was one woman whose father was so overcome that they stood embracing in the aisle for what seemed like at least five minutes. For the men, the custom seemed to be for their wife or a female family member to grab the diploma, hold it high with pride, and turn around a few times for all to see before finally sitting. I felt sorry for the handful of students with no one present to cheer. The families and the students were justly proud of their accomplishment, and seemingly looked forward with pride to national service.

Then came the gift presentation for those who had excelled in one way or another. Again various ministers and officials were called up to do the presentations. It seemed that nearly everyone in the government, and the heads of the Supreme Court, National

Assembly, and so on, were all involved. The French ambassador was summoned, which struck me as appropriate since there had been a reference earlier on to French aid to the school. But then I heard "Ambassador of the United States," and there was the protocol person to escort me, too, up to the side of the dais. I presented a gift to one of the few young women who actually looked attractive and well fit in her uniform. One woman, a sort of valedictorian, received two prizes and was loudly cheered by all the other students. She was slightly lame, and I wondered if her colleagues knew of special hardships she'd endured. The newspaper report headlined her by name as leader of the Abderahman Dadi Class.

The last word was left to the prime minister for closing things down. He made a brief speech. (Another nice thing in Chad is that people generally keep their remarks short and focused.) He appropriately referred to Abdelrahman Dadi, who as both a graduate of the school and briefly as its director, was the perfect role model for the new graduates. And when the prime minister departed for a moment from his prepared comments, one could again detect a strain of real national pride undergirding all the usual injunctions about service to country and people that are customary on such occasions.

Yeah, it's a good thing I showed up for this one, even if the titular host didn't. It was truly gracious of the emcee to include me and a couple of my diplomatic colleagues in the proceedings. Moreover, I would have missed the valuable reminder that there is a sense of nationhood growing up here, even if it is still in childhood or adolescence. And seeing it through the prism of a national loss showed me as well something else Chad now has in common with us. Last, I was reminded of how much things we Americans take for granted still mean in a place like this—higher education, for example.

Regards,

Ambassador Chris

Being the Ambassador: Three Sides of a Coin

February 24, 2002

Dear Friends:

This will be the last planned Chad letter. That doesn't mean something won't crop up that I must relate in my final months, but here I will try to draw together some final thoughts on my experience as an ambassador in nearly three years here. I'll circle from the personal to the professional and back to the personal. [I didn't know as I wrote this letter that I would remain in Chad some eighteen months longer, writing many more letters, and setting a record for tenure as a US ambassador to the country.]

Been There, Done That

Overall this has been a fantastic experience for reasons I'll get to below. But being an ambassador on a daily basis hasn't always been a good fit for me. I will not seek a follow-up ambassadorship as many do. Why not?

First there is the small stuff—inconveniences, lack of privacy, being on call at odd times. Speakers at the ambassadorial seminar I attended told us that a car and driver were ours at any moment we were in country to take us anywhere, because we were always considered to be "on duty." They also warned us to block out some time each week as our own private time, which is easier said than done. Phone calls and invitations respect no such schedule: official dinners on Sunday evening, Saturday afternoon summonses to the Foreign Ministry, etc. And there is the lack of privacy at home— with four servants in a not overly big house, I have the place to myself only evenings (because I stopped having them come back to serve my dinner) and Sundays. Even on Sundays, there are gardeners running around the grounds, whom I could dismiss but to what avail, since I can't dismiss the guards that patrol the rear of the yard, which is the perimeter of the embassy compound?

And the security. I stopped running at the stadium when I learned the RSO [regional security officer] was sending someone to watch over me. And I'm told I don't dare travel unless either the

RSO or his assistant comes along. I don't see the threat here, and to me this is oppressive. And it is obvious to those outside—two days ago, one of the missionaries called to extend an invitation to an event at his house, expressing in advance his understanding if my security concerns wouldn't let me come into that part of town! I went. It is true that I usually manage one afternoon/evening of delicious solitude in the weekend. But which day often doesn't depend on me, and I have to plan aggressively during the week to shelter one or the other of them.

And there's the stuff I don't enjoy doing. Events: I've never enjoyed large receptions and dinners. I invest hours and hours here to just be seen and to pick up the odd tidbit of news. But folks are offended if I don't show for most of them. I'd do all this gladly if I felt there was a positive dividend, if the functions weren't an add-on to long parts of the business day when I already feel underutilized in this presence post, i.e., if they were truly an extension of the kind of busy work day I had back in Washington.

Then there are the tangential responsibilities: the American school and American club. These have posed the most intractable problems of any I've dealt with here. Essentially, we are trying to maintain both because they are absolutely key to morale, on a customer base that can barely support them. Through constant gyrations we keep our heads above water. But it is deflating that my most difficult managerial and intellectual challenges should be so ancillary to the issues of economics and politics I'd like to be grappling with.

The isolation of being ambassador also tells. I spend a great deal of social time with my Americans, judging my attention critical to keeping morale up, keeping their off hours occupied. But there is always the distance of being "Sir" or "Mr. Ambassador." And they don't invite me if they really want to unwind. With my peers, other ambassadors, it is little better since there is also an inevitable official side to the relationship. Nor do the Chadians warm to foreign ambassadors. Only once have I been invited privately for dinner, and the experience of my French and EU [European Union] counterparts is similar. My closest acquaintances have been with chiefs of the World Bank and similar institutions and a couple of the missionary or expat business families.

The dimension of life here that I'm even more cut off from than other expats is ordinary life. In Nigeria I used to enjoy going to local bars and restaurants, markets, and I had three or four Nigerian friends who would ask me in. I could glimpse a little of their life even if it was that of the better-off. Here, even in the *marchè*, I am recognized: *"Excellence! Excellence, ici!"* And if I went to some of the places at some of the times that I used to in Lagos, the regional security officer would have a heart attack. Ambassadors just don't go there. This in N'Djamena, which is much safer than Lagos was.

But all this is little stuff. It would evaporate in an instant if it weren't for The Great Frustration. This is that I will leave after nearly three years, having almost no concrete accomplishments. I can point only to one agricultural development project, financed with USDA [US Department of Agriculture] food aid, which I can say was my initiative. But the US government isn't really a player in Chad's economic development, and because of that we don't have much policy impact either. So for nearly three years I've been trying to show interest in Chad, protect US policy interests, and avoid raising expectations we cannot meet. So three years of maintaining a delicate holding pattern, treading water in a sea with an undertow. Someone who has made a career within the State Department derives satisfaction from that institution's imperative of maintaining a relationship. They would find it easier to accept this as the main part of the job. But in my career, I've grown too fond of getting concrete things done, and for me, the adjustment has been difficult.

A Meeting with No Agenda

On about my third visit back to Washington, two years into my term here, someone finally said it directly: "Chad is a presence post," meaning that my embassy's purpose is maintaining a US presence as opposed to accomplishing any specific US objective. Of course, we are to try to advance US policy, but Washington does not invest significant resources here and doesn't have great expectations of us. No senior official told me this before coming here. No one ever stopped or corrected my team here when we spoke or sent cables about what we should achieve here, or when we put it all down in our annual planning documents. This is, of course, the root of The Great Frustration. Only now, as I'm wrapping up, may this be changing a tad.

With this gripe as backdrop, let me then talk a bit about Chadian-American relations and how I have tried to relate to my Chadian contacts. And how I think the American ambassador should relate.

Beyond the general strictures of our Africa policy, the United States has one specific interest in Chad—the oil project—and one amorphous one, which is regional stability. The Chadians share our interest in furthering the oil project, and have a further specific interest in using the bilateral relationship to generate as much US aid as possible. These interests frame the communication that is at the core of my work here. In my first several months, discussion of the oil project dominated. But once the World Bank loans were approved with US support in June 2000, our relationship devolved into a meeting with no agenda. Small issues come up and I am tasked to make representations to various ministers a few times a month, but there is no programmatic structure to the relationship. We attract Washington's notice only when there is some crisis, for example, a recent student riot in which an American citizen's car was stoned.

So how do I try to forge a constructive dialogue under these circumstances? What I can give the Chadians is respect and my own attention and interest, up to the point where it would begin to build expectations of something I can't deliver. My colleagues and I maintain a steady schedule of calls, a handful each week, following the major developments in the country. We use whatever opportunities to interact our meager aid does give us, for example, the financing of the farmer-herder conference mentioned a few letters ago. Frankly, I could do a lot more and keep a lot busier running around town to see folks. But to what point? More cables won't help anyone back in Washington, and I would risk raising expectations here and eventually wearing out my welcome. Perhaps most important, one thing I don't do is lecture or demand. This sets me apart from the other Western ambassadors and heads of the international agencies; I believe it has won me the respect of my Chadian interlocutors, and perhaps makes them more attentive when I do express a viewpoint.

From the Chadians, in return, I feel respect, a certain appreciation, but a warmth that goes only to a certain depth. Is theirs the cool reserve of the northern desert? A lingering resentment of the departure of USAID [US Agency for International Development] and the Peace Corps before I got here, or simply the sad lesson Chad has learned that it cannot trust any foreigner? Outside N'Djamena, you know by now that the warmth goes deeper and is sincere; but that is the tradition of hospitality first, and appreciation for the visit of the American ambassador only second.

So what would I change? You know already—I'd like our encounter to have an underlying agenda. I'd like the United States to be more involved bilaterally in development here—it would serve American interests as much as Chadian. But I don't mean that I want to see just the normal run of typical aid programs. That would get us a seat at the table to intensify our policy dialogue with the Chadians, but at the risk of introducing the condescension and rancor I see in the relations with the French, European Union, and multilateral organizations. If it were up to me, I'd first multiply severalfold our self-help program where we actually deal with grassroots development efforts by local associations. And then I'd like to see us take the lead in tackling the great unknown middle zone of development in partnership with the Chadians, i.e., the gap between policy and capacity building at the government level, and the grassroots. This would all be a very different approach to bilateral aid, but it is the kind of leadership the United States should be exerting in developing countries. It would cost a lot less than our current aid programs and have much greater impact. But USAID prefers not to spend much on things that, however efficient, have low Washington visibility. So the bureaucratic obstacles are probably insurmountable.

The Ultimate Voyeur

I began this letter saying that this has been a fantastic experience, and then jumped into a litany of tepid complaints. So what is it that has salvaged the experience for me and made it all worthwhile? Chiefly, the vantage to observe this country that being the American ambassador has given me. It's unique. I can talk to anyone in the country at will, the president on down. The range of contacts is endless—ministers, opposition leaders, business people, association folks, journalists, other diplomats, and the list goes on. And I have an entire staff in the embassy dedicated to keeping me informed about what's happening throughout the land. And I have to admit it, here the detachment that comes with the lack of program I bewailed above is a plus.

Perhaps a metaphor will describe my observation point better than a description. I'm a Peeping Tom, circling the house, looking in one window after another. First a business perspective, then a human rights opinion, then a political window (the curtains on that one have been torn to shreds by the government and the opposition pulling in different directions). If there are some angles that are denied me because of my visibility, the entrée my job provides far outweighs them. I've been able to travel everywhere in the country except in the rebellious Tibesti. Even in N'Djamena I've had rare peeks into the squalid mud-brick compounds in the *quartiers*, usually going to wakes.

But the voyeur is always more titillated when the stripper retains a shred of her clothing. There are things this Tom sees, only distorted like the light refracted through a double-pane window. I've noted above the places where I can't go without notoriety, or where I don't get invited. There is also everything that people won't tell an ambassador, or do tell him hoping he'll actually believe it. And the flattery that makes me so uneasy. There are two Chadian ambassadors currently on assignment at the Ministry of Foreign Affairs, both protocol officials. I see them frequently and genuinely like them—but aren't their jovial handshakes and embraces, the inquiries about my health, always just a bit exaggerated?

And there is that side of Chadian life that no expat sees, save perhaps Les or Ace, the inscrutable family life. The blank walls and distortions are just enough to accentuate the thrill of my observations from my rare aerie.

So what indeed has been so enthralling? Can I summarize in a few words the essence from what I've relayed to you in over thirty letters? The country is one of beauty and variety—soaring in the Ennedi, soft and still in the watery plains of Zakouma. The difficulty of getting around is part of the enticement and satisfaction.

Barren in places and rich in others, Chad's resources are poorly exploited but nonetheless keep eight million souls alive. The sharp differences of the desert of both crags and sand dunes from the forested south just begin to suggest the essence.

The people sharpen the contrast. I still mourn the loss of the suave statesman **Abderahman** Dadi, who left behind too many grasping, venal scoundrels in offices too lofty for the country's good. The ordinary people are overwhelmingly friendly, if reserved in giving their hearts to outsiders. Their hospitality is inverse to their means—my skimpiest meals were the state dinners; in the countryside, people always put everything they had on the table, and on occasion gave me their own beds to sleep in. Much of what I've seen has been sordid and distressing—people living at the edge, beyond any redemption of comfort, and rarely complaining. And, God forgive me, it is fascinating for a well-off American to see it so closely. I've learned as well how much, in a pinch, I can do without. For most here, life is raw and elemental. Even the elite can't guarantee their comforts if they move through the land or return to visit their home villages.

It is most of all this sense of divisions and contrasts and their dialectic that I take away with me. Seeing from my vantage what is good and bad about this country only scratches the surface. Seeing what is good and bad in man is harder but more rewarding.

And here it is easier than at home, for life isn't subtle here. The dishonest official may hang out an alibi or excuse, but everyone knows him and he can't really hide his peculation. And in contrast, the honesty and self-respect of Chaibo, my driver, or Alphonse is positively uplifting. Yes, here you see the essence of humanity so starkly—nearly naked, rarely modest, good and evil blended inextricably in the same personality.

These past three years (almost) I've stared at it, often unable to divert my eyes, sometimes feeling I should and a little sordid myself when I can't, like a voyeur. I've tried to describe and interpret it for you, to tell you what it has awakened in me and how I have appreciated it. There is something intangible, a sense of growth and satisfaction, I feel I have stolen from this experience. Perhaps this, and not The Great Frustration, is ultimately why I chose not to seek another ambassadorship. This experience couldn't be repeated in another country. Nor should it be.

Best regards,

Ambassador Chris

Jogging in N'Djamena and Giving Blood

August 8, 2002

About six weeks ago I bit the bullet and began jogging again. I'd intended to do it when I moved back to DC. But if I'm going to be in N'Djamena several months (perhaps a year, it now seems) longer, I don't want to put this form of exercise off any further. So I do it the only way I can—I rise early (5:45 a.m.) on Tuesdays, Thursdays, and Saturdays, and do a leisurely two to two and a half miles up and down the paved road in front of the embassy. Any later and the street is too congested and it gets too hot.

No one in America would run on a track like this. The "sidewalk" is a sandy expanse, irregular and uneven, interspersed with piles of garbage and obstacles like holes in the concrete grill over the deep drainage ditches. Keep eyes peeled to avoid broken ankle! The street is little better, the pavement potholed and eroding. Perhaps the best compromise is the edge of the street where the sand has piled up a little, filling gullies and cushioning the asphalt, at least when there aren't vast puddles.

You may recall that I tried running when I first came, driving down to the National Stadium at about the same time, also three days a week. But I hated having to drive to where I run. And the final straw was when I learned that the RSO was sending a plain-clothes guard to watch over me. But times change, you live and learn.

Now I tolerate the security in the interest of the greater good. There's a car that follows me. I hate it, but, hey, what are you gonna do? For a couple of days, there were two cars sandwiching me, one fifty feet ahead and the other fifty feet behind. I squawked. Now there's one car that follows maybe 500 feet behind. Often, as I make my little circuit, it's on the other side of the street. That works OK.

When I first started this, out in the street, the first things I noticed were sights, smells, and sounds. I pass several of N'Djamena's principal sights—the Rond-Point de l'Unité with its three mosaics portraying life in Chad's desert, Sahel, and Sudanian zones; and the National Reference Hospital and City Hall, across the street from the Monument Éboué-Leclerc. But the people are most interesting. There are already plenty on the road, mainly coming from Moursal, the middle-class residual area to the southeast. Most walk—miles it seems. Some bike, a few have motos or ride minivans—not so overcrowded at this hour. There are yellow taxis too, and a handful of private vehicles. Here and there it seems a vendor has slept by his stand.

The smells were overwhelming the first day or two, but you get accustomed to it, tolerant. N'Djamena's major arteries are lined with deep drainage gutters, often infilled with trash and sand. They collect liquids and everything else. You smell the rot in the heat, including waste, animal and human. Sometimes you see a guy urinating in them, but not every twenty feet, like back in Nigeria. And the little piles of garbage no one removes smell as well. It's the rainy season now, so the moisture awakens the odors. But after several days I hardly notice.

The people I pass rarely smell—or rarely smell bad. Men and women both favor floral scents that disguise days without bathing. Remember that household water is mostly carried blocks from a neighborhood well in plastic or metal cans—on the head, dangling off either end of a yoke, etc. Or it's bought dearly from a water boy. It's amazing that these people keep themselves as clean as they do.

The sounds are gentler at this hour: voices calling to one another, the mumbled words of people munching breakfast beignets over tea, the whir of a car or bike. At one point I heard the splash of water—and looked up to spy the leakage in the low water tower at the National Reference Hospital. Loudest are the frogs, croaking up from the drains in this season.

In some ways this is as close as I've been able to get to ordinary city life. I see a certain segment—the street vendors—as their day begins. Many in this neighborhood are purveyors of street food. At this hour they are setting up, it seems, for their own breakfast before opening for sales. Tea is boiled or poured from thermoses into little two-inch glasses. There are big bags of beignets—fried, square doughnuts with no holes. These folks are gathered in groups. Later, one or two will move over to mind the stalls. What do the others do?

The vendors I see seem to divide into four or five groups, of whom I've already mentioned the food vendors. Suffice it to add that later in the day, the beignets long gone, the women will bring hot stews and boule in enameled metal pots resembling toleware. Then there are the washermen. They have huge piles of clothes tied up in sheets. I can't tell if these have just been fetched from people's houses, or if they are what had been collected and washed the previous afternoon, now ready to return to the owners. The outside wrap always seems rather drab, but some of the garments inside explode in riotous color in the dim dawn—undoubtedly the *peignes* of the women. Then there are the sundry sellers—cigarettes, detergent, little odds and ends of daily life. And last, the fuel hawkers—diesel and gas for the motos in one-liter bottles, and larger drums with basic pumps for cars. The vendors are mainly men, with women dominating only with food sales. In other parts of town you see different product mixes, and in the Christian quarters to the southeast, more women. Then, working harder than any of these folks, are the charcoal porters pushing their two-wheeled carts, laden with 200 pounds perhaps, into town to the market.

These poorer Chadians have good habits. One thing that struck me was the honesty you see in small places. The vendors have no qualms in leaving their primitive chairs and tables, and sometimes their merchandise, overnight. There is one plant seller I pass who leaves his hundred seedlings in the open, abandoned at night. The limit here seems to be the vehicle fuel, which is carted away at day's end and brought back in the morning. But, all in all, it is a sharp contrast to the major corruption we hear about in high places.

In addition to being honest, these folks are tidy. As I jog by, I see that several of the vendors have already carefully raked the trash away from their simple stands. And afterward, they swept the sand into neat, fanlike patterns spreading out from their rickety tables. I try not to disturb their handiwork, and move out onto the street to run by these stretches. Alas, there is no system for collecting and disposing of the tidy piles of refuse. As like as not, in the rains it drifts into the drainage channels, or back toward the vendors' stalls, to be swept away anew the next morning.

I'm hardly anonymous when I run. From the first, the guards at one or two compounds I pass would shout "Bonjour, Excellence!" Now even the kids along the route mostly recognize me. Yesterday there was a big group of traffic police at a roundabout I circle (the end of the month is ticket time here too!), and one of them called out, *"Bon courage, Ambassadeur!"* Lots of people say *"Bon courage,"* and I feel no danger or discomfort as I lope along. A few days ago a couple of the guards from one concession, with elaborately exaggerated gestures, joined me for a dozen paces to our great mutual laughter. But people must think it strange to see a jogger—I've seen only a couple of Chadians running, though when they are in town a couple of Canadian oilmen I know run at this hour and sometimes pass me.

Which brings up a metaphysical point. Calories. I run in large part to burn them. None of the toiling Chadians I see, already approaching their places of labor at this hour of dawn, are heavy. These are working blokes whose meals don't come easy. They'd love to own the extra pounds I'm trying to shed. And so, ever again, even in this simple exercise of running, I come back to the strong contrasts here that so fascinate me.

I noted above that my route takes me past the National Reference Hospital, a couple of blocks from the Embassy. This is Chad's best hospital, save for the one at the French air base. And perhaps this is as good a time as any to describe the blood donation we made there a week or so ago.

A couple of weeks ago an article on the front page of the only daily paper, highlighted the scarcity of blood. There were only five pints in the national blood bank, all donated and reserved by family members for their own sick relatives. This got Marty, our nurse-practitioner, thinking: could the embassy organize a mini–blood drive? And of course, for me guilt overcame apprehension—I decided to give as well. In the end, twenty of our folks, about half, and half Americans and Chadians, took the plunge (of needle into arm, that is).

The hospital is a sprawling complex of single-story buildings scattered around a huge compound. Only the entry drive and an oval amid four or five administrative buildings are paved. The rest of the buildings are separated by sandy tracts that, in this season, harbor huge pools of malarial waters.

Arriving at the hospital, we disembarked from several cars and someone led us back to the blood bank at the very rear of the compound. Kay, my public affairs officer, complained loudly that the hospital's rear gate, almost opposite the embassy, hadn't been opened for us—we could have walked, avoiding the floods. But we threaded our way between mosquitoey puddles and arrived before the blood bank building. The last steps required a leap halfway across a huge puddle onto a teetery brick, onward onto the foundation of a hole in a fence, and finally onto dry land. We scraped the mud off our shoes as best we could and tramped into the facility.

I'm inured by now to the dingy squalor of Africa, even dirt in a hospital. So let me translate the commentary from the newspaper, regarding the sanitary conditions we met:

"It is necessary to point out that, despite the goodwill of the personnel of the blood bank, the site is disgusting. This building, at the east end of the hospital, behind 'Medication 5,' is ramshackle. The rooms are tiny, the floor rutted, the walls damaged, the paint dim with age. The ceiling is warped by the oozing rains. Visitors and donors are received in the hallways. There is a sad lack of modern equipment. That which exists is much deteriorated. The blood bank has a storage capacity of 200 pints for a population of 500,000." Let me add only that I saw the same little piles of trash in corners here that I see when jogging; and that the population is really more like 800,000.

Of course, we took our own supplies and equipment as necessary to ensure our safety. But the Chadian hospital staff was good—gloved, the technician examined first one arm and then the other, and needed only one stab to get a good vein in my left arm. You pump faster in the ninety-degree-plus heat, and I'd guess that within five to seven minutes my pint was collected.

The format here is a little different here than back home. Modeled on the French system I assume? The cots weren't bed style, but recamiers—you reclined with the upper portion of the body elevated at nearly ninety degrees. Marty spread our own sterile covers on the beds. And the collection bags were below, hidden from sight. Mine dropped onto the floor when the technician tried to attach it, and Marty insisted that a new one be brought. These are imported from France, double sealed and sterile.

And naturally I felt smug after giving. Don't you always? At least a little? My newly arrived deputy chief of mission spent some time talking with our Chadian donors afterward. Several were first-time donors, and one or two indicated that they wouldn't have given except that the ambassador was doing it. Makes you feel pretty good.

Here, too, I can't help but wax a bit philosophical. A few years ago in the United States when I tried to give blood I was refused. It was because I'd lived in Nigeria for over six months nearly fifteen years earlier. Chad, I noticed, was also on the list of suspect countries. So I probably can't ever give blood again back in the US of A. Why? HIV/AIDS? Malaria? Both, I'm told. I'm glad that I've been able to give here—if ever I need a transfusion back home, I'll feel justified in that my own pint has helped a Chadian.

Our donation made headlines here, of course. It was the lead story on television that evening, and on the morning following there was a photo of myself, sleeve rolled up, on the front page of the daily paper. Our goal wasn't PR only, though we saw the obvious benefits. We discussed the publicity with the hospital—they wanted it, hoping that our example would stimulate other donations. Let's hope it did. The story also ran on radio, the most influential media here. And speaking of smugness, I take a certain nationalistic pride that the French embassy would never do this kind of thing. The government of Chad was so grateful that they sent a diplomatic note to the State Department thanking us. The grand imam called on me at the embassy with a delegation—an unheard-of departure in protocol—to thank me. Weeks later, when I met the new health minister at a reception, he brought it up as well.

The day after we were bled was my jogging day. I ran up and down the street before the embassy. And when I came to the hospital, I saw that the rear gate was open. Kay would have been furious had she known ... I didn't tell her.

Best wishes,

Ambassador Chris

2

The Country: N'Djamena and the South

As a child in the 1950s and 1960s, my family drove across the United States numerous times, generally from our California home, to visit my grandparents in the East. I was the typical impatient, "Are we there yet?" child. In Chad, decades later, I grooved on every move outside N'Djamena.

Long hours on rutted *pistes*—dirt tracks. Here was the chance to see how 90 percent of Chadians lived. Talks with local officials and the ubiquitous citizens' groups. A look at the local agriculture, the towns, and the rare historical or economic site of interest. This travel was what I loved best in my years in Chad.

The letters in this chapter describe my visits to two of Chad's climatic zones: the moist south and the central Sahelian belt. These encompass the bulk of the country's agriculture and other economic activity, except for herding. Thrown in for good measure is my description of my first visit, very early in my tenure, to the Waza game park in nearby Cameroon. My first conclusion: Chad's flag should be blue, beige, and green, representing the bright sky and the two seasons, dry and wet.

Thematically, you may find in these letters several things. Beyond my own joy in traveling the countryside was the impact it makes for the American ambassador to appear in a remote village. Also apparent is my fondness for Zakouma, one of my two favorite spots in Chad, and my hopes for its prosperity.

I hope you will get a sense for why I valued these treks. For example, meeting the village people who form associations to better their lot with our meager self-help funds exposed me to the automatic and heartfelt hospitality of people who had so little for themselves. Also intriguing is the enigmatic role of the central government, guiding and cooperating with local notables and the villagers, not strong enough to dictate unless crisis forces intervention. The Gong and Lamido, traditional rulers, remain local powers, balanced by the local administration of *préfets, sous-préfets,* and *chefs de cantons* [village chiefs].

Here also you will see surprises: the expat eccentrics, largely European, that gravitate to Africa, like Kuhn at Waza: the well-functioning Baptist Hospital at Koumra; the petrified forest and the incredible range of vibrant birds.

Between the lines you may read the reason for my dedication of this book. The "Les McBride network" and the guidance Les offered served so many ambassadors to Chad so well. His understanding and love for the country, the depth and breadth of his contacts, and his advice were invaluable.

Driving in N'Djamena, or, a Tour of the City

February 2000

So you've come to N'Djamena for the weekend. Why not? People from out in the bush do it all the time. To make the best use of your brief time here, we'll spend a lot of it in the car taking my personalized tour of the city. Assuming we wrap this up today, Saturday, tomorrow we can run over to Koussérie in Cameroon, squeeze in church at SIL, and perhaps get out into the country just a bit.

To begin with, you should know that N'Djamena is laid out roughly north to south along the Chari River. It spreads inland a fair bit in the middle. The directions are only approximate and, as in many American cities, the gridlike streets divide at geographical breakpoints and head off in different directions, making any sense of direction confusing.

We'll start off where the city started, with General Lamy. He is credited with having conquered Chad for France in 1900, although he was killed in the decisive battle over in Koussérie. His companions decided to found their own city on the right bank, named it Fort-Lamy in his honor, and buried him in what became the main cemetery in Farcha, a northern suburb. We begin at his simple but honored gravesite, where I was taken on Veterans Day by the French ambassador to lay a wreath—nearby is a tomb to the unknown soldier. The cemetery has both Christian and Muslim portions. The graves are dug shallowly, with more earth piled high above the ground. Many are marked only with wooden crosses. I wonder what happens when the rains come.

Farcha is an important part of N'Djamena. Much of the city's trivial amount of industry is there—for example, the flour mill, which has been closed since the civil war back in the 1980s. There is a functioning abattoir that I've purposely avoided visiting since my cook buys there. There is also a women's weaving and embroidery cooperative where we stop to do a bit of souvenir shopping. The only truly unique Chadian handicraft item I've discovered is the loosely woven ecru cotton cloth embroidered with designs adapted from the rock paintings in the north. A "must" stop is the Coca-Cola Bottling Plant, since we're in the neighborhood—the best place in town to get wine (French, medium quality, about the same price as comparable bottles back in Washington, DC).

As we turn down toward town, we pass Camp 27. This military base, named for no one knows what, is the site of our demining school. The training of the deminers, with centers both here and up in Faya-Largeau, is the largest US bilateral assistance project. If we can talk our way onto the base (unlikely, unless we're in the official vehicle with flag), you will see the low pyramids of earth back away from the housing to where test mines are detonated. But if you've ever been on an American base, what will strike you most is the scores of family members milling around with the half-in-uniform soldiers. Women, children, men with and without weapons, all just hanging out. The women thread their way across the test minefield, vessels on head, making for the single outdoor faucet alongside the school building, where they chat, fill their containers, heft their infants back up into the cloth wraps on their backs, and go off again carefully balancing the now full containers on their heads.

But I said this is a driving tour. Out in Farcha you have been in a different world from N'Djamena. Most all the buildings, if fairly run down, have been stuccoed, painted, and set in ample yards a little back from the road. The road itself runs parallel to the river and is tree lined and, by local standards, broad. We have threaded by a few stopped minivans, and the odd tricycle peddled by someone who has lost a limb to a land mine or polio, but the driving challenge still lies before us. The Farcha road does have an inappropriate number of speed bumps, put in a year or two ago to slow down the police chasing the smugglers, who had caused many accidents and several fatalities. But this roomy neighborhood with its nearly defunct agricultural research station and the sprawling French air base isn't the real N'Djamena, however important a component it is of the city's economy. Let's head south into town.

Coming in from Farcha we twist and turn, come back adjacent to the river where you have a pleasant view of the exotic mud villages on the Cameroon side, and file down a narrower road past the Novotel. Also known as Hotel Tchadienne, it is one of the two in town where we put visitors. Several scenes from Romain Gary's novel *The Roots of Heaven* take place here. Along this stretch you will begin to appreciate the difficulty of local driving. I had thought that after the aggression and congestion of Washington driving, this would be a piece of cake—not many cars in this relatively small city of 800,000 with its modest distances. Boy, was I wrong.

Driving in Chad is a lot like what I imagine driving in the United States to have been like around the time of World War I. To begin with, there are not many paved roads. Most are dirt and, I'm told, many nearly impassable during the rainy season. They're bad enough in the dry season—narrow, garbage filled, rutted, with the worst little obstructions hidden by the black plastic bags that are littered ubiquitously. And the paucity of motor vehicles doesn't atone for the increased unpredictability. Most people, including my driver, drive at a pace guaranteed to frustrate a Washington driver to the point of madness—rarely above twenty-five mph [miles per hour]. At last, I admit this is prudent. Many of the people from the bush drive even slower, and have no concept of other vehicles moving around them. They stare straight ahead, trying to avoid the pedestrians, animals, mopeds, etc., of which more later. But then there races by—well into the oncoming lane and oblivious of oncoming traffic—a city driver, likely a government notable or someone from

Nigeria. And the crumpled yellow taxis are forever lurching across the lane of oncoming traffic to pick up a fare on the other side of the street. Nor can you tell when the car in front of you will simply stop, dead in the middle of the road, to discharge some rider.

But the cars aren't really the half of it. Take the animals. There are animals being driven along by herders. There are animals being ridden by people—camels or horses, usually. There are the dogs—often sleeping right in the middle of the street with no consciousness of the passing traffic. And there are the animals pulling carts. These are often enormously laden with anything from straw to big sacks of sugar or charcoal. And the mopeds—this seems to be the favored means of transportation of the Chadian middle class, meaning, for example, my driver or my household servant. Most seem to have a maximum speed of fifteen to twenty mph, which does not stop the drivers of the "fast" machines from swinging out to pass the drivers of the "slow" machines with no attention to who or what may be coming up behind them. The principle seems to be that caution is the responsibility entirely of the other guy. And this goes for the pedestrians who make up a large share of the street traffic. I've often seen people, singly or in groups, plunge out into the midst of a busy intersection without looking, confident that the cars, mopeds, and bikes will all avoid them. Does this begin to convey the enormous difficulty of adapting from a practice where roads themselves are the sole property of cars and trucks, and where the rule is to go as fast as conditions permit, to one of completely random traffic of every kind of creature and conveyance? Trucks? More of them later. Let's get back to our touristing.

Now that we're coming into town I explain to you that N'Djamena calls itself "La Ville des Rondpoints," the city of traffic circles. Actually, it may be *ville de fontaines*—the fountains in the *rondpoints*, but since none of them function, the point is moot. The idea is that N'Djamena is a planned city, however overwhelmed the plan may have been by subsequent unchecked sprawl.

I've described for you before the depressing uniformity of the city's mud-brick architecture and the monotony of single-story structures behind equally drab compound walls. I'm told it wasn't always like this—the defensive posture developed, not surprisingly, with the advent of relentless civil war over three decades ago.

But today that's neither here nor there. Let's focus on the sites of the city during our drive through town, and on what makes it vital.

Coming in from Farcha we are entering the administrative quarter, ironically the only neighborhood in the city without a name. It is here that most expats, including my embassy colleagues, call home. That doesn't mean that there aren't squatters setting up housekeeping in shanties on the vacant lots between compounds, but this is the prosperous side of town. We drive around the first of the fountains, the Place du Maréchal Leclerc, with big golden bulls' heads around its base. Leclerc was the French officer who led Free French troops across the Sahara from N'Djamena to join up with the North African campaign in World War II, ensuring a soft spot for Chad in the hearts of all good French imperialists. Appropriately, the Place radiates streets in a design modeled on the Place de l'Étoile but in miniature. And most of them are unpaved.

We take one of the spokes, turn a couple of times and double back to the road called Avenue Charles de Gaulle, the main street of the Westernized part of town. It is this that I described in an earlier letter as the Main Street of a 1950s western. I think a little more kindly of it today, as my eyes have learned to pick out the whitewashed or stuccoed buildings with their shady arcades in front. There is the Chinese restaurant and Restaurant N'Djamena, the best in town, with so-so French cuisine. And lining the arcades are the vendors of tourist items interwoven with merchants of vegetables, tins of food, and beer. After about three blocks, as we near another rondpoint, we pass a half-block of vendors selling nursery stock. And then we are in the circle, marked on the east by the finest building in town, the Bank of Central African States, some seven or eight stories tall. We make a right turn out of the place and in a block come to one of the city's two stop lights. We exercise caution to avoid the open gutter that runs dangerously close to the edge of the narrow paving. At the light we make a left, but then swing sharply right into the gateway of the National Museum. Here we will pause for a half hour, long enough to exhaust the collection's four little rooms. Traditional handicrafts, regional culture, N'Djamena history, and the archaeology digs in the north are the four themes. While small, the collection is of such enormous scientific interest that the best fossils are reproductions—the French who dug them have refused so far to meet their commitment to return the originals to Chad. In a newer, larger exhibition hall behind the museum proper, there ran for three weeks an art exhibit, where I purchased my first Chadian painting.

Resuming our drive, we pass on the left a monument to Lamy in a little park overrun with squatters, the Catholic Cathedral, and then quickly on the right the Presidential Palace, a.k.a. le Palais Rose. It is a complex of three detached pavilions, the grandest and centermost of which is the actual residence, replete with reception rooms. As palaces in developing countries go, it is not too extravagant. The grounds aren't very well kept, but there are a few gazelles roaming around. And if we crane our necks to see through the grated grill to the little dilapidated guards' hut by the entrance, at least one of the guards will be sprawled out asleep in the shade of a tree—perhaps with a family member or two.

Soon, on the right, we will pass a monument to Leclerc and Félix Éboué, the independence leader for whom the artery is named. Like that of Lamy, it has seen better days and is now behind a locked gate. But the outline of what were once pleasant gardens remains. We are now nearing the familiar US embassy compound, but will make a left turn to head towards the Grand Mosque and the center of the Chadian city. The mosque is a large, attractive rose stucco structure with two tall minarets. It was financed by the Saudis, who also sprang for the appropriately named Faisal University next door. Adjacent to the mosque is the main market, closed now as it is being totally rebuilt, again with Saudi development assistance funds. Some of the vendors have moved out into the sidewalks and street, so you will be able to fill most needs, and enjoy the myriad colors of fabric and plastic ware, without going out to the temporary market farther south. Our driver can stay with the car (there's no parking), and we disembark long enough to stroll the crescent around the mosque and stick our heads into one or two carpet stores to see if they have any Chadian kilims hidden away beneath the gaudy, machine-made Middle Eastern ones that seem to be more popular. Many of the latter are brought back from the hadj and sold by the hadjis to defray their travel expenses.

Again in the vehicle, we head out Avenue Mohamed Gaafar al Nimeiry. This is the main street of the Muslim quarter. It is lined with handicraft and utilitarian shops. Lots of hardware dealers, some of auto parts. There are many makers of wooden furniture, which is of plywood lacquered in a variety of monotones, but with little touches of decoration that look oddly art deco in style. The street teems with commerce and stretches a good two miles before it jogs a half-turn to the right and enters a less dense, more residential neighborhood. Eventually it will dead-end into another artery on the outskirts of the city, and before us is the National Assembly, termed "Palais du 15 Janvier" for an event on that date which I haven't yet tracked down. Chadians seem to like naming things with numbers. For example, most streets in town are named with numbers in a complex pattern that gives no clue as to location — with the result that no one uses street addresses in giving directions.

We turn right on the artery that will snake us through a typical *quartier* where the people live. We see a vibrant market on one side, offering even a few animals, unlike the one downtown. As we come closer to the river again, we are in Moursal, a section inhabited by largely Christian people from the south of Chad. To the trained eye, the buildings are a little more open. As we turn back north on Félix Éboué just opposite the single-lane bridge over the Chari River, we note the number of native cafes with little wooden benches and tables out in front. They have names like Galaxie-Annexe, Bah-Sam Bar, and Discotheque Oxygene. I remember on New Year's Eve seeing the throngs of drunken partiers lurching from one to another (and out into the street) as I drove home around 2:00 a.m. The southerners are definitely more outgoing than the northerners in Chad.

After a mile we will pass the National Stadium, built by the Chinese before Chad flip-flopped and recognized Taiwan. It isn't anything fancy, just a good basic soccer field surrounded by a decent track. For a while I tried coming here to run at 6:00 a.m. But having to drive to get here, and the insistence of the regional security officer that he plant an observer beginning a half hour before I arrived, and then arriving half an hour late in the office, were between them conditions I couldn't deal with. Next we go off the main road and make a brief stop at the temporary main market (the RSO wouldn't like that either, but we can't stay in the car all the time). New, it is about the cleanest I've observed in Africa. Laid out in a nice grid, the merchandise roughly sorted out by alleyway, it has most everything you would expect to see in any African market, perhaps a little less variety in foodstuffs, but plenty for us to enjoy strolling through for half an hour. And after this we call it a day and close the mile that leads us back out to Félix Éboué, through the last of the rondpoints (that of national unity with three huge concave mosaics depicting the harmony of Chad's three climatic zones), and at last to the embassy compound and my residence.

Sunday. This morning we don't sleep in since we have only this day to finish your tour of N'Djamena and environs. At 8:00 a.m., or as soon after as is deemed civilized, we jump into the car and head back to the southern end of the city. We turn right over a single-lane bridge and enter Oualia, the section of the city between the Chari and Logone Rivers before they merge. This is the route that will take us to Cameroon.

After about fifteen minutes, we have reached the border. We're crossing into the other country for two reasons: so you can add another country to your list, and to sense the contrast of this better off but still developing country.

Our driver is Chaibo—my own—who is the best. We linger in the car as he puts our papers through immigration and customs. It may take fifteen minutes—or an hour. Even on a Sunday morning, we will observe a circus while we wait. There will be the vendors—sheets of eggs piled five or six deep and balanced on the head, kola nuts, tubers of every description, dates, citrus, and groundnuts are the visible food choices.

Small Peugeot pickups will inch along in either direction, piled to nearly three times the height of the cab with cargo, the wheels bowed out surreally, limiting their speed to a crawl. This pattern will be echoed by larger trucks, motorbikes, and even bicycles. The bikes will have as many as three enormous sacks of grain or charcoal perched precariously above the rear wheel, nearly as wide as the bike itself is long. And the cars? Once I saw one with two men in northern robes in front, and four live goats in the rear seat. They stopped just in front of me; a customs official came along and they opened the trunk and, lo and behold, there were four more goats!

So as we wait you will see every conceivable kind of portage—truck, car, head, hand, bike, moped, charrette, tricycle, and of course camel. If you look a little farther, you will see the uses of the river as well: fishing, water source, kitchen and laundry room, irrigation source, bathroom, etc.

Our Cameroonian visit is only a token. To the trained eye, the contrast with Chad is clear. There are several *châteaux d'eau*—water towers—for a much smaller population. More buildings are stuccoed as we wind our way into Koussérie. And the two or three blocks of the main street are competitive with N'Djamena. This and a few other streets are paved, unheard of in small towns in Chad. While we're here, I'll run into one or another of the food stores and buy a case of wine—about a third less in price than over in Chad, despite the supposed customs union. It's also a good place to buy a Chinese-made bicycle.

And having obtained a Cameroonian stamp in your passport, and having tried to see a little of the contrast between the merely poor and the destitute countries, we return. At the border we'll pause again while Chaibo does his thing with the passports. You may notice this time the variety in garb: men in Western dress or flowing northern robes, the so-called "boubou"; women in a huge range of dress, from Western skirts and blouses, to northern wraps that enclose the body and include a matching shawl over the head, to shifts of various descriptions. What is most striking is the variety itself, and the contrast between the colorful female outfits and the drab male ones.

Back in N'Djamena now, it is nearing 11:00 a.m. and time to hurry off to church. The Sunday service would not normally warrant notice, but we are attending the ecumenical Protestant services at SIL. SIL is a religious, private, voluntary organization that works to record local languages (remember, there are 120 in Chad), develop primers and dictionaries for spreading literacy, and eventually introduce the Bible in the people's own idiom. But the church service (in an instructional hall without so much as a cross), is remarkable in and of itself. With no basis for unity of rite among all the missionary sects represented by Americans in Chad, a very loose and informal service has emerged. The ministry shifts among various missionaries. Usually there is a good portion of hymn singing, several readings of scripture, and sometimes a sermon. Often a fellowship lunch, picnic style, follows. You will see that there is little ritual, but much personal feeling toward God. While I come from an Episcopal background of considerably more formality and structure, I have to admit that somehow, here in Chad, it works for me. It communicates.

We will mingle briefly and I will introduce you to several of the missionary families, including some from Canada, Australia, Korea, Europe, and other countries. But we will apologize for not being able to stay for lunch, and take our leave.

Now we are off to the north, an hour's drive to one of the inselbergs being about all we can still squeeze into your weekend visit. We head north, passing the French air base on the right and the garbage dump on the left. The road is narrow, two lanes only, but with very little motor traffic. There are many of the hazards I've already mentioned—animals, pedestrians, mopeds, and the occasional truck stopped dead in the middle of the road for repairs, no warning sign at all.

Our first stop will be Dougia, where we'll return for a very late lunch. It is now half past one, but we'll stop at this little resort on the Chari River to order the meal and pick up a guide.

The guide helps us navigate another few kilometers along paved road, but at Karnal we turn off into the bush. Chaibo puts the car into four-wheel drive because the tract has deteriorated into sand. In fact, driving here several weeks ago was my first real experience with four-wheel drive. I got stuck once, but managed by rocking back and forth to break out, back up to where I could get traction, and to race over the dunes ahead. Elephant Rock is our goal, a rock formation some ten miles beyond Dougia.

Elephant Rock is probably an inselberg itself in strict classification, but in our book it is a fun place for a half-hour rock climb. You will be able to clamor up it with a minimum of exertion—it takes only twenty minutes, and there are only one or two steep points where it is hard to get traction with shoes or hands. From the top there is a beautiful vista over the Sahalean scrub plane, but also a neighboring inselberg and a few birds and villages. From this, you have gotten an impression of the Sahel, but also of the fragility of life here in Chad. The land we are on is productive now, but it wasn't back in the drought of the eighties when the country was dependent on food aid. On the way out, we pull around to the rear of the rock, and you see that it forms the perfect outline of an elephant, trunk and all. And during even a pause only long enough to take one photo, children will appear from the bush asking for a *cadeau* [a small gift].

We are just in time for our very late lunch at the Dougia resort, admiring the sun and shadows over the river, before we return to N'Djamena. Dougia is a veritable garden spot on the banks of the Chari, some sixty or seventy miles downstream from N'Djamena. From the shade of the tall trees above the outdoor tables, we see the blue line of the river. Between it and the softer blue of the sky are two parallel bands—one the beige earth, increasingly broad with the advance of the dry season, the other the green belt of shrubs and trees lining the far bank. The darker profile of a pirogue or two completes the placid scene.

In the growing dusk en route back to town, we encounter the last great challenge of driving here. Driving after dark poses three hazards that can be summarized as trucks, trucks, and bicycles. The first menace is oncoming trucks without headlights. It isn't the Chadian custom to replace these when they burn out, so most trucks lack at least one. And the exact position of the oncoming vehicle will be further disguised by the tendency to drive in the middle of the road, perhaps in an effort not to unbalance the inevitable mountainous load. Of course the truck will see you, and in a last-minute effort at equity will turn on its high beams just in time to blind you as you swerve toward the right shoulder. The second menace is the stopped truck, again with no lights, disgorging innumerable passengers who mill across both lanes of the road, oblivious to other traffic. And last, the bikes: Few have rear reflectors or headlights and, like the people, roam all over both lanes of the road. So if you see one in your lane in time to swerve left to pass it, you are just as likely to take out one in the oncoming lane. Similarly, the people in the villages we pass through will sit on the edges of the asphalt oblivious to the vehicular traffic.

Back in N'Djamena by early evening, you can say that in two days you've done the town and its environs—and experienced the challenges of driving from a totally new angle! N'Djamena is far from a tourist mecca, but does sport its handful of novel sites and neighborhoods, as must any agglomeration of 800,000 humans.

Best regards,

Ambassador Chris

Jet-setting around Chad

December 6–9, 1999

First, I'd better 'fess up that it wasn't a jet, but that was better because it would go more places. This week I had available the regional defense attaché C-12, a small executive jet that seats about eight passengers. So I spent three days traveling to and back from the "urban centers" of Chad: Faya-Largeau in the north, Abéché in the east, and Moundou in the south. In all, it gives me a good visual impression of the country early in my tour, and the chance to meet some of the local leaders.

Faya

Faya is an oasis in the Sahara. An old town, its palms begin to break the orangish Saharan sand from a distance, and you quickly become conscious of how extensive this break in the desert is, in fact. The palm groves stretch nearly twenty miles north to south, but in a narrow band like the irrigated land along the Nile. The impression of the Sahara itself deepens as you get into it north of N'Djamena—the scrubby bush yields to drier and drier country; the tree dots disappear, and the sands alternate with protruding rock as far as the eye can see. To the west of Faya, the landscape is mainly rock, eventually rising from 1,000 feet in elevation to the huge 11,000-foot crater mountain of Emi Koussi a hundred miles away. But the air is laden with sand to an altitude of a few thousand feet, and we couldn't see the mountain. To the east, the rock is sparser, the blowing sand ruling all. The wind must be very uniform in its direction, since the dunes and the eroded breaks in the rock all line up in parallel lines, stretching out to the murky horizon. As we approached Faya, we saw a caravan of about fifteen camels heading out from town south of the landing strip.

You don't have an impression of Faya itself until you land, for its single-story buildings are mostly obscured by the ubiquitous palms. From the ground, it is like a diminutive, even poorer N'Djamena, but with an exotic desert atmosphere. The mud brick is lighter in tone, the erosion slower since annual rainfall is in the single digits. A few of the buildings are stuccoed, on a handful the stucco brightly painted, peeling on the rest. I compared N'Djamena's main street to the main street of a town in an old western; Faya's is like the caricatured Mexican town in the same movie. The streets are of blown sand, the handful of vehicles in the town of 13,000 all four-wheel drive.

My first stop was to call on the préfet, the equivalent of governor of this province of only 60,000 people that stretches over the entire northern 40 percent of Chad. I pretended to understand his mélange of French, Arabic, and muttering. I hope I understood enough not to insult him, and to pose a few basic questions that didn't ask what he had just related. The préfet hadn't been told of my visit by the interior ministry, as he should have been, but he behaved with the impeccable politeness of these people and became my guide for the four hours I was in the town. Faya is where the demining (as in land mines) effort in Chad is focused, and demining is the largest US bilateral assistance activity, so I wanted to see the center, which is being constructed, and the hospital that will support the deminers in case of accidents. Those things have to be completed before the fifty-two deminers the United States has trained can get out into the fields to clear mines. We waited over tea, soft drinks, and cookies as the préfet sent messengers to arrange our tour.

The hospital seemed staffed by a single administrator and one doctor, both of whom dropped everything to show us around. They showed us the single-bed operating room, which had less equipment visible than my doctor's office back in the States. Cleanliness suspect, dedication not. There was an x-ray, but it was out of service due to a missing part. We were shown one recent mine victim, a youth of sixteen or eighteen who had scars from the shrapnel all over his chest and right arm. He was lucky; it only took two days to get him the 300 miles here from where his mule had tripped the mine, and he was healing well. But no way was this clinic satisfactory for local needs, let alone reaching international standards for deminers.

We drove then through the market. The old market, also called the Women's Market, near the main mosque seemed to be largely food products. We hurriedly walked through, amazingly avoiding anyone's produce as we trod. Faya, by the way, has twenty-two mosques, four churches, and one synagogue. There was no religious strife, the préfet, whom I was beginning now to understand a bit better, assured me. The newer market had the usual array of vehicle needs, animal feeds, and a street of little open-faced shops with housewares. Somewhere there was a camel market; later I learned that the livestock market didn't open until afternoon, when it was too hot to work any more.

I had no clear idea where we were headed next, as the cars took us through town and in a direction that I want to say was south, although I forgot to note the sun and it could have just as well been north. We passed palm gardens, irrigated with groundwater. The water table is two meters; we were told this was a problem, however, since the latrines in town also drained to two meters. This stopped the recently constructed *chateau d'eau*, or water tower, from operation; the groundwater it pulled was all polluted. We got out from town and followed the line of palm groves on our right, with the desert opening up again on our left with alternating rocky bluffs and orange dunes. We drove over sand and rock. It became apparent we were headed to a natron (think rock salt) field, natron being, along with dates, the principal product of Faya. After a ride that would have done my colleague Frank proud, we halted in front of a group of four men and six camels. The men were digging and breaking up the chunks of natron rock, putting those rich enough to be worth the haul into huge leather sacks. These men had traveled on camelback two weeks here from Biltene, further east, were nearly finished after two days of mining and would be on their trek back home the next day or so. I saw that the camels each had its left foreleg doubled back at the knee and secured with a soft woven rope; thus hobbled, they would not run off. Did I want to climb on one of the camels? Regretfully, not in the suit I was wearing.

On the run back into town, I began to appreciate why all the locals wore exotic head turbans that wrapped around their mouths and noses, leaving only the eyes exposed: I became conscious that the wind was blowing the grit of the Saharan sand into my mouth, no matter how hard I tried to avoid it, and coating my exposed forehead and cheeks as well. At one point, our vehicle floundered in the sand. I was not allowed to climb out to lighten the load, but we went into four-wheel drive and five men from the other car came to push and we got going. With the taste of the grit, I smelled the burning of rubber the rest of the way back into town.

We made a brief stop at the demining center, which will be perfectly satisfactory as an administrative unit and hostel for the deminers when it gets finished. The local director presented me with a baby gazelle, Chad's national animal. I held the little critter for a few moments—all of six or seven pounds with its two-foot length, clean and soft to my touch—but couldn't keep it since we couldn't take it on the plane. What a Christmas gift it would have made for John or Nicholas, or Michael and Katherine, children of my closest friends! And then we bid farewell to Faya, the ever-loyal préfet making us stop at his home for a stand-up, ten-minute lunch and accompanying us out to the air strip.

We had purposely hurried off to have time to make an air tour of the north before heading back to N'Djamena. About two hundred miles northeast of Faya is Chad's salt lake district—several inland lakes of varying hues, depending on the exact chemical content of the water. We saw greenery and the straw huts of the north, made entirely of palm fronds. There are four lakes, surrounded by desert, nearly contiguous, each looking to be several miles in diameter. We swung low, noting the presence of military vehicles here, only 200 miles south of the Libyan border and at a strategic point due east of the hills that shelter the rebels. Earlier in the century, the encampment was an outpost of the French Foreign Legion for fifty years, at one point occupied by the Libyans, and now of course by the Chadians.

We raced southeast now, looking for Fada, a smaller oasis where we wanted to get a look at the airfield. As we approached Fada, we approached the Ennendi—a moonlike landscape of broken-rock formations that darkened from the orange that I call "Sahara color" to a brownish red to nearly black, like dried blood. The closest *be-griff* [concept] for Americans is probably Bryce Canyon. After circling Faya and the airstrip a couple of times, we all, including our pilots, became mesmerized by the erosion-formed cliffs and buttes. We engaged in a series of "low levels," sweeps along the rock formations that brought us within a few hundred feet of them and kept us below their tops. I kept my eyes peeled for any signs of rock art, said to be present here, but saw none. We banked and soared and, alas, our Chadian demining colleague lost the lunch he'd greedily scarfed down back at the *préfet*'s. Ah, well. So it goes. Demurely, we leveled off and headed back to N'Djamena over hundreds of miles more of Sahara. Yet it was not quite barren! As I watched, I noticed that the desert was laced with wadis, and that now, in the wake of the rainy season, little dots of trees or bushes speckled the lines the wadis made through the waste of sand and stone.

And just to let you know that an ambassador's life isn't all touristic fun, I'll boast that when I got back to the embassy at 5:30 p.m., I went in to an hour-and-a-half meeting on how to balance our perimeter access security concerns with the sensibilities of the other ambassadors, a couple of whom intimated to me that they are offended by having their cars searched for bombs when visiting me.

Abéché

The flight to Abéché was uneventful. We did dip low over one large lake, Fitri, but it was nowhere near as exotic as the landscape yesterday up around Faya and Fada. Just brown scrub brush as far as the eye could see. Hazy up to several thousand feet with the incipient harmattan.

Abéché is Sahelian, whereas Faya was Saharan. The ground is completely covered with thin grass, dried now to a tawny straw. In the wadis, where there is no foliage or where the land has deteriorated into patches of sand, it is much more tan or beige than the orange-brown Saharan sand. There are fewer camels and more donkeys, a few horses. There is scrub brush and the odd tree along a dried watercourse, but everything is much drier than, say, Waza. I believe that I was looking at desertification in process. I could see how thinly the dried grass held the soil, and wherever the earth

was bare, for example, the track our Toyota followed, it was deteriorating into sand. I'm not optimistic about what I'll see here if I return in ten years, or even five. The white, four-wheel-drive Toyota
SUV is, by the way, *the* vehicle in Chad. Everyone has one; it's what
the embassy uses too—all configured with folding seats in the rear
to hold four extra passengers in lieu of (or in addition to) baggage.

Abéché is a desert town, with somewhat the air of those I drove
through as a child when our family went cross-country—maybe a
Lovelock, Nevada, or Tucumcari, New Mexico. I had mistakenly
heard that it was a big town, 100,000, whereas it really has only
about 20,000. It isn't an oasis like Faya, but a small commercial
town trying to be an agricultural center where crop production
is precarious. It has the architecture of N'Djamena, but the streets
and clusters of houses are interrupted by sandy, dry wadis. Sanitation services are provided by the goats. Abéché is an old city by
Chadian standards, going back a couple of hundred years as the
capital of the Ouadai sultanate. The one departure in construction
materials—more use of red brick as opposed to only adobe—was
explained to me as an old Ottoman influence. Similarly, the metal
doors of the compounds and houses seemed to be more brightly
decorated than elsewhere.

My visit began with the obligatory courtesy call on the préfet.
As is the case in discussions with the northerners, there are long silences between comments, which embarrass no one. It is simply the
way—not every moment needs to be occupied with conversation
and I imagine these folks would find animated dinner conversation in a Washington home positively grating on the eardrums. We
talked largely about agriculture, which the préfet knew, and when
I asked him about other industries in the town, he simply said there
weren't any. The rest of the day was appropriately devoted to a review of the Africare development project, the largest US aid effort
after the demining.

We started with a briefing on the project, which begins with
monetized wheat flour and involves improving agricultural
production skills, marketing of fresh produce, and both storage
of fresh products and processing into a preserved form (largely
drying) for sale out of season. But the main effort of the project
has been land reclamation. We bounced out eighteen kilometers

into the countryside in the Toyotas. There, several years ago, a long retaining dike had been constructed across the exit of a wadi. The result is that when the rains come and the wadi is fed, the water is retained in an area measuring 350 hectares. The silt flowing down the wadi has evened the land surface and in contrast to the bone-dry fields and scrub bush outside, the area behind the dike is still green. Tomatoes will grow here until the end of March, making for an eight- or nine-month season where the rule is four or five. I looked at the green, bushy tomato and okra plants sprouting every few feet from the dry, cracked soil. The trick is that they had been planted in a trowel-sized hole a full foot into the ground, where the water remains to feed the roots. The first green tomatoes were evident on the plants. The plan is to expand the project with an additional 700 meters of dike, which will add between 100 and 150 hectares more. Indeed, the contrast between the barren bush beyond, with the odd withered field of sorghum or millet scattered into the gullies most appropriate for water catchment, and the even, green cover within was impressive.

Impressive also, however, is the poverty. We were told that over thirty villages with a population of about 5,000 try to scratch a living from the parched soil. Given the limited yields on 350 hectares, even semi-irrigated in this way, it ain't much. Nonetheless, as we toured the dike, construction site, and production areas, the peasants greeted us heartily. The men were lined up to shake hands, all wearing white robes and speaking only Chadian Arabic. The women, colorfully garbed, gave out their traditional yodel-like yells from the back of the throat as we approached. The people were particularly cheerful this day because water had been struck just the day before at a well Africare was digging near one of their villages; the people in five of the villages would now have potable water within an easy walk of two or three kilometers as opposed to going back fifteen kilometers into Abéché, or almost that far. And just a few months ago the forestry service had planted 7,000 tiny saplings that eventually would form a tree hedge to keep itinerant cattle from the fields during the transhumance. Some small steps of progress were coming together!

The day concluded with méchoui, roast whole goat stuffed with couscous and vegetables. Not too bad. Most ate with the hands, but I was allowed a knife and spoon. The agriculture minister who was my guest for the excursion courteously pulled some of the best morsels from the animal for me. In the shade during this coolest of seasons, it was actually quite temperate and pleasant; I sweated only because I had to be so formal as to keep my suit coat on. The only two Americans in town not affiliated with Africare had been invited—a doctor and his teacher wife, who had been in the region for nine years. He confirmed my impressions from the day before's hospital visit in Faya, but said he'd seen improvements over the years: for basic types of surgery, his facility was adequate. There were more doctors in the outer reaches of the country than before, when all but a dozen had been concentrated in N'Djamena. And by coincidence, I learned over the chop that the local Africare director had gotten his BA [bachelor of arts] at the State University of New York at Plattsburgh while my Dad had been teaching there!

Small world as it is, I departed less certain about the future of farming around Abéché. Will the dedicated work of both development workers and the farmers themselves be able to preserve their productive niches of land against the advancing desert? It made me think of the first Chadian painting I have purchased, *Mécontent dans un champ de riz*. It is a picture of a farmer standing in a field of lush, sprouting rice plants with a scowl on his face. Symbolic of the plight of farmers in Chad: Even a good harvest is scant cause for celebration because the grower is forced to sell it for a song, or it is only one good year among several bad ones. And ironically, as we came back into N'Djamena, we were delayed in landing due to air traffic (two other planes coming in, i.e., a ten-minute delay) and we swooped low out over the plains of Chad and Cameroon along the Chari and Logone Rivers. Plains still flooded from the rains two months ago with all the water that would have made the difference for those farmers up in Abéché.

Moundou

After skipping a day to do some real work back in the office, I flew off again, this time to Moundou in the south, *le Tchad utile*, or "the useful Chad," as the French call it in a backhanded slap at the north. This would take me to the third, smallest, and most productive of

Chad's climatic zones and to the country's second-largest city. The country was more interesting than the dry bush of the Sahel, and we spent about half the flight flying low along the muddy Chari River so the military guys could photograph the bridges. The country is greener as you move south from N'Djamena, especially as we got within about fifty miles of Moundou. The transition in the village and field structure that we could observe along the way was fascinating. A hundred miles south of N'Djamena, when we began to descend, I saw expansive areas of cleared bush with alternating, irregular patches of beige and green hue. This probably reflected both water table and harvesting or planting a second crop in the fields. But the villages were unlike anything I had yet seen here — tiny circles, each made of several one-room thatched huts, scattered around the large expanses of bush like the lone trees further north. These must have been individual family settlements, since the little rings couldn't have held more than a few people, little more than a large nuclear family — a rare pattern in this Africa of the extended family. The population was intense along the river, but diminished a mile or two inland. Quite soon the village changed back into the larger, irregular jumbles of square and round adobe huts I'm used to seeing in this country — large enough to hold numerous families, with lots of space in between settlements. As we got well into the "useful Chad," a third pattern appeared: large square fields, obviously measured, and much larger villages or small towns with oblong houses with tin roofs, a little like some parts of southern Nigeria. Was this yet a third traditional settlement pattern, or was this step in the direction of Western order the result of the sometimes violent resettlement by the French when they forced the people of this region into cotton production some seventy years ago?

The country around Moundou is savanna, with taller grasses and greener from the air in spite of the hazy atmosphere. The defense attaché had described the city of Sahr, where he was the day before, as open in contrast to the northern towns. I didn't understand what he meant until we circled low around Moundou before landing. But it was immediately clear. The city was laid out in large blocks in a grid pattern, with the houses scattered anywhere around the perimeter of the block. In contrast to the northern cities and N'Djamena, there were no compound walls! The buildings also tended to be from red bricks, the same shade as the iron-rich soil along the road. Moundou's streets are of the same dirt, except for the paved main drag that runs from the airport to the Cotontchad operations. More churches and Christian organizations are in evidence here in the south. More of the roofs are tin. More trees, everything a little greener and with a more tropical feel, if still fairly dry.

Things are a bit more laid back in Moundou, reflecting the more open appearance. There was no welcoming committee at the airport. A lone representative of one of the private voluntary organizations was there to greet us. The préfet was coming, he told us, but we could start into town. Midway, we encountered the *préfet's* small motorcade, and stopped to put things in order. The préfet had been the ambassador in Paris, having returned only in March, and was clearly more worldly and quick than the other two I had met. But at his house we saw the same reception room—large, square, lined with chairs and couches (most of these residences were put up by the French back in the forties). He and I shared a single couch at one end, with the rest spread out along the two sides. He made no pretense of having a serious conversation, but in polished French asked his assistant to phone around regarding our schedule for the day, and after about an hour sent us off with his assistant. Tea had been served, but only to the visitors since this was the first day of Ramadan. Our schedule would include the cigarette factory, the brewery, and Cotontchad. We'd return for a meeting with reps of the NGOs.

At the cigarette factory, which we hadn't requested to visit, we saw one of those typical, riveting assembly-line processes that are characteristic of many agricultural processing industries, and which haven't changed fundamentally in a hundred years. The machinery was old, seeming to have been imported decades ago as a turnkey operation from Germany. But the operation was efficient with its hundred employees. The impressive technical director led us around, speaking as if he gave the tour every day. The factory is actually owned by BAT [British American Tobacco]. At the brewery we saw the home of the famous Gala beer, as well as its offspring, the lighter and less alcoholic Chari. The brewery is owned by Heineken, and contained a hodgepodge of machinery, a lot of it older but some of it fairly new, of various national origins.

Employment, nearly 200. Both facilities had their own water wells and electric generation, not wanting to rely on the public supply for either. In both facilities about half of the raw materials (tobacco and rice) were local, and the rest imported along with fancy stuff like material for the cigarette filters. One surprising thing was that no expats were in evidence in either place. This is a change from what I saw twelve or fifteen years ago in Lagos where the managing director or technical director would always be an expat who called all the shots. Does this represent some developmental progress over time, or simply that Chadians are more capable than Nigerians? (The former, I later concluded with satisfaction.)

At Cotontchad, a government-owned parastatal, we saw a different sort of operation. Rather than a simple processing industry, it is a vertically and horizontally integrated cotton industry operation. It provides inputs and extension services to the farmers, and the technical director who showed us around complained loudly about the problems that have developed since the company extracted itself from rural road maintenance in the production zones. Cotontchad gins and markets all the cotton lint. It crushes the seed, selling the husks for livestock feed, extracting the oil and either refining it for cooking oil or making it into soap. We saw the gin, the classing facility, the oil extraction plant and the soap factory. And the "workshop": This is a huge facility that does everything from manufacturing spare parts for the machinery to rebuilding engines for the machines. Nothing that can be done in-house is contracted out. As elsewhere, water and electricity are self-produced. There were a handful of expats here, but not in the highest jobs. And, of course, Cotontchad has been running terrible deficits for years; the total must equal a high percentage of the country's gross national product. Including families, some two million farmers and an additional million people in related services are dependent on the cotton industry—well over a third of Chad's population! The privatization of the enterprise that the IMF [International Monetary Fund] and World Bank rightly demand is *the* major economic issue in the country after the oil development.

Frankly, Cotontchad reminded me a lot of the enterprises that I had seen in the former Soviet Union, in their expansive scope of activities, in their paternalism toward employees, in their organizational rigidity, overemployment, and mismanagement implied by the mushrooming losses. Cotontchad had no cotton to gin or process today, a month after completion of the harvest, because it has just reduced the producer price to only twenty-five cents per kilogram, or roughly one-quarter of the world market price; in most developing countries, farmers get 60 percent, and in the United States, perhaps 80. Chad's farmers are for the moment refusing to sell. They recognize that they are being asked to absorb the cost of decades of mismanagement and corruption. But like my mécontent farmer in the painting, they won't be able to hold out for long and will have to take the meager prices offered. In thinking about the parallels with the old Soviet factories and state farms, I was reminded that the parastatal industries of Africa were set up during the twenties and thirties by frustrated socialists from Britain and France who went into the colonial service because they found themselves shut out of significant government jobs by the conservatives back home. Their model failed just as miserably here as in Russia, and again at the expense of the lowest tier of workers it was supposed to protect.

Back at the *préfet*'s, he joined me for the meeting with the NGOs. He asked each to give an overview of its activities, just as I would have, but expressing himself better in French. And we heard a lot about rural development, health, and education, all of which only reinforced that the needs are just as great here as in the other parts of the country. A number of these get a little US government funding and appreciated my assurances that I would try to see that it continued. And then we left rather hurriedly, wanting to get back early to N'Djamena so that we could get all the plane servicing done before everyone knocked off work to celebrate Ramadan. On the way out to the airport, I noticed something new: Everyone at the side of the road stood in respect as the first car of our little motorcade, led by a car of soldiers, rolled by. And yet another type of hut: rectangular adobe buildings with gables and sloped roofs— native or a European adaptation? The flight back was uneventful. My Chadian guest quickly fell asleep, and I spent it needling my defense attaché relentlessly about not being allowed to keep my gazelle earlier in the week.

For me, the week provided a brief opportunity to see something of each of Chad's three principal climatic and economic zones early in my stay. I hope I've been successful in conveying to you a little of the fascinating contrasts.

Best regards,

Ambassador Chris

The Waza Game Park

December 6, 1999

Waza is one of the more accessible local attractions. Reputed to be the best game park in Cameroon, and one of the best in Central Africa, it lies some two hours' drive—100 miles—south of N'Djamena. But you don't always reach Waza easily.

Our group consisted of about half the American staff at the embassy—myself, several officers with a few family members, and three of our seven marines. We left midmorning on a Friday, delayed by a *tapis rouge* (i.e., red carpet). A *"tapis rouge"* is when the presidential guard and police shut down traffic for a "movement" by the president or the military. Just like back home in Washington, everyone is inconvenienced. Rumor had it that this tapis rouge was to permit transfer of the guard's heavy equipment north to combat the insurgency, which is getting more serious. (Speculation is that after months of unproductive negotiations, and losses in two recent skirmishes, President Déby has decided that he really must cajole his recalcitrant soldiers into action and tamp down the rebels. If they can.)

So we set off around 10:30, half an hour late since people had to take circuitous routes to meet up at the embassy and to leave it—one of our drivers led us, driving our personal cars through the back streets, which were still open to the southern end of town, to the bridge to Cameroon. We were on our way—almost!

Customs is located at the second bridge, the one over the Logone River, which is the actual border with Cameroon. It is a typical

African customs station, complicated by the single-lane bridge. As you approach, buildings line the road set well back from it—the highway is slightly elevated so it won't flood in the rainy season, even though the buildings will. The road is narrowed, however, by the commerce of motor scooters, pedestrians, hawkers, and market merchants. Myriad colors and products. Especially interesting are the egg men, carrying square trays of about two dozen eggs, stacked layer upon layer (no pun intended) on top of one another, all balanced neatly on the head—Look, Ma, no hands!

On the right hand side of the road the mud-brick shops gradually yield to a couple of large, walled compounds. Some private, some customs yards, these are for large trucks and petrol tankers that pause in crossing. Finally, the inevitable customs and immigration offices—a little building with a row of rooms all open to the road, awaiting the typical sequential process of having your passport and vehicle documents examined first by one, then another, officer and finally subjected to a smudgy hand stamp by the fourth or fifth functionary down the row.

Our administration, or admin, officer thought it would expedite things if the *douaniers* [customs officers] knew that the ambassador was of the party. So I was ushered in and introduced. This meant that the high commissioner of the customs station in turn invited me into his hot, dingy office, and it was up to me to entertain him for the next twenty or so minutes. He was actually an interesting chap, having been to the United States recently, who had been particularly impressed by Niagara Falls. Our admin officer, escorted by the deputy commissioner, took our little stack of passports from office to office, and returned fairly quickly. And we were on our way—as far as the bridge!

At the bridge was a line of vehicles—cars, minibuses, trucks, and what all—waiting to go to Cameroon. We joined in, being the tenth through fourteenth vehicles. Not bad. We had to wait while a line of a dozen or so vehicles, including two huge trailer trucks, entered from the Cameroon side. An enormous throng of pedestrians, bikers, motor scooters, and disabled people on tricycles moved both ways, milling among the vehicles and keeping their speed to a crawl. Thank goodness Chad is too poor to support any more than light vehicular traffic, or we would have been there all day. How anyone official keeps track of this enormous foot and bike traffic is beyond me. The answer, probably, is that no one bothers to, except for the motor vehicles with big cargos.

And the cattle. Oh, yes. A herd of several hundred cattle—the typical local breed somewhat reminiscent both of Brahmans and Texas longhorns—was waiting to get across. Our real challenge was to beat them onto the bridge and avoid another hour's delay while they crossed. We learned that they would be driven on the hoof across Cameroon to Nigeria. Cattle are a major Chadian export, and the country is a resource for the markets of Nigeria, Sudan, etc. Back in the sixties and early seventies, before the civil war got bad, it used to go as value-added fresh or frozen beef. But the roads and abattoirs deteriorated, the air service ceased, and today the practice approximates that of the Old West.

There was a further delay. One of our party, with a foreign service national [FSN], had come early to the border, supposedly to grease our transit. Now he, car, and family were over on the Cameroonian side, where they'd determined that we didn't need to be cleared in and stamped since we were traveling under a diplomatic *ordre de mission* and coming right back to Chad in two days. Should they come back to escort us across the bridge? No. Heavens, no. Not necessary. Problem was the FSN was already on the way back across on foot to look for us, since we were now an hour or so behind schedule. Would we wait for him? We looked at the cattle. No. We'd come on into Cameroon. If we didn't spot him, we'd radio him and the lead car would wait until he made his way back on foot. We went on, avoiding the bikes and pedestrians, across the still rain-swollen river, which lapped against the lowest mud-brick houses, flooding a few of them. We made our way easily the few miles to Kousséri, the first town in Cameroon. There we stopped just short of the single paved shopping street to wait for the other car. Then we could be on our way—as far as the convoy.

In Kousséri, we were theoretically supposed to meet up with a Cameroonian military convoy, which escorts travelers daily from Kousséri down to the town of Maroua. Lots of *coupeurs de routes*—armed bandits—on this road. Did we *need* to go with the convoy, I asked? It wasn't clear. I could, of course, make the decision not to. The regional security officer, also along, merely explained to me that he recommended the convoy, although it was fine if I wanted to take the risk for the group, including the women and children, etc., etc. I decided that we should wait long enough for the other car to catch up and then go, escort or no escort. By now we'd spent fifteen minutes driving and an hour and fifteen minutes waiting on one thing or another. Since there was no sign of it, I figured that waiting for the convoy would cost us at least another hour. In five minutes our last car arrived, complete with the missing FSN, and we were ready to be on our way—and up came the Cameroonian escort officer. Rats!

He graciously welcomed us, reinforcing my impression that the officials here are incredibly polite (at least to ambassadors). He applauded our wisdom in accepting his escort, jumped back into his car, and led us off—to the convoy? It wasn't clear. No, as it turned out, to his company headquarters, where we would hold in the yard until it was time for the convoy to depart. It had been due to leave Kousséri at 11:00 a.m., and it was now nearing noon. No one seemed concerned, or to think that this lack of military precision was anything unusual. We spent about half an hour in the company compound, chiefly trying to scope out the departure plans for the convoy. Were we it, with a special guard? Were the other vehicles expected to come here? As it turned out, they were all formed up on the main road about two miles away. Discreetly omitting the security officer, the rest of us put a hundred francs each (sixteen cents) into a pot and bet on our departure time. Twelve-thirty-one, and we were on our way—to as far as the rest of the convoy.

Mercifully, after a five-minute drive to get to it, the convoy took only ten minutes to integrate us, and by 12:45 p.m. we were on our way—really, at last!

The trip itself was uneventful. The road was good, for which we paid a tiny toll (CFA 500) just as our convoy at last set out. A narrow two lanes, paved and with few potholes, the road threaded its way among swamps and scrub, with a handful of villages thrown in for variety. The villages here were mostly different from those in Chad. The mud-brick huts are round and have pointed thatched roofs, in contrast to the square, flat-roofed dwellings I saw lining the banks of the Chari. We rolled along at a good clip, considering the long line of vehicles, some fifty mph or a bit better. At one point we came to several large oil tankers pulled over to the roadside on our right. The drivers had clambered up to the roofs of their cabs and were sitting there in the hot sun for some unapparent reason. Just beyond them, our column ground to a quick halt, like an accordion imploding. Our military escorts climbed out of the little white minivan they were riding in and fanned out along the road. Over to the right, a patrol of soldiers was coming out of the bush toward the road. They waved at our guys, and our guys waved back. We waited until the first of the patrol drew near, conversed briefly with our chief escort, and in a few moments we were on the way again.

You know you are at Waza when you see three steep hills thrusting up from the otherwise pancakelike plain, not unlike the big rock south of Abuja, in Nigeria, only not quite so high or steep. The convoy paused in the little village of Waza, where the escort would change. We rolled on a few hundred yards and turned off to the west to the encampment at Waza, where we would lodge. It consisted of a tranquil group of round huts scattered midway up the smallest of the three hills. Just to the north was the second, and the third was across the road, marking the entrance to the game park itself.

The hostel was comfortable, if spartan. You had to get used to climbing up and down the slopes of the hill to get from cabin to cabin, or from the cabins to the eatery. This was a large, open terrace with a magnificent view out over the plain. In clearer moments, the view was miles in depth. It was a pale green blanket scattered with little water holes and a network of darker green trees standing solitary and, from this distance, tiny. No game in sight, however. The cabins themselves were basic—each had three sagging beds and a tiny desk and a nightstand with a mosquito coil and a candle. There was electricity with an overhead bulb of the forty-watt variety, and running water in the little bathroom (sorry, cold only). Clean towels and sheets I didn't hesitate to sleep on. There was an aroma, mixed from the toilet and the smell of the burning of the bush, which we would observe when we crossed over to the park. You get used to the smell after a bit, and what more could you ask for $25 a night? About the first thing I did was to climb up to the top of the hill and get the view out in all directions—the same, except in the direction of the adjacent, taller hill. It was now nearly 3:00 p.m., and some wanted a bite of lunch. The choices were the plat du jour, always some grilled meat with french fries, or an egg sandwich. Most opted for a cold drink and whatever snacks we had brought with us. We wanted to get to the park in time for an afternoon game run.

So, 4:30 p.m. found us concentrated in three of the cars, all SUVs, negotiating for guides. The entrance fee was $8 a head, good for the weekend, and each car was required to hire its own guide at about $5 for each game run. We got Ali, a wizened gentleman with forty years' experience working in the park. A trace of gray mustache touched his upper lip; tribal scars traced the bones that led down to his sunken, chocolate cheeks. His eyes were still keenly alert, we would find, even if he was a tad less adventurous than his younger colleagues. We made a total of three game runs, covering forty, seventy, and thirty miles each. I discovered that Frank H., our public affairs officer, loved to drive, including on the dirt roads through the bush. That was just fine with me—he had the job for the duration! And drive he did, as you will hear. Frank, you should know, is sixty-five and a rehired annuitant; he was allowed to take his job for a year when no one from within the existing USIA [US Information Agency] workforce bid on it. He is also the best tennis player in our little community of N'Djamena.

The first afternoon run was relatively uneventful. We stayed out close to two hours, until it became dark. We made a circuit, some of which would become familiar, through the scrub bush. Waza isn't known for the beauty of its landscape. It was mostly browned grass, broken by a scattering of acacia trees and fairly frequent copses of shrubs and taller deciduous trees near the waterholes and streambeds. The dry season had begun, and much of the range was dusty and dry, but with occasional stretches of still green grass where the underground rock shelves had trapped moisture to create a high water table. That, I guess, is why the game comes here. Lots of the bush had been burned off—Ali confirmed that this was deliberate, done by the guides and rangers, but he didn't seem to know quite why. I assume it is for the same reason the subsistence farmers here burn their fields: to restore a little nitrogen to the soil, and to encourage the regrowth and rooting of some of the grass before the dry season gets too advanced and makes that impossible. The highlight of the afternoon was a family of giraffes, male, female, and a colt (is that what you call a young giraffe?). We also saw antelope called *damelesque*, a pair of jackals, and countless varieties of stunning birds, including the *rolliers* with their dramatic powder-blue back wings. Frank did well by us, getting us back safe and sound as dusk darkened into night—one of the marines, however, remarked that his racetrack driving over all but the biggest potholes made the trip seem like one enormous boxing round in which the opponent threw nothing but kidney punches.

It was Frank who also made the acquaintance of the Belgian. The Belgian, first name Kuhn, is riding his Suzuki motorcycle from Europe to South Africa. Thirtyish, he'd been planning this adventure ever since he graduated from law school and started working in whatever the Belgian equivalent is of contract law. When he'd asked his boss for three months off, and the boss refused, he had quit, and here he was some eight weeks into his journey and running ahead of schedule. He had come down through Morocco, joining a convoy to get through the Polisario-infested southern portion of the country (western Sahara) to Nouadhibou. From there, with a guide, it had taken three days of tortuous sand riding to reach Nouakchott. His subsequent course had brought him down to Dakar, across parts of Mali and Upper Volta, into Niger and down through northern Nigeria. Only in the latter country had he felt any sense of danger, he commented. From Waza, he would work his way through Cameroon to Douala over the next couple of weeks, and from there seek a boat down to Namibia. The war in the Democratic Republic of the Congo makes overland transportation impossible for the foreseeable future. Quite an adventure, though Kuhn seemed no worse for the little discomforts and illnesses he described. One meets such people in Africa.

After the evening meal of french fries and grilled meat that tasted an awful lot like pork, we determined to retire early and be up and at the game park gates when it opened the next morning at 6:00 a.m. Our community liaison officer who was along volunteered to awaken everyone at 5:15 a.m., although somehow during the night the duty became delegated to one of our poor marines. And somehow the cold early shower and lack of coffee were tolerable at that hour.

Our morning run, Saturday now, began uneventfully. Kuhn came with us since the park officials refused to let him into the park on his moto. We went back out through the same route, turned at the first water hole, and made a large circuit similar to that of the previous evening. By the end of the day, however, we would cover seventy miles of track, inviting Frank to add new ground to his repertoire. After a good hour, we were wending our way back toward our starting point, having seen almost no animals, just some of the ubiquitous guinea hens, more birds, and one *cob du Buffon*. I was beginning to think that Waza was a bit of a disappointment, perhaps too poached-out over the years. We'd been badgering Ali about our desire to see elephants all morning, but now that dawn was brightening into daylight, we seemed to have missed them. We'd stopped a couple of times to look at spoor, but saw no signs of the beasts themselves.

As we turned back toward the first water hole, we saw her— profiled on the ridge behind it, her full leonine length stretched out against the bluing sky. We raced the car through a copse to try to get closer, approaching from the east. We were too far for a good photo, and as we broke from the copse and rounded the water hole, the other two cars in our group had also spotted the lioness, as had someone in an old blue Peugeot 504. We came around the water hole, each car from a different direction, and circled the ridge. The lioness had gone behind some bush at the crest, midway between the steep edges. We circled and circled, trying to see her clearly, when the blue Peugeot went right up the softest slope of the ridge, straight toward the brush where Her Majesty was hiding. No sign of her, however. We came around to the western side of the ridge, it now between us and the water hole. And then we saw her crash downward below the reckless Peugeot, toward the base of the steep slope which she had no problem descending. She disappeared again, but had to have been only a hundred feet or so from us. And then we saw her again as she determined to break across the open space before our vehicles to another patch of denser bush a quarter mile away. So there she ran, tailed at top speed by our three white SUVs, the blue Peugeot, and a white minivan that had appeared out of nowhere. Poor animal, I thought, to be so tormented by us, even if all we wanted to do was to watch and photograph her. But, reaching the cover of the bush and the trees that blocked the vehicles' further ingress, she slowed again. We saw her lurking confidently in the undergrowth, not too far for us to get our shots. And finally, she ambled slowly off beyond where we could see.

The lioness turned out to be only the first of a full morning of animal sightings. We drove off in a new direction to the north of the water hole. We saw more antelope, birds galore, and as we were coming back around 11:00 a.m., happened upon a herd of giraffes. I counted fourteen, all within perfect vision. Stately, now hurriedly, they moved across the road in front of us and off into the distance. A mile beyond where they had appeared so suddenly, we saw a herd of ostriches, and there were monkeys, a mongoose, and some smaller animals as well. At one point we saw the carcass of a dead giraffe, the patterned skin still taut over the bones in places. The stench was horrific, and I asked Ali how long it had been there—three months, he said. I was struck during the chase after the lioness, how much more approachable the game was here, even if nowhere near so abundant as in Kenya. We lurched along, windows open and sitting on the sills, our bodies mainly outside our cars to better our view. We came within feet of the lion where a Kenyan guide would have kept us back, and we drove freely over the open bush at will.

But we were disappointed in one thing—we'd seen as yet no elephants. We determined to go out one more time, that afternoon, looking only for the elephants. We reached the portal around 3:45 p.m., and headed in along the familiar route. The other car was in the lead, now, and its guide seemed a bit more adventurous than Ali. Just as Ali had told us to keep to the normal route, the lead car turned onto a different track, dryer and more barren, heading in a southeasterly direction. In a mile, the car first stopped, then turned out overland across the bush for a few hundred yards, and stopped. We followed. And there they were—a largish herd of elephants just barely within eyeshot. But they had seen us as well, and headed off briskly as only elephants can move in the rough bush, further south and east. We noted a second herd as well, farther away than the first. We trailed after the first bunch, losing sight in only a few minutes. But still the guide in the lead car kept pointing us through the rough ground, over tree trunks and the huge declivities the trees had left as they had fallen. We must have spent half an hour at this, Frank guiding the vehicle superbly through the rough country. Then we rounded a corner, and we saw them. I think it was the second herd, not the first, which we'd reached, but there they were, some thirty or forty animals, only a few hundred feet distant.

They began to move off, and we followed. After several minutes they stopped, and like covered wagons, formed themselves into a gigantic circle, all facing outwards, the big tusked bulls taking up staggered positions around the perimeter. We looked at them and they at us. We clambered up onto the roofs of our vehicles, children included, and took photos to our hearts' content. And finally, after an additional half hour, we decided it was time to give the poor animals their peace for the evening, and we found our way back across the barren bush to the road. This third viewing had been our shortest distance out, only thirty miles or so, but we'd seen our elephants! You can't do it this way in Kenya.

That evening we dined on guinea hens—big birds, the size of an American chicken, tasty, not gamy or tough, and standing up well against the inevitable french fries. In the night, making my way carefully over the angular trail back toward my cabin, I happened to look up at the black sky. The stars were stunning, so profuse here away from any artificial light. I could easily make out the Big Dipper, Orion, and the brash Milky Way. Only the deep desert is better, I'm told, if you camp there.

On Sunday morning, a few from the group who hadn't made the last run went back to look for elephants, but most of us had determined to climb the hill adjacent to our encampment. It has a rise of perhaps 1,500 feet from the plain, not more and perhaps a little less. I had been eyeing it carefully, and thought that it would pose just the right degree of challenge: by swinging north toward the gentler slope and making a switchback, we could come out along the ridge and gradually reach the topmost elevation near the steep slope, adjacent to the encampment hill. It would make a nice hour's hike without undue exertion. So we set out at 7:00 a.m., seven from our little group, plus Kuhn, walking down the little hill of the encampment, across the few hundred feet to the taller hill. Our three fit marines quickly took the lead—and determined that we would go right up the steep slope immediately before us! Our group quickly broke into two subgroups, the leaders (the three marines, Kuhn, and the wife of our admin officer who teaches aerobics) and the followers (yours truly, Frank, and the admin officer). And I must confess that my mild fear of heights exerted itself a couple of times when we clambered up thirty- to forty-foot expanses of exposed rock face with only small irregularities to cling to, and nothing to break a potential fall. I slowed the followers still more, I fear, in catching my breath after those—for me—harrowing moments. But pauses notwithstanding, in little more than half an hour we were all at the top. And there, before us as if to mock our pride in our achievement, was an extended family of baboons, perhaps twenty individuals. They moved off to a clump of rocks just down from the pinnacle, which we claimed. They looked at us and we looked at them—reminiscent of our standoff with the elephants the day before. Then, mission accomplished, we moved off down the little mountain, descending along the gentler slope that I had wanted to ascend in the first place.

It was now time to leave Waza, and we needed only to determine whether we'd again go back by convoy or on our own. One car from our group had already gone off, in any event. In the end, the local garrison dispatched a couple of its effectives with us, and we departed at noontime without waiting for the entire convoy. The captain of the local garrison was pleased to do this for the visiting diplomats and ambassador, and came with us himself as far as a village midway along our route to Kousérrie. This point, where the Nigerian border abutted the road, was the locale of most of the banditry. As far as I know, the captain extracted no bribe or "special fee" for this service, but I have yet to confirm this from the regional security officer. ...

So, uneventfully and with less delay than in the coming, we returned to N'Djamena after a fabulous weekend at Waza. We even stopped in Kousserie to buy wine and expat merchandise—it is far cheaper there than in N'Djamena, only two miles away. We will recommend Waza to all our friends and colleagues who haven't yet been. It's well worth the extra bit of process and palaver in getting there!

Yours truly,

Ambassador Chris

Zakouma and Sarh

March 26, 2000

With an irony possible only in the developing world, the Zakouma game reserve with its primeval marshes and endangered species is a place of the future, while Sarh, a European-founded city that just celebrated its first century, is all about what was.

My second overland trip was occasioned by the visit of Richard R., who works on programs to save elephants at the Fish and Wildlife Service. The trip was another Les special, and before I knew it we were joined by Dr. John H. from the World Wildlife Fund and Dr. Conrad H., an old Africa hand and conservation specialist from a European Union organization. Also along was Debbie L., our State Department desk officer out to check up on us. Zakouma was our objective, but I wanted to add a day and swing through Chad's third largest city, Sarh, which I hadn't yet visited.

I'll spare you another saga of the roads. Suffice it to say they were better, nearly all dirt but freshly graded. We touched 120 kilometers per hour at times, and did 725 of the 750 kilometers in just twelve hours. This doesn't count an hour lost at the park entrance (don't ask: drivers are sometimes more trouble than they're worth!). En route we passed one of Chad's leading natural wonders, the inselberg Abtouyour. It is an abrupt little mountain, the name in local jargon describing the great white storks that nest on its peak, and whose guano has imparted a white crown to the crag. The birds were an omen of what we'd find in Zakouma.

An hour or so short of the park, we made a last rest stop just beyond Abou Deïa. There we found a manmade wonder. On an exposed granite slope 100 meters in from the road, we saw the refuse of a threshing operation—stubble and grain from the sorghum, the wooden mallets strewn around the surface, and deep pockets worn several inches into the stone from centuries of pounding in the same place with these soft implements.

And then, coming into the park just after dark after our delay, there was of course the préfet, wanting to do the right thing and greet me. He was headed into the park just ahead of us at 8:30 p.m., and we fell in behind him, our missing vehicle having already somehow found its way into his little motorcade ahead of us. With a park speed limit of forty kilometers per hour, we never figured out why the préfet drove at twenty all the way, delaying us even more. But at last at 9:30 p.m., after now not twelve but fourteen hours on the road, we reached the encampment. The préfet ordered drinks for our refreshment and made small talk. With no particular haste, after some time, he inquired about dinner. Then there was a fuss about lodging since there were reservations for us, but not for him and his guards. Eventually dinner arrived around 11:00 p.m. We ate quickly and retired, for we would be up at 5:30 a.m. for a game run in the morning. Not the préfet, of course, so we bid our adieus before retiring.

Zakouma has it all over Waza as a game park. And to tour it with three naturalists was sheer bliss. We saw elephant, lion, giraffe, crocodile, a great monitor lizard, half a dozen kinds of antelope, including the rare red-fronted antelope and the great kudu — scarcer still since Hemingway shot them all (poetic license; actually he shot them over in Kenya, but they've always been very rare here in central Africa). And warthogs, mongooses, baboons and patas monkeys, jackals, and the footprints of small cats. And I heard all about the habits and attributes of the beasties. Can *you* describe the difference between hindgut-fermenting and foregut-digesting mammals? And their relative ecological survival advantages, and which are more archaic and more modern traits? (Hint: rhinos and elephants are hindgut guys, humans and hoofed animals are foregutters.)

And the birds. It was Conrad who introduced me to bird watching practices and lingo, even if Richard was better at identifying what we were seeing. Bird sightings are informally classified as ticks, twitches, megatwitches and cosmic-orgasmic (Conrad used a slightly different construction) twitches. Tick comes from checking off the species on a list. A twitch is rare enough to make your head turn, and so on. We eventually counted just over 100 species — a pretty good start for me on a life list, although determined bird watchers get up to 6,000 to 7,000 species pretty easily within a few years. And our 100 didn't include a whole bunch of "LBJs" (little brown jobs, i.e., common small birds) we didn't try to identify. My favorites were probably the bee-eaters: green or crimson, they are beautiful in color, elegant in shape (with a long bifurcated tail in flight) and in song.

We must have spent over twenty hours in two days on game runs. During the less interesting stretches, Conrad and I discovered that, in addition to crackerjack ability to identify mammals and birds, Richard was a whiz at classical music trivia. "What romantic composer wrote a symphony, one movement of which was named for a tarantula, and why? ... Look at that roller over there, or is it just another Abyssinian? ... Yeah! Nope, not Schubert. It was Mendelssohn—the fourth movement of the fourth, or "Italian," symphony, so called because it imitated a peasant dance called a tarantella." This as we bounced over the dirt tracks of central Africa's best game park.

But this was a business trip, not a vacation. So during the game runs and back at the encampment we spent numerous hours in discussions with the European Union guys who seem to be managing the park and its recovery. A French-Belgian team, they seemed in total control. There was a nominal Chadian park administrator around some, but he said all of about three words. Had it been an American aid effort, there would have been a heavy emphasis on "capacity building" and the expats would have stood back a little. But here it was again, the familiar story—a French show with us filling in some at the margin. At least with the funding Richard contributes we are large enough to be appreciated.

The Belgian project director was incredibly hospitable, accompanying us almost without pause, and seemed very competent, if not quite ready to entrust the park to Chadian management. He reported on the careful progress in rebuilding the park, especially its guard force, since poaching remains the biggest threat. Our contribution so far has been radios so the guards can communicate with each other during their several daylong horse patrols. And animal numbers are up for all mammalian species and the birds. Poaching is down, if not under control, and relations with the surrounding populations are improving. So the park has been stabilized and is on the upswing from its disastrous state at the end of the civil war. The next step, which we are also supporting, is to give it sustainability through revenue generation from tourism. And my naturalist companions were realists, seeing that without this element, the long-term fate of the park would remain in doubt. It will be a long time until countries like Chad can afford to subsidize animals, so parks need to generate some tourist revenues.

Among the Frenchmen, the most interesting was probably Dr. Pierre P. The former head of the French Museum of Natural History in Paris, he is seventyish and retired, and here on vacation. He had cut his professional teeth on the central African game parks decades ago and likes to keep his hand in. Affable and charming in the relaxed way of upper-crust French, he was here with his thirty-something female assistant. They shared the same *boukourou* (bungalow), but there were also rumors of a wife of similar age—not the same person, since she was said to be Chinese. Conrad couldn't resist a Viagra joke, while the ever-respectful Richard grimaced.

For me, the game-watching highlight was undoubtedly the ULA (ultralight aircraft) flight. Going up in this two-seat, twenty-foot-long, open cockpit job made me think I was at Kitty Hawk with the Wright Brothers. But what a view of the park from 500 feet! We tooled nearly noiselessly over lush green meadows with stands of antelope and buffalo. At one point, we encountered an enormous herd of elephant my companion pilot estimated at 500. Along the Salamat River we saw countless crocodiles sunning themselves on the muddy banks. But the application of such a craft for monitoring both animals and poaching is obvious.

I could go on and on about Zakouma, but I'll close with a word about the accommodations. Another of our projects is to rebuild the restaurant, so I toured the kitchen and quickly saw the reason for the long delays in meal service. Seating nearly fifty, the staff prepared all the meals on two tiny four-burner stoves the size you find in temporary apartments. Not to mention the need for better storage—the vegetables were piled all over the floor. But this too will be improved—my admin officer will sign the contract for restaurant reconstruction shortly, helping to ensure that Zakouma is indeed a place with a future.

On our third morning away from N'Djamena, 7:30 a.m. found us piling into our two vehicles and heading southwest for Sarh. Here I will describe the roads, for their decay was in a way a precursor of what awaited us in Chad's third-largest city. Through the park, and for the first couple of villages beyond, we were able to track our way with landmarks shown on our maps. But at some point, these evaporated and we were following the sketchiest of tracks, comfortable in our direction only from the position of the sun and the reassurances of villagers whom we asked along the way. It seemed we were now in the remotest depths of the country—away even from the influence of Islam and Christianity, to judge by the occasional bare-breasted women working in the fields. The villages showed no touch of outside hands—no dispensaries, no stucco schools. I don't believe we saw more than three other vehicles during the first four hours of our trek. This stretch of the journey reminded me for all the world of the descent I made from the Gongola Plateau of eastern Nigeria, equally remote, some fifteen years ago.

Then suddenly, after over seven hours on the road, we rounded a bend, entered a village, and found ourselves looking at the ferry over the Chari River, only a dozen klicks from Sarh. As always, the ferry itself was entrancing. The piles of soggy coffee beans to the side of the approach and the overturned truck trailer in the river told their story. So did the posted tariffs for crossing, indicating the charges for trucks, cars, motos, cattle, camels, goats, etc. The river itself was picturesque—shades of blue, green, and beige making up a limited palette. If I were to redesign Chad's flag, it would be in these three colors, so pervasive do they seem in all parts of the country. Hey! Not a bad idea, given the need for national unity here! Reaching the far side of the river, we cajoled one of the six or so waiting trucks to lend us its power air pump to inflate a weak tire on our second car—its third flat for the journey, adding still further to my doubts about that particular driver.

And then, in no time, we were in Sarh. Neither the préfet nor the préfet adjoint [assistant prefect] were awaiting us, but Les left his card at the house of the préfet adjoint, with whom he'd been in touch. We were free to go to the hotel and check in. There was some hubbub at the Hotel des Chasses in coming up with enough rooms for us and our drivers, but it was managed. According to Les, old movie buffs would recognize the hotel as the setting for the novel and early 1960s movie entitled *The Roots of Heaven*. When I read the book later, the hotel turned out to be the Novotel in N'Djamena—

perhaps in the movie the setting got moved to Sarh? In the old days Sarh—and the hotel—were the jumping-off point for big game hunting southeast of here. The movie is about the unsavory characters who hung around here back then for that purpose. The hotel's setting, with its terrace bar and restaurant and dozen or so rooms, all having a view over the Chari River, is picturesque if not downright romantic. Despite the decay. And the restaurant later in the evening produced a tasty capitaine with frites for dinner. The rooms, however, were dingy, mine characterized by a big, mosquito-inviting hole in the window and the lack of a toilet seat in the bathroom (for that sin I declined an apartment back in grad school days in Cambridge).

Soon the préfet adjoint showed up and was prevailed upon to give us a half-hour tour of the town in the waning sunlight. The perfect motif for seeing Sarh, for if Zakouma with its recovery in animal numbers and bright future was a surprise on the upside, Sarh was everything I'd heard with respect to its decay and dependency on a failing parastatal, Sonasut [Societé Nationale Sucrière du Tchad, now Compagnie Sucrière du Tchad], the sugar company.

We began what would be a large quadrilateral route by turning inland from the river, traversing the administrative quarter. Here we saw mainly old, rundown French colonial structures with their thick concrete walls and tin roofs. A few were maintained, but more were mildewed, roofs rusted out, some with big chunks missing from the walls. All had unkempt gardens. We turned left at the empty airfield and made our way along a broad road that divided the French from the African town. A row of pharmacies and bars to the right marked the beginning of the quartiers populaires [popular neighborhoods]. Sarh has been for some time a city of 80,000, now growing more slowly than Moundou, the other major southern town, which overtook Sarh a few years ago as Chad's second city.

We passed landmarks: the main mosque, the Catholic cathedral (an ugly, looming, oval, concrete gray structure). We skirted the teams of cattle in the street, turned right and penetrated the quartiers enough to see the large animal market. We remarked along the way the network of neighborhood wells—some identified only by old tires, some by elaborate circular adobe or concrete walls and a superstructure for drawing the water. Everywhere, it seemed, children were playing soccer in the broad, carless streets.

Going back toward the river now, we saw the hospital—impressively modern—and several institutes of higher learning. These were mainly of the high school or junior college level. But in a way Sarh is the educational center of Chad. And flowers had been planted at the major intersections for the recent centennial celebration. Passing back by the main drag, we saw the préfet's large residence, a presidential palace erected in the old days of southern domination by President Tombalbaye, who hailed from here, and the residence of National Assembly leader Kamougue. Then back to the hotel. The préfet adjoint had described to us the problems of the failing Sonasut, COTEX (the city's sole textile factory, which was barely operating), and its general lack of job growth. Visually and economically, we saw a town with a past more prominent that its future. Along the riverbank and around the half-abandoned buildings, nature seemed to be reasserting itself, overgrowing them. Only the *quartiers* seemed vibrant. In contrast to Zakouma, this city, which had only just marked its centennial, simply didn't seem to have any future. Maybe its educational institutions could produce something, maybe processing the fruit of the ubiquitous mango trees? But otherwise, …

The next morning we called quickly on the new Institute for Agricultural Sciences and Environment. It was struggling even in its birth and its staff begged us for books. Then a courtesy call on the préfet, who, for lack of anything better, gave me three ostrich eggs produced by the pets roaming his ample compound. What to do with them? By 9:30 a.m. we were on the road for N'Djamena.

The road to N'Djamena was mediocre, neither the best nor the worst of the unpaved highways I've traveled in Chad. As we rolled along, I couldn't dismiss from my mind the contrast of Zakouma and Sarh. At Zakouma we had seen an age-old, if not primeval, wilderness inhabited by countless species of beasts for countless eons. After severe damage by men, and now with man's benevolent intervention, the prospects for nature's survival were positive and hopeful. At Sarh we saw a town that had been built for men out of the wilderness on the basis of colonial administration and an extractive agriculture a century ago. To a degree successful in the shelter of an exploitative colonialism with tight links to France, it has now declined under the pressures of a real world environment. So which is more powerful? Nature, which preserves itself only with man's help, or man's edifice, which cannot resist nature's eroding reflux without the heavy, expensive hand of government? Ancient Zakouma seems ascendant, while youthful Sarh is ailing. Not to wax too philosophical, this much seems clear from this minidrama of central Africa: Just as nature here will not prosper without the benign intervention of man, so men's efforts will not flourish without in turn recognizing the rules laid down by nature and economics—an elegant, platitudinous statement to result from a five-day trip! Can we take it any further? For the moment, I think not.

Best regards,

Ambassador Chris

The Midsouth

April 24, 2000

I had been planning a swing through the southwestern portion of Chad for some time, but when our little time of troubles arose at the end of February, I decided I'd best remain in N'Djamena. But now, with the passage of time, things seemed more relaxed and I determined to salvage at least part of the trip I had intended. Chad's midsouth or southwest includes the préfectures of Mayo-Kebbi and Tandjilé—fairly densely populated, dotted with towns of secondary importance, and largely dependent on agriculture and livestock with a little commerce thrown in for good measure. So guided by Les and focused on stops at three of his self-help projects, we set off for a two-day jaunt.

You always see something unexpected when traveling in this country. This time it was the camels. We were about a hundred miles south of N'Djamena, still on paved road, when we saw them strung out along the highway by the hundreds, mostly munching on the fronds of scrub palms. Why here? Probably because it was proximate to the Chari River, which still has a little water in its bed as we near the halfway point of the hot season.

My travel always has its formal quality, such as the calls upon the préfets in the provincial capitals—in this instance, Bongor and Lai. In both cases the préfets themselves were traveling, but I was by no means put out in having to be content with the préfet adjoint [assistant préfet]. The first gentleman, in Bongor, had been transferred recently from the presidency in N'Djamena. He was a lively if not weighty conversationalist who knew colleagues of mine back in the embassy, and we passed a pleasant half hour. In Lai I found a rather perfunctory and bureaucratic reception. I had more pressing interests in the town and was content to make this the briefest of courtesy calls.

What really made this trip a trip was the informal reception we received at the village level. Les had tried as best he could to pass word of our coming to each location where we would stop. The first was the village of Djoumane. Here we, together with the local association and the European Union, had financed a project to plant trees and otherwise improve the facility of the local high school. As we neared the site, I was surprised (but Les wasn't) to see a crowd in front—the chief of the village, the school's headmaster, and about twenty local notables and an equal number of students. All were waiting for us to arrive. We were greeted and immediately given a tour of the project—the garden of scraggly trees, the two wells that had been dug to produce water to keep them alive, the school buildings, and the site for a future henhouse to generate a little revenue for the school. We were taken to the teachers' room, into which about forty people crowded. Drinks were served, including beer—we were in the non-Muslim south, after all. The village chief spoke through an interpreter and two school officials added remarks, as did I. I was presented with a hoe and a set of metal boomerang-like items which can be used for both hunting and self defense. Their rude, rustic quality made me appreciate the level of development here, or lack thereof. But these folks had plans. The headmaster explained what future development he envisioned for the school, including a grove of citrus trees to earn a little money and help the students learn something practical along with the book learning. Our hosts had planned a light grilled meal for us, to be followed by a more lavish repast at an expat highway construction camp nearby. But we had to excuse ourselves and make our way down to Lai.

In Lai, our real business was to meet with the Americans from the region. There are two families and a single woman, all missionaries. They had been alerted to our coming and had gathered at one of their homes. They were incredibly grateful that we would spend half an hour and had prepared tea and cookies. More than anything, I was struck by how poorly informed these folks were about the greater events in the country. They asked avidly about the troubles in the north, and were relieved to learn that the government still held Faya-Largeau and all the strongpoints surrounding the Tibesti. They described briefly their work here, indicating that they preached in languages I'd never heard of, and didn't really work very much in French or Arabic.

And then it was on to Béré. Here we found our way to the home of the sous-préfet, an old friend of Les's. We had anticipated a brief visit with him and then a drive twelve kilometers out to the village where we had paid for the installation of a rice mill. The question was whether the citizens association had upheld its end of the bargain and built a permanent shelter over the mill. The sous-préfet observed all the courtesies—he had invited the local gendarme commandant and a handful of other notables; he served first *sucréries* [the term Chadians use for soft drinks] and then a little plate of chicken. When Les began to hint that we'd need to drive quickly out to see the mill and be on our way, it became clear that it wasn't to happen so smoothly. Seems that all the women from the village had come into town to greet us. A thank-you ceremony had been prepared. So, not wanting to disappoint, we followed the sous-préfet (who promised brevity) across the open area in front of his compound toward a couple of buildings a quarter mile away. As we turned a corner, we saw some of the women in their colorful, flowing gowns waiting for us to file between them. As I approached, two or three jumped in front of me poking menacingly with umbrellas and dancing, leading our little group forward. They cried out chants of greeting, ending in throat yodeling.

A few feet later, others were squatting on the ground awaiting our coming. A series of about five short speeches had been planned, which the sous-préfet immediately announced would be curtailed in view of the need for us to move along. The village chief spoke, as did the mayor, of course. Naturally the upshot of both comments was the need for more developmental help. Someone translated their French into the local dialect so the women could understand. I was asked to make my second impromptu speech of the day. And of course it was the women's spokesperson who got cut off the agenda. But they were clearly grateful.

Then we were in the car again and off across a track toward Piti, the village. And there, after twenty minutes, was the mill. No shed had yet been built, but our guide pointed out that the bricks were already there and swore that the structure would be completed in another couple of weeks, well before the rains. Heading back, we began to see what looked like rain clouds off on the flat horizon. I hoped the construction would beat the seasonal clock. Back in town, just before leaving, I was introduced to a small group of the women's leadership and at last got to hear a few words from them directly.

Les explained as we sped away that there was one more travel hazard to be overcome before reaching Kélo, our goal for the night: the little ferry. And, as if on cue, we came to it and saw only another vehicle waiting to cross—no ferrymen anywhere in sight. It was about 5:30 p.m., and we figured that what with the few drops of rain and all, they had probably knocked off early for the day. Someone, we were told, had been sent to call them. First one came to the far bank, tried to talk us out of wanting to cross, and then clomped away. After about half an hour, he reappeared with his colleagues, four men in all, and we crossed.

Not five miles down the track was the last of the projects we wanted to visit this day, an irrigation project premised on a pump that lifted water from a small river onto the higher fields nearby. And sure enough, as we came to it, there was our greeting party. About 200 villagers, including the children, who sang a series of songs, in one of which I could hear the word "ambassador." And the sous-préfet of Kélo was waiting, a former student of Les's, and he introduced us to about forty of the village elders who lined the road. We took a quick hike down to see the pump and the irrigated fields, and then bid farewell to the villagers and headed for Kélo.

The sous-préfet led us to his residence. The military escort in the lead car (a Toyota pickup of course) blew a whistle as he rode and all the people of the town stood in respect for us to pass. There were a surprising number of soldiers and gendarmes patrolling the roads. For my security, of course. I'd have thought they all would have been up north, but apparently a lot of them just refuse to go to the front. At the residence we could anticipate more *sucréries* and a meal. But there was something else as well—rain! The first I'd seen in five and a half months! We scurried into the house as it began to fall, the servants dragging in the furniture and food that had just been brought outside to us. You can't imagine the pleasure I felt in hearing the thunder, feeling the wet breeze through the glassless window at my back, and hearing the splatter of the heavy drops. I don't believe I've ever gone so long without seeing precipitation. And then it was off to our lodging, the Cotontchad guesthouse, which was perfectly adequate.

Friday morning dawned. We had one event awaiting us before our drive back north to N'Djamena, graduation exercises at Gaston's preschool, the Barbara Schell Center [see "Is It Hopeless" in chapter 5]. He had adjusted the date for our convenience. Driving out, I was reminded of how flat this country is, and how the soil absolutely refuses to drain. The hour-long rain of the previous evening had created huge ponds in the streets through which we drove. After a few minutes we reached the school, and the adjacent "American Fermer" [sic] experimental farm that Gaston is putting in beside it. These tots will be called on to pitch in on the family plots at times during the year; might as well give them some skills. And here, of course, there was another little ceremony. The sous-préfet spoke. So did the mayor, Gaston, and yours truly. This time I'd been forewarned and had prepared a few comments. Then the children read a few poems and sang a little song—in English, no less!

Gaston's school was pretty primitive—so far, just a straw shanty. But here again there was a pile of bricks waiting to be molded into a permanent building. Indeed, throughout this part of the country we seemed to be seeing a replacement of adobe by fired brick. This was the result, Les speculated, of three years in a row of heavy rains and flooding. Everywhere we saw the bricks being fired on-site: first a bed of firewood is laid down, and the raw clay bricks are stacked in a pyramid on top. The whole thing is coated with adobe mud, save a smoke hole at top. The fire is then lit underneath, and the bricks bake for a day or two until the slow fire burns itself out.

Heading north, we followed a new road not yet paved, so we drove partly on the gravel underbed and partly on a now muddy track beside it. But with luck it will be paved before the rains, giving that much more of Chad all-weather communications. I wondered how far north it had rained, and was able to track the standing water until almost to Bongor—only 200 miles south of N'Djamena. It is amazing how quickly the seemingly dead grass greens up here with just a few drops of moisture. And even where the rains hadn't come, there were signs of spring—several varieties of the scraggly Sahelian trees had leafed out, and we saw over and over again large shrubs that had burst into yellow flower like forsythia. So even here, there are a few faint signs of the turning seasons.

Ambassador Chris

April 24, 2000

P.S.

As if to confirm the musings with which I closed, it rained in N'Djamena on April 27, less than a week after my return.

Waiting for Rain: A Last Swing South (and North)

June 27, 2000

Could we do it? Squeeze in another trip to the southern part of the country before the rains? Perhaps two? It seems that we are always waiting on something here, now the rainy season. And there was some question about a road trip, since by the time June rolls around it can rain heavily up to N'Djamena or even north of here.

I wanted to go south for several reasons. First and foremost, in my most recent meeting with the president, he had suggested that we invest food aid proceeds in an agricultural development project near the site of the oil project. Chad cannot afford to forget its agriculture, no matter how rich its oil reserves. It would make a nice fit, he said, for the US government to be doing ag development near the American-led oil exploitation. So I wanted to visit with agriculturists and development folks in the region to see if this made sense, and to look at the specific project the president had in mind. And I wanted to treat myself to a few days looking back at my old realm of agriculture! But I also wanted to visit the American-supported hospital at Koumra I'd heard so much of, and to check firsthand into rumors of disorder in the southern countryside.

But could we go? Weather-wise, Les had his doubts. He researched the weather data with the FEWS [Famine Early Warning System] project people—an AID-supported regional project that projects drought and famine throughout West and Central Africa on the basis of weather monitoring. The intertropical convergence, he learned, was pushing up against the sixteenth parallel, some 100 or 200 miles north of here, which meant that rains could be heavy anywhere from N'Djamena south. And we had three successive days of storms in the capital—the Saturday, Sunday, and Monday before our proposed departure. To go or not to go? We finally decided we could only try it, and if the roads were bad once we got off the paving, turn back.

My defense attaché wondered if the government would intervene and try to dissuade me from traveling to the midsouth just now. The opposition press had been full of stories of rebellion breaking out in that part of the country as well as in the north. We knew that some troops had been sent south, confirming the newspaper reports. And the president, in a two-day swing through the very areas I proposed to visit, was careful to lay out the rationale for a military presence in the region and the need to reconcile the rebels to permit its withdrawal. Was there a security issue as well? When the foreign office failed to react, we decided not, especially in the wake of the president's visit.

We departed early on a Wednesday morning. We'd added a back-up car, but made the decision only the day before so there was no real opportunity to add anyone to our normal overland duo. I had remembered the Sarh road that we took from several months ago, returning from Zakouma—very rough to within a hundred kilometers of the paved road at Guelengdeng, and then recently improved. Now it seemed that the improved portion had worn a bit, but the work had continued further south and the route was in good condition all the way to the outskirts of Sarh, where we hung a right for Koumra.

Koumra, our first destination, is the site of the hospital supported by the American Baptist Church about which I've written before. It is the work of Dr. Seymour, a sort of Albert Schweitzer of Central Africa, and equally famous and revered within Chad. I was delighted that, thanks to our second car, we were able to haul a load of supplies down to the hospital and in a small way repay the warm welcome we received from both the expat and Chadian administrators.

We began with the requisite stop to visit with the sous-préfet or assistant governor. Under Chad's recently announced decentralization Koumra will be the capital of one of Chad's twenty-eight *departements*, which will replace the current fourteen préfectures, or provinces. Some, including Les, think that in theory smaller territorial divisions make sense in this country of enormous distances and poor infrastructure—but for the cost, which the country clearly can't afford. In Koumra, we found the old sous-préfet still in charge, and the newly named "préfet de *departement*" not yet "on seat." And the sous-préfet had a tale to tell. When I asked him about all the publicity about rebellion in the region, he scoffed. It was more fear than fact. If we wanted to know about the real conflicts in the region, listen to his story of a farmer-herder struggle that had just taken place and claimed nine lives. Seems that, as is often the case, some cattle wandered onto the land of a farmer in a nearby village just as he was getting ready to plant. He went after the beasts, and the herders who followed them, and before anyone could intervene two of the herders were dead. Then, of course, the remaining herders gathered up their companions and returned, and the village farmers massed in opposition to them. By the time nightfall dampened their ardor, the death total had reached nine. In the evening our préfet heard of the troubles, and at break of day was at the village with six gendarmes, interposing himself between the hostile groups. After three days of patient mediation, a shaky peace had been established, from which effort he had just returned.

At the hospital we were met by a line of 100 or more of the full employment and many associated supporters. I proceeded along the line, shaking hands and nodding as the director presented individuals by either name or function. The director then made a brief presentation in a voice so subdued that I could hardly hear, never mind the folks strung out behind us. I answered in just a few sentences, and the director led me in for a tour of the entire, sprawling facility. The crowd scattered, but many of the folks would turn up again as I visited the individual buildings of the huge operation.

The hospital was cleaner and better equipped than the Chadian military facility I'd seen only a day before. This was clear from the storerooms of medications we saw, as well as the general degree of sanitation—had we not been honored guests, shoes would have come off as we climbed from the damp, sandy grounds up to the hospital buildings themselves. But the hospital was also a study in contrasts: In the building with the famous eye clinic, sought by people from countries all around, we heard of experimentation with laser surgery during the most recent visit of the American specialist. In the radiology department, however, we saw an x-ray machine that had been in continuous use since World War I! Spare parts were still available from the United States. This disconnect was somehow symbolic not only of this facility at Koumra but also of Africa itself.

Dinner at the home of the Chadian hospital director and chief physician that evening was also a disconnect. He and his wife had gone out of their way to prepare a feast, but had carefully blended a variety of western dishes—pizza, macaroni and cheese, salad—with Chadian boule and other typical Chadian dishes like broiled chicken. The doctor had invited the only other expats in the region: his European deputy, an American administrator, and a visiting team of Bible translators. Dry, of course, yet it was nonetheless a jolly evening.

Our lodging was very similar to the cabin I've created for Grant Thomas, the Peace Corps volunteer protagonist in my recently completed novel—austere but blessed with occasional electricity and basic plumbing. I confirmed the accuracy of my intuition with a series of oblique questions to Les about the resemblance to his Peace Corps digs two and a half decades ago. The beds were comfortable even if the rooms hosted a diverse population of bugs.

In the morning there was a hearty American style breakfast with the other expats. Afterwards, I received a brief visit by two of the local Baptist pastors who wanted to express their gratitude for the help both the hospital and their missions received from the United States. They hoped that I could somehow ensure that the support continued. And then, after a bit of the normal confusion over transportation and destination, we went off to visit a women's cooperative with which we have just signed a self-help agreement. They are basically a group involved with manufacturing garments from locally available cloth, but with our funding want to branch out into processing of mangoes and other local fruits into jams and juices. Precisely what southern Chad needs! Back at the hospital we had to wait first for the sous-préfet and then the chief doctor, to say our formal farewells. And then we headed off for Doba.

At Doba, I looked for the préfet, and in his absence was received by the secretary general of the *departement*. Seems that this title will be the number two position under the new provincial structure. When I inquired about the rebellion rumors, the secretary general indicated that there were problems in the neighborhood, but that they were confined to a small, heavily wooded territory just south of town. His story, later confirmed by the local workers of the American private voluntary organization World Vision, was that this was one of the few areas of southern Chad that hadn't been deforested because it was rougher terrain. Hence, whenever southerners took to the maquis, this was where they went. All of the few dozen rebels and the military forces chasing them were concentrated in this little area. The préfet, joined by his compatriot (a presidential chum) from Logone Occidental, had gone into the region seeking to negotiate with the rebels and talk them into coming back to civil society. (They had some success, we learned upon returning to N'Djamena a few days later.) So much for the rebellion in the south.

Our main focus in Doba was agricultural development. We wanted to see and hear about the World Vision Area Development

Program. And we wanted to see Casier C, the project that the president hopes we will revitalize. Early in the afternoon, we sat down at the World Vision base camp and were given a very well-organized and thorough presentation on their projects both north and south of the town. Theirs is a tripartite effort at integrated rural development. Essentially, they seek to graft production improvements and social development onto the subsistence agriculture village structure. Education efforts begin with school construction. Health goals involve wells for clean water, as well as village sanitation. I paid the most attention to the food security effort, which involves a series of activities ranging from providing improved seed varieties, through extension to grain storage at the village level. After the charts and talk, we took to our vehicles and visited a couple of villages north of town where work was under way, as well as a site where they would love for us to invest some resources to permit water retention and farm development.

And then, prior to a modest entertainment on the terrace of the absent préfet's residence, the secretary general drove us out of town to see Casier C. It was a dismal picture of a failed, overly technological enterprise, which reminded me of nothing so much as a Russian state farm. The fields were now abandoned, the buildings for administration and housing administrators were in decay, and the irrigation system was totally defunct. While in recent years farmers had squatted on the fields to produce a rain-fed crop, in the most recent season they had skipped even this modest effort. No, Les and I quickly concluded, we don't want to get involved with Casier C—at least not with its old model of inappropriate technology.

So back we went to drinks on the terrace. There was the mayor, a lady more comfortable in Arabic than French, and a handful of other notables. It was pleasant and relaxed even though, after a few minutes, I abandoned my soft drink to the several flies that had found their way into the open bottle. And after the requisite time, barely more than a half-hour, we excused ourselves and went off to the lodging that World Vision had organized for us. It was a motel-like camp that had been constructed by a German firm that is doing roadwork throughout the region. The setting was idyllic—low buildings on a bluff overlooking a bend in the meandering

Pendé River. In the twilight, the few souls below on the banks of the stream, the rain-greened foliage, and the aromatic flowers outside our cabins made for one of the most attractive settings I've yet seen in Chad. And, despite a few bugs quickly dispatched by the spray supplied by ever-thoughtful Chaibo, I had a quiet, sound sleep. Just watch out for the snakes if you wander around in the morning, Les warned.

We were up again early the following morning and ate quickly. This time we had to wait half an hour until the camp's sole expat could be troubled to bring our bill. When he finally appeared, there was a mild altercation and we had to persuade him not to charge our rooms and meals to World Vision, as he'd been instructed. And then we were on our way.

Our first stop of the day was Bébédjia, where we would visit two of our self-help projects and Chad's most important agricultural research station. The sous-préfet here was another old friend of Les's; it seemed that every ambassador visits here sometime during his tenure. We went first to see the self-help projects. The first was an orchard project. A civic association wanted to plant 1,500 trees on about ten hectares. The first plants had gone into the ground last fall, and we were escorted to the shade of a huge primeval tree on the fringe of the cleared land where the group had begun planting its orchard. We saw a combination of mangoes and citrus trees, most about two feet tall after weathering their first dry season. Losses had been high, about 25 percent. But the enthusiasm of the group was undiminished; they'd replant for the losses and extend their area from three to seven of their ten hectares this coming year. Of course, they had developed a small program for us—statements by the association officials, the mayor, and the sous-préfet, and they expected an impromptu word in return from yours truly. The women of the association presented me with two painted calabashes, one with a primitive American flag that would have done Grandma Moses proud, as well as a third wood-burned calabash filled to overflowing with guinea hen eggs.

The people at the second association were not so far along. Their project was a plant nursery and orchard development. The nursery was already there, and we looked at a charming garden surrounding a well, laid out under shady acacias and mangoes almost like a parterre. Our funds would go toward planting an adjacent hectare or two with the tiny saplings we saw being nurtured and grafted in the nursery. The treasurer of the association was introduced during the formalities and proceeded to read his entire roster of bookkeeping entries for the past eighteen months, clearing his throat to emphasize each time that the association members were hit up for an additional contribution. The association, it seemed, had no particular money-making goal, but was intended chiefly as a source of plants for reforestation, city beautification, and small growers who wanted a fruit tree or two for raising salable produce.

Then it was off to the research station. It had originally been a French-supported facility designed to support cotton cultivation. Now it was Chadian run and had evolved two additional focuses— grains and sustainable agriculture–natural resource protection. The facility does some decent work, has relationships with the American Collaborative Research Support Program, but clearly suffers from lack of funds. A particular weakness seems to be the extension of what it does to the farmers. Only nine village districts are the experimental, small-scale recipients of the center's results. But we saw some impressive plantings of mangoes and citrus, multiple varieties of each with varying harvest periods. Between the two, produce could be expected for nearly eleven months a year, which would be important if we could ever find an American company interested in investing in fruit processing here, in Chad's richest agricultural region.

We left a little after noon for Kome, the base camp of the petroleum project. There I had hoped to hear about the initial development steps once the rains are over. But we were greeted by—Are you surprised?—a twenty-five-year veteran of the project who just happened to be an in-law of Les's, Soulyman. And he wanted to take us out to see the first well that had been drilled here some twenty-five years earlier, which had proven definitively that the Chadian reserves were significant enough for exploitation. And off we went under an increasingly ominous sky which reminded us that, however lucky we'd been up to now, it was nonetheless the rainy season. And reaching the well, we hadn't the heart to tell Soulyman that it turned out to be the same one that our drivers had pointed out to us on the way in a couple of hours earlier. But we admired the century-old tree nearby that Soulyman bragged hadn't been in the least disturbed by the oil discovery. And en route back to the camp, it began to storm as it can only in the tropics: wind, and rain heavy and almost horizontal, blinding so that our vehicle slowed to a crawl.

Back at the camp, we tried to divert ourselves from the thought that the rainstorm might well keep us here an extra day, or even two. But Ellen Brown was waiting to receive us and give us the briefing we had sought. Ellen is another one of the handful of Americans who have been associated with Chad for a generation. Peace Corps initially, she is now a professional sociologist and for the past several years has been handling Esso's relations with the villages that will be affected by oil production. She has visited them all, interviewed the headmen, worked with them on compensation for the land and mango trees they will lose along the route of the pipeline and where the oil wells are to be drilled. Not surprisingly, she could tell us as much about our agricultural interests in the region as the first steps with respect to oil development. As we continued into our second hour, a young man in a rain slicker walked by the open door of Ellen's office and she hailed him. He turned out to be an archaeologist Esso has employed to do a survey of the pipeline route just in case the construction will interfere with any historical sites of cultural interest. Turns out that a site not far south of Kome was a major premodern iron-smelting center, adding to Chad's list of archaeological highlights. And the agriculture? Ellen agreed that doing something here was a good idea; she echoed our conclusions in panning anything too high tech. And, oh, yes, the oil project: Next season's work would begin on October 18, and focus on installing the infrastructure that Esso will need to support the pipeline construction and well drilling later on.

By dinnertime the storm had subsided to a drizzle, but the residual water still worried us in connection with our intended departure the next morning. Relaxing in my cabin, the deluxe model of two container-like structures joined together, I had noticed water leaking in at the seam. The meal was tasty and hearty, even though a lot of it obviously came from cans and boxed mixes. We lingered long over the table after the dishes had been cleared, chatting idly with Ellen and Soulyman. There isn't much to do in base camps in the evenings, and I can see how they can easily become oppressive. A little after nine, we all retired to our cabins; only a drop or two of rain still fell, giving me hope.

As if charmed, we saw that the weather had turned by morning. A bright blue sky basked over the damp, reddish earth and verdant bush. After breakfast, Souleyman led us out of camp over a short-cut that saved us a half hour in getting back to Bebedjia, from which we would turn west towards Moundou before going north on the best road. The roads were damp, but the reddish laterite held up well and the guards at the rain barriers all let us proceed after noting the license plates of our vehicles. The country was beautiful — tidy, clean villages with rectangular compounds and houses, shady trees along the highway, and fields just being turned for planting. I noted numerous horse- or oxen-drawn plows here, even if fewer than half of the farmers seemed to have them. Elsewhere in the country, cultivation is done almost entirely with the hand hoe. And we rolled along nicely. In little more than an hour, we reached Moundou and turned north. The roads were fine, if dirt, and I had to caution Chaibo against going too fast (I'd take my chances, but Les is probably right in saying that we should keep to sixty or six-ty-five mph on unsurfaced roads). There was only one stretch — a long detour through wet fields with deep tracks about halfway along — that was onerous. To make a long story short, we were back in N'Djamena by around 4:00 p.m., only nine hours after we'd left Kome. Les commented on how much better the roads were than just a few years earlier.

Two trips did I say? I'm writing the last of these words a week after our return from the south, on Sunday, July 2, on the heels of a day trip to Massakoury, the market town a couple of hours' drive north of here.

The preparation for this trip and our Fourth of July reception dominated things at the embassy last week. I had originally envisioned the day trip as a chance to take some of the more adventurous newcomers up to the market which, you will recall from my

earlier description, is one of the most exotic in Chad. Our community liaison officer advertised the trip, and before I knew it, some
twenty folks had enrolled. And the numbers kept growing. There
were official visitors in town — they wanted to come. Les had coordinated the trip with the Ministry of Foreign Affairs, and Dr. Haroun,
the head of North American relations, who hails from Massakoury,
wanted to guide us. The Whitehouses would come with their dozen
adopted Chadian children and both their pickup and van. And so
it went. In the end we were close to forty, leaving only a half dozen
of the official American community who didn't participate (there
are three or four Chad haters among our folks who never participate in anything, to my increasing chagrin; they're bad for morale
at a small post, and I'll be glad to see them go this summer). Even
Les's wife decided to join in, wanting to check this southernmost of
northern markets for a certain kind of ghee.

Did I think that this would be a simple market visit? No way.
Dr. Haroun, the ministry official, let it gradually become known
en route that he'd prepared the way for us. We were expected by
the sous-préfet, and there would be some kind of a meal. And my
timing was off as well, of course. When I'd envisioned this convoy
as three or four cars, I'd thought of Chaibo's familiarity with Chadian roads and thought it would take two or two and a half hours
each way, plus an hour or two in the town. But we ended up with
ten cars in the caravan, and some of the drivers had never driven
long stretches over dirt roads. So, despite an 8:00 a.m. departure,
we pulled off repeatedly to wait for the slower cars to catch up, and
it was nearly noon by the time we got to Massakoury. The sous-
préfet had abandoned his sick wife in N'Djamena to hurry back
to greet us, along with the National Assembly representative from
the district, not to mention the mayor. The deputy's car met us a
few miles out of town, and the musicians intoned their traditional
instruments as we pulled up to the sous-préfet's residence. I'm sure
that part of the warm welcome is attributable to the fact that we've
done a series of development projects in the town over the years — a
well three years ago, a school enlargement two years ago, and this
year a reforestation project. But it was mostly just straightforward,
outgoing Chadian hospitality.

At the residence, the sous-préfet met us on the steps, and

gradually all of our group filed into the little reception room. We were indeed a motley crowd, with even a couple of our marines in t-shirts and shorts. But no matter. It was quickly decided to send most of the group off to tour the market; Les and I would stay behind to conduct business. And our business? Viewing the nursery for the trees for the reforestation project, and turning over the documents by which we'd agreed to fund it. Oh, yes, our hosts had planned for me to ceremonially plant two trees in the town's main square, just outside the sous-préfet's compound. Eventually, the mayor opined, he would like to show us the city's abandoned abattoir, the subject of a future funding appeal. And we wanted to see the well we'd paid for a couple of years earlier, the prototype for a project we're about to embark upon to install wells in a dozen or more villages. So, after retrieving one or two folks from the market, we headed off to see the development sites. Les, always vigilant, had us also stop at the place where the trees from our reforestation project would be planted.

Back at the residence, it was about 1:30 p.m., and clear to me that far from my original expectations, we were looking at a 3:00 p.m. departure. With luck. A few folks began to talk about heading back earlier, but most of us waited and at last lunch appeared—2:15 p.m. At this point I learned that, indeed, a couple of cars had started off back to N'Djamena, but some roughneck kids had stoned the cars exiting Massakoury—breaking the windows in one—and that the entire group was back. Sadly, such things happen. I thought momentarily of the kids on Washington-region overpasses, hurling stones and bricks and concrete blocks on the cars passing below.

But we enjoyed our meal, protein heavy with poultry and eventually mutton or goat (I couldn't tell which). After some small talk with the local officials, it was time to go. The drive back was uneventful. I'd arranged for Dr. Haroun to be with a visiting elections specialist, and they had lots to go over. So, entranced, tired, content, nonplussed by the broken car window, we arrived back in N'Djamena.

Oh, yes! I became a parent of sorts on this trip. Once again I was presented with a gazelle. Before I knew it, the little critter was all tied up in the back of the car, and withstood the bouncy ride amazingly well. But once released in my garden, it was clear that he was terrified—he quickly hid under a thick shrub. When I checked on him the following morning he seemed to have ignored the food and water I had put out, and not to have moved an inch from his refuge. But later in the afternoon he let me reach in and pet him, and he eventually stood to stretch his elegantly reedy little legs.

And now I'm back to waiting on the rains. I'm waiting to see what it will be like to be isolated in the city for months at a time. Professionally, we're waiting to see how the Chadians organize for their elections next year, and whether American groups like the National Democratic Institute will be willing to come in and help. Always waiting on something, here in Chad.

Best regards,

Ambassador Chris

The Gong and the Lamido

December 15, 2000

I hope you are not tiring of my travelogues. This week I took my first domestic trip of the new dry season, going into southwestern Chad, that little arrow of the country that points into Cameroon near the town of Léré. My main objective was to see the natural beauty of that corner, home of Africa's only freshwater manatees, where I'm trying to entice the cooperative involvement of an American environmental organization. But there were the normal handful of self-help projects to review, and people to meet as well. Les was along, of course, but also Denise, our embassy nurse-practitioner, and Justin, one of our marines.

We set out at 7:30 a.m. on a Monday and stopped first at Bongor for a courtesy call on the préfet, who was charming and agreed to arrange our accommodations for our last night en route back to N'Djamena. An hour south, we split off from the main road onto a dusty track and arrived at a village where we had sponsored the construction of a dispensary (actually a health clinic). We were expected, and saw the modest structure, as yet uncompleted. But it was enough to assure us that our funds were well spent; the nurse was in training in Niger and expected back in February, at the same time that the building would be complete. Some of the equipment had already arrived in N'Djamena. Success—these 11,000 people would at last have a medical person in their midst, and thanks to their own initiative, not government. Denise was encouraged by the attitude, but saw that our contribution was no panacea.

Hospitality is heartfelt in Chad. But if I had any doubts that it makes it nearly impossible to keep to a travel schedule, this trip removed them. We drove another hour south, headed toward the major town of Kélo, where we would spend the night. At Gong, a village along the newly completed highway en route, we were to meet local folks and see another of our self-help activities, a reforestation project a few miles off the road to the east. And we recognized Gong, indeed, by the group along the side of the road awaiting us, including the local deputy from the National Assembly and the sous-préfet, whom I'd met on my trip through last season. But instead of going a few miles to see our project, the préfet had decided that we should come directly into Kélo. We did, arriving at around 3:00 p.m. There was a warm welcome, of course, and conversation and a meal. Afterward, a visit to the one self-help project we wanted to see in town: a rice mill. But at 5:00 p.m. we were delivered to the Cotontchad guesthouse, our lodging for the night, and left to our own devices until it was late enough to bed down. Since it was Ramadan, some of our party took a car into town to break fast at around 6:00 p.m., rejoining us later. Talk (we'd not thought to bring cards), reading, and an early night.

Up early the next morning, we were taken to the préfet's for a bite of breakfast (chicken and noodles, bread and an omelet) before being off to our first stop. I thought we were headed to the reforestation project we'd missed the day before, but we headed due east from town. In forty-five minutes we found ourselves at the edge of a stream reviewing one of our projects that I'd visited the year before and had no need to see again! The préfet's party bought fish. We then cut north through the bush on a rough track, passing village after village that I hoped would be the reforestation project. After nearly two hours, we spilled out of the bush onto the main road we'd used to enter Kélo the day before. A couple of miles north, a couple of miles off the road to the east, and there we were at last!

My frustration at the three-hour wild-goose chase was high, but what I saw in Cheriot, the village we entered, melted my rancor. A couple of outriders on horseback awaited us at the fringe of the village and, when we came through the fields of dried grass, immediately took flight for the center to announce us. As we worked our way into the middle of the village, we found ourselves awaited by an announcer with a portable, handheld loudspeaker and a crowd of about 300. The spokesman blared through his microphone in both the local language and French to greet us. We alit and walked into the village center, where we sat in waiting chairs in the shade of an enormous mango tree. With its brother, it shaded the entire meeting place of the village. The local chiefs and notables were there, as was the sous-préfet. It was the first time the préfet, newly appointed, had visited as well. There were brief speeches, including by yours truly, off the cuff, and the local deputy to the National Assembly. Clearly, my visit was a major event in the life here.

After a brief skit demonstrating the local methods of planting, we were off to tour the sites of our aid. The deputy took charge, and it quickly became clear that he was milking every move for the upcoming election—just like a politician back home! We stopped here and there to see where the trees would be planted, the storehouse, and a local dispensary that the association we were supporting had built. I could tell that Denise was doing her mental evaluation, including of the chances of survival of one tiny infant with respiratory problems. This is rudimentary development at the bootstrap level. But we saw more and more people as we went along, and before we left, I had touched nearly 400 people with my presence. For an investment of $8,000, we had generated an incredible amount of goodwill for the United States, since we were supporting the things that the people here had decided for themselves they needed, and for which they were willing to invest their own scant resources to go along with ours.

A little before noon, we were off to Pala, a hundred kilometers west. There, as expected, the préfet met us, and after a brief refreshment, escorted us off. He knew that we needed to reach the far western edge of his jurisdiction by evening, and would accompany us. We stopped in town to view a grain mill we'd financed, and then went off to the gold mine. Chad has some gold reserves in this region, and a South Korean firm is analyzing whether they are worth commercial exploitation. A half-hour drive off the main road got us to the site. We met the three Korean expats, who were clearly a lonely crowd. We toured their small-scale extraction facility. They told us that next year's experience in running the mined soil through their extractive facility would tell whether the reserves were worth development. If so, this would become Chad's second largest industrial facility, after the oil project.

The rough road out underscored the loneliness I'd seen in the faces of the Koreans, but in a few miles brought us back to the main road east. There was one more detour—a mile off the route to see Chad's petrified forest. Not protected and intermittently vandalized, it is nevertheless a goal suitable for touristic interest. We saw only the edge before heading onward. To my chagrin, a sample chip found its way into my possession, courtesy of the préfet.

The town of Léré with its calm lake and sandy-colored hills was our main attraction in the far southwest. Denise said it reminded her of several in the east of her native Oregon. But I get ahead of myself.

Dark as it was, we were met at the edge of town by the sous-préfet and local notables. As we drove in to town, it was clear that we'd been expected for hours. People milled in the dark streets, stepping to the nonexistent curb to wave and shout as we passed. Some chanted greetings. Here and there we saw improvised American flags. You can't imagine the heart twinge that gives, here in remotest Chad! If I'd dwelled on it for a moment, my eyes would have teared. Yet the people had been told to turn out for us. How long had they waited? What of their daily duties had they neglected?

Courtesy and protocol demanded that we proceed first to the sous-préfet's residence, where we were paraded through the ranks of local administrators, seated, and given drinks. As we relaxed, we learned that we'd put up at the local Cotontchad guesthouse, and that the Gong, the local traditional ruler, expected us for dinner at 8:30 p.m. at his palace. After a brief stop chez Cotontchad, where I donned a sports coat and tie, we proceeded to the Gong's palace. As we turned off the main road, I noticed high mud-brick turrets spaced along the long, curving wall we were rounding. The palace entrance was obvious from the gap in the walls and the small crowd of retainers awaiting us.

The Gong himself met us. Les was high on this sultan, who was young (i.e., my age), little more than a year in office, and seemingly dedicated to trying to do something for his subjects' well-being. His flowing white robes flashed in the moonlight and guided our way as much as his flashlight through the dark, litter-strewn grounds of the palace. After a tortuous turn or two, we scaled some steps and entered a small, fairly new house to the side of the main, decaying, mud-brick palace buildings. And what a surprise! In its intimate living area, with only a modicum of generator-driven lighting, blared CNN in English from a satellite dish! We were all immediately riveted upon the American news, with its still inconclusive report on our election. There I was, trying to make polite conversation in French with the Gong, and more interested in overhearing the TV in English just behind him.

The Gong himself seemed very much a mixture of old and new—hence Les's enthusiasm for him. He received us comfortably in what would have been very much a middle-class home in the United States. But the grace and dignity were not lost in the warmth of his welcome. We chatted, and after a little while repaired to a heaping dining room table, serving ourselves, and returning to our seats in the living area to eat. After we dignitaries had served ourselves, portions of the buffet began to disappear, as is typical to satisfy the hunger of retainers and servants outside. It was a surreal scene: being received in this modest living room by the exalted Gong, in remotest Chad but with CNN omnipresent, and all this within the 200-year-old enclosure of the mud-brick palace, where, we later learned, 300 people reside. By 10:30 p.m., we could gracefully take our leave and repair to the Cotontchad guest quarters to sleep off a long day's travels and events.

Our program for Léré kicked off the next morning at 7:30 a.m. with breakfast at the sous-préfet's. We were served méchoui, cold, and I suspected it had been prepared to welcome us the day before in anticipation of a noontime arrival.

Moments later, we tramped across the compound to an administrative building where the director of the local nature park awaited us. We had brought a donation of camping equipment for the park rangers down with us from N'Djamena, and its presentation was the main benefit we were bringing to Léré. But our cars had gone off to gas up, and we needed to fill the awkward gap until their return with conversation. I'm always amazed at how long it can take to do something simple like get gas in this country. We quizzed the park director about his reserve. In season, it harbors a wealth of animals transiting this narrow spit of Chad between two game reserves in Cameroon. There are antelope, crocodiles, elephants, lions, and even Chad's only rhino. The préfet and park ranger debated the handling of the herd of elephants currently destroying farmland a few miles to the south. Then the cars arrived and we unloaded them, signed a note commemorating the donation, and moved off.

I didn't mention manatees. But Lake Léré is the home of the only freshwater manatees in Africa, and these were one of the primary interests of our visit. So off we went to the lakeshore, and a beautiful, restful sight it is. The dark blue of the twenty-mile-long lake is nestled against soft blond hills enlivened by occasional copses of dark green trees, and all this is arrayed against the gentler blue of the expansive sky. The promised capture of a manatee for our visual pleasure didn't materialize, which I found just as well. But the park director assured us that the numbers were on the increase for the moment. The great threat was the silting of the lake, which is only ten meters deep, whereas it had in places reached a depth of thirty meters some decades ago. Ideal habitat for the huge sea cows today, it won't be in another few decades—unless my efforts to attract the Nature Conservancy or some similar group to help salvage it meet success. Walking to the shore, I confirmed the diagnosis of the problem; in a few feet, I went from dry grassland through mushy bog to water grass, where I dared not step.

Then we made a stop back at the palace. The Gong conducted a brief tour. Along the exterior wall were a series of dwellings. We saw an empty one, a three-room apartment like each of the resident matrons possesses—a living room, a storage room, and a combination kitchen/sleeping room. And each has a grain silo, to boot.

The Gong doesn't know who all the residents are, the wives of his father, uncles, etc., and their children. And, of course, he wants money to restore the palace. He reinforced his plea with the gift of a traditional robe, and by anointing me the Gong of all the Mgong people who have emigrated to the United States—if there are any.

Our hosts were well aware of the rugged road that awaited us and sent us off promptly with an escort toward our intermediate stop at Binder, fifty kilometers to the north. After nearly two hours of harsh bounces over nearly nonexistent road, we came to a village where a welcome party awaited us in the shade of a neem tree on our right. I was greeted by a new préfet, who had traveled a hundred kilometers of rugged track already that morning to be here to greet me. And Binder's traditional ruler, the Lamido, was there with other local personalities. We were in their hands now, and I was escorted to the préfet's car to ride with him. We headed for Binder proper, stopping only briefly to see a weaving cooperative where a famous local cloth is produced; I gratified my love of textiles and bought two bolts for about $20.

Even more than in Léré, it was clear that the Lamido was the critical local figure. We were escorted to a house that was cleaner and in better repair than any I'd seen in rural Chad. It was not the sous-préfet's, but the Lamido's. Here we cooled our heels until it would be time for us to be received by him in his traditional palace. I asked to use the restroom, and here there was an anomaly. I was taken through an adjacent bedroom to a tiny adjoining closet. In it was no toilet, not even a latrine-style hole in the ground, only a tiny hole in the exterior wall at floor level, with a tiny trough in the floor leading toward it. This must have been a nighttime recourse for when one didn't really want to tramp outside to the main exterior latrine.

My reception by the Lamido was a bit more formal than that by the Gong. As I approached and alit from the car, I could hear the traditional musicians with their horns and drums. Behind them, to my right, a small contingent of colorful horsemen waved their swords and paced their mounts in rough time to the music. The Lamido approached, shook my hand warmly in both of his, and proceeded to introduce me to a dozen court notables on my left.

The Lamido led me through a gate, around the side of the palace, and into a shady shelter of sekko (woven straw). These guys never want to receive you inside the palace itself, it seems. We sat in waiting chairs. The court notables filtered in and sat on mats on the ground opposite us. There were formalities, interpreted into the local language by a court spokesman, although both the Lamido and I spoke in French. The gist of the Lamido's message was that my visit was as if President Clinton himself had come to this remote corner of Africa, and they were grateful. I responded as best I could to such encomiums. As at Léré, the Lamido presented me with a traditional robe, this one in the local Binder woven cloth with embroidery. The courtesy call lasted only a few minutes, and we were escorted back to the modern house where a meal was served for those of us not fasting for Ramadan. The Lamido showed up, more comfortably garbed, and we were on the road again heading eastward.

The préfet had complained already about the state of the road, or trail, as it might better be described. We lurched over rocks, tried to choose among conflicting sandy paths through the bush, and crossed wide sandy wadis in four-wheel drive. After perhaps an hour, during which we covered somewhere between twenty and thirty kilometers, the Lamido, in the lead of course, stopped and walked back to my car. We were nearing the end of his realm, and he advised against a detour to see a famous waterfall a little off the road to the south. Only a few klicks away, between driving and hiking it would take some hours. I demurred and, somewhat relieved, the Lamido bid us adieu and headed back to Binder. A mile or two further we found a pair of park rangers awaiting us, just in case we had determined to try to see the waterfall.

With the préfet now escorting us, we continued on toward Fianga, the next major town. The track was the same for many miles. We were still in the huge Binder-Léré Faunal Reserve. The scrub was not particularly attractive, but I had to judge this one of the least-inhabited parts of southern Chad I'd encountered. Off to our right, the orange sun sank lower, and after seemingly forever, we came out of the upland plateau we'd been navigating. We passed more and more cultivated fields, and suddenly we were in a fertile, farmed place of enormous fields of recessional sorghum. We stopped briefly to admire a thin blue finger lake off to our right. A looming inselberg that I later learned reached 2000 feet above sea level told us we were nearing Fianga. We'd done eighty kilometers in three hours. We swept into a little village—and there they were, another welcoming party led by the sous-préfet of Fianga. Dashed were our hopes of a quick jaunt over the better road ahead to reach our evening destination, Bongor. It was now 5:00 p.m., and the Fianga folks had been waiting for us since 2:00 p.m. We couldn't not stop.

I was feeling more and more like an old colonial district officer on tour, but I have to admit that the Fianga welcome epitomized those that I had been receiving along the way. The sous-préfet, along with the mayor and other notables, met us outside the edge of town and, after brief greetings, led us back to his compound. A sekko shelter awaited us with a single upholstered couch behind a low table, and hard chairs and benches splayed out to its left and right. As we sat, servants brought soft drinks with the normal nervous awkwardness. The préfet introduced us, emphasizing our need for haste. The sous-préfet spoke and introduced the chefs de canton who were lined up opposite us. The mayor said a brief word. The sous-préfet was clearly disappointed that the stopover would be a brief one, as the préfet harried him about being sure we had a key to the gate on the bridge over the Logone River we needed to cross to our east, since it would close at 6:00 p.m. After a polite half-hour of desultory conversation, just about the point at which I thought we should rise to excuse ourselves, the préfet disappeared. Signs of food began to appear. Uh-oh. I then noticed that the Moslems among us were praying on mats laid out behind the chefs de canton; my driver was among them. It was the moment for evening prayers and the breaking of the Ramadan fast. We couldn't leave now. The préfet returned. We ate. The préfet told me that two things delayed our onward progress: The escort car had had to go find some gas, which would take a while, and the search for the key to the privately owned bridge had not ended. (As it turned out, there was no key—when we got there, we'd have to negotiate with the guard, but that should pose no problem since we would have the Fianga gendarmes with us.) At last, a little before 7:00 p.m., we were off, cutting through the darkness over the good road.

But the unexpected stop in Fianga was only the first in a series of little calamities. After half an hour, Chaibo abruptly pulled the car over to the edge of the road. Flat tire, he said. I hadn't noticed a thing, but sure enough he was correct. Another brief delay. We spent the time admiring the magnificent sky full of stars, here so remote from any ground lights. Les revealed another of his skills by identifying the constellations for us. On warm nights when his family sleeps on the roof in their *quartier*, where the electricity usually fails, they study the sky for amusement as they chat.

And then we were again en route, hurtling through the darkness—until we came to the bridge. The gate was barred as anticipated, but contrary to promise the guard was nowhere to be seen. A couple of the gendarmes went off to look for him at the gatehouse on the other side of the bridge, and back down in an encampment on the riverbank where a little fire was burning. No luck. But just as we were trying to decide what to do next, he appeared out of nowhere. Wherever he'd been, he must have seen the lights of our cars stopped up on the bridge. And then we were off again for Bongor. With no further interruptions, we reached our destination around 9:15 p.m. Typical of Chadian hospitality, our host, the préfet, had kept dinner waiting for us.

And I should perhaps close with a brief dissertation about the préfets and sous-préfets whom I've mentioned so often in describing my travels. Let me start with their houses, for, if we arrive in town at or after lunchtime, it is there that we repair. The houses are by no means identical, but they have an overwhelming similarity. We will enter into a large reception room, airy, with high ceilings. There will be a horseshoe of couches and chairs in the largest part of the room, with a couch in the middle for the préfet and his chief guest, and the rest of the couches or chairs to the sides. Mostly built in the late 1940s, these run-down stucco dwellings persist as the nerve centers of regional administration, yet well built they were, to survive a half-century with minimal maintenance. To the side of the main room there will be another sort of living room or two, and beyond it the bedrooms and bathrooms. The toilet may or may not benefit from a seat, and the porcelain is usually orange with rust. There may or may not be running water in the washbasin. The kitchen is often in a separate building out back. These poor houses suffer so because they have no real owners! The préfets are the most temporary of residents, changing office even more frequently than American ambassadors, and they have no real interest in keeping them up.

But the administrative system itself is in much better repair; it is, in fact, impressive. The préfets, sous-préfets, and chefs de canton form a tight network. Somehow, despite no phones and a dearth of vehicles and radios, they communicate well and keep their fingers on the pulse of what goes on locally. It is a system that blends the modern and traditional: the préfets and sous-préfets are centrally appointed officials of the Ministry of the Interior. The chefs are traditional authorities, sometimes holding their offices hereditarily, sometimes appointed from leading or eligible local families by the central government. And rulership is blended as well. The préfet will decide certain matters, but much is left to the chefs and their interpretation of local custom. This becomes very interesting where both national and customary law may be involved, since they can often be in conflict. And depending on the quality of the chef, the hand of authority may be firm or very light in districts remote from N'Djamena. But down to this level, the network itself is tightly run. So let no one tell you that developing countries are incapable of well-organized administration. Indeed, I wonder if in Chad, where I've pointed out before much remains unchanged over centuries, anything else would work. This must have been the conclusion of the French who set the system up. But it is the Chadians who have maintained it for now more than forty years. And I realize as well that only with time—indeed, only at the end of this latest trip into the country—have I come to understand the system and how well it works.

On our last morning, as we rolled smoothly along the paved road from Bongor to N'Djamena, I pondered changes in my own attitudes during my time here. It did not, for example, strike me at all strange to learn of the final result of our presidential election (i.e., the Supreme Court decision), from RFI [Radio France International], the French equivalent of Voice of America. And I find myself much more relaxed about travel arrangements. I can remember traveling in Nigeria, when the one thing I was always fixated upon was knowing exactly where, in what hotel or guesthouse, I would spend each night. Now, in Chad, I've adopted Les's attitude: The préfet or sous-préfet will provide, and give us the best accommodations available, however humble they may be. If not, we have camping gear in the vehicles. I can even imagine myself overnighting in a pinch in one of the mud-brick houses—now that I've been in enough to see that some of them can be clean and bugless. In fact, my eye is becoming trained to evaluate which of these adobe buildings are well made, and which not. I found myself subconsciously judging them to pass the time on our last few miles back to N'Djamena. As I thought back over that last courtesy visit in Fianga, I realized that I am becoming less impatient, more tolerant of delay and "African Time." Not always, you understand, but occasionally. Mentally, I often fault Les for being too accepting of the vagaries of African Time and the préfets. Am I headed in the same direction?

Best regards,

Ambassador Chris

Day Trips

October 31, 2003

Four excursions out of N'Djamena in a month's time. Is there a theme? Perhaps only the unexpected, always here in Chad, and the relief of being out of the city. And maybe the extremes represented by these events.

The Oil Project Inauguration

Friday, October 10, a long and gala day, was the official inauguration of the oil project. Diplomats, after having hung around at the airport until 8:00 p.m. the previous evening to greet arriving heads of state, were to be at the airport before 6:00 a.m. to fly down in the painful net bucket seats of Chad's C-130. I had special dispensation, however, an invitation to go with the Esso folk on their comfortable Dash-8. With Vinny, my commercial officer and consul, I arrived at the airport at a leisurely 7:00 a.m. There was the "in crowd" — World Bank and IMF folk, Esso folk, etc. We waited around a while for the French ambassador, who never did show, and then we were off.

I didn't know the day's program down south in Kome, the heart of the oil fields, but trusted fate in the African way. The one glitch occurred just as I got off the plane: Esso had a car ready to whisk me and the French ambassador off to a second airfield where the heads of state would be arriving, to join their welcoming party. Vinny and I went there and spent some minutes greeting the president of the National Assembly and various ministers. But the Chadians hadn't anticipated us being there, and quickly made it clear that we weren't welcome. So we went back to the ceremony site and joined the waiting throng of nearly 1,000.

By now it was just short of 10:00 a.m., and the program was scheduled to begin at 11:00 a.m., which I knew it wouldn't. Protocol people ushered us to the diplomatic section, but I found that the Esso folk had a place for me reserved much nearer the stage. Vinny took my diplomatic seat, next to the Central African ambassador, our doyen, whose nephew he'd denied a US visa only the day before. Poor Vinny. *Mais c'est le Tchad.* For me, there was plenty of time to network with oil consortium folks, Bank and Fund people, Chadian dignitaries, etc. The Fund rep and I placed a bet on the real starting time: She said 11:30 and I said 12:30. Guess who won when it got under way at 12:20 p.m.? She still owes me lunch.

The formalities were what one expected. Speeches by each of the reps of the three consortium members, two World Bank speakers, then a representative of "civil society" — someone from the group the government had set up to offset real civil society's continued criticism of the oil project. This guy's fatuous flattery of the president was the only thing I found distasteful during the long day. It smacked a bit too much of the typical African personality cult.

Then came the president's own speech, not too self-congratulatory, and then he left the hall with a handful of officials to turn the spigot symbolically to start the flow of oil to the coast. I say symbolic because the first oil entered the pipeline in early July. But watching on a big-screen TV, the president's turn of a wheel and the thick black oil pouring through a glass pipe made very good visuals.

Lunch followed, in the "senior" dining hall for the president and 200 of the rest of us, in another locale for the other 800 guests. I remember the salmon appetizer. The meal broke up even as dessert and coffee were served, various guests needing to get to the two airstrips and roads for the trip back to N'Djamena. My group got to the airport at 3:30 p.m., but we had to wait—there was a rain shower. This late in the season that was very good news, and made me ponder whether the black liquid would be an equal blessing for the Chadian people.

We took off finally at 5:00 p.m. The flight was uneventful, save for one thing: Approaching the N'Djamena airport, we had to circle for twenty minutes because of traffic! Another first. I recalled that, taking off in the morning, I'd counted an incredible seventeen planes on the tarmac. It was a whole day of firsts here in Chad.

But it was far from over. Still to come was a state dinner in honor of visiting heads of state. At Kome I had discovered that by some mix-up the World Bank hadn't been invited, and I had gotten the head of protocol to pass them an invitation. Now I found that the oil consortium folk hadn't been included either. To their relief, it was too late to get them included (these events are no fun). This one, mercifully, wasn't too bad. Only one head of state stayed for it, General Bozize of the Central African Republic. The event began an hour and twenty minutes late, just as the oil ceremony had. The adulation of the president was distasteful, but there was something to eat this time, and it all ended by 11:00 p.m.

This had been a great day for Chad. The country is now an oil producer and will remain so far into the future. This is the most important positive event in the country's history since independence. But getting the production on stream may well turn out to be the easy part. Managing the oil revenues according to the innovative revenue management plan, by which they will be invested in the country's development, has still to play out. That is the challenge of the coming years.

The following week, on Wednesday, October 15, found me visiting my Peace Corps volunteers at their training site at Darda, an hour and a half's drive south of N'Djamena. I say "my" volunteers because I view the return of the Peace Corps to Chad as my greatest accomplishment in four years here. It wouldn't have happened (at least not so quickly) without 9/11 and President Bush's subsequent decision to double the size of the Peace Corps. But because of my groundwork, Chad was first in line for a new program, and is the first new country to receive volunteers.

Darda, a facility of Chad's Ministry of Agriculture, provides a great transition from the Western comforts of the volunteers' homes to Chadian life. They sleep four to a room (three volunteers and one Chadian instructor). Food varies—boule and lizard stew some days, roast chicken in honor of my visit. The goal is to introduce the volunteers to everything they will experience, except the isolation of the village. For that, they do a one-week advance visit to their village, along with their local host, and then return to Darda for the final training and a couple of weeks of trial teaching. Our initial bunch of twenty volunteers is a great group. I'd welcomed them earlier by giving them my city tour and lunch at the residence. Now I saw them working and thinking and anticipating *in situ.*

My presentation was on the history of US-Chadian relations. I wanted also to convey a sense of Chad's bloody history since independence, and to blend in some information about the country's history with the ups and downs of our relationship. I began with US interests in Chad—oil and Central African stability. I described our accordion-like aid relationship through the years: modest after independence, strongest when the Libyans invaded, then cut sharply and now growing a little partly because of them, i.e., the Peace Corps's return. I interwove the country's own history with its twenty-eight years (by my count) of civil war.

These smart young men and women asked good questions. Would Chad really use its oil revenues wisely? How did we reconcile our aid to the Habré regime with its human rights violations? Were the French helpful or harmful vis-à-vis political reform? Were there rebel groups in the countryside that should concern the volunteers? What were our views of the current government and its honesty, commitment to democracy, etc.? I answered them directly, holding little of my own opinions back.

After more than two hours of discussion my time was running short. Noelle and Mousa Kébir, the training coordinators, picked up on my hints and drew things to a close. A group picture was de rigueur. As I began to withdraw, one young woman approached me: "Mr. Ambassador we don't want you to leave Chad. We want you to stay here for our tour. Thank you for everything!" I thanked *her*, noted that I'd be here a few months longer and hoped even to visit some of the volunteers in their villages. Inwardly, my heart swelled. These words and the smiles of the volunteers are my greatest reward for four difficult years in Chad!

For Chadians, Ouadi Doum is *ein Begriff*, a concept or reference point everyone knows. Here in 1987, then-Colonel Déby's Chadians developed an aggressive tactic so effective that they soundly defeated the more numerous and better-armed Libyans and began their expulsion from Chad. With only light Toyota pickups with machine guns mounted atop the cabins, they poured into the Ouadi Doum basin, where the Libyans were holed up behind a barrier of land mines around the airfield they'd built. The Chadians drove the Toyotas across the minefield so fast—sixty to seventy mph—that the mines detonated behind the vehicles, and the gunners mowed down the unprepared Libyans within, killing 4,000 to 5,000.

Today Ouadi Doum is only an obstacle on the main trade route from Faya-Largeau up to Libya, and as such it is a focus for our demining operations. On Monday, October 20, I flew up to have a look at the work in progress and at the instruction being carried out by a visiting US team. Two things were of interest to me: the changing climatic zones I would observe from the air so soon after the rainy season, and the progress of the demining operations themselves.

It has been a very good rainy season this year, the best since the year I arrived. From the air, I could see ample evidence around N'Djamena—empty gray fields just harvested, green patches planted with a second or "residual" crop, or standing pools of water. Moving north, I got perhaps the best range of moisture conditions I've seen from a flight north. There were many shades of green where things still grew, but they gave way to yellow and beige where the grass had already dried. The higher elevations were still drier, darker brown to red. The sky, in contrast, faded from a sharp blue to a soft white at the horizon.

As we reached Massaguet, a half-hour north, and then Massakoury and beyond, I saw the water pools and splotches of vegetation begin to thin and eventually fade. At last the desert began to encroach on the Sahel. It begins imperceptibly. Where can you draw the line? For me it is when there are no tufts of dry grass, but only the sand with its isolated shrubs. Even these continue the transition, becoming ever thinner and lower, until finally they exist only in the wadis.

Nearing Ouadi Doum, we saw salt pans and stretches of thin sand, as well as pebble fields, for this had once been a lake bottom. Then there were three large hangar-like buildings, the first large structures we'd seen since Massakoury. We alit noisily on the long black airstrip, constructed from interlocking steel panels. I was immediately struck by the ruins—a burnt-out tank, the burned tail section of a plane—remnants of war not cleared these past twenty years. And I sighted a more recent carcass: a small white plane from the air taxi service that had been crashed by the sole Chadian pilot the government forces the company to employ.

Colonel Donai, the local military commander, greeted us. I will remember him for his aluminum teeth (perhaps Russian work) and his determination to bring a school to Ouadi Doum for the children of the soldiers and deminers. Our flight had run longer than predicted, so we would have barely two hours on the ground; we went right to the minefields.

The deminers had finished for the day. They knock off around noontime, as the heat then becomes too intense. Several had stayed in the field, however, to demonstrate their work for us. The mine belt around Ouadi Doum is forty to seventy kilometers in circumference, depending on whom you listen to, but only a few hundred meters deep. A major trade route runs right through the wadi, providing the economic justification for clearing it.

Three Chadians and Aimé, a Frenchman from the international NGO Help International, took us around. They escorted us into cleared lanes and explained that the stakes indicated where it was safe to walk, and described what kinds of mines had been found in the cleared areas. The colors and band patterns tell whether the mine is or was antipersonnel or antitank, and whether it's been cleared or not. We were always in the cleared lanes, but Aimé stooped once at the edge and brushed the sand away from a still live mine about three inches from the lane. He explained the two patterns of mine distribution found here, both combining antipersonnel and antitank mines to defeat any kind of attack. The mines were an eclectic bunch, of Yugoslav, Belgian, French, and Soviet manufacture. The Belgians seemed to excel as mine makers. There was also some old ordinance around—we saw an unexploded, 500-pound Soviet bomb.

From the minefield, we went to one of the hangars (left from Libyan days), where an American instruction team was training the Chadian deminers. Our guys had been here a month now and were just wrapping up. They raved over how well the Chadians had done and how skilled they had already become.

With our fast paced inspection over, we again fell into Col. Donai's hands. He walked us quickly through his headquarters, two mud huts with no equipment. Then it was off to the village for the inevitable hospitality. No matter how poor, Chadians always entertain us with their best. Here it was a goat méchoui with a stew of variety meats and rice, but no bread or vegetables. We enjoyed the meal for its warm hospitality and bade quick adieus. I noted that all the huts in the village incorporated steel panels from the airfield as walls or roofs. Asking, I was told that one end of the strip had been bombed, shortening it to a still usable 10,000 feet and freeing up all this building material!

You've heard me say fate is resolute in Chad. We're going to build Col. Donai his school, although it won't be until next year's funds come in, and he will still have to find a teacher—perhaps one of the soldiers who can read and write and can help the kids get the fundamentals. But for Aimé and five Chadian deminers, fate struck more quickly. Ten days after our visit, they were killed in an explosion while preparing UXO [unexploded ordinance] for demolition in a huge pit on the fringes of the minefield.

Sunday, November 1: I'm up at 3:30 a.m., shower, grab a cup of coffee and a granola bar, and am out the door at 4:00 a.m. We're going birding. Casey, my deputy chief of mission, is an avid birder and has become acquainted with Pierre, a Frenchman at a local transport company, who is even more fanatic than she is. (Does going with them at this hour make me a fanatic as well? The difference is they do it every weekend.)

We go north by road, and then west beyond the little resort of Dougia. After just over an hour, we go off the paved road and stop in a little village to pick up Mohammed, our local guide. After a couple more miles on the road, we turn off again and in barely a kilometer are near the banks of the Chari River, still at flood stage after the rains. It is nearly six o'clock and suddenly daylight.

This is another world from N'Djamena, so remote and relaxed. The bush here is fairly thick with scattered clearings, mainly acacia, palm, and some unidentifiable trees of up to fifteen feet. Shrubs and grass below are already dying back only a month after the rains have ceased. The air felt incredibly fresh, and something in flower gave it a sweet perfume; in short sleeves, I felt a touch of chill.

Casey began to set up our base in a clearing by the road, and Pierre asked if I wanted to come with him, Mohammed, and the driver to set the nets. Of course I did. We thrashed through the brush, pushing some bushes aside and ducking under the lower branches of trees. It was harder going, and I was clumsier, than I'd anticipated. Part of the problem was that I was breaking in new hiking boots with soles much thicker than any others I owned. We found our way to the broad, placid river with only a couple of pirogues in motion on it. The nets were strips of nylon mesh, not too finely woven, stretched between poles. We worked the poles into the ground thirty to forty feet apart in five pairs near the water. When their extensions were up, the poles hoisted the net to a height of nine or ten feet. I stumbled back to our camp with a hole in one knee of my jeans and thorn cuts on my nose and forehead.

To call Mohammed a guide was a concession to local custom, since he really didn't show us around at all. But as long as there was someone local escorting us, the nearby inhabitants would leave us alone. He was, however, a very good assistant for Pierre. He and the driver would go together to check the nets for birds that had flown into them. They would work each into a cotton bag measuring six by eight inches, closed with a long drawstring that could be looped over their heads and dangled on their chests as they moved on to the next bird. They would come back after half an hour, each wearing three or four bags, which would then be carefully hung on a long horizontal pole.

I came quickly to feel a little rush of anticipation as Pierre would prepare to extract the bird from each bag. What would it be? He would sometimes show Casey just the head, making her guess the species. For me, it was simply the beauty of the plumage that was exciting. Pierre would carefully examine each bird, and with Casey in the role of secretary, call out the Latin name. Next he would band the bird, carefully slipping the metal ring around the ankle and calling out to Casey the band number. He then measured the length of wing, beak, and tarsus. Next he would blow gently to ruffle the feathers on the stomach and, probing with his fingers, announce whether he felt any accumulated fat as well as the "sexual state," that is, whether he saw indications of pregnancy or recent egg laying. Both would be rare in this, the migration season. Last of all, he would put the bird into a sheer nylon sack and weigh it. This day our birds ranged in weight from nine to fifty-three grams. No very big birds.

Handling the birds is a separate skill. I was terrified at first lest I harm them, but a rudimentary ability came fairly quickly. The bird is grasped in two places. First you slip the first two fingers of one hand over either side of the head. Then the same fingers, or a finger and thumb of the other hand, are used to grasp the little legs as high and close to the body as you can get—too low can damage the feet. If the second grip is firm enough you can remove the upper hand to get a better look. Casey describes the feeling you get from holding these creatures, which are normally seen only from afar, as almost religious. It is awe inspiring, and something else. If you cup your hand and place the bird there on its back, it will be immobilized and unable to fly away. The stillness is such a contrast to the creature's usual quick flitting.

And what did we see? Chad lies astride the Central African flyway, with migratory birds attracted by the wetlands around Lake Chad during the European winter. Literally hundreds of species can be seen here. We tallied twenty-three species over four hours, until the heat of the day had driven the birds into the shady trees or undergrowth. Pierre was pleased; our take brought his band list up to 1,350 individuals over the past year or so. He sends his records to the University of Bordeaux to become part of a major database.

Not surprisingly, our birds were small wetland types. Even the LBJs (little brown jobs) are exceedingly beautiful close up. My favorite was the malachite kingfisher, which I've also seen in Kenya. Ours was a juvenile with the blue feathers of his crest sticking out wildly in all directions. Nervous, he rotated his head constantly in little jerks almost 360 degrees. The blues and greens of his wings and back shown iridescent in contrast to the orange breast. The black-headed gonolek was also impressive, with the night-dark head and wings contrasting with a body of scarlet deeper than blood. Both of these species cawed incessantly, the only of our birds to complain. There were several fire finches, both a pygmy and a grey-headed kingfisher, an indigobird, and a nightingale.

The birds we didn't catch were also impressive. Along the river, in the sky, and in ponds near the road we saw maribou storks, sacred ibis, a carmine bee-eater, kites, pied kingfishers, and a Senegal coucal. Casey saw two yellow-ringed parakeets from the car, but I missed them.

People complain of nothing to do here in N'Djamena, but that's only if you measure activity in terms of concerts, the theater, and movies. Like tennis, the birds are infinitely more accessible here. No advance arrangements at parks and nature preserves is necessary, just CFA 5,000 a pop for Mohammed.

In a like way, getting out of N'Djamena is one of the keys to enjoying Chad. The variety of the country and the sharpness of its extremes register regardless of the purpose of the excursion—as does, in the case of our poor deminers, the precarious balance here between life and death.

Best wishes,

Ambassador Chris

Photo Gallery

Official Activities

Presentation of credentials to President Idris Deby, October 1999.
Credit: Government of Chad

Ambassador Goldthwait was at the time one of only four foreign
ambassadors to have received an award from Chad's Superior
Islamic Council, January 2004. *Credit: Superior Islamic Council*

160

With the Sultan of Kanem-Bornu in Mao, March 2000.

An embassy self-help project at a village near Kome in the oil region of southern Chad, June 2000.

At the Residence with Hallebassa Soubiene, the Chadian ambassador visiting from Washington, September 2003.

A donation of surplus Department of Defense equipment, 2003.

As vice-doyen, Ambassador Goldthwait delivered the diplomatic corps New Year's greetings to President Deby one year when relations with the doyen's country got testy, January 2002. *Credit: Government of Chad.*

With Chad's first returning Peace Corps class, 2003.

Scenes of the South and Sahel

The Chari River near Sarh, March 2000.

Ferry fees on the Chari for vehicles and animals, March 2000.

The author ascends in an ultralight aircraft at Zakouma National Park, March 2000.

A giraffe at Zakouma, March 2000.

Ambassador Goldthwait receives a letter of "doleances" from villagers in southern Chad, June 2000.

Hippos on the banks of the Chari near N'Djamena, 2000.

Ruins of Dar Sila in east central Chad, March 2002.

With Ambassador Mattie Sharpless, visiting from the Central African Republic, at Elephant Rock, 2001.

Avenue Charles de Gaulle, N'Djamena, November 1999.

Scenes from the North

The livestock market at Massakoury, March 2000.

Les McBride and visiting desk officer Debbie Lopes da Rosa in front of Abtouyour, a leading Chadian tourist attraction, March 2000.

Embassy staff at the ruins of eighteenth-century Ouara, the former seat of the Sultan of the Ouaddai, north of Abeche, January 2001.

A typical scene in the the Ennedi, January 2001.

The oasis town of Bardai in the Tibesti Mountains is one of the few places in Chad where deciduous fruit can be grown, September 2002.

The seven-million-year-old hominid skull, Toumai, was unearthed by Ahounta Djimdoumalbaye, a member of the French archaeological expedition, west of Faya Largeau, July 2001. *Credit: French government employee*

Street scene, Faya Largeau, November 2003.

Overland transport in the Sahara (and possible inspiration for the Sand People vehicle in the original *Star Wars* movie), November 2003.

172

Ounianga Kebir's salt lake and old French Foreign Legion fort, November 2003.

The Sahara Desert, November 2003.

Camels at a desert well, November 2003.

Scenes from the Letters

Captain Guardi with his burned-out tank, January 2001.

With Gaston at the Barbra Schell School, Ambassador Goldthwait delivers the proceeds of a benefit he held at the Residence for the school, 2001.

With visiting godson Tom (left) and the rest of the Block family, 2000.

Moussa the gazelle in the backyard of the Residence, June 2000.

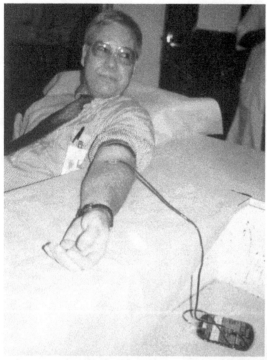

Giving blood at N'Djamena's main hospital, July 2002.

Rock art at Toukou, not far from Fada, November 2003.

The rolled-over vehicle at Ounianga Kebir, November 2003.

In a nomad's hut,
December 2003.

With the nomads near Mao, December 2003.

A late dinner with the nomads, December 2003.

3

The Country: Le Grand Nord

Think of Air France posters of the 1930s and 1940s, with the plane or its wing silhouetted against the stark and rugged landscape of North Africa. What is it that makes the Saharan zone, and its Sahel borderland, so exotic and enticing?

There is the remoteness, and the star-spangled nights. In Fada, there's the Crusader castle straight from the days of the French Foreign Legion. Around the town is the rock art in the Bryce Canyon–like setting. All that, yes, but it doesn't quite capture the mystique of *le Grand Nord*. Perhaps the most surprising thing is that here you are in the middle of the Sahara, and people and evidence of them are everywhere. And how the people live in the north! In an earlier letter I wrote of how travel here brought me closer to the essence of life, and that is surely the heart of the mystique.

Then there is the journey itself. It is often a hardship, yet I thrived on it. The trek was much of the message of these tours of the north, as in the Odyssey and other classics about journeys. There was something metaphysical about traveling in Chad.

Last, there are the great sites of the north. The sculpted, rugged Tibesti and Ennedi. The rock art. The eighteenth-century ruins of Ottoman-influenced Ouara and Sila. The salt lakes like Ounianga Kébir. Zakouma Game Park (not really northern, but I visited during a largely northern swing).

And the surprises: A durbar [reception] organized for me in a village near Adré, on the Sudanese border. The use of Sudanese pounds as currency in Tiné. Captain Guardi's burned-out tank at the roadside. And the men in nomad *ferricks* pleading for girls' education!

Overland to Mao and Bol

March 5, 2000

The trip to Mao was Les's idea. He manages our pitiful development activities (which I mean to augment). Married to a Chadian, Les has been here for a quarter-century, since Peace Corps days. He had been egging me to get out of N'Djamena, which he says you must do to appreciate what the country has to offer. A needed review of two of his tiny self-help projects in Mao would be our pretext. Or was it really that he wanted me to appreciate the depth of Chad's *enclavement*, or isolation, on this four-day swing?

We left early on a Thursday morning and the first hundred miles should have taken us over a third of Chad's paved road system. No such luck—as soon as we got north of the turnoff for Dougia and Lake Chad, we were routed off the paved road, which is being resurfaced onto a temporary parallel dirt track—my introduction to what was to come. At the town of Massaguet, we turned north on the route to the strategic Faya-Largeau. Massaguet, a place of a few thousand inhabitants, struck me as dismal and remote. From here to Massakoury, the road deteriorated—it showed no sign of work in several seasons, and we spent more time on improvised tracks beside it than on the rutted-out road itself.

In Massakoury I had my introduction to the civilities of rural travel in the form of a call on the sous-préfet, or county administrator. We entered the front room of his house where he normally receives guests. It was typical—high ceilings, tawdry furniture, the hospitality of sucrees or soft drinks, and sweetened tea. Then in came a huge plate of roast chicken and rice—inescapable. We asked after the local school where we'd constructed a few classrooms a couple of years ago, and promised a longer stop upon our return, Sunday, for a look at the famous cattle market.

From Massakoury, we plunged off onto a road that isn't on my map (1974, latest edition), and two things struck me immediately. First, after a few miles, our road dissolved further into a sand track. It seems to take only a few passages over these fragile soils by tires to transform them into beds of wispy desert. Thank goodness for our experienced local driver with his knowledge not only of the geography but also of sand driving! Second, the animals: Strung out all along the route, some led, some tethered or hobbled, some roaming—many more beasts than humans.

The deteriorating track distanced us quickly from civilization, despite the agonizingly slow pace. Through hours of increasingly parched countryside, I developed my own code for what I was seeing. The occasional stretches of tallish dried grass—six inches to a foot and fairly dense—I called steppe. The next drier category is the predominant one—true Sahel where the dried grass is thin, a few inches tall only, and the plain is sprinkled with scrub shrubs and low-growing acacia trees at intervals. Finally, there is the almost desert: only the wispiest, shriveled grass of lawn length—you notice that it exists only when the car slows for a rut and you get a closer look. And then the dunes begin, splotches of true desert sand, encroaching and blowing.

En route we began to notice the villages. Frank, our public diplomacy officer, had joined the expedition as well, and described the unique architecture that had been highlighted in a pamphlet he'd found at the National Museum. First, the adobe is grayer here, not mud colored, but of a gray-white color washed out like the eroding surface of the brick. And the dwellings wear horns—little acroteria on the corners of the eaves, and a middle one above longer walls. One village we passed has gained a certain notoriety for its school. Founded by a local Muslim woman with hard-won support from the local authorities, she ensures that at least a rudimentary French education is available to girls and boys alike. Her efforts were eventually recorded in the *New York Times,* and of course Les, whose records are impeccable, was able to produce the article for me as soon as we got home—and a copy of a letter from former Senator Paul Simon who had sent a donation when he read the article.

Mao itself is built on the top of a sand dune; in approaching it, we came upon a huge sand field blocking access. With only one false start, our driver was able to scale the steep slope and, sliding as much sideways as forward as we lunged along the broad sand streets, delivered us up in front of the office of the préfet for the necessary obeisance.

As I hinted at back in Massakoury, my first stop as a visiting ambassador must always be upon the local administrative authority. This is both courtesy and necessity for, if all else fails, it is incumbent upon the préfet or sous-préfet to find us food and lodging during our visit. Besides, Les, steeped in Chadian protocol over the years, wouldn't let me omit the courtesy, despite my unambassadorial desire to move around without hubbub. And here the préfet was expecting us, notified by the Ministry of the Interior by radio, and had gathered around him the local notables—mayor, chief of police, chief of the military detachment, and a couple of his administrative department heads. After a friendly twenty-minute chat, we were dispatched with the mayor to wherever—it turned out to be the local station of the World Food Program (WFP), which has a fine, US-supported base here that would be our headquarters.

And then it was that the sultan took charge of our visit, exhibiting the strong power that traditional rulers continue to wield in remote northern Chad. The immediate emblem was a modest durbar organized in my honor. As our cars—now a small cavalcade— rolled into the WFP compound, a conglomeration of people on foot and horse- and camelback crowded around the entrance. We were discharged at the far end of the yard, where a long row of chairs was arrayed, and I, of course, recognized the sultan, turban and flowing blue and white robes, as the only seated party. He rose and shook my hand with several friendly "Ça va?"s, upon which my WFP host took me by the arm and led me along a line of local notables and functionaries standing respectfully at a right angle to the chairs. I then returned, nodded respectfully to the sultan as I sat, and the fun began.

The crowd I'd noticed outside began to pour in through the gate playing drums, horns, and primitive stringed instruments. Half a dozen camel riders filed in and lined up to our left, matched by an equal number of horsemen on the right. The crowd of cheering commoners remained back by the gate, but we heard them. As the sultan and I exchanged repetitive pleasantries, the tone of the music changed and suddenly the riders were swinging their swords in time to it in a precise, swirling motion as their mounts executed a ceremonial pace. As these loyalists executed the "Dance of the Swords," a couple of the local officials began to file in a small circle before them, raising their clenched right fists in a salute reminiscent of the Black Power signal of the 1970s. At a prod from the ever-watchful Les, I followed them, leading in turn all the rest of the on-lookers, save the sultan himself. The cavalry reacted with motions of renewed vigor and broad smiles. Both groups, first the camel riders and then the horsemen, rode forward and saluted the sultan and me and retreated beyond the gate, where the crowd of commoners erupted in new yells. Last, the musicians came forward, saluted, and withdrew. Thus my durbar! Now we could go in for a cold drink!

Hours later there was dinner, perhaps the most typically Chadian meal I'd had to date. The national dish is *boule*, French for "ball," a big, round ball of doughy sorghum, millet, or other grain. You pull off big hunks, dip them in an oily meat or vegetable sauce, and enjoy. Hands (even the left on occasion) are the usual utensils, but not to worry—servants bring around a little kettle of water and a basin with soap and a towel before and after the meal. There were also whole roast sheep and goat. They seem to taste almost the same here, the latter perhaps a tad stringier. Also served were some vegetable dishes; moist, soft bread; more chicken; fish; and various sauces.

Over dinner I began to get more of an impression of the sultan. Sixtyish or beyond, he relaxed the stoic northern facade and greeted me and the other notables with courtesy, even joking and laughing. He teased the local military commander half-seriously when the latter showed the disrespect to come forty-five minutes late. The sultan understands French well, but seemed less comfortable in initiating conversation, or just didn't find it needful. Often when I would hazard a comment, he would respond "*C'est ça!*" and go on to repeat the gist of my remark. While protocol clearly dictated that I remain by his side, I felt relaxed with him. I studied his traditional dress more carefully: an elaborate white turban which could be adjusted to hide all of the face but the eyes, flowing white robes over a medium-blue surplice of floor length. Pointed white leather shoes and a silver-headed cane—almost a scepter in the way he wielded it—completed the costume. His family has ruled in the Kanem and Bornu for 400 years. He waited only a moment or two after the eating was done to rise and excuse himself, followed out by nearly all the Chadian guests.

I awoke the next morning conscious of a chill; the bed had had only a thin top sheet. After the inevitable cold shower—you get used to them—I stepped out onto the enclosed porch-*cum*-corridor to find it swirling in the dust of a full harmattan that had blown in over night. Visibility wasn't a hundred feet out into the yard.

Les had been up a little earlier, and deserves more biography than I have yet given him. Two words to describe him would be loyal and thorough. A few years my junior, he looks at least a decade older. Perhaps unfairly, I can't but think his quarter-century here has aged him more than the time would have at home. He began his Peace Corps stint here in Biltine in the 1970s, retreated a year later for security reasons to Abéché, re-upped and was transferred to Sarh in the south, and eventually went back to N'Djamena as Peace Corps headquarters staff. He had married a well-connected Gorane woman from Faya-Largeau by the time the civil war brought the fighting to N'Djamena—first for a few weeks in 1979, and then more seriously in 1980. He missed the embassy evacuation because then, as now, he lived in one of the *quartiers*, and didn't get notice. He, his wife, and his child holed up in the deserted embassy compound for a couple of weeks living off the mangoes and papayas. When things got hotter, they made their way across the river to Koussérie by pirogue. There Les went to work in the USAID refugee assistance effort and his second daughter was born in the lean-to he erected for shelter adjacent to the USAID office.

When the embassy in N'Djamena reopened, Les came back, worked for USAID for a while, survived its pullout, and is today our only officer who devotes his time to development assistance. He combines an odd devotion to both Chad and the United States. He believes in our goals for development and democracy, but is skeptical about their success even as he (like me) desperately wants to do something to better the life of people here. Through his wife's and his own Chadian friends and contacts, he is one of our best sources on what's going on in the real Chad, beyond the expat circles. But his wife is wary of the linkage to us; I have yet to meet her.

Now out to see Mao! Let me try to paint the town and its environs for you in five or six images. If my art is successful, you will see its aspects, but also sense through the haze of the blowing sand the *enclavement* here.

When I try to conjure up the memory of the town itself that morning, I see a soft blur of pinks, browns, and grays. The air itself, heavy with sand, is ecru but with a hint of pink, and the obscured sun an orange circle. The ground sand is a darker beige, from which loom up the washed-out grays of the edifices, their outlines only a little stronger in the fog. Here and there the dot of a more brightly painted sign breaks the ethereal gloom. It is an image that Turner might have brushed onto his canvas, or perhaps Whistler.

And you must look to appreciate the unique adobe architecture of the city. I disagree with Les, who says it is as distinctive as Timbuktu, but it is unique. The grey coloration of the adobe, the ornamental roof finials—more elaborate than what we saw in the villages en route—the multistoried structures of the sultan's palace and the city museum, an old fort—all add to the enigma. It is an old city, by Chadian standards at least, dating to the time over a century ago when the capital of the Kanem-Bornu empire was moved to this dune from a more exposed locale some fifty kilometers distant. Then it was a city of straw huts. Now, the adobe buildings threaten to be the town's undoing, since they catch and channel the water from the rains, causing erosion down most of the streets. Indeed, we visited the ravines that have nearly bifurcated the little city—only two streets remain, which connect its eastern and western halves. And soon, if nothing is done, the city will need to relocate again!

The next picture will be a photo from a wide-angle lens in the realistic style of Gordon Parks. It is of the malnutrition program of *Action Contre la Faim.* From the doorway where we are standing, we take in the courtyard on the left and the interior of a clean but barren room on our right. The courtyard is filled with huts made from mats woven from the straw of sorghum sacks. Here dwell the mothers of the malnourished infants with whatever other children they could not leave at home in their village. The doors are covered by blankets that retain a little warmth from the blowing harmattan. One blanket is ajar, allowing us to see that inside the hut are several children on mats spread over the sand, and a little brazier of charcoal and incense, which casts its cleansing scent through the air. Across the yard we see the adobe structures of the latrines, and a well that, we are assured, conveys potable water.

To our right, inside a small building, the central figure is Jeanine, a Frenchwoman in her late thirties who is the director of the project. With her are a couple of her local staff, but the real focus of our attention is the tiny women sitting on the mats on the earthen floor with their even tinier babies. Here the malnourished babies are brought, weighed, and put on a liquid diet of eight feedings a day, tapering over three weeks to three solid meals as they recover. In Jeanine's hands are the weight charts—2.5 kg, 2.6, 2.9, until this child has reached 80 percent of the height/weight norm, the goal for release. The mothers are alert, and you can tell that they are catching on to the feeding treatments. One suspends her infant on a hanging scale. In the arms of one of Jeanine's co-workers is a child with the telltale puffy swelling of ankles and wrists that indicates kwashiorkor.

The project has fifteen clinics around Mao. Our picture will not show the kitchen where the mothers are given lessons on preparing the dry rations for the children at home who are less severely malnourished. It has a typical brazier, modified to conserve firewood. Nor do we see the bags of corn-soy mix, the basis of the nutritious ration. The stolid, hardworking farmers I used to visit in the Midwest would inwardly thank God if they knew that their crops were the basis for the porridge that is saving the lives and restoring the health of these children 6,000 miles from Kansas and Illinois. For myself, seeing the wretched poverty and distress of these tots and their diminutive mothers, I couldn't help feeling a little like one of the fat overseers at Oliver Twist's orphanage. And the malnutrition itself is, in a way, a measure of the *enclavement* here, for the diet is entirely restricted to what can be produced locally and stored without refrigeration from season to season.

We moved off in the inevitable Toyotas, military escort *de rigueur*, to the site of our third picture, a little village where the United States has sponsored a reforestation project and, cooperating with the World Food Program, a school feeding program for girls to get them to stay in school. The fifteen-minute drive over dunes and through foggy gullies only deepens the sense of isolation and poverty.

Our photoscape this time is a broad, sloping hill rising from the left to the right across the canvas. Against the murky mauve background of the harmattan we see the tiny trunks of the newly planted trees before us; uphill to the right are a couple of houses on the outskirts of the village, and further up an established plantation of trees. The new plantation consists of sprigs barely visible in the haze of several varieties of acacia planted at three-meter intervals. Sheltered from the goats by a bramble fence, these trees are hand watered until they become established. Most seem to remain alive six months after planting, but from the few tiny green leaves they sport, you wonder if they will ever thrive. But look over to the right of our picture at the older plantation, which, after only five years, has created a nice canopy of six- to ten-foot trees. There is hope! Dividing the two plots in the center of our painting is a sloping field leading uphill to the first village houses. Like most of the territory, the sloping field is chockablock with animal dung. You can't avoid it and, after a day, cease trying to step around it. Even out in the remote bush, it peppers the entire country; here it stands out in black globs against the grayish sand. At the back you see what we hope our new forest will stem—the shifting dunes of sand encroaching and nearly burying the outrider houses. The picture is not complete without a few goats and sheep, and the local village headman who has come to greet us and thank us for the new trees. But they are stark, solitary figures barely emerging from the mistiness of our canvas.

An understanding of Mao isn't possible without a snapshot of one of the ouaddis, or wadis. They are the lifeblood of the city, its source of food. We look down into Ouaddi Youlo from a higher dune, since most are in declivities that drain the scant rainfall into their artesian roots. The ouaddi covers several acres, and its foundation plants are the tall date palms and mangoes that create the skyline-*cum*-canopy beneath which the activities of the oasis thrive. Peering into the cool gloom below the taller trees, we will see an ancient well, the water extraction delivered by beasts of burden. The water tumbles from the wooden buckets into earthen troughs, which distribute it throughout the ouaddi. There will be a handful of wells here, perhaps ten-feet deep. We can tell that it will be cool beneath the trees, even when the harmattan isn't painting the sky pink above. Looking with microscopic care from our vantage point, we will see other crops growing in tiny plots both under the canopy and to its left—the outskirts of the plantation where more drought-hardy plants are placed. All in all, we might make out wheat, millet and sorghum, citrus, papaya, peas, guava, garlic, onions, tomatoes, peppers, potatoes, and more. And nowhere else have I seen wheat production on little five-by-ten-foot plots, but forget not that this is family subsistence farming, the goal being a little surplus of everything to sell right there in the market of Mao. Some of the locals tried to ship their dates out, but found that the quality couldn't compete with those from the true desert oases further north. Similarly, a handful of outside foodstuffs make their way into Mao's market, but not enough to be a real part of the diet. For all intents and purposes, the region is dependent on what can be produced and stocked from these lush little ouaddis.

We were to have lunched picnic-style in the ouaddi, but the harmattan nixed that. Instead, after a couple of additional stops, we returned to our base camp for a very late meal hosted by our guide, the mayor.

The last picture of Mao you should carry off is that of my courtesy call on the sultan. Right after our 4:00 p.m. lunch, we hurried off to the palace. Making our way slowly through the throng of retainers who had reassembled and made all the noise they were capable of, we entered the sultan's compound. The palace, dating from the 1940s, is of the same gray adobe in the local style, but bigger than any other structure in the town and two stories in parts. Alighting, it took me a moment to realize that we were not going into the main palace, but to a side courtyard where the sultan was waiting.

So grasp this picture: As I approach, the sultan is seated on a tatty old brown couch that could have come from the reception room of any préfet. But the entire yard is strewn with oriental carpets (new machine-made variety, just purchased on the Hadj last year). I kick off my shoes and approach the sultan, who stands, smiles his slightly leering grin, grasps my hand with both of his, and pulls me down beside him. Then silence. I'm looking perplexed, not sure if I should kick off the formalities, or await a signal from my host. He chats amiably with Les at length, not at all concerned for any protocol. Meanwhile I have sent Frank out to retrieve our finest remaining gift book; does the sultan know, and is he waiting until my delegation is complete before launching the formalities? After an interminable time, Frank appears, passes me the book, and more silence ensures. Once or twice, I've made courtesy comments to my host and brief exchanges have resulted, replete with "*Ça va?*"s and repetition. Then drinks and dates and nuts are served. It is clear that we are into the ceremony. And then a second course made up of poultry on a bed of deliciously seasoned couscous and whole roast sorghum. The best flavor of the trip! Then the sultan rises suddenly—the call is at an end. I present my book, and receive in return a fine kilim carpet, most likely from Libya. We shake hands warmly, and I retreat over the carpets, retrieve my shoes, and withdraw.

Only later did I learn of the side plots of my colleagues. Les, it seems, had been importuned by the sultan at length for money to repair the eroding palace. Frank, a full ten minutes in seeking the book, had been greeted effusively by the retainers in the street, decided that they were far more photogenic than any of the animals at Waza, and taken several minutes to video their antics. I would have until sometime the next morning to decide what to tell the wealthy sultan about financing the restoration of his house.

I could give you other pictures of Mao as well. For example, shots of the great, twenty-foot ravines that are eroding this city on a sand dune, having already cut through all but two of the east-west streets in the town. Or the high school where we stopped to donate books: rooms so dark you could hardly see the blackboard; roofs sagging, and in one little building collapsed, putting it out of service; a new classroom wing built by parents at their own expense, but eroding in its unfinished state because they could afford no tin for the roof and therefore stopped with the walls about a foot below their intended height. And no latrines for the 300 to 400 students.

Early the next morning we were up and ready to be off to Bol, on Lake Chad. But there was a complication: the sultan would have us stop en route at a lake in the middle of the semidesert, which he hoped we'd help restock with harvestable fish. It was impossible to refuse, so off we went following a car of his retainers. It was along that route that I began to appreciate the residual power of the traditional rulers in the backwaters of Chad. The sultan himself had passed along the route about an hour ahead of us, and along the way were villagers lining the road to cheer us along. And when we reached the village nearest the little lake, there was a huge throng like what he'd produced back in the city: chanting, shouting, playing musical instruments—only no camels and horses out here. The lake itself was charming—a little oval of blue in the middle of the blowing sand. A green necklace of date palms encircled it. It was clear that in most years there would be water year round. Before us, for show, there paddled a local on a papyrus canoe, and a little straw pavilion had been constructed for the sultan and me to relax and talk, with the vista of the oasis lake before us. Idyllic even in its isolation! Realizing our impatience to be on our way, the sultan kept us only fifteen minutes before sending us off, guided by a car of his retainers straight through the bush, for surprise! the lake wasn't exactly on the road to Bol. And in parting, I muttered something innocuous to him about considering the funds for his palace, but that it would be difficult since it was an individual, not a group project. (Later I learned that he'd also requested money from the French!) Les will tell you that during this stretch, my frustration at not being in control of where I was or where I was going or how long it would take finally got the better of me just a bit—or was it that after several pauses for ceremonial tea and soft drinks, it was nearing noon and, in contrast to everyone else, my excellent, center-of-attention self hadn't been able to sneak off into the bushes for a quick leak since breakfast.

Released finally upon the main road, we drove for a couple of hours over track that was slower going than the overland route had been,

ultimately reaching Bol in early afternoon. We proceeded immediately to the préfet's house and, sure enough, in his absence the
préfet adjoint was awaiting us. He had evicted the préfet's family
from the house for the night and it would be our hostel. The préfet's
wife was relegated to a small outbuilding in back, but that didn't
diminish her hospitality in ensuring our meals and comfort.

We had come to Bol wanting to see the lakeside agricultural
development projects, at the suggestion of the minister of agriculture. The préfet adjoint, mayor, et al., were determined, of course,
to show us their development assistance priorities. So we saw a
decaying water tower the Italians had put in twenty years ago, a
pathetic abattoir, the market, which lacked shade structures, and
finally the *Maison de la culture*. This is the closest thing to a library
the major towns of Chad enjoy. There are usually a few shelves of
books—not more than a few hundred—and a reading room where
some of the children also come to play Scrabble. In bigger towns,
there is an effort to have a bigger room or outdoor space for showing films or TV on special occasions, such as key soccer games. The
plea here was for funds to restore a room whose roof and wall had
fallen in, rendering it unusable.

After this, our hosts took us on to the agricultural projects we
wanted to see. It was for the development of polder works from the
lake—large floodplains which had been contained and fitted with
year-round irrigation with lake water. Enormously productive, this
land was growing vegetables, corn, and wheat. Various cooperative farmers groups—mainly women—were undertaking the work.
With modest state subsidies (all Chad can afford), the project was
pretty much a success on 1,000 hectares, with 1,500 more due to
come on-stream in the next season. Just one catch: Where's the market for more than double the production? N'Djamena is a dozen
hours away by truck, days more by the more common pack animal.
So it remains unclear if the added production will yield added income for the locals, or have any impact whatsoever on the country's food deficit.

The business portion of our visit concluded with an hour in a
boat on the lake. It contrasts a little with the southern shore—there
is less floating grass, and more solid islands, meaning that we didn't
reach open water. But the same exotic birds and fishing and trading

boats were here. Here also we saw the unique Kouri cattle, which have enormous, thick horns, as big at the base as a man's head.

And when we returned to the préfet's, all four of the resident Americans had gathered to meet us (actually, three Americans and a Swede). Two, both middle-aged single women, have been conducting a literacy project on the lake islands these ten years. They have developed a writing system for the language of the lake people, instruction manuals so that it can be taught and perpetuated, and eventually they will produce a copy of the Bible in the local idiom. The others, a couple, have been doing church work—serving the burgeoning community of southern Christian immigrants into this northern community. After a chat, a meal, and another chat mixing our Chadian hosts with our American callers, we retired. The bed in my room had been made up with only a spread, no sheets—which didn't prevent me from sleeping soundly.

The morning brought absolutely the worst road I've seen yet in Chad. It took us four and a half hours to do the 130 kilometers back to Massakoury. What was so frustrating was that it should have been a good road—Italian engineered some decade or two earlier. But it was impossibly pitted out, so we drove off to the side. The most diverting thing during the excruciating drive was the nature of the traffic—many times more animal trains than trucks. Horses, donkeys, but especially camels! No doubt but that the pack animals were the prevailing conveyance.

Les had carefully timed our return so we would pass back through Massakoury at midday on a Sunday, when the livestock market was in full swing. After swilling a Coke with the sous préfet, the mayor led us through the market. We came first to a huge corral of camels, horses, and donkeys. I'd have thought this was the cattle market itself, but no, only the pen where the visiting merchants put their riding animals while they were in the market. We went north and turned west and came to huge fields reserved for each species—camels, cattle, sheep, goats, horses, donkeys—literally thousands of animals for sale, by and large in very good condition. It is the second or third largest animal market in Chad.

But the rest of the market was equally fascinating. There was a section of artisanal metalworking, and we saw the resulting harnesses and hardware items, even spearheads and arrowheads for bows and arrows. The leather section sported mainly containers for salt, water, and anything else you might need. The aroma of the fresh tanning was enticing. And there, at last, I saw gum arabic—used stateside as an emulsifier in many food and household products. It is Chad's third largest export, some $20 million per year. I tasted it—tasteless. From one of the varieties of acacia, it looks a little like amber, but it is malleable when you squeeze it. And, of course, the market displayed the normal array of foods and spices. All in all, this was one of the least spoiled and most interesting markets I've seen in Africa.

The stop having been worth the time invested, we then made tracks for N'Djamena, arriving around 5:00 p.m. on our fourth day of travel. As I began to recognize the familiar scenery north of N'Djamena, it seemed to me truly that I was climbing back from a remote world of far away and long ago. Mao, a hazy never-never land where the traditional authority of the sultan seesaws with that of the titular administrative authority, the préfet. Bol, a newer creation, seemed almost an artificial colony whose burgeoning produce costs as much to extract as to grow. And the market of Massakoury existed unchanged for generations. In Chad, anachronism is reality.

Best regards,

Ambassador Chris

The Ennedi

January 21, 2001

The vast north of Chad looms mysteriously over us here in N'Djamena. It is a scantly populated land whose people nonetheless wield undue influence over the destiny of the nation. Made up of rugged mountains, orange Saharan sand, and rare green oases, it seems from a distance impenetrable. Parts, such as the Tibesti, were never under the firm control of the colonial French, and even today that massif is held by rebels who draw the greater part of their strength from the local Toubou tribesmen. But with ageless geological marvels, the sites of man's eldest australopithecine forebears, and thousands of years of rock art, this is Chad's most intriguing region.

Thus it was with both excitement and a hint of trepidation that I led a small party east and north to the Guéra, Ouadai, and finally the magnificent Ennedi, the oasis town of Fada being our ultimate destination. Les, our perpetual guide, nurse Denise, and Daryll, a sergeant in the defense attaché's office, joined me to make up the party—not to mention the faithful Chaibo and Adoum, our other driver.

We had, of course, specific objectives for our week-long journey. Important among them was assessing the need for expanding Chad's demining program to the region northeast of Abéché, along the Sudanese border, and further north near Fada itself. We also wanted to hear about the impact of the failure of last season's rains and the threat of food shortages in this part of the country, said to be the hardest hit. But I am also learning how travel can be its own objective. This is good, since one invests a lot of time on the road here for very little at the destination. On the one hand, the mere fact that the American ambassador would come overland to the remote hinterland has a tremendous impact on the officials and people I meet. On the other, psychologically for me, the process of movement itself comes to be as important as what I do upon arrival—rather like the young backpackers for whom the experience of travel to a more primitive world is its own ultimate fulfillment. And indeed, this trip gave me my most archaic travel experience in Chad and brought our little party closest to living for a day or two as rural Chadians do themselves.

Leaving in two cars, our first day's destination was Mongo, capital of the Guéra Department, where we hoped to meet with the préfet and inspect a self-help project, a plant nursery. Making good time along the 450-kilometer route, we lunched in the shadow of the crag called "Abtouyour," one of Chad's leading tourist attractions for its dramatically spiked peak stained white with the guano of the birds that nest on high. From a certain angle, it looks almost like a huge maned lion. We continued eastward. A few miles further, at Bitkine, we had just turned south to drop in on some Australian missionaries I knew when a car overtook us and told us that the préfet had come out to meet us and escort us the 60 kilometers into Mongo. So, sooner than we'd anticipated, we were swept into the Chadian pattern of escorted hospitality. I joined the préfet in his car and it was soon clear that he, like me, is relatively introverted (I'm especially introverted in French), and we jostled along the rough road exchanging the odd comment, but neither embarrassed by the long silences in between.

Reaching Mongo, a dusty place like most Chadian towns but surrounded by high jagged hills, the préfet took us into the airy reception room of his residence and we discussed the program. We would see the nursery project we'd supported yet that afternoon. We could then rest a little while, and eventually there would be a dinner. The préfet had gathered the local notables, and asked if I would address them and hear their concerns. Of course I would, and I listened now to the first reports about poor rains, failed crops, and impending hunger. We went with the flow, and in a little while we were off to the nursery site where, again, a small crowd awaited us. The association leaders guided us through the acre or so of grounds. We saw the propagation of seedlings, some test plots, and the well that watered the project. As elsewhere, the people were grateful for our support and even more thrilled that we'd come to visit. I like to think we reinforced their pride, their sense of the importance of what they were doing to better the community, and strengthened their determination. Our money—and time—had been well spent.

After an hour at the guesthouse where we were lodged we returned to the préfet's residence for an ample, relaxed meal. We munched and chatted. The repast included méchoui, boule, sauces, salad, a side vegetable or two, and chicken—the typical Chadian banquet fare. It was good, if plain. As our trek continued, I'd remark a diminution in the variety and quantity of what we were served, but never in the fervor of the hospitality. The préfet had invited not only the town notables but also the ten or so Americans from his region. I was able to chat with them as well, getting some idea of their local work, largely in the study of indigenous languages, with an ultimate end after several years of developing a written form, codifying the grammar, and eventually translating the Bible into them.

The next morning we were up with the light. Somewhat to my chagrin, for it always slowed things down, the préfet had announced he would accompany us to the furthermost town in the *departement*, Mangalmé. So off we went around the northern end of Mount Guéra, and east into the bare Sahelian plain. It was slow going, the military escort leading at thirty to forty kilometers per hour, not half the speed Chaibo and Adoum would have managed. We threaded our way along half of Mount Guéra's western side and across all of the pointed northern reach. It rises abruptly from the plane, reaching nearly 3,500 meters. It is characterized by enormous, towering piles of erosion-rounded boulders, piled atop one another, the upper ones leaning eerily askew in seeming defiance of gravity. Back home this would warrant protection as a national park or monument with a suitably descriptive name like "Teeterstone." We had actually begun seeing these rock piles a hundred miles west at Ngoro, but Mount Guéra's were more dramatic. At intervals, we would come upon such outcroppings all the way up to the Ennedi, where they would become more dramatic still, with sharp, harsh formations coming to outnumber the softer worn ones.

After an hour and a half, we found ourselves in a fairly dense acacia forest, a little short of Mangalmé. Suddenly, the pickup truck of military men at our head slowed and stopped. A couple of the company jumped out, shouldered their rifles, and fired into the bush up ahead. Gazelles! There were no hits, thank goodness. I mumbled something to the préfet and, embarrassed by this breach of discipline, he ordered the party to advance. We soon found ourselves in Mangalmé, where we greeted the sous-préfet, bid adieu to the préfet, and were released to find our own way east to Abéché.

Something noteworthy occurred on our return trip when we paused again in Mongo to pay our respects to the hospitable préfet. He was ready for us with a lunch that, after some days in the north, we found varied, tasty, and welcome. As we finished he rose. He spoke, he noted, in the name of each of the local representatives of authority, and of the minister of the interior and the president. He formally apologized for the incident with the gazelle, also on behalf of the local military leadership. Days later, in N'Djamena, the interior minister again repeated the apology to me when we met by chance at an event. The apologies were, first of all, a reflection of the impeccable Chadian sense of courtesy. But also, I dare believe, they were an example even here in Chad of civilian leadership exerting its control over military leadership. In some small way, our trek had contributed to the country's plodding democratization.

We arrived in Abéché in midafternoon and went directly to the préfet's compound, as is wonted. Even before we saw the préfet, the representatives of Africare met us on his steps. Africare is a developmental, private voluntary organization (PVO) that has the largest (two–three million dollars annually) bilateral US aid project in Chad. Its major activity is around Abéché. Then the préfet himself was on the steps to greet me and escort me into his residence. He was newly arrived and hadn't officially assumed his function, but greeted me warmly and served us all with the ubiquitous soft drinks. We talked for some minutes and he politely relinquished us to our avid Africare hosts, a review of whose operations was our chief interest in Abéché.

The Africare presentation took the remainder of the afternoon. These folks knew that I was interested in seeing what they had done with respect to food processing. In this overwhelmingly agriculture country, everything is marketed right from the field: Cereals may be threshed and groundnuts shelled, but little more. So it seems to me that the only way forward developmentally is to stimulate food processing, or "transformation," first artisanal and eventually commercial. And this is an increasing focus of the Africare project. At their main compound, they had gathered their staff for a hands-on presentation. The projects were described and examples of packaged goods ready for sale, as well as the resulting meals, were there for our examination. The dishes made from the dried mixes were tasty. It seemed to me that a great deal of progress had occurred on transformation and nutritional fronts since my first visit some fifteen months earlier. Denise commented positively about the nutritional aspects of the products. Then we were off to view the workplace of a women's co-op that packaged dried and powdered tomatoes. The ladies awaited us and showed us two simple mills of Indian origin that they relied upon. Each of the building's three or four rooms corresponded to a step in their simple transformation process. The resulting "high value" product was marketed in N'Djamena and beyond with success, and the women are saving for a new mill to grind groundnuts (peanuts). This is real economic development at the grassroots level.

Come evening, there was a méchoui back at the guesthouse compound. I was content that this project was on track, and glad to have Africare as the lead PVO in a new agricultural project in the oil region of the south for which I'd arranged funding, drawing on my old USDA food aid programs.

Breakfast the next morning was deceptive, fresh bread and little packages of French cheese from the local French military unit. This was the last Westernism we'd see until our return four days later.

There were two events in Abéché that hadn't been worked into the previous evening's schedule. First was my call on the sultan of the Ouadai. He received us not in the palace, but in a rather ordinary compound nearby. The one concession to his dignity of office was the series of murals around the walls of the porch-like room where he received us. One was of the ancient capital of Ouara, to which we'd be off shortly. The sultan applauded the various interests I'd expressed in his realm. He apologized for having missed the dinner the previous evening, but explained that he was just recovering from a bout of malaria. I sympathized, and departed at what seemed the perfect time—after about ten minutes.

Our last Abéché stop was the local hospital. We were conducted by the director and Dr. Louis Sutton, an American missionary attached to the facility. Denise confirmed that the basic structure was sound, better than the hospital in N'Djamena. But the broken equipment and lack of basic medicines were shocking—a theme we'd see echoed throughout this part of the country in coming days. And there was a horrible problem with stagnant waste water: The drainage canals were improperly bedded, meaning that liquid waste—blood, guts, latrine waste—didn't drain, but sat stagnant in three open troughs that ran between the wards of the hospital.

The Africare folk insisted on accompanying us as far as Biltine, some ninety kilometers to the north. It was here, I would judge, that the process of travel began to assert itself over the object and control our progress. Somewhat in the mode of nineteenth-century explorers or contemporary backpackers using "public" transportation, our movement increasingly came to be stage by stage, dependent on directions or a guide to the next stopping place.

We probably would have found our way to Ouara, the ancient capital of the Ouadai, some half an hour west of the road to Biltine, since Les had been there several times. But the military escort in the lead missed the turnoff; it was our Africare hosts who stopped them and got us on to the sandy side road. Arriving, I saw the wide ruins of a walled, fired-brick city that still reached to two or three stories above a sandy bowl toward the encircling, rocky hills. Defensively sound, this Zimbabwe of Chad had been relinquished only in view of the failure of the springs that had fed the site when it was founded in the seventeenth century. We wandered through the several acres of ruins, picking out the structures with a map from the first ever guidebook of Chad, loaned to me by the author the day before our departure. What impressed me the most, perhaps, were the 300-year-old palm trunks that served as lintels and supported the towering superstructures. Might they collapse as I ducked under them? The refined architecture might have nurtured a more lengthy and sophisticated history had not the water given out, leading the dynasty to move to Abéché around 1850.

Our image of Chad prior to colonization—or at least in the nineteenth century—is of a largely empty space without organization and with intensive settlement only in the far south, the region designated by the French as *"le Tchad utile,"* with a pejorative implication regarding the rest of the country. Ouara is proof to the contrary, with its solid walls and delicate keyhole portals. It betrays a highly sophisticated state with some Ottoman influence, contemporary with the European baroque.

We regained the main road and headed north to Biltine. Les shared with us what he could recall of his impressions and anxieties as a young Peace Corps volunteer, heading over the same track nearly thirty years earlier as he traveled to his first assignment in Biltine. He contrasted his old worries with those of his own son, now gone to the United States after being raised in Chad, and facing the opposite problem of adapting to life in the world's most advanced society.

Once in Biltine, we sought out the préfet, but he hadn't been informed of our travel, a failure by the Ministry of the Interior that we'd regret come evening. Further, the *departement* was in the midst of a change of leadership—a new préfet was present but hadn't yet assumed duties from the old. All this gave us the reprieve of leaving for the northeast unaccompanied. We headed off into a region that I can best describe in American terms as chaparral. The land was rolling, sometimes quite rugged. It was loosely cultivated or forested, and occasionally in drier spots gave way to short grass cover, wispy straw in this season. It was fun driving as we rounded hills, scaled slopes and then descended, crossed wadis, etc. We knew we were on the right road chiefly because of the steep, paved concrete fords in the wadis: Only the main route would have them. We stopped twice along the way, both in Am Zoer and Guéréda, to drop off boxes of schoolbooks. I was quickly tiring of all the interruptions during these long days of driving. We were further delayed at Guéréda by the confusing road out of town; we had to go back into town twice for directions before we were securely routed out into the dusk.

Our entry to Ireba, our destination for the night, was marred by a wrong turn that led us off toward Tiné on the Sudanese border (we wanted to go there, but not until the next morning). To reinforce our new dependence on guidance, we found a rider in a truck who was changing a flat tire, and he was willing to ride back with us to where we'd gone astray and point us in the correct direction. So, in the dark, instead of arriving in Ireba at a civilized 8:00 p.m., we rolled in at 10:10 p.m. The town seemed to be locked up tight for the night. The only lights were for security at the Zaghawa sultan's palace. And, horror of horror, the sous-préfet had not been informed of our arrival, either days earlier by the Ministry of the Interior or that day by the préfet in Biltine. We got him out of bed. Nonplussed but aware that it was his duty to provide for us, he finally took us to an unfinished office building that in a month or two will become his headquarters. It was commodious, with doors and windows, if not yet up and running in the plumbing department. We spread out the cots and sleeping bags with which we always travel. Dinner was whatever dry food we'd brought with us—chips, an apple, nuts, and dried fruit—but no one had much appetite. Before bedding down for the night, we couldn't help noting the magnificence of the desert sky, undisturbed by any ground lights. Les pointed out some of the constellations. As I drifted quickly into sleep, I began to sense a remoteness different in character and degree even from that of N'Djamena.

Now solidly in the north, we were already becoming accustomed to a new daily cycle. For one thing, with no electricity, schedules depend entirely on the natural light of day. We awoke early, before 6:00 a.m., and the sous-préfet was not long in joining us at 6:30 a.m. We wandered over to his office (no breakfast you understand) and sat to discuss our schedule. We would stop briefly at the hospital where Denise had equipment to deliver, call on the Zaghawa sultan, and then move off east to Tiné. The sous-préfet would accompany us.

At the hospital we roused the director who, it seemed, was getting his beauty sleep at just past 7:30 a.m. He gave us a quick tour, including the maternity ward that we'd paid to rebuild a couple of years earlier. Denise surrendered her supplies, and the director was suddenly glad to have been disturbed. Afterward, we rushed around the back to view a burned-out tank, remnant of the civil war of 1990, into which had been stuffed a lot of unexploded ordinance—a clear indicator of the need for the demining program in this neck of the woods. Then to the sultan. It surprised me that he was ready to receive us at a little past 8:00 a.m., but so much the better. We were very welcome—it seemed he was another former pupil of Les's. He apologized for not receiving me with a durbar, as was my due, but again the lack of notice.... We chatted a little. He asked if I wanted a horse (the appropriate gift of courtesy for an ambassador). He knew I would demur, but gave me instead the cane he was wielding, made of horn and dark wood. He was a charming gentleman, despite the harsh reputation of the Zaghawa.

We were then off to Tiné, where we'd almost ended up the night before. Along the way, the sous-préfet, knowing our interest, pointed out burned-out vehicles and random unexploded ordinance, and described a little of the 1990 civil war that had brought the current president west from Sudan to expel Hissène Habré. He described some twenty injuries, including eight deaths from mines and UXO during his two-year tenure, and higher animal losses. Clearly, the issue was a priority. I was suddenly glad we'd turned back before reaching Tiné the night before, instead of trying to find our way through the town and back to Iriba in the dark over this infested road. After some ninety minutes, we spied a minaret and some adobe buildings, and descended into the town that was separated from Sudanese Tiné by only a wadi.

In contrast to Ireba, which even in the morning had seemed dead as a doornail, Tiné is a thriving border town. The local administrative officer received us. He would take us to the local clinic and the school, and, finally, to see the two wells down in the wadi that we had supported financially. What we saw was really sad. At the clinic, serving a regional population of some 30,000, there was a nurse with a four-room facility. Two of these were for overnight patients, and in one was a woman with respiratory problems. In the other was a twelve-year-old boy whose hand had been blown up by UXO, with the permanent loss of two fingers. Graphic proof of the problem I'd come looking for. At the school I saw the worst teacher-to-student ratio I've encountered so far in Chad: two instructors, one trained and one not, for 310 students divided by age into three classrooms. The oldest group, teens, numbered only fifteen to twenty, including a single girl. Our wells were an enigma. They were dirty, serving mainly livestock, and we trod across muddy dung to approach them. But in this year of failed rains, they were all that provided the townspeople, as well as the animals, with drinking water, literally keeping the town alive. The wells were a critical contribution, but how far still from satisfactory sanitation!

I had expressed an interest in visiting the market in this border town, and replete with wares it was. With prices denominated in Sudanese pounds, it was clear that we'd crossed a continental divide, and that here the orientation was east toward Sudan and the Middle East, not west to Douala [Cameroon], as in N'Djamena. Abéché itself may be on this eastern side; judging from what we'd heard, I suspect that the true divide may be back at Mount Guéra.

The market administrator had been showing us around and he insisted that we pause for a cool drink of delicious, milky guava juice and an early lunch of roasted meat, lamb this time. While we ate, the cars were gassed up, and after sending some food out to the drivers, we were ready to be on our way. Just one more thing (there always is one more courtesy or delay in this country): the sultan of Bahaï, to which we were next headed, and incidentally the younger brother of the president, was in town, so we had to pay a call on him as well.

By now we considered a guide to the next stopping place to be essential. We could plan only as far as that next point, recognizing the need to pause and invest the time to organize our further progress once we got there. From Tiné, the deputy mayor had been dragooned into accompanying us as far as Bahaï, some sixty or seventy kilometers north, from which the sous-préfet there could be helpful in pushing us further toward our goal of Fada. So off we went, again observing countless examples of the detritus of war as we threaded our way along the sandy track. It was our drivers' first extended stretch of sand driving, but they avoided getting stuck.

Bahaï, where we arrived in early afternoon, is a newly created sous-préfecture. It lies just north of the border with Biltine *departement*, into the Ennedi *departement*, of which our destination of Fada is the capital. The secretary-general (a new name for the deputy to the préfet) was there to solve some administrative problem and welcomed us. The locals were again ignorant of our visit, but not so surprised since my European Union colleague had passed through just a couple of weeks earlier. He and I are the travelers among N'Djamena's small diplomatic corps. We drank the obligatory *sucreries* and tea, and explained our need to get further toward Fada that day. It seemed that a truckload of soldiers was headed to the intermediate village of Kaoura, and we could follow. Upon our cajoling, one of them was held back to ride with us while the slower military pickup truck went on in advance. After the minimal period dictated by courtesy, we rose to follow with our guide.

Bahaï, like Tiné, was smack dab on the Sudanese border, so in leaving we headed pretty much due west, and eventually a little north. My new compass and Daryll's GPS told us that we were headed more or less in the direction of Fada, but little more. The track we followed didn't seem to correspond to the roads shown on the map I had—but no matter, we trusted our guide.

The country we headed through was rolling plains, marked by the thinnest sort of grass cover, akin to what I'd seen in the Kanem a year earlier. After a couple of hours with no distinguishing features, we began to see isolated buttes, and then stronger hill formations. Then we were into the real Ennedi, with its stark red-brown cliffs alternating with softer piles of boulders. We threaded miles and miles of alternating plains and upland plateaus encircled by the coppery tors. Finally, we entered yet another valley, with a cluster of white stucco buildings encircled by adobe huts. It was Kaoura.

It was only 5:00 p.m., but fairly clear to us all that we would have to stop here for the night. It seemed that only Chadian Arabic was spoken here, and Les entered into negotiation for a guide. When the confusion was clarified that we didn't mean to get to Fada yet that night, it seemed that someone could be found. A price of CFA 30,000 ($40, or a good month's salary) was agreed upon, with a 5:00 a.m. departure. We had instinctively headed for the complex of white stucco buildings, which turned out to be a school. Another group of travelers had staked out the yard amid the structures, but we were offered the interior of several empty classrooms. It seemed that there had never been any desks, and that the failure of a school lunch program had discouraged the rural population from sending their kids to school, so the rooms were essentially unused. A slogan drawn on the wall of the room I slept in said, "We welcome all who help to ensure that we are paid without delays." It recalled rumors I'd heard before leaving N'Djamena that rural government salaries hadn't been paid for two months. Our drivers joined the other travelers for evening prayers. Their fires burned low, and they chatted into the evening, some eventually throwing sleeping mats onto the sandy ground. A goat showed up led by a slightly disoriented (or high?) gendarme, and there was talk of butchering it for our dinner. Thank goodness, it didn't happen (a four- or five-hour procedure), and we ate again from what we'd brought with us. For me, it was canned stew heated on a camp stove, with only half spilled on the ground when the burner tipped over. And again we opened our cots and sleeping bags. That night the stars were, if anything, even more magnificent than the night before. We admired them before retiring, slept soundly, and were all up again in time to see the Southern Cross, Scorpio, and other morning constellations before the new day dawned.

Our guide, of course, didn't show up at 5:00 a.m. as promised. But we were, amazingly, all ready to go only a few minutes thereafter, and irritated that he hadn't showed. Les chatted with the other group of travelers who had passed the night in the yard, who related that the guide had let on he'd be here around 6:00 a.m. And a moment or two thereafter, he appeared with the chef de canton, i.e., village chief. But now there was an argument over price. Now the guide wanted CFA 50,000. Against Les's advice that we accept, I demurred. They stalked off, but when I saw them peek around the corner of the school building at us, I knew we had them. So CFA 30,000 it was, and by 6:30 a.m. we were off.

I haven't yet given you much of a sense of the Ennedi and its spectacular mountains. It bears a certain resemblance to the American southwest, if you don't push the analogy too far. The Ennedi isn't really true desert; rather, most of the lower country supports an ever so thin, fragile grass cover that at this time of year is dried to a pale yellow or yellow-green. Against this undulating foreground with the occasional, spindly dwarf tree, rise up the mountain cliffs. They are sometimes in buttes, sometimes on all sides of you. They are a stark red-brown. It seemed to me that they took two forms. First were the harsh, abrupt ones: all square, boxy substructures topped by stoutish round towers that looked like so many chimneys on a Tudor roof. The softer, older structures were in the same red-brown, but worn into rounder, softer forms by the winds of time—like the Guéra, but grander. I wondered why these two forms were so distinct, but everywhere in juxtaposition. Each formation was different, and many of them looked as if the highest lopsided stones might tumble hundreds of feet to the ground at any moment. Teeterstone, but sharply different from the Guéra.

In an odd sort of way, the contrasting types of hills might give you some insight into the two sharp aspects of the personality of our guide, Captain Guardi. He spoke little French, and Les and

Chaibo communicated with him largely in Chadian Arabic. He was, we learned, about thirty-six, my height more or less, and of the thin, sinewy build of northerners. His face looked younger, with its thin chin, high round cheekbones, and a delicate wispy mustache. He wore long beige trousers, a matching knee-length overshirt like a caftan, and a white turban that obscured all his head but the face. He reminded me of the pictures in nineteenth-century history books of the indigines of the Caucasus, or perhaps the warriors of the Khyber Pass. He began the trip with typical northern reserve, but warmed to us and was soon giving Chaibo hints on sand driving and eventually sharing tales of his past as we got into the territory of his youthful exploits during the Libyan war. He was, it seemed, still in the army, but sort of drifted in and out of duty, taking long periods of leave when personal business—his forty head of camels or his millet field—demanded.

Nearing Fada, we began to again encounter the detritus of war, this time of the 1987–1988 Libyan campaign. Guardi described a skirmish that took place here or there as we rolled along. At one point, we entered a high upland plateau surrounded by the stark red-brown cliffs on nearly every side. We came to a row of three burned-out tanks. Guardi pointed to the nearest, which we swerved to avoid: "That was my tank," he said, "and I was the only one to escape alive." It would seem that the delicate face, thin frame, and polite demeanor masked a character of steel and determination—at least where fighting Libyans was concerned. But Guardi had warmed to us, as I said. He asked if he could travel south with us the next day to Kalaite, below Fada and well along our way back to Abéché. We concurred, of course.

Perhaps this is the time to describe how Chaibo learned sand driving. Adoum, the driver of our second car, was supposedly the embassy's best sand driver, and he had worked in this region of the country years ago as well. But Chaibo had little experience with sand driving. He did well enough on the little stretches where the road had worn down but was ignorant of dunes. Guardi gave him one or two pointers before we hit the big time challenge—a huge dune, over which the road ascended 300 to 400 feet in elevation. The orange sand literally poured out of the red-brown rock formations. With no particular effort, Chaibo got half way up but then stalled.

Guardi coached him back down while we all alit and waited anxiously at the midway point. Daryll had found some spent shell casings from a firefight Guardi later described to us, and was in seventh heaven. Chaibo deflated the tires, locked the front wheels and shifted into four-wheel drive, got a running start, and gyrated the steering wheel in the best form as instructed. The car sailed up, up, up and over the ridge to beyond the danger point. Lesson learned. But I could tell that it was all a bit intimidating, for Chaibo kept in four-wheel drive the entire rest of the day, and kept gyrating the steering wheel even on the clear stretches of road. We would get stuck three or four more times in the next two days, but I never again worried that we wouldn't eventually get free and advance.

In the morning hours we also saw lots of gazelles, individuals, pairs, and one or two herds of thirty to forty individuals, grazing the upland plateaus. It was marvelous, confirming in my own mind the appropriateness of designating this as Chad's national animal. Seeing the animals in the wild always conveys to me a certain relaxation, a feeling that man's depredations notwithstanding, life is fundamental, the world turns.

I knew from contrasting our bearings with my map that we were not taking the main trail into Fada. Eventually Guardi confirmed that, indicating that the old road through the mountains was mined and impassable these last dozen years. We went way to the southwest, then turned north, and finally northeast into the town. We knew we were there when a huge Crusader castle loomed up from the sand—something right out of the French Foreign Legion, really and truly. It had a low battlemented outer wall, a higher inner curtain wall, and in the center a high tower from which the Chadian flag fluttered. We rolled past it and into Fada's main square, with the market on one end and the administrative buildings (i.e., the military camp) across from the castle. Driving into the yard of the sous-préfet's residence, we found the newly created préfet and local National Assembly deputy awaiting us. The préfet had arrived only three days ago, the Ennedi having just been elevated to a full *departement* as opposed to a sous-préfecture. But he inherited the old residence just the same. He welcomed us into his living room, barren but for one corner, which had a Western couch and a few matching armchairs. By this time, I felt totally comfortable in this milieu—hell with the French language and formalities. We took refreshment and the ebullient deputy began to plan our program for the time we had in Fada.

Yes, ebullient, for Deputy Bodoumi was outgoing and bubbly in a most unnorthern way. Fortyish, he seemed to get along well enough with the préfet who was older, self-confident, and a southerner. But his talkative manner and evident impatience to call the shots would have offended his northern peers if he hadn't instinctively reined in these tendencies a bit with the elders among them. But to us, of course, he was immediately sympathetic. Before we knew it, he had outlined a full program for the remainder of the day. We would tour the hospital, local (empty) grain warehouse, and an oasis garden on foot. We'd return to rest in the heat of the day, and in the late afternoon head out of town to see examples of the ancient rock paintings for which the Fada region is famous. The other famous site, Guelta Archei, would be left for morning on the way out of town. And this indeed became our program.

But more important, perhaps, is how we lived that day and night in Fada, for I felt that we really lived as our hosts did. It came as close as any experience I've had to living as the locals do. Our first event was a meeting with the local *sages*, elders and chefs de cantons. We knelt with them on carpets spread in the living room of the little house and heard them recite their plights. Their complaints weren't a whole lot different from what I'd heard elsewhere, perhaps a little refreshing in their lack of political correctness. The most senior spokesman began with the need for a senior mosque in Fada. There were other points about the lack of school meals and water—wells were a big priority. They mentioned the lack of rain to recharge the wadis and the approaching hunger. And two or three *sages* mentioned the need for poison to kill the wild animals that were menacing the regional herds, or, lacking poison, guns.

The préfet politely excused these notables and we went off for a walking tour of the hospital, grain storage depot, and an oasis garden. They differed little from what I've described in other locales, but I must allow that Fada had a nice, small-town urban feel to it, a charm unexpected in Chadian towns. After we'd walked to the hospital, etc., we lounged on the same carpets, now spread beneath a stand of palm trees before a little square reservoir of water in the public garden just north of the préfet's house—a tranquil moment made tantalizing by the aroma of the sweet blossoms of the palm trees. There were pillows as well, and of course tea and soft drinks. We lolled, awaiting the hour when we could move again—roughly 4:00 p.m. Then we were off for the rock paintings, driving by a fenced-off minefield en route. Our first stop was a small, deteriorating ruin that had been the first French colonial structure in the region somewhere around 1905 or 1910.

The first site of rock art was a high cliff a few hundred meters further to the west. We scrambled out and quickly reached a sharp rock face. The préfet and I, among others, paused as we reached the steep ascent. Not knowing that this first ascent was the most trying, we declined the climb. I silently cursed my security cocoon, which has deprived me of jogging and other exercise, and hence the agility that would have made me feel comfortable with the climb.

Les, upon return, pushed our guides to take us on, dusk notwithstanding, to a nearby second site. We rolled over the sand around to the northern side of the hill we'd just assailed. On the next ridge beyond was another site, this time at ground level. There were simple red stick drawings—archers, horsemen, spear carriers, and a few victim animals—in all, perhaps two dozen specimens on a ten-meter stretch of rock face. Even I took photos! Some fifty meters away was a low rock hut—a slab atop natural supporting walls, all naturally formed. We squeezed under on our backs, in turn, and saw more of the paintings on the low ceiling above us. Enormously impressive! I was sorry I couldn't spend several weeks here searching out all the drawings of the region.

Returning for dinner, the rugs were back inside, and we squatted on them and helped ourselves with our hands from the common dishes, consuming chicken, boule, and meat sauce, and a tiny bit of salad and one or two other vegetable dishes. The village women had brought in the meal, which was enough but certainly not sumptuous. After we'd eaten, visitors came through the dusk to call on the préfet and on ourselves—representatives of a women's co-op, local schoolmasters, etc. And Guardi showed up among several others who seemed to be half-supplicants, half-retainers of the préfet's. I was given the room that the deputy had been occupying—the only one with its own bathroom (no running water, of course, but a good, sit-down toilet). Later, I was brought a big bucket of cold water for "a shower." You can't imagine my joy—the first time in three days I'd been able to do a thorough wash, even if it was only a sort of sponge bath! I knelt trying to wash my hair in splashes from the bucket. I luxuriated!

Afterward, I strolled back out to the main room. About a dozen men were lounging about, a radio or two still blaring. It was apparent that these guys would spend the night in the big room. Daryll had claimed the couch at the far corner in preference to another night on a cot. I silently relished the ambassadorial perk of the privacy of the bath and bedroom, devoid as it was of furniture, save the cot and sleeping bag I'd brought along with me.

Breakfast the next morning reinforced my sense of partaking only of the local fare. First there was warm milk, sweetened. Then tea, sweetened a lot. And then bouille, a sort of watery porridge—milk and water, with some rice or millet cooked in it, sweetened not quite as much. NOT the breakfast for someone who dislikes sugar as much as I do, but it was authentic. I do understand the love of sugar here, for there is a dearth of nourishment and the flavor and quick energy of the sugar have value.

So we set off south, and what for me became the most frustrating part of our trip began. I had anticipated a quick drive back to Abéché, and subsequently, a quick drive back to N'Djamena. Not to be.

On the outskirts of Fada we paused to say farewell to the mayor. We then drove on for an hour and a half to Guelta Archei, where we reveled in the natural beauty for a good forty-five minutes. It is a gorge beneath 200-foot cliffs, with a spring-fed, year-round freshwater lake that harbors its own species of crocodiles. There was a huge, high cave that we explored to its 200-meter depth; insects had coated the ceiling with their nests, and their trails were etched on the hardened sand beneath our feet. We saw the little pond amid the cliffs—never mind that the sand was paved with the dung of goats, camels, and who knows what else. We couldn't get to the crocodiles—it would have required rock-climbing gymnastics or an hour-long hike around the cliffs, neither of which we could manage in our limited time. We drove back out of the narrow valley, bid adieu to the préfet and deputy, and, with the deputy's driver as guide, headed out overland toward the main north-south road and eventually Kalaite to the south. Guardi was along as well.

As we continued southward, my frustrations increased. We needed to stop first in Kalaite, and, since we were discharging passengers there, we had to call on the local sous-préfet. He spoke no French, but delayed us with drinks. Next we drove into town to deposit Guardi at the compound of some friend or relative. And then, a little outside of town, we needed a rest stop, the first of the day. Moving on, we headed for Aréda, but got stuck in the sand a few miles short. Finally in Aréda, we paused to turn over surplus Department of Defense camping gear to the local representative of the park service. Twilight fell as we sat on the sous-préfet's terrace, with its striking view out over the low mud-brick town. And then, an hour later, we stopped in Biltine to leave word for the préfet (who was out) that we were passing back through his city on our way back south to Abéché. To the annoyance of ever-dutiful Les, I complained that you couldn't go fifty miles in this country without stopping to pay a courtesy call on someone.

That evening back in Abéché, arriving around 8:30 p.m., we wondered if a dinner invitation from the resident American couple, the Suttons, would hold. They would, of course, still be delighted to see us, lateness notwithstanding. So we had a nice American meal—a Texmex casserole, green beans, salad, and a couple of other vegetables. After three days in the north, great!

Our final morning on the road dawned more leisurely. We'd lodged again chez Africare. I'd told the drivers to sleep in a little, that we wouldn't leave before 7:00 a.m. I knew they'd been up late the night before working on tire repairs. It was nearly 8:00 a.m. by the time we'd said our goodbyes and packed up. We still needed gas, and filling up Chadian fashion took forty-five minutes for the two vehicles. I watched a disfigured leper woman begging as we waited. And then off we went.

If the previous day's stops en route had been frustrating for me, today's were the pits. We headed out by around 8:30 a.m., and made good time to Oum Hadjer some 150 kilometers west of Abéché. There the drivers wanted to stop and buy straw mats to take home, which I of course agreed to. And then we drove on two hours more, stopping midway to Mongo for bush visits and a bite of lunch. In Mongo, of course, we had to look up the préfet, who was expecting us and gave us a heavier lunch. Then we were off, just short of 4:00 p.m. now, wondering if we should stop for the night in neighboring Bitkine or push on to N'Djamena. To my question, no one objected to pushing on. Alas, short of Bitkine we had a flat—perhaps the fifth of the entire trip. We changed it and Chaibo insisted on replacing the inner tube of the flat tire. We'd need to stop yet again to inflate it. After one false start with a roadside truck, Chaibo stopped in Bitkine, finding a huge, flatbed road-maintenance truck that would help us. (Big trucks here always carry air pumps.) This huge truck ported a Caterpillar grader on its trailer. Up front of the Cat earth-mover on the truck's trailer, a little camp of family members had settled. One woman seemed to be nursing a babe.

Alas, it was only another hundred kilometers through the deepening gloom before Les indicated that we needed to stop again—to inform the préfet in Bokoro that we were passing through his district doing night driving. Reluctantly, I acquiesced, but was pleased when we found the préfet away from his house. We drove on. It seemed to take twice as long as before to get from Bokoro to Ngora, and then on to Massaguet, where the paved road started.

Coming at last to the paved road at around 11:00 p.m., I thought we would be home free, able to zip right into N'Djamena. But then we lost the second car in our rearview mirror. Returning, we found that its spare tire had broken its traces and blown off the roof; I instructed that we abandon it and continue. Then, barely five minutes later, we again lost our following car. This time its engine had simply died. After massaging its fuel pump (bad gas), we got it started, but its headlights wouldn't light up. So we limped along the last 100 klicks at sixty kilometers per hour. The second car followed us closely, seeing what it could of the earth around us through our headlights. And so it was that at just past midnight on Friday evening, after exactly a week on the road, that we regained N'Djamena. All this, and no harm done.

In a week we'd covered 3,200 kilometers on Chad's primitive roads, and at least a century in lifestyle. We'd shown the flag in remote regions, learned a great deal about the need for demining and drought relief. And we'd seen the successful results of numerous of our developmental assistance efforts. All in all, it was a great week.

Perhaps our desire to push all the way through to N'Djamena reflected a degree of overload after this incredible, week-long trek. How then to sum it up? Certainly, as I said at the outset, the process was to some degree the message. Our mere presence, i.e., showing the flag, had an enormous impact on the people we met—they so appreciated that we'd come. And the ruggedness of the travel brought home to us the remoteness of the outlying parts of the country.

But we learned much more. We learned, for example, how administrators cope not merely at the end of a very long supply pipeline, but beyond where it ends—the case in all the hospitals we visited north of Abéché. We learned of the primitive simplicity of life, even for the seniormost people, in Fada. Eating plain fare with them on the floor, providing our own bedrolls afterward, while the locals sprawled out with only a carpet to soften the hard floor. And along the way we'd seen three of Chad's leading tourist sites: Abtouyour, Ouara, and Guelta Archei.

But perhaps the most enduring memory is indeed one of process—the seemingly endless driving, mind-numbing bouncing, really, over 3,200 kilometers of road, only 200 of which were paved. And the great north itself? Its mystery was both diffused and intensified. Diffused because, with our step-by-step, guided approach we'd been able to penetrate it, see it, and live for a day or two as do its people. We realized that we could, if we had to, adapt and live as they do. It gives you a sort of confidence in ultimate human adaptability—intensified, however, because you realize that you have only skimmed the surface of the lifestyle, culture, and the beauty and grandeur of the environment: It seems almost tragic to acknowledge that you may never again have an opportunity to come back.

And that's the north of Chad, such as we may taste it!

Best regards,

Ambassador Chris

Old Haunts and New Territory

January 27, 2002

Dear Friends,

Can you feel true nostalgia coming back to a place you've seen only once, and then briefly? Perhaps, if it is beautiful. Perhaps, if you may never see it again. And perhaps, if to you it means something bigger than itself.

This past week was another travel marathon for me. On Wednesday, I joined a government–UNDP (United Nations Development Programme)-sponsored day trip, by air, to Fada and Faya, to review the demining program's progress. On Friday, I set off on a three-day land trip to Mao and Moussoro, returning only this afternoon. Two thousand klicks by air, nearly 700 by car. This was mostly a reprise of earlier travels: Only Moussoro and a brief stop at Mechimere en route were new; Faya, I've been to several times.

As many do, the invitation for the Fada and Faya trip came suddenly. It would be a single day, by air, for field demonstrations of the demining program, the complement to a half-day seminar for donors in N'Djamena. There were countless professional reasons to go—we are the largest bilateral donor to the demining effort, to show US interest in the north when Libya is meddling up there, etc. But I'll confess—I really went because I didn't want to leave Chad without seeing Fada and the Ennedi again!

We were to leave last Wednesday at 7:00 a.m. It was a complex arrangement. Most of the large delegation would leave even earlier, at 4:00 a.m., in a C-130, land at Kalaite, (a three-hour drive from Fada), and rendezvous with us VIPs who traveled in two small planes directly to the softer landing strip there. And in true Chadian fashion, the rendezvous worked perfectly because both parties ran into difficulties: the big group ran late because their drive was really four hours, and the VIPs left an hour late because a harmattan was blowing over N'Djamena and we had to wait on daylight and radio communication to confirm that visibility would allow the small planes to land in Fada.

I'll deal only briefly with the demining program. After refreshments at the préfet's house in Fada, we drove to two sites. At the first, we were shown a collection of unexploded ordinance and the demining contingent that had gathered it. We were whisked away to a safe vantage from which we watched as it was detonated. The second site was more interesting, a narrow defile through which the main north-south road (which my party had avoided a year earlier) passed. The mines had been cleared some years ago to a nine-meter width; the project now was to widen the route to a safer twenty meters. The commander of the (US-trained) demining detachment explained the whole operation from six to eight flip charts in crisp, Western military style. He walked us 500 yards down the road, pointing out where four mines—not yet blown—had been found. For effect, a deminer to our side was sweeping a metal detector over an uncleared area with typical slow, rhythmic motions. Hours later in Faya we got an office presentation only. Operations in Faya had concluded months before, so what we heard was a report on what had been accomplished, as well as the status of work at Ounianga Kébir, the little salt lake district 150 miles northeast of Faya. I'd say, all in all, that the progress was satisfactory, if not stunning.

What was stunning was the expansive beauty of the Ennedi! From the air or the road or the hill from which we saw the detonation, the rugged rocks and cliffs stretched to the end of our sight. Rank after rank showed forth, retreating to the horizon. The nearest were a dark red-brown shadowing the sand; this faded to a warm rose in the distance. Here the formation was a huge field of Tudor chimneys, there an enormous butte with a 1,000-foot cliff rising straight up from the orange Saharan sand. All these tall, harsh features were confined only by the endless light blue sky. The sense of peace and nature's majesty was overwhelming, strong enough not to be broken by the French and Arabic chatter of my companions in the Toyota 4x4, or the rough bounces as we lurched along.

The impression was of a vast wilderness, forbidding but enticing and comforting. Yet it was wilderness no more, for here surely man's hand has touched. If you lowered your eyes from gazing at the cliff tops to the sand and desert brush at hand, you saw it: parts of burned-out vehicles, metal refuse, and shell casings. This remote stillness had been a war zone twenty years ago, and that's why we do demining here. Nature's sublimity and man's sordidness in one landscape!

***

For the Chadians with us, memories of those glorious battles near here, where they had bested the mighty Libyans, might have set hearts and minds off in a dolorous direction, especially considering that sacrifice back then brought the country no permanent peace. But for us expats, the Italian honorary consul said it best: "I can't help but think of the journey we made up here with Amine Ali," she said, recalling the horrible loss of Chadian statesmanship in the crash of that little plane over in Koussérie. For me, another wave hit as soon as I entered the préfet's house in Fada, for here a year ago my little party had overnighted in such good spirits brought on equally by the paucity of comforts and the warmth of our hosts. I glanced across the living room where twenty had slept that night to the door to the préfet's unfurnished bedroom, which he'd ceded to me, and thought of my cot and sleeping bag and the little bathroom where a large bucket of cold water to bathe in had brought such relief after three days of sweaty driving. And later in Faya, I sat for the fourth or fifth time in the préfet's reception room and recognized the cook who brought on the méchoui and busied himself with our comfort. The Italian woman knew him too from her three- to four-year residence in the north, and we each greeted him in turn. There was little dust that day and the air was marvelous, and it wouldn't have been sad at all but for the thought that I might never get back here again.

Then came the adventure of the C-130 flight. I already knew that our two light aircraft would rest in Faya that night, and that the big plane, Chad's only C-130 transport, would come to Faya as soon as its earlier occupants had made their way back to it from Fada by road. Then all of us would fly back to N'Djamena. Just as I was becoming a little irritated at the inevitable delays, word came that the plane was airborne from Kalaite, and we could make our way leisurely to the airport.

We boarded, and it was immediately clear that this was the airplane equivalent of those huge trucks that thread Chad's roads, with dozens of people atop loads that are themselves already twice the stated capacity of the trucks and trailers. If I had any small disgruntlement at the delays left, any residual doubt whether the day had been worthwhile, it vanished immediately upon stepping aboard, for here was glorious chaos! A natural circus so dynamic as to restore the faith of any doubter in the irrepressible human spirit! The engines revved as we strode in. Everywhere were piles of baggage and men milling about—many more than there were seats. Some settled on sacks in the open space before me. I grabbed one of the sling seats near the door as it closed—only to reopen three or four times more to admit yet more passengers. The vehicles that had been transported for the drive from Kalaite to Fada were aboard, secured to the floor of the plane. As the engines whirred ever more shrilly, the crowd dispersed, seeking seats. Men scrambled into the two cars, taking every seat within. Before me, two men, an expat and a Chadian, sat back to back on an ice chest; as the taxiing began, they rose long enough to each hoist a soft drink from the chest, and then settled down on it, splaying their legs out to brace themselves as they leaned against each other for the takeoff. The plane roared ever faster down the runway, the two cars rocked against their lashes, and I wondered if they'd hold. They did, thank God, and then we were airborne.

This constituted my first real experience with Chadian military operations, and the review is mixed. The demining folks had told me that the Chadians had wanted to organize the whole operation themselves, with no French help (well, not quite: One of the two small planes was that of the French Cooperation Service). But otherwise, it was a Chadian operation of moderate complexity, and it all worked out with perhaps an hour and a half of delay. Not bad. But the chaos aboard the C-130 was another world entirely. It was rollicking fun, but dangerous. It amply displayed Chad's poor military discipline and the army's tribal nature, as we saw who did or didn't get to hitch a ride from Faya down to the capital.

Only two days later, on Friday, January 25, I headed out on another nostalgia trip. This one was to Mao, one of the first places I'd visited overland back in December 1999. This time I would also go to Moussoro, to see the military training facilities there.

We pulled into Mao around 5:00 p.m. on Friday afternoon, having left N'Djamena around 9:00 a.m. in the morning. We had stopped in Massaguet and Massakoury to look at self-help projects—a peanut-crushing oil press and a reforestation plot, respectively. It was my third visit to Massakoury, and it was the people there who gave me Moussa, the gazelle. I consider them almost friends by now. So it should surprise no one that they had lunch waiting. From there, we launched out over the sandy track that in four hours brought us to Mao.

In Mao we were welcomed at the edge of the town and taken to the World Food Program compound, where we would overnight. There the sultan waited to greet us. After a half-hour of Cokes and greetings, our hosts withdrew, the acting préfet indicating that he'd return with dinner around 7:00 p.m. He did, and we ate together, and he withdrew. A little later we made an early evening of it, everyone turning in before 10:00 p.m., when the generator would go off, depriving us of light.

Our main focus in Mao was the reinauguration of the local high school (*lycée*), which we'd paid to refurbish. For $16,000, we'd constructed a new building with two classrooms, built a wall around the entire complex of two–three acres, paid to reroof and replaster several older buildings, and constructed three latrines for boys, girls, and teachers, respectively (there'd been none before). Money, you can see, goes a long way here. It was the US Department of Defense's Humanitarian Aid Program that footed the bill. The *proviseur* [headmaster] took us on a brief walking tour of the facility. The sultan, for whom the school is named, was waiting when we wound up, and we held our brief inaugural ceremony. Comments by local officials and me, with a "cocktail" soft drink at the end, ran barely half an hour. After warm adieus, we were free to be on the road again.

Always there is tension between moving right along and stopping where duty suggests. My instinct is to travel, but that often isn't politic. Before leaving Mao, the acting préfet whispered to me that he'd informed the officials in Mechimere that we'd be passing through. That meant that we'd have to stop there and pay our respects. Mechimere is a sous-préfecture, the only sizable town (a cattle center of perhaps 5,000 souls) between Mao and Moussoro.

And it's a good thing we did stop, however reluctantly, because the local chef de canton is important. One younger brother was the longest-serving Chadian ambassador in Washington, and is now employed by the World Bank. Another younger brother is the new minister of livestock, whom I'd just met on the trip up to Fada and Faya. Mechimere is a prominent town, considering its size, remote location, and the inability of its notables to use French (Les spoke with them in Chadian Arabic). We spiked their idea for an afternoon feast, Les explaining our tight timing. A snack was substituted, and in our quick departure I was gifted with a rug in lieu of the fuller meal.

We made good time the rest of the way. Leaving Mechimere, we loped over sandy hills with a scattering of wispy shrubs. These alternated with greener wadi bottoms with more verdure including acacia, date palm, and the occasional stubble of a millet patch. Here the road was packed hardpan and we could edge up to eighty kilometers per hour. The wadis gradually predominated, and the last hour of our drive was across the flat Bahr el Ghazal, with its traces of wet-season moisture.

We pulled into Moussoro around 3:30 p.m. and went to the préfet's house, where his deputy was expecting us. Over the inevitable soft drinks, we chatted and indicated our programmatic desires—to see the training camp of the Garde Nationale et Nomade du Tchad (GNNT), as well as to meet with a civic group that we knew had been confronting the serious problem here of violence in the schools. Our hosts told us that, like Mao, Moussoro was cut and threatened by erosion ravines. They wanted to show us, and we said we'd welcome a spin around the town before sunset. They also told us that we'd be lodged on the base, and we should go there first to drop off our bags.

At the base we came to an abrupt halt before the gate. We would enter on foot through a defile of sentries and review an honor guard just inside. The commander, a colonel who couldn't have been very far into his thirties, met us and led the way. I knew immediately he was a Bidyate (i.e. of the President's tribe). He seemed a little unsure of how to approach me, and took refuge in orienting the review of the guard towards my Defense Attaché, his fellow soldier. Fine by me; I paced the rank quietly with them.

We then moved on to the guest house. It was a spacious facility just like a suburban American three bedroom house. It was well appointed, including a 12′x24′ Chinese carpet in the living room, the finest rug I've seen in Chad, saving the antique Turkmen I brought back from Turkey. The house could only have been constructed for some Presidential visit in the past two or three years.

The colonel then seated us in the commodious living room and we were brought more soft drinks, peanuts and dates, succeeded by sweet tea. After we had sat a while, civilian and military authority made eye contact, arose and departed the scene. I knew our plans for the afternoon were changing. Military authority, of course prevailed. Our hosts returned and we sat a little longer. The colonel then invited me to follow him. He led us to a small dining room and we sat. More soft drinks, nuts, dates, tea. When we didn't rise immediately I knew a meal would follow. And indeed, punctuated by the brief ride into town and a meeting with local PVOs, the rest of the evening was an exercise in enduring the colonel's sincere but almost stifling hospitality, with its surfeit of sweet drinks. The meal was familiar: tasty roast chicken, a stew of mutton or goat, rice, a vegetable dish or two. More tea.

Then, at last, our foray into the little city of 17,000 souls. First we stopped in front of the locked-up-tight city hall; there the mayor presented me with a gazelle. I made excuses and declined the creature; he would be "kept for me" so that I might pick him up on some future visit. We moved on to a ravine—a steep city street that channeled the infrequent rain so as to become an arroyo, the erosion undermining the foundations of the houses on either side. Then we stopped to see the butcher's wagon, a large, horse-drawn flatbed trailer, which carried meat from the town's abattoir to the main market. The need was to enclose it to ensure sanitation and deflect the sun, thus protecting against spoilage. Then more ravines. We saw where a Swiss aid project was attempting to terrace the streets, adding steps and thereby turning them into pedestrian passages. The Swiss were tackling fourteen of the twenty-six stricken roads, leaving a dozen that the mayor hoped we might take on. And by then it was past 5:00 p.m., the hour that had been fixed for seeing the PVOs.

Back to the fort and the guesthouse. The PVO meeting was now to be a group session with about eight organizations, and we could hear them gathering outside. But they could wait—first we needed to be offered another round of Cokes and sweet tea. When we got under way with the PVOs, it was a good session and went until nearly 7:00 p.m. It was impressive but typical for Chad that, here in this remote town, there were so many civic groups, each trying to address some social or economic need—AIDS, women's jobs, the school violence issue, etc. We heard from each group in turn and explained how to apply for our Ambassador's Special Self-Help Program's support.

After wrapping up, it seemed that at last we'd have a moment to relax. The houseboy pointed to the dining room, noting that there was a terrace outside. One by one, as we finished a minimal unpacking, we drifted out, and what we saw was both spectacular and serene. The house was set with a westward view from the hill on which the fort sat, looking across the town toward the Bahr. It was past sunset now, but a pinkish band lingered on the horizon, darkening gradually into first a medium and then a cobalt blue. Not more than half-a-dozen lights broke the darkness beyond the fort's wall, some 300 feet below us. Stars came out, Orion and Cetus. We sat transfixed in the absolute silence, broken only by our occasional mutterings, for nearly two hours. The colonel joined us intermittently, and of course there were rounds of soft drinks and tea. We'd been out only briefly before a snack arrived—it looked like a nice macaroni and cheese, and I dug in—only to recoil as it turned out to be macaroni in a sugar sauce! Reluctantly, around 9:00 p.m., I realized that the only way to arrest the continued bouts of Cokes and tea would be to go in. The colonel demurred, indicating that a *casse-croute* [snack] was en route. It was bouille, a brothy milk porridge, not quite so sweet, so I drank a cup. It had become chilly, and I was glad to go in to read for a few minutes and turn in at the early bedtime hour of rural Chad.

The next morning, Sunday, had been fixed for our tour of the camp. We were told it would start at 8:30 a.m. and end promptly at 10:00 a.m. I told myself 11:00 a.m. The program began only a few minutes late with a demonstration by a troop of the Nomadic Guard marching in formation. They marched in, presented arms, ran in place, presented arms again, went through two or three maneuvers, and at last burst into a vibrant, swinging sort of African dance, accompanied by whoops and yodels. This was the dance of joy when the unit returned to camp from weeks in the desert. Next came a five-man detachment atop camels, the beast of choice for the GNNT. The animals carried huge saddlebags with their riders, and a hill of carpets as well—all a nomad would need for two weeks in the field. They galloped in, formed up, galloped again, and turned back to us. Now it was our turn—the highlight of the day! We mounted the camels and were led out and around the entire perimeter of the fort. It must have been a mile or more, during which the poor condition of the perimeter wall was pointed out, along with another ravine.

Returning, it was felt that the brief trial by saddle warranted a round of soft drinks and tea. A second breakfast followed, then our discussion of the camp's activities, centered mainly on the needs for equipment and funding, etc. Then gifts: First, one of the carpets from the camel I'd ridden; and then, alas, another gazelle, and one for the defense attaché as well. Mine was so tiny that I wondered if it would live without nursing. I was tempted out of mercy to take it, however much I hate to encourage the practice of hunting down these babies for gifts. But the problem resolved itself—the mayor had explained somewhere along the line our rationale for refusing his gazelle the day before, and all the animals stayed in Moussoro.

The last event, time now beginning to press, was a walking tour of the base. And tour we did, every nook and cranny. The dusty storage rooms for the camels' saddles and gear; the officers' billets; the doorless and barren, sand-floored rooms for the trainees; the meager clinic; the generator. Lots of contrast with the tidy guesthouse, where the shower even had hot water (a first for me outside of N'Djamena or Kome). Finally, hurrying along now, we were given certificates and insignia to commemorate our camel-riding skills—usually reserved for nomadic guards who completed 600 kilometers, but ours had evidently been a very successful crash course. A group picture. And then we exited on foot past the honor guard to our cars that awaited without.

We were in the cars right at 11:00 a.m., as I'd predicted. And on our way? Well, no, not quite. We needed to stop and see the dilapidated school for the children of the troopers. And, interservice rivalries being as strong here as at home, we had to stop and pay a courtesy call at the army base in town as well. But we made good time once on the road. I noted that between Massakoury and Massaguet, considerable road grading had been done just since we'd passed on Friday heading north.

I said that these two brief trips gave me my best look to date at the Chadian military. Can I draw any conclusions from so brief an exposure? Perhaps just the overwhelming sense of contrast. The demining trip was an ambitious expedition of a certain complexity that more or less succeeded, with small delays. But compare this with the very unmilitary chaos of the C-130. Moussoro was similar. Some of the base structures (not just the guesthouse) were smart and well maintained. The colonel and his deputy, who was in charge of camel-riding training, seemed to know what they were about and to have an intimate knowledge of their operation. But the recruits themselves were expected to throw their bedrolls on the sandy earth and rely on minimal latrines, showers, and medical services. Those deep dichotomies are, as by now you know, so characteristic of so much of Chad.

This letter is an interjection amid my wrap-up letters. But in reviewing it, I see that these pages serve as well as the others in summarizing my experiences here, and that is where the nostalgia comes in. These trips north remind me of what I have loved best about Chad: the spectacular scenery and expansive sense of nature; and the primitive and difficult conditions of travel here, which contrast so much with life at home and Western travel. Even so, I move, protectively encapsulated in my 4x4, centuries—nay, millennia—back to the level of human existence I see outside the vehicle in the mud-brick towns like Mechimere. These trips illustrate clearly how much of Chad's charm is due to what isn't here: it is the absence of lights in Moussoro that permit the serenity of watching sunset from the bluff of the military camp. But I come back always to the human element and its contrasts: the lavish hospitality from limited means, the difference between my comfortable guesthouse bed and the mat on the dirt floor for the GNNT trainee. It is mostly this rawness, the way these contrasts give me a feeling of being closer to the essence of life that I will take away. It is these things that will be hard for me to ever touch again—unless I become a backpacker tourist in my old age.

Best regards,

Ambassador Chris

P.S.
February 10, 2002

In yet another throe of nostalgia, only a week after the trip to Mao, my travels took me to a conference in West Africa, my first return to haunts of my Lagos years. I visited both Douala and Cotonou.

In Douala, I remembered immediately the airport; its long, elevated fingers hit me with the same familiarity they had last July. Driving into town, however, I recognized little. The overall impression was of a metropolis merely shabbier than before, starting with the dismal brown grass in front of the terminal as I sped away in an embassy car to the center. What surprised me most, perhaps, was how little I recalled or recognized.

The layout of the town had been refreshed for me by a map, and after pondering some minutes, it fell into place as we drove: the bluff with the administrative quarter on one side of a deep gully, formed by a tributary of the Wouri, that separated the rough port and hectic business quarter.

But visually I remembered little. The carnality of West Africa was there: the fleshier, more rounded people; the crazy woman lying stark naked on a street corner right downtown; the men urinating anywhere for all to see. But mostly I saw piles of trash, which I hadn't noticed fifteen years ago, and dirty storefronts so layered in grime that the facades beneath must have been there when I'd passed this way before. Weren't they cleaner, brighter back then?

The next morning, the only American officer in the embassy branch office in Douala took me out on a brief driving tour. We spent lots of time looking at the port where all the official cargo for N'Djamena comes in, and where I saw pipes for the oil project stacked up. Here, more was familiar: I remembered the thin office tower that held the cocoa and coffee parastatals, where I'd always called during my visits. I saw the flour mill and the container port, the latter much larger now. But the old consulate building rang no bell, even though the region of the Sawa and Meridien hotels, where I'd always lodged, felt familiar. But mostly everything just felt shabbier and more crowded. It made me envy Chad just a little, where we think things may be on an upswing. For here, beyond any shadow of deception from the distance of fifteen years, I was looking at a city that had declined and decayed.

The Journey to the East

March 24, 2002

Les sprang it on me one day in a staff meeting. He was planning a trip to eastern Chad with our political/economic officer and a member of the defense attaché's office to look at development projects. Where exactly? Les indicated a region east of where I'd been before, and where I wanted to go again before leaving Chad. My appetite whetted, I committed almost on the spot, eschewing my usual day or two of hesitation and checking potential conflicts.

It was also true that I looked forward as well to traveling with the company that would make this trip. Beyond the old master Les, Catherine (the political/economic officer) and George (the defense attaché's rep) were among our younger, newer staff, and they were joined by Robert, one of our information systems specialists. These were twenty- or thirty-somethings, and Catherine and Robert are in their first overseas tours. I welcomed the chance to spend time with young people and get to know these colleagues better.

Before departure, Les outlined for me the itinerary, and after the first two days it was tough indeed. Leaving on a Saturday morning, we'd overnight in Mongo, where the préfet is a good friend, and where we have self-help activities. We'd continue on Sunday to Abéché, where we wanted to see local officials, Africare's operations, meet the Islamic leadership, and visit the branch of the university to which we'd just donated some DOD surplus furniture and equipment. The next day we'd go out to Adré on the Sudanese border and back, taking in a side trip to a school that DOD had constructed in a remote village. The following day looked especial-ly grueling: from Abéché to Am Dam, where we had a project, on through Goz Beïda and Am Timan to arrive at the Zakouma Game Park encampment—almost 600 kilometers on dirt roads. We'd then spend a full day at Zakouma reviewing our assistance projects and sneaking in a couple of game runs. Thursday would be another long driving day, bringing us 800 kilometers back to N'Djamena, though over better road. When Les hemmed and hawed about whether the trip might spill over to a seventh day, I knew right where it would happen: on the long, rough route from Abéché to Zakouma.

To deal with the worst first, this trip was a hardship in every pos-sible way. Most fundamentally, there were the roads, if you can call them that. The stretches from N'Djamena to Abéché and Zakouma to N'Djamena were relatively good by Chadian standards—aside from one rough stretch of 150 kilometers, they were in reason-able repair, with the occasional gully or pothole. We could bounce harshly along, averaging seventy to eighty kilometers per hour, sometimes a little more. But Abéché to Adré was just a rough track over rocky ground. Abéché to Am Timan was a little better only because in a few spots the stone was interrupted by sand. Of the 2,600-plus kilometers we covered, only 160 kilometers, 80 kilome-ters coming and going right outside N'Djamena, was paved.

In retrospect I am amazed that our vehicles, rugged Toyota 4x4s, held up so well. But they too had problems. George's car took on some bad gas in Mongo, or had a bad filter on the reserve tank, and started conking out the second day. And surprise, surprise, it developed problems with a shock absorber as well. My car lost its headlights just as we were starting from Adré back to Abéché at dusk. George had a cigarette lighter–powered super flashlight that he held outside the vehicle, allowing Chaibo to creep the last 150 kilometers back at about 30 kilometers per hour. Only twice did the vehicle come close to toppling over into the gully alongside. The Africare folks have a good garage in Abéché, which fixed all the problems. The most persistent vehicular problem, however, wasn't mechanical: My car was fitted only with bench seats in the rear, and with baggage bouncing all over with each bump, it was nearly impossible for anyone to sit there. Les began the trip in my car, but quickly abandoned me. Had Robert not devised a way to make a tolerable nest from the sleeping bags, I'd have ridden alone the whole way and been a very unhappy camper. Chaibo was there, of course, but I didn't dare distract him with conversation from his focus on the road.

Our accommodation confirmed the wisdom of always traveling with your own cot and sleeping bag in Chad. Most nights we had rooms of some sort, but it is the hot season and they were stifling. Les and Robert preferred to put their cots up outdoors in Mongo and Abéché. In Goz Beïda—where yes, as I'd predicted we broke the long route and overnighted—we were guests of the local sultan. He took us to a guesthouse on the grounds of the Taiwan-built water tower. It was unfurnished and unventilated, and he advised us to sleep outside. Mats were spread and we slept, all five of us, in a little row on our cots, Chaibo and the other driver on theirs just a few meters away. With donkeys braying, bats squeaking, one companion snoring loudly, and two planes passing overhead (from where?), I slept little, but I've learned to relax and rest even if I can't fall asleep—a useful skill here!

And never in my trips around Chad have I been less fed. The préfet in Mongo and Africare folks did well by us, but most days we were offered only lunch, which our road-cautious stomachs sampled lightly, and otherwise depended on what we'd brought. George was well supplied with MREs (meals ready to eat), at 3,000 calories a pop! I had my granola bars, which I shared with the drivers, and Robert had brought the more contemporary equivalent, power bars. I'm not sure what Les and Catherine lived on, although I bought bread enough for everyone when I could along the road. When we reached Zakouma, we were overjoyed with the meals at the restaurant we'd paid to refurbish, although on our last day—the long trek back to N'Djamena—we again subsisted on bread and granola bars. And water! I drank an entire 1.5 liter bottle every single day, plus all the tea and soft drinks we were given.

I'll spare you a blow-by-blow travelogue this time and focus only on the highlights and on what was new and different, like my meeting in Abéché with the local Islamic Council. This was Catherine's idea, and it turned out to be our most useful business event of the trip. We didn't talk weighty affairs, but they were complimented that we wanted to see them—even the sultan of Ouaddai, titular head of the council, came to the préfet's for the meeting. We learned that Abéché is the center and font of Islam in Chad. We heard that Islam is a religion of peace, and the events of 9/11 were inexcusable. They asked that we keep in touch with meetings like this every six months or so. The préfet concluded the session with a neat statement about the equality of religion as enshrined in the Chadian Constitution, and the need for harmony and communication between faiths.

The same day we drove first to Adré, and then over a rough country track thirty-four kilometers more to reach the DOD-funded school, threading our way through a pass in a high bank of cliffs reminiscent of the Ennedi. As we neared the school, I spied a couple of horsemen who came up on either side, riding hard to match the pace of our vehicles. In the distance we finally saw the little two-room building, with a dark mass enveloping it. As we approached, we were suddenly surrounded by dozens more riders, some in battle dress, some with fancy harnesses, and one with his horse in chain mail! Nearly all had swords. Then we could drive no closer and had to alight amid the throng. The hundreds of women were dressed in their finery and danced, shouted, and throat yodeled. Some had percussion instruments, some empty calabash bowls (whose purpose I learned only later). The crowd parted instinctively before us, revealing a circle of half a dozen men doing a battle dance. They squatted and jumped, heaving their swords and spears menacingly at each other. The préfet from Adré introduced us to the village elders who approached, and we were escorted to shady seats beneath a *hanger* adjacent to the little school. The women shouted and danced, the horsemen paraded before us presenting arms or saluting in an odd sort of way, the battle dancers feigned their combat anew. Finally, a bewildered-looking man pushed a wheelbarrow heavy with bricks across the open space before us. Looking awkwardly out of place, this was meant to symbolize the school construction. Then we were escorted into one of the schoolrooms and served a tasty meal of roast chicken, goat shank, and a couple of vegetable dishes. The crowd outside continued its celebration—the people had waited for us since midmorning and had a lot of pent-up energy to release. After tea, we indicated our need to get back on the road to Abéché, where that préfet expected us for dinner (both he and we failed to show, as it turned out). As we exited the school, I saw that horse races had broken out, and fast they were! I made it to my car along with Robert, but it was mobbed by the women. I rolled down my window to wave—they grabbed my hand and some reached in, placing their calabash bowls over my head (I hope someone got a photo)—a gesture of capture, denying my intent to depart. Chaibo couldn't move forward now without running over several of the ladies. At last a local official cleared a path and we drove off.

A day later in Am Dam, our welcome was equally warm, if less spectacular. Here we had financed a grain storage facility for a women's co-op. The members were all decked out in Sunday best with a banner to welcome us and a little display of sheaves of sorghum and millet to indicate what they stored in the warehouse. Again we had a tasty meal, lavish by local standards, confirming once more my hypothesis that the humbler the host in Chad, the grander the meal. After eating we went to see the building itself—a sound structure filled with sacks of grain and peanuts. The women gave us their *doléances*, wishes—in this case, a vehicle to use in marketing their produce around the region. Everyone here keeps asking for vehicles, and fearing diversion for personal use, the donors hate it. But given the isolation and difficulty of travel, I can understand these requests. And Am Dam itself deserves a word. Nowhere in Chad, not even in old Sarh, have I seen such a rundown, gutted-out collection of colonial ruins as here. It is as if the colonial past with its facade of stucco is fading and the real Africa reasserting itself, in its traditional guise of mud brick and thatch.

The same evening, an hour after sundown, brought us to Goz Beïda, seat of the sultan of Dar Sila, who, in the local préfet's absence, welcomed us. After trying two or three compounds, we found his. First there was a bear hug for Les—the sultan, like so many Chadian leaders, had been in school in Abéché when Les taught there as a Peace Corps volunteer. The sultan escorted us into his compound. He had a generator as well as a satellite dish, and there, in his courtyard, was a large TV receiving a French program. What a non sequitur, here in the back of beyond! The sultan was warm and voluble, and we had a good chat typical of what I'd exchanged with other senior officials en route. What of the upcoming legislative elections? Yes, people were mobilizing for them, but only a few districts were contested, the ruling MPS [Mouvement Patriotique du Salut] party having no competition in the others. What about rumors of banditry and rebel groups operating here over the past year? There had been some bandits, but no real rebels; the government had cracked down on the highway robbers, and now all was fine and calm. What was really important was the prior harvest, fairly good despite some insect depredations; the livestock situation, again, was fairly much okay, but with some tensions between herders and farmers. And then the sultan indicated his willingness to escort us to the chateau to overnight—not another palace of his, I soon realized, but the grounds of the Taiwan-built *chateau d'eau*, or water tower, where there was a rude guesthouse.

The next morning the sultan was back at 6:30 a.m., half an hour early, to escort us to Sila, the ruins of the ancient capital of his kingdom. We rushed our packing, and Robert barked at me because our drivers hadn't been fed as we exited with the sultan. We drove a dozen kilometers south and then off-road, a flat on the sultan's car stopping us a few hundred yards short of the entrance. Sila had been a fortified palace ringed by high hills, with two successive ramparts closing off the only level access into the basin formed by the hills. We hiked a half-hour in, and there we saw ruined walls of stone—selected for shape like a New England stone wall, but with an improvised mortar. Here, from sometime in the sixteenth or seventeenth century until 1872, the sultan's family had had their seat. Population pressure—including from slaves captured further south—had led them to relocate from here to Goz Beïda's more open site. The sultan escorted us back to the main road, and we were off to Am Timan and Zakouma. That evening at Zakouma, with a real restaurant and bar, we unwound a bit, eating and drinking heartily after days of stinted rations.

At Zakouma, the next morning I had perhaps the best game run of my life. In the car were Chaibo, Robert, myself, and Charles, our guide. Robert and I had tried to dissuade the exhausted Chaibo from rising with us at 4:30 a.m. to do it, saying we could drive. But the stalwart Chaibo wouldn't hear of it—if I was fit to ride, he was fit to drive! And it was less difficult driving since we went slowly, pausing often to look. We saw everything—giraffes, elephants, warthogs, ostriches, birds galore, crocodiles, baboons, monkeys, nearly a dozen types of antelope, and small things like mongoose. Finally we happened upon a lioness with two cubs. Reluctant to anger her, we turned around and retraced our path back. Then the highlight of the day—sitting quietly where we'd passed half an hour before, a spotted leopard! The first I'd seen in all my twenty years of living and traveling in Africa! And there was a third cat as well, most likely a civet, that Robert had scared out of the bush when walking out from the car for photos. Alas, the other car saw no cats that morning; we consider ourselves to have been very lucky!

I confess: I'm masochistic about traveling in rural Chad. Having never endured hardships or even camped out while growing up, I love testing myself with the privations of travel here. But I'm often surprised by the reactions of my companions. This time I was also a little disappointed in my young travel mates. Catherine is former Peace Corps, and George told us of the deprivations he suffered in forty days in the desert during Desert Storm. But the evening we reached Goz Beïda, both were thoroughly done in and irritable. George complained loudly about the roads, implying that our itinerary was too tough. Catherine was moribund and unapproachable. Only Robert, who hails from my own sort of comfortable background, was as unfazed as the veterans—Chaibo, Les, and myself. Even George's driver, Hassan, was fairly fried by now, although it was Chaibo who had spent four hours driving rocky tracks without any headlights the night before. Sadly, I felt our group divide for a day or so into the camps of the exhausted/cranky and the strong/ silent. Reaching Zakouma the next afternoon, with its full meals and bar, healed the little rift, and we sat up until 11:00 p.m. over an enormously expensive bottle of poor red wine. But it was well worth it to have folks back in good humor.

But for the most part, our eyes were set by the sun. As early as Mongo, it was clear that the evenings would be as void as usual. The préfet gave us an early dinner and sent us home before 8:00 p.m., splitting us between two hot, rude guesthouses. At the one,

Les retired immediately while Robert and I played cards and chatted a bit. Only that one lingering evening in Zakouma broke the
pattern, and otherwise our clock was that of rural Chad, i.e., the
sun, moon, and stars.

And on this trip we were unusually cut off from the news, for
Les didn't dare to listen to the 5:00 a.m. news broadcast as usual.
Our sleeping quarters were too close. With an information systems
specialist along, we kept in much better contact with N'Djamena,
but were oblivious to what passed in the greater world without.

Humorously, when I first decided to join this trip, I dubbed it the
"Journey to the East," with mute apologies to Hermann Hesse. But
I must admit that traveling in Chad reminds me of all those great
stories where the journey is itself much of the message: *The Odyssey, On the Road, The Lord of the Ring*, etc. For here also the mere accomplishment of the trek is a major result. The ambassador merely
showing up a thousand kilometers from N'Djamena is what impresses folks. And the portion of time spent actively doing business
is very small compared with the long hours in the car—long hours
to talk idly, or to cogitate. Ultimately, there is something metaphysical about a road trip in Chad.

Is it the adventure and unpredictability? The hardship itself,
which I've confessed to thriving upon? Or the sharp contrasts that
are so much a part of all of life here? All of these to a degree. But
more perhaps the parallel between our daily trek over the incredibly tortuous roads and the daily life of the rural Chadian, struggling just as hard to be able to put boule on the table for the family
each evening.

I'll deeply miss traveling in Chad!

Regards,

Ambassador Chris

It Rains in Bardaï

September 15, 2002

Dear Friends,

You know that ever since coming here I've wanted to get to the Tibesti, the rugged massif in the northwest that has harbored a rebellion throughout my tenure. I toured all other parts of the country long ago. Last Thursday and Friday, I finally made it to Bardaï, the largest town in the Tibesti, thanks to the periodic visit of the C-12, a USAF aircraft rather like a small private plane.

We planned this trip, the defense attaché and I, with some apprehension. We judged it possible only because of the months of relative calm that have prevailed since the signing of a peace agreement with the rebels back in January. A final settlement has remained elusive, however, and we still feared up to the moment of our departure that the government might decide conditions were too unsettled and deny us permission. For cover, we invited the minister of defense to come along, although in the end he couldn't make it.

This area is home to the Teda, or Toubou, tribe, which spreads west into Niger and north into Libya (one of the reasons Libya feeds the rebellion just enough to keep it alive). The Toubou have never really been subject to outside control, not by the French or by any government since decolonization. Their fierce independence is as big a factor in the rebellion as the broader political goals. What happened to Kallibou, who was to have been our escort officer, says a lot about the Teda. Kallibou is one of the few from the tribe to hold high public office—he is the deputy chief of the demining commission—and one of the few Teda trusted by the government. A family incident involving him, a cousin, and a knife took him out of commission just days before our departure. It seems that the cousin was wavering over whether to join the rebellion, and the family sent him down to N'Djamena, to Kallibou, to prevent this. They quarreled on the way home from the airport, and the cousin drew his knife (all the northerners carry long, sharp knives, sometimes concealed inside their pants). Kallibou managed to deflect a thrust toward his heart, but the weapon caught his thigh and he needed twenty stitches.

The night before we left I had a visit from Mark O., one of three American missionaries who had lived in Bardaï for several years before the rebellion, practicing medicine and learning Teda with the eventual goal (it takes decades) of developing a written version of the language and translating the Bible into it. Mark remains in contact with Bardaï through the N'Djamena Teda community, and he'd reproduced a map of the region for me, and on the back he'd drawn one himself of the town. He pointed to where Togoïmi, the rebel leader, had been badly injured two weeks earlier when his Toyota hit a land mine. He indicated a broad swath of mountains south and east of Bardaï, the core of the Tibesti, which remains rebel territory. The rebels hold one village less than ten miles from the town, but Mark doubted we'd have any problems: It is the season of the date harvest, one of the few annual events that always takes precedence over fighting.

Why, aside from seeing the only corner of Chad I hadn't, did I want to take this trip?

Professional reasons were several. First, I wanted to confirm that the fighting had calmed to the point that we could realistically consider demining operations in the region. And I wanted to explore the needs of the population after several years of civil war, both immediate humanitarian concerns, and what was needed for rebuilding and kick-starting the economy. Last, I flattered myself that the demonstration of US interest in this part of the country might give the Libyans pause, and strengthen the weak Chadian hand against them just a tad (it did, at least according to the resulting chatter in the opposition press).

On September 12, we boarded the C-12 for a 10:00 a.m. takeoff. We'd thought to bring food—me, a few power bars, the DATT, some MREs. The Chadians brought a freshly butchered sheep that we crammed into layers of plastic bags so it wouldn't drip blood on the plane. Kallibou was replaced by his boss, and the minister sent a staff officer to represent him. We would make the 500-mile flight in two and a half hours, nonstop each way. It's a little tricky flying into Bardaï, which sits at 3,500 feet in an open bowl on the northwest edge of the Tibesti. We would fly over the 10,000-foot core of the massif, and I kept waiting and waiting to see the mountains. Finally, we hit the abrupt line of tors just after we began our descent, in the last twenty-five minutes of airtime.

As the little plane bounced in the air currents, I craned my neck to see the famous Tibesti landscape through holes in storm clouds that we hadn't expected in the far north. It was spectacular, the mountains mirroring the black, gray, and brown of the clouds. It was starker and sharper than the Ennedi, with tall mystical cones that took me back to *The Lord of the Rings*. The bulky crests below the spires were gashed with incredibly narrow ravines. How could a slit so deep be so thin, and still the work of water erosion? A few broader valleys showed a handful of trees, but no sign of human habitation. So what if the rebels controlled it all? At one point, to our general surprise, we flew through a spitting rain for two minutes. Then the mountains began to dissolve here and there into softly sloping rubble, shoulders of black rock that ran down to little fields of drifting orange Saharan sand. And then the gray-beige of the open bowl that we knew contained our airstrip. We saw it, turned a couple of times to lose altitude, and hit hard. The pilot said the sand was very soft, and he'd needed to catch the very edge of the short strip.

As we alit (me first, of course), not knowing what to expect, it was the preponderance of uniforms that struck me. Several clumps of soldiers and one small formation, and only a couple of civilians, were in view. One of these, the préfet, stepped forward to greet me, and a few more civilians emerged from somewhere: the chef de canton, the sous-préfet, the head of the local demining office. The commander of the military region of Bardaï led the préfet, me, and the DATT off to review his little honor guard. From their build and facial features, I could tell that these troops hailed from all parts of Chad; most of the other clumps seemed to be northerners, with lots of Bidayat and Zaghawa (the president's tribe and their closest allies).

By the time we'd walked back to the plane, our gear had been loaded into a couple of Toyota pickups. The soldiers were clambering in on top of it, and the préfet motioned me toward a Land Cruiser with the plate "HCND 001"; it was one we'd given the demining program three years ago. It was now here, attached, I was told, to the newly opened demining office, although I suspected it had been flown in just for my visit. We headed off on the ten-mile track to Bardaï town. My regional security officer and one of the pilots joined the soldiers in the back of one of the Toyotas. The weather was overcast, and the scenery only a little less bleak than the mountains. The beige sand was hard enough for us not to need the 4x4, interspersed with lots of black, hand-sized rocks. A tall black butte to our left was the probable source. Its sharp walls dissolved midway down into sloping piles of stone like what I'd seen from the air. As we bounced along I began to spy the rugged, gray-brown cliffs Bardaï is famous for, wind-carved into amazing chimney-like shapes. Along the ground I saw unexploded ordinance here and there.

When we got to town, the préfet took us to his house and offered soft drinks, dates, and peanuts—typical Chadian hospitality. Did we need to rest? No. The préfet didn't seem to know quite what to do with us. Through the pleasantries I tried to push the talk in the direction of planning out our brief time. Finally the préfet pulled himself up in his chair and launched into a standard sort of welcome. He was a southerner, from Logone Oriental, I judged by his features and speech, which could have made him my butler's brother. Mark had told me he'd spent little time here, perhaps accounting for his hesitancy. In my response, I stressed our two main goals—looking at prospects for demining and how best to help the civilian population recover and reintegrate after peace was achieved. We bounced on around the table with courtesy speeches.

Eventually we got down to business and had a good half-hour discussion of my topics, relying largely on the sous-préfet, whose Arabic had to be translated into French for my benefit. It was clear that the demining effort was critical: nearly all the roads (read tracks) are heavily mined starting perhaps ten kilometers out of town in any direction. The office was revving up, but actual work would begin only when the peace agreement was finally implemented. Fair enough. From Bardaï's encircled isolation flowed the most pressing humanitarian needs: medicine and food. Everything gets flown in at irregular intervals. There is virtually no medical care, and food is five times the cost in N'Djamena, with selection very narrow. Longer term, the needs for reintegration and economic development were less clear. The best prospects seemed to be tourism, commerce, and oasis agriculture. Demining and infrastructure seemed to be the keys to all. And yes, the military situation had been calm for some months, although vigilance was still advised. What to do next? I asked if there were things we could see to better understand the needs. Yes, how about starting with the demining office?

We walked a few hundred yards to Maison Staewen (about which, more later). It looked like the demining folks had moved in yesterday. The sign outside was stenciled on sheet cloth; labels on the office doors were handwritten on paper. But our hosts duly led us through a suite of rooms in an outbuilding, explaining the function of each. There was a modicum of equipment. The préfet explained the dearth of tables and chairs: They were the ones we'd been sitting on at his house! Things were indeed at an infant stage, although the local demining director later averred he'd been in town two months.

Now what? Did we want to rest now? Still not. Did we want to see the defunct dispensary? Of course we did. We walked the half mile and entered a room with dilapidated walls in which only three years ago Mark had treated his patients. Now it seemed that our hosts had caught on. During the next hour and a half we visited all the public sites in town: the market, the high school, the grade school, the military hospital, and a well. Then we were content to go back to the préfet's to eat the goat we'd brought; I tried to grab for well-cooked chunks and eschewed the liver and tripe. It was now past 3:00 p.m., and didn't we really want to rest now? We consented and moved back to Maison Staewen where we would overnight. We were now in the heat of the day when the Chadians normally sprawl out on mats and cushions in the shade of a big tree and chat idly and snooze, their charming equivalent of a siesta. The préfet murmured something about seeing us again at 7:00 p.m.

Resting diverted us for maybe half an hour, maybe less. Rudy, one of our pilots, suggested a stroll to see more of the village and its "gardens," and to take some pictures. The RSO and I joined him, and as we set out, the local demining director and a lone Chadian officer came running. I was afraid they'd constrain us, but *au contraire*, they opened every gate and we had a delightful and informative jaunt. It was the only time I can remember being able to wander at will through a town outside of N'Djamena. Here in Bardaï of all places!

The gardens we wanted to see are plots of enclosed, irrigated land smack dab in town. The town itself is, indeed, a jumble of these oasis cultivations with houses adjacent, plus the market, mosque, and a few administrative buildings. The largest garden, that of the chef du canton, was maybe an acre. Some others were as small as a large living room. An enormous variety of plants were being grown—wheat, date palms, vegetables, cotton, grapes, and herbs, to name a few. I'd always heard about the deciduous crops up here, where winter temperatures will fall into the high twenties and ice will form. The cotton surprised me—big perennial or ratoon bushes, the source of stuffing for cushions and pillows, I was told.

As we reached the edge of town, our military escort suddenly came to semiattention and pointed to his own house: Did we want to have a look? Of course. We passed a demurely smiling woman vendor with a little selection of cloth and sundries as we entered. A wife, perhaps. We walked quickly around an ample mud-brick compound with five or six rooms ringing an open space in which was erected a temporary structure of sekko. The soldier poured water into a stainless steel bowl from a tightly stitched animal skin. Water seeps slowly through the leather, moistening the outer surface of the hide, and the evaporation keeps the water inside cool. The demining director drank, the rest of us not. Another wife had brought the skin, smiling. The rooms had only mats, no furniture, though one had a raised ledge that might have been a bed. Both wives had simple, sunlike tattoos on chin and brow. Outside the compound we photographed the two women, giggling slightly in an embarrassed dignity. As we strode away, I noted the heavy clouds that were beginning to soften the afternoon heat; a few raindrops fell.

We went on to another garden or two and eventually came back to the market. There were a few sekko stalls, but mostly single-room mud-brick buildings with a single door in one wall to admit both clients and light. The wares were uniform—sorghum, rice, beans, a few other dry foods like noodles. Some spices and a few canned goods. Sundries—soap, laundry powder in tiny bags, razors and blades, toothpaste. And cigarettes—Marlboros even here in the Tibesti! Soft drinks, of course, and I suspect something stronger hidden away for those in the know. The prices quoted us were prohibitive—a *koro*, or large cup of sorghum, that cost FCFA 500 ($0.75) in N'Djamena cost 2,500 here. Periodically one of the Chadian Air Force C-130s takes the market women down to N'Djamena, where they buy and bring back enough to feed Bardaï for another week or two. I didn't learn if the high prices were because the women had to cough up the fuel cost for the plane, or whether it was simply what the market would bear.

By sometime between 5:00 and 6:00 p.m., we were back at Maison Staewen. It is a famous site in Chad's history, one of two places in Bardaï raided by Hussein Habré in about 1975, when he took Dr. Staewen and Mme Claustre hostage. This began his bloody march to power, and the struggle to free and eventually ransom the hostages was a cause célèbre for the following two years. More recently, the house had sheltered a French detachment that had been assigned to Bardaï until three or four years ago. The main room was lined with the shields of the units, insignia, and murals incorporating names. The house was on a high point, and from various angles of its porches we took dusky photos of the bowl of crags surrounding the oasis. We had been told that the toilet in the house no longer worked, and the lack of a latrine worried us a little until we discovered the Jeep built into the wall of a roofless outbuilding; the latrine pit was aligned with the driver's seat, from which the bottom had been cut out—the French military sense of humor.

Eventually a couple of servants wandered by with a simple supper of bread, macaroni, and two bowls of sauce in which to dip the bread. After that, the préfet and sous-préfet appeared and we chatted amiably for an hour about the needs of the district. And by 8:00 p.m., we were left to ourselves for the night.

We slept outside, beyond the veranda of the house, on a flat sandy expanse held up by a retaining wall. Our hosts had carried mats, carpets, and cushions from the house's main room and spread them around for us earlier in the afternoon. The DATT strung a hammock between two pillars of the veranda.

Sleeping outside this way is delightful, though I confess I never sleep well the first night or two, perhaps because, in its way, the experience is very sensual. Looking up, there is nothing between you and the vast sky. The sounds are few here, but the cry of the odd child or the bleat of a goat is riveting. By 9:00 p.m. the town was in repose, and I heard only the flapping of the flag against its tall pole. A gentle warm wind wafted over legs, arms, and face. A delicious stillness. As I lay in semislumber, I felt two or three more raindrops on my cheeks. Sometime after midnight, the clouds all cleared off, and when I opened my eyes for a moment, the sky was lit with constellation after constellation of stars standing out with dramatic clarity.

As I drifted back to sleep, it struck me that the prospect of peace in this part of Chad, the premise of my trip, was like the scant rain that had fallen on us. It comes unexpectedly, and you have to grab and hold what of it you can. It isn't strong enough to yield a truly good crop without the help of groundwater. There's just enough to keep life and hope alive.

Best regards,

Ambassador Chris

P.S.
October 5, 2002

Since I penned the first draft of this letter, war and peace have been much in the news here. There have been skirmishes in the south, on both sides of the border with the Central African Republic (CAR). With Libyan help, one Abdoulaye Miskine, a former Chadian rebel, has been raiding into Chad, and tensions are high with the CAR, which can't control its northern zone. Then we heard that Togoïmi, who had been recuperating from his mine injuries in Libya, had died. Would this at last permit the implementation of the January peace accord? Last Wednesday, we got good news about the CAR: It seemed everything had been patched up, Chad would expel a CAR coup plotter it has been harboring, and the Libyan troops in the CAR would be replaced by more neutral peace keepers. For an evening and a morning, it seemed as if the clouds were clearing as they had that night in Bardaï. Peace at last on both fronts? Then, Thursday afternoon we heard that a rebel force had boldly raided Faya-Largeau's airport and blown up Chad's only two transport helicopters, just as if to say that Togoïmi's death isn't the end of the rebellion. Yes, peace in Chad is elusive. It's like hoping for just a little more rain, now in October, at the tail end of a rather weak rainy season.

Visiting the Neighbors

May 30, 2003

Dear Friends,

When I welcome embassy newcomers, I tell them that the hardship of life here isn't the obvious deprivations—those we compensate for with generators, water trucks, and enormous expenditure on importing and maintaining infrastructure. It's really the lack of diversion, the need to be creative in finding entertainment. After nearly four years here, I'm a firm adherent of the advice expats of long residence give—get out every six months to Europe, America, or eastern or southern Africa. Only now am I finding that weekend excursions to neighboring countries help as well. This letter describes two jaunts—one to Maroua and Rumsiki in Cameroon, one to Maiduguri, Nigeria. These were great little trips, but don't get me wrong: They aren't weekend escapes to your favorite B&B, but very much part of the African experience.

After logging between 10,000 and 15,000 miles overland in Chad, I firmly believe that in principle you can drive anywhere in Africa. It is rigorous and takes time, you have to be well provisioned and you need to check in with the locals for directions and advice at each stage as you go. Vast swatches of territory move on or off limits depending on political events. Until eight months ago, I was considering an overland trip to Bangui, Central African Republic, where my friend Mattie Sharpless is ambassador. Then, last November, there was a coup, the government changed, we closed our embassy, and the entire north of the country fell into anarchy. Guess I won't be doing that trip anytime soon.

If most routes stay open and relatively safe, why is overland travel still intimidating for most of my colleagues? I can think of several reasons. First, when you leave N'Djamena you are a stranger and a minority divorced from your support network. The tourist infrastructure is primitive, although basic lodges and hotels exist in the neighboring countries (but not in Chad, except for Zakouma and Sarh, so you have to take lots of your own gear). The roads are poor, often dirt or so badly potholed that you're reduced to ten to twenty miles per hour for long stretches. The border crossings can be difficult for the inexperienced, although a diplomatic passport helps. Finding your way with inaccurate maps and no road signs is a challenge. Banditry looms in the background, a greater or lesser threat. Food is unpredictable and tummy troubles crop up frequently.

So why bother? Most don't, but for some of us the change of scenery and taste of the exotic are worth the trouble. It's lot's better than another Sunday afternoon watching a VCR. And to a degree, as with backpackers, the medium is the message—the experience is its own reward. Even the discomfort and hint of danger can be exhilarating. In our embassy community of about fifty, at any given time perhaps a dozen are game. On these two trips I was joined by Robert, our information systems specialist, and Janis, a Canadian teaching at our American school; and for the second, by another teacher, Patricia.

The trip to Rumsiki was last November. This village lies in the rugged Mandara Mountains of northern Cameroon abutting Nigeria. We left on a Friday afternoon, as quickly after the embassy's noon-time closing as we could manage. Robert, not trusting my aged Toyota Corolla, offered to drive his 4x4 SUV.

Handling the border formalities was my job on our excursions. While exiting Chad, I chatted with the *commissaire* of immigration, who is by now an acquaintance. He has participated in various of our training programs over the years. Entering on the Cameroonian side, I met my colleague, the ambassador from CAR. I lamented the rebellion that had broken out in his country only two weeks earlier.

He said he was taking his son to school in Cameroon, after which he would make his way down to Bangui. He said he didn't dare go across the Chad–CAR border directly, since Chad was apparently aiding the rebels who occupied northern CAR.

We drove as far as Maroua, some four hours. The road was fine as far as Waza, but the rest of the way to Maroua it had deteriorated sharply since I'd last traversed it eighteen months earlier. We found rooms, enjoyed a relaxing meal at the Relais de la Porte Mayo, and arranged for a guide, Victor, who would come with us to Rumsiki the following morning.

Victor was a great guide, and cheap at FCFA 10,000 per day. He told us en route what we could see and do in Rumsiki, elaborating on the exotic scenery and hiking promised by my twenty-year-old guidebook. The road was paved as far west as Mokolo, the good infrastructure in and en route to that town the result of the town's being home to the mother of a former president.

At Mokolo we left the paving behind and the road turned sharply south for the remaining thirty miles. We began to glimpse afar the moonscape scenery of rugged little hills like fists and thumbs that erupted from the rolling plain. As we came nearer, the plains gave way to sharp folds and high arêtes that made for magnificent views when the road passed their crests. Now the entire horizon, in an arc from southeast to northwest, was dominated by the fingers and mesas of inselbergs—tough cores of stone that rose several hundred feet from the hills, having resisted eons of wind erosion.

Rumsiki's campement is not unlike Waza's—round, white *boukarous* (cabins) with spartan furnishings, cold-water showers, and clunky aircon. It was noon. We lunched, rested through the heat of the day, and set out around 3:30 p.m. on our hike. We circled north of the lodge and began a sharp descent into one of the declivities in the landscape. At the bottom of this narrow valley, Cameroon met Nigeria. Foot over foot, we went down rapidly, honing to a steep, thin, rocky trail down several hundred feet in elevation. For me, trying to keep pace with my colleagues, all much younger, the issue was balance.

At the bottom we found fields of sorghum and corn, and paused in a tiny village—now on the Nigerian side—for a Coke. We had turned and were now a mile or two south of Rumsiki, looking back at a spirelike inselberg that I could see from the stoop outside my room. Victor told us that if we'd had a whole day, we could have climbed it, too. Maybe, I thought to myself, maybe not. Now we turned quickly back to the Rumsiki side, seeming to scale a forty-five-degree precipice. Step after step, breath after breath, for an exhausting forty-five minutes. At rare moment-long intervals, we paused long enough to notice the scenery, which was spectacular. Finally the slope softened, and we were again amid fields and dwellings, nearing Rumsiki; in a few minutes my breathing was normal again. Later I asked Robert how this compared with Kilimanjaro, which he'd climbed some months earlier. He allowed that the slope was similar, but in place of forty-five minutes, think six to eight hours a day, and in rarefied air at high elevation. Hmm. One of those cold showers, a hearty dinner, and a cold beer did marvels to restore us.

The next morning we did touristic Rumsiki, beginning with the crab sorcerer. We had already gathered a crowd of children as Victor led us to his hut. This shriveled, wizened diviner would answer questions about our future by interrogating his crabs. He took a clay pot perhaps eighteen inches in diameter, with mud up nearly to the top. He stood little wooden planks in the mud and reached for his crabs. He placed two or three in the vessel, put a lid on it, and moved it around over his lap in a level, circular motion while incanting a spell. Placing the pot on terra firma, the sorcerer removed the lid and read the answer to our question by how the crabs had moved around on the surface of the mud and which of the planks they'd knocked over. Victor translated the man's local tongue into French, and I took it back into English. Janis and Robert were reassured regarding future romantic interests, and I was promised a good job upon regaining Washington.

Victor took us next to the weavers' cooperative, where we saw how the local cotton makes its way from raw lint to finished garments and household items. The results aren't elegant, but they are impressive in their way because of the primitive implements used to make them. As a textile junky I couldn't resist a couple of small souvenirs. And then to the market. There didn't seem to be anything unusual for sale, but it was a lively little mart. What I remember most is the groups of people in drinking stalls: men over here, women over there, many already soused at 10:00 a.m. on sorghum beer. Retreating toward the lodge to pack and depart, we were pursued by more youngsters peddling toys. We bought little sculptures in gray wire of men on bicycles, and tiny cars made of balsa twigs.

After gassing up and dropping off Victor in Maroua, we turned north for N'Djamena. The main amusement of the long ride back was the rather futile effort of my companions to educate me about contemporary country-western music.

It was only a week ago that we made the trek over to Maiduguri. I'd been wanting to get there these past two years. My interest began with a desire to better understand the trade between Chad and what seemed to me to be its natural market for ag products, Nigeria. And, of course, I just wanted to get back into Nigeria after all these years. Last, in recent months I've begun work on a murder mystery drawing on some of the events and controversy surrounding Toumai, and to protect the guilty, I've decided to move the setting from N'Djamena to Maiduguri. So I needed to get over there and jumped at the chance when Patricia, Janis, and Robert were willing to come along.

I did the best advance work for the trip I could, asking various folks about the roads and travel time: three or four hours, roads paved except for one short stretch, no problem. Thus spake Les, Anne-Nicole (my language tutor who goes there on church business), and a couple of others.

We set off on Friday afternoon, a little later this time, but still seemingly in plenty of time. We were crossing the border around 3:30 p.m., and my friend the commissaire provided a reassuring forecast of the travel time: Banki and the Nigerian border by 5:00 p.m., Maiduguri two to two-and-a-half hours later, so only the last few miles in night driving. I sighed, relieved.

Off we drove, taking the turn for Fotokol, the border town shown on my map. The road, however, was dirt and seemed to take us much further north than my map showed. We kept on, landmarks falling into place, and asked once or twice in villages to be sure we had kept to the main road. By dusk we were crossing into Nigeria. At the border, the officials were welcoming and friendly, telling me that this was a different Nigeria than the one I'd known so many years before. The immigration office itself was farcical. I entered the front room, which was deserted. Hearing sounds beyond, I went deeper into the building, finding a chamber where all were watching an American movie on a battery-powered VCR. I greeted the apparent boss, who looked up and responded politely. He took our passports and sent minions scattering. Someone took the passports off to an adjoining room. Space was made for me to sit and enjoy the movie. The fellow with the passports returned in a few minutes, and there began a team effort to process them: one person to thumb through and find our visas, one person to stamp them, and a third man to hand a pen to the second so he could initial over the stamp he'd just placed. It took all of twenty minutes, but there was no hassle.

My map showed paved road the rest of the way to Maiduguri, and we'd already done fifty kilometers over dirt, so I assumed that was the bad stretch and we'd coast from here. Wrong. The road was paved, but greatly deteriorated—more potholes than clean surface. We stumbled along in the fading light, on and off the paved track, following a parallel power line as our directional. Night fell and then our crisis hit. We came to a stretch where the day's rain, the first of the wet season, had totally flooded the main road. The roadbed was a mere trough filled with water, just waiting to bemire any vehicle that approached. The shoulders on either side were higher, but were only ridges of soft sand. The oncoming shoulder was totally blocked by trucks coming out of Maiduguri toward Chad, which were all stuck and stopped for the night. By great luck, the right hand shoulder was open, if treacherous. Patricia and I dismounted to have a look. The sand firmed beneath our feet as we walked on it. Robert shifted into 4x4, and we moved forward steadily, countersteering as the vehicle veered from side to side, narrowly avoiding the oblivion of a lurch either into the wet trough of the main road or off the sand and down into the swampy fields below. There were two stretches like this of perhaps a kilometer each, and then the road really was paved. We all congratulated Robert on his superb driving skills.

From Dikwa, thirty kilometers in from the border, the road was fine. It even had a dotted white line separating the lanes. Approaching Maiduguri, the map in the *Lonely Planet* guide was good enough for us to find our way to the Deribe Hotel, the city's shabby best, without a wrong turn. This was probably the same hotel I'd stayed in back in 1985, and which I remembered for its mosquitoes. Multi-storied, it had a tidy parking lot and a welcoming marble entrance; a plaque noted that President Shehu Shagari had inaugurated it back in 1983. We passed under a concrete awning, through a glass double door, and things deteriorated from there. The lobby seemed dingy and nondescript, whether from poor lighting or decay, I couldn't quite judge. The rooms were cheap enough—$30—but not quite worth the price. At least the sheets were clean.

At dinner at 9:00 p.m., we were the only guests, but stains on the table cloth belied the presence of others earlier. It took a long time for the kitchen to rev back up, and we weren't served until nearly 10:00. But the main disappointment was the lack of a longed-for Star beer. Bornu State has Sharia law now, and alcohol is available only in speakeasies.

As I got ready for bed, something else was puzzling me, my friend the commissaire's reference to "Banki." The name had rung a bell, yet we hadn't passed through any town of that name. Looking at the map now, I saw a Banki on the border some seventy-five miles south of Fotokol where we had crossed. Hmm. Was it possible that most people took that much longer southern route? Did we take the slower truck route, where only the savings on fuel would force the truckers to endure the poor road? I thought back to my reconnoitering. I'd talked to at least four people in recent months, and their descriptions of the road and travel time had coincided nicely. But no one until the commissaire had indicated that they meant the longer route through Mora, Cameroon, and Banki, rather than the shorter route that was more obvious on the map. In Africa, live and learn; nothing substitutes for firsthand experience.

The next morning we were up early and went out to see the sites of the town. Like N'Djamena, it is low and spreading, and it has the same vibrant street commerce. But it is distinctly more prosperous: It has graduated from mud brick to concrete and tin. Working streetlights hint at a deeper infrastructure. The downtown is more densely populated with both cars and people. But a lot of the squalor, filth, and decay are the same.

The main attraction was the zoo. We spent a pleasant hour

looking at monkeys, antelope, birds, and a friendly elephant who let us pet his trunk. It was very run down, but they were feeding the animals. En route to the market district, I noted that there seemed to be a state office for every imaginable purpose, a lingering residue of the socialist tendencies of British colonialism. Driving by the market, the exterior stalls and shops were shoehorned so tightly together that they formed a fortress-like wall around the hidden core. Crowds and merchandise spilled into the street, narrowing four lanes into two that we could still barely get through. A man pushed a cart of meat beside us as we inched along—were those long, thin haunches beef? Ostrich? They looked almost human.

At the museum we found only a caretaker with broken English. It was closed on Saturdays. But we found the university and drove around it enough to give me a mental image for literary purposes. It is very Sahelian—low buildings rambling around a campus of tall dry grasses with a few low trees, and faded lawns nearer the structures. Short-order food stalls had been constructed pell-mell between the classroom buildings. The brick walls of the latter were pockmarked where entire bricks had eroded away, leaving holes.

Our plan after Maiduguri was either to head back to N'Djamena or to take a second day and drive down to Gwoza, a town on the Nigerian side of the Mandara Mountains, somewhat north of Rumsiki. This would imply an eventual crossing into Cameroon at Banki. I detected a certain skepticism regarding my navigational skills as my companions hesitantly agreed that we'd give it a try and see how the road was. But first we'd need gas, and here we encountered the essence of modern Nigeria. There were tidy, modern filling stations along the road south from town every half mile or so, sometimes clumps of two or three. We stopped at five or six, and none had gas. At some, empty cars in a fifty- to a hundred-long line awaited the eventuality of fuel. At one, an attendant waved a notebook before us that listed thirty or forty license plate numbers of cars not present but "in line" for the next fuel delivery. Yet traffic was heavy—people got gas somewhere. What to do? It was touch and go whether we had enough gas to get back to Cameroon. Well, beside each gas station there was a sidewalk stand with plenty of gas in big five-gallon jugs. No line, no problem. Reluctantly, we decided we'd have to risk using this stuff. We stopped by one stand,

and a youth of fifteen or sixteen sucked the air out of a siphon and filled our tank. It was expensive but not outrageous—$1.75 a gallon. What explains the juxtaposition of dearth and plenty? Officials at the Nigerian refinery get bribes to divert fuel from the legitimate downstream retailers to black market wholesalers. Result: empty pumps, but ample supplies at a markup from street vendors. No beer in the restaurants, but lots if you know where to go. The whole country runs this way. It may be worse today than when I was here before.

Resupplied, we tooled along toward Gwoza. The road held, and we pretty much determined to take the Banki route across to Cameroon that evening or the following morning, depending on what we found at Gwoza. Indeed, the town seemed much less than promised by the guidebook—it wasn't in the mountains yet, and they seemed too distant for a short hike—and the promised guesthouses weren't anywhere to be seen. We drove a few miles further south, all the time on good paved road, to get an impression of the mountains. They reminded me of Chad's Guéra—tall, red-brown piles of rocks with soft, wind-eroded surfaces. Nothing as spectacular as Rumsiki. Turning around, we decided to head for the border and overnight in Maroua.

It was an easy two-hour drive to Banki, but as soon as we got into town, we got lost. A guy on a moto kept following us and waving—perhaps we'd inadvertently cut him off and he was angry? Finally, we realized we'd missed the border, and stopped. Up came the guy from nowhere, and he offered to lead us back. As usual, I took charge of the formalities. While scribes copied and stamped, I chatted with the local head of immigration, who wore an Alcohol, Tobacco, and Firearms Control lapel pin commemorating training he'd had in the United States. He was longing, of course, for another trip to America.

I should have known, however, that you can't make four border crossings in Africa without at least one minor crisis. I had the passports in hand, shook hands with the immigration officer and scribes, and turned on my heel to walk back to the car. Then another official approached me. What about our health cards? (God! How foolish could I have been *not* to have brought health cards—didn't I remember how sensitive Nigeria is about them?) The man motioned me to follow and led me through a back door out, around a corner, and into another building. He sat, I sat. He picked up a huge ledger, opened it, and began to ask me about the cards. Especially for the two Canadians, he needed to see the cards. No one had asked to see them coming into the country, I countered, why did he need them for us to exit? He grunted and began to page through the ledger. I could see all the signs of a major dash (bribe) developing. Our passports were already stamped, I knew, and I'd just developed a nice relationship with the immigration guy. I decided to play hardball. I grabbed the passports and strode out firmly, not too quickly, smiled and waved at the immigration folks again, and went right to the car. "Robert, we may have a problem. Drive right to the border crossing, quickly." And there, sure enough, a young man raised the barrier for us to cross into Cameroon just as the dazed health official was coming out the door after us. I told my friends what had happened. Patricia and Janis, it turned out, had remembered to bring their health cards.

On the Cameroonian side, I made small talk with the officials about the rain and directions to Mora and Maroua. What they told me turned out to be accurate, but I was mildly concerned because the route out of town seemed to be taking us southwest, back toward Nigeria, rather than more easterly toward Mora. Abruptly, the road swung east in a little village, and there was an old mileage marker—Mora four kilometers. Again, the map was only indicative.

What is it we all love about Maroua? The smallish city has a relaxing ambiance, with broad, paved streets, and it has a little more in the way of western shopping than N'Djamena or Koussérie. And it has the Relais de la Porte Mayo. This rustic inn has *boukarou* rooms a little more comfortable than Waza or Rumsiki, and definitely cleaner. But the highlight is outdoor dining, with a kitchen that serves French, local, and Vietnamese dishes. After hitting the largest western store and the artisans market, we returned for drinks and a leisurely dinner. "All of our trips ought to end here!" someone said. Somewhere in the lingering conversation, and after a second beer, Robert admitted that years earlier in high school he'd liked to go mud racing—hence his excellent driving through the rough spot on the road to Maiduguri. Relaxed now, we laughed over the exploit and it became lore, part of the travel experience in Africa.

As we left town and headed north, back to N'Djamena, I reflected on the diversion offered by these little trips, and how even an old hand like me can misjudge things. The essential elements and incongruities stay the same across the borders of the three countries we'd traversed. It had rained again during the night, the second storm of the season. Where we filled up with gas, the attendant could talk of nothing else. Along the road, grass was already sprouting where all had been barren a day or two before. Villagers were out in their fields, lines of four or five people working their way across the fields in unison, making holes for planting with their short hand hoes. An hour north of town, we were stopped by a herd of cattle crossing the road, already turning north after the first signs of a change in the season. The enigma of it struck me yet again. We watched this timeless pattern of primitive people farming, as they had for millennia, from the comfort of the vehicle with its air-conditioning and CD player. No, our little trips can never provide the relief from Africa that most of my colleagues seek in order to relax. But in an odd way, the experience both explains and deepens the mystique of this gripping place: an Africa you can get away from only with a jet, but even then you take something of it with you.

Regards,

Ambassador Chris

Le Grand Nord

December 4, 2003

My long-awaited trip through Chad's great north, in which I invested leave time and treasure, was spectacular, but it was not the leisurely vacation I had expected. Although it was more ordeal than relaxation, I survived it safe and sound and, in retrospect, the adventure will become part of my overall Chadian experience.

What We Saw

To begin with the positive, our trek covered the intended route with minor detours and we saw most of what we had hoped. And I had great travel mates. It was a military group: my Defense Attaché Col. Scott W.; his wife, Captain Rebecca C.; their four-year-old son, Sam; Chris H. and Brad L., who are on temporary duty in Scott's office; along with Bill M., the regional security officer. With their talents, humor, and tolerance, we endured our plague of car problems.

The scenery of the Sahara and its mountains is awe inspiring and magnificent. Sweeping beige or orange sand dunes are broken by red-brown eruptions of rock twenty to thirty feet high. The vastness seems endless, yet changes constantly in the wind. Looking afar, you feel remote and isolated, yet a skilled guide can read your location without a compass. Looking down, you are rarely without some sign of man. The rust-colored buttes and cliffs are most spectacular in the Ennedi. Often resembling massed Tudor chimneys, the spikes are taller and more rugged, each unique. Here the cliffs seem to ring the acacia plains on all sides. The oases, however, break the dry tones with green belts of palm or denser acacia.

Ounianga Kébir was my favorite spot, and one of our two or three prime objectives. It is a salt lake three or four miles long in the remote north, barely a hundred miles south of Libya. The blue water reflects the morning sun with all the sparkling intensity I remember from Lake Champlain. High, pinkish cliffs surround the lake on two sides, and one promontory is topped by an old fort recalling Italy or the Holy Land in a charming, painterly manner. With a dense copse of green palm climbing from the lakeshore toward the heights, it was my favorite image from the trip. We camped on a high dune with striking views of the lake through the palms as the sun rose at 5:00 a.m. Unrivaled beauty.

Guelta Archei, a few days later, was similarly a water spot in the waste. It is a year-round pool surrounded by cliffs, deep in the Ennedi to the southeast of Fada. It is home to a unique species of crocodile. I'd been here before, but only to the outside edge of the lake where herds of animals water and defecate. This time we camped behind the pool's remoter ridge and hiked, or rather rock climbed, in at dawn to see the serene interior pond. It made for a rugged hour plus, but the view down on the lake with its surrounding papyrus reeds was a worthy reward. Alas, it was too early in the day for the crocs to be out sunning.

The rock art was the other treat. Bill found the first example when we were broken down 100 miles east of Faya: several cows etched in white on an outcropping of rock in the open desert a few hundred feet from the road. Later, in the Ennedi, it was everywhere. We saw important examples at Toukou and Terkei: Men galloping on swirling horses, huge cows, and smaller camels. Women in long, flowing robes, and giraffes. We saw little scraps everywhere we explored on foot—handprints or single bovines. But we could have seen more if our guide had known the area better, and it would have been nice if he could have told us a little about what we were looking at.

The Sahara

Is your picture of the Sahara one of light brown, shifting sand dunes under a beating sun? That's only half right, or not even half. The shifting dunes are perhaps only a quarter of the Sahara, at least judging from Chad. Equal shares are composed of vast pebble beds that were once lakebeds, gray-white expanses of salty hardpan, and shallow sand bogs only a few inches deep. As we drove, I could distinguish each soil type and welcomed any territory but the high dunes.

There is always a wind in the desert. It can be a mild breeze, enough to keep you alert and squinting, or a heavy gust assaulting you with tiny bullets of sand. On even the mildest days, the dunes have a sand fog a foot or two high that disguises the surface of the ground and walks the dunes thickly across the landscape. Even where there is no fog, for example, in the pebble beds, there is sand in the air and you inhale it and taste it and can't keep it out of your mouth. It seasons all our food. On the worst days, I wore a scarf and turban like the local folk, which helps somewhat.

I noticed that the sand has two distinct colors—the slanted dunes are a definite orange, the flat surfaces beige. Are the sands different, or is it only the angle at which they reflect the sun? Nor is the desert empty. Everywhere are human signs—the dung of their animals, tire tracks, and refuse. Much of the refuse is military: ruins of military vehicles from Chad's rebellions and the war with Libya, live artillery shells and their casings, AK-47 shells.

Eventually I began to analyze the dunes aerodynamically. They are long and gentle mounds on the windward side, a sort of sweeping half circle. But on the leeward side, they form steep clifflike crescents. These drop at a sharp angle to the flat sand floor below. One night we camped inside one of these crescents, and it was very sheltered and placid.

It seems you are never alone in the desert. After driving and seeing no cars for an hour, you will stop in an oasis or a wadi, and in five minutes you are surrounded by children with outstretched palms begging, *"Donnez-moi un cadeau!"* No, the Sahara isn't the empty, pristine wasteland you imagine.

People en Route

We were items of curiosity everywhere we went, especially Sam. Chadian children from his own age up to ten or twelve seemed fascinated by the aspect of a white child, and engulfed him at every stop, sometimes reaching in an open car window to touch. With groups of four or five, Sam returned their overtures and at longer stops played with them. Larger gangs he found intimidating and would avoid.

For myself, I am not especially outgoing when on vacation, enjoying in part the chance to be offstage and anonymous (or at least not "Mr. Ambassador"). But I made a few acquaintances and observations along the way, mainly in the early days before the continued car problems drove up my frustration level.

At Moussouro, where we stopped the second morning to gas up, I fell into conversation with a *métis*, who seemed naturally to seek out any white visitors. His French father had paid to educate him in Nigeria, and he spoke fair English. Now he was stuck here in this last population center on the road up through the Sahara. He told me that the town's big news was its selection as the site for an upcoming holiday celebration of the regime's ascent to power. But this chap clearly wanted more of a future than working on the fringes of a one-day event. How does a young man, clearly better educated than his peers, break out of the confines of this backwater? His only chance would be to get to N'Djamena, but if his father is gone and his mother has no relations there, that route is blocked. I gave him a lapel pin of the crossed Chadian and US flags; he seemed delighted.

That same night we camped in the sandy borderland between Sahel and Sahara, a few hundred yards off the road. While we were still pitching the tents, a nomad approached. Only Nasour and Gerome (driver and cook) could speak with him in his dialect of Chadian Arabic, but he seemed quite at home with all of us and shook hands all around. He spent much of the evening at the camp-fire Gerome made for cooking, around which he and the drivers lolled away an hour or two before retiring. At one point he went away and returned with some very dry dates, a hospitality offering. In the morning he was back at dawn. Just before we drove away I saw that Gerome had given him some tea and sugar. His wizened, weathered features were broken by a grin of ecstasy as he poured the white granules into his own sack.

Reaching Faya two days later, we were held up all day for car repairs. The one scheduled tourist activity was a tour of the town's markets, and two local guides, one a soldier, had been engaged to show us through it. We holed up at the house of someone acquaint-ed with our tour company's director, and when we got back from the market the guides hung around. They were helpful initially in beating back the horde of kids that tried to climb the compound gate to get to Sam, but afterward we sat in the shade of the palms and the military guy began to ask my advice about a recent busi-ness deal. He had given a Nigerian he had met, who was going to Dubai, FCFA four million ($7,500) to bring back a digital camera, a personal CD player, and some other item of electronics. My first question was where a soldier not over thirty would get so much money, but I didn't ask. The Nigerian was to have been back in two months, and now four had gone by. Did I think our guide had been cheated? (Is the sky blue?) I told him his only chance was to show up on the guy's doorstep in Kano. I was baffled by this interchange. The guide can only have gotten his boodle through some swindle or extortion, and then he trusts it to a barely known Nigerian who is going to go shopping for him three thousand miles away?

The other personal exchange of note didn't involve me, or at least not directly. It was the clear, north-south tension between our chief guide, Nasour, and the interlocutor on our little team, Gerome, the cook. We'd been told Gerome was the point person, but it soon became clear that Nasour had all the expense money and all the papers we needed to present to local officials along the way. He pulled the strings of our little party. But since he spoke only Chadian Arabic, we could speak with him only through Gerome. He ignored Gerome, and it didn't seem to make any difference if Gerome was speaking for himself or for us. It soon became clear to me that, with the arrogance sometimes seen in the northerners who run Chad, Nasour would simply do whatever he wanted. I even resorted to an African tactic to communicate directly with him, a show of anger. Even this had little effect, and we remained at the man's mercy.

How Not to Travel the Sahara...

...is in broken down old clunkers; with arrogant, ignorant guides with no common language; and with drivers inexperienced in the sand.

Where to start with our tale of woe? The second day we heard suspicious gear-grinding noises in my car as we went in and out of four-wheel drive. The next day the front differential went out, leaving us with no 4x4 for the last 300 kilometers into Faya. We were, fortunately, beyond the worst of the dunes, but didn't know that, so we worried just the same. Leaving Faya two days later, the rear differential went out on the same vehicle, stranding us for twenty-four hours in the open sand while the vehicle that still ran returned to Faya for parts. The next day, having gotten the car back on the road by noon, we rolled into Ounianga Kébir late, around 6:30 p.m. The driver inexplicably took the accursed car down a steep sand bank to where we intended to camp and rolled the car, which then was out of commission once and for all.

Using our cell phone, Nasour got permission from the company director to hire a replacement car locally. Driven by its owner, it was filthy and had no spare tire, no muffler, and no shock absorbers. On the other hand, the driver was the best sand driver we had the entire trip. The director sent two replacement cars to meet us in Fada, and that proved to be his only wise action of the trip: The second of the vehicles we'd had leaving N'Djamena proceeded to lose its right side brakes, the gas filter, the muffler and manifold both, and the steering engagement on the right-hand side as well. It was relegated to limping after the two replacement cars. I won't bore you with the minor stuff. Suffice it to say that we spent about forty hours of daylight doing car repairs, four days' worth of what should have been driving and sightseeing time.

I've mentioned already our communications problems with Nasour, his contempt for the southerner Gerome, and his general "Father knows best" attitude. Worse yet, he didn't know the Fada region and the main tourist sights. First there was a great detour west from where we had overnighted due north of Fada, before swinging south and directly east again into the town. Was that geography driven? To avoid landmines? Our maps suggested a much shorter route, but we couldn't communicate clearly with Nasour to clarify. In the Ennedi itself, he had no idea where the principal rock-art site of Terkei was, circling a butte for an hour and a half only to find it five or six miles from where we'd camped. To no avail, we argued for using the GPS coordinates we had to go overland (it was a straight shot). And of course he didn't have anything to tell us about what we were seeing, but only took us to the sites themselves.

Philosophically, I mused to myself during the long drive back to N'Djamena, in one way all the headaches demonstrated what a Chadian company was capable of when it had no expat involvement. I had purposely chosen the local firm over the one other tour company, Italian, that does the trek, and had had an excellent recommendation from one friend who had had a good experience with them. But I couldn't help thinking that the local firm hadn't been able to maintain consistency in its operations. And that it wasn't equal to the challenge over time of managing organization, maintenance, and a customer orientation—the concepts being foreign to African cultures generally. I hope I'm not letting my own poor experience reinforce a stereotype.

But the negative memories fade quickly beneath the positive impressions. Everyone got home safe and sound, and no one got sick.

We maintained the intended route and, by driving through lunch and up to dusk every time the cars were working, we saw perhaps 90 percent of what we'd hoped to see, including all the major sites. Just today I picked up my photos.

Best regards,

Ambassador Chris

Life among the Nomads

December 14, 2003

It was back in May that the embassy was first contacted by the Association of Nomadic Herders. Some 5 to 15 percent of Chad's people are nomadic or seminomadic, depending on whose estimate you believe. This young association has established itself over the past six or seven years as the primary interest group representing these oft-forgotten folks. It has a central body in N'Djamena, and is trying to organize local associations in rural areas. It focuses on the several major needs of the nomad community, but has a particular emphasis on education. The group wanted a relationship with the embassy so that we would become attuned to this particular population and its needs, and so that we would support its development activities.

One of the group's first suggestions was that I visit the countryside with its leadership to see myself how the nomads live. The trip was finally organized for the week of December 8, for four days, in the Kanem region north of Lake Chad. We would go first to the main town, Mao, after a stop at a village en route. Our second day would be mainly around Mao, but would take us to overnight in a nomad *ferrick* (encampment) an hour outside the town. We would go on to an upcountry village, more nomadic settlements, and finally back to N'Djamena. Contrary to all our instructions, nine members of the association showed up to cram into two cars with me, Julie (an embassy colleague), and our two drivers. The chief organizers were Achta, an official from the Livestock Ministry, and the association president, Moubaschar.

So how do the nomads live? Very simply. On the road north from N'Djamena we passed several groups on camels, beginning their annual trek south. A family will have five or six camels and donkeys, and somewhere behind, a herd of cattle, goats, and sheep. The materfamilias sits atop one of the camels in a wicker cage, screens of cloth and hide protecting her from sun and view. Her perch can be wildly colorful. The household's all is packed on her camel and one or two other animals, including the poles and covers that make up the family home. There is no room for surplus goods. Any wealth is on the hoof or in the carpets and blankets atop the camels.

At one of our stops I was received inside a typical hut. It is perhaps twenty feet long and a dozen across. The support is a framework of poles that rise from the ground up to meet a ridgepole that runs the length of the structure. The ridgepole is supported by five or six thin upright posts that are painted with a curious design of dots and lines. Various tarps and blankets are thrown across the structure to complete it; sometimes the covering is of large screens woven from palm leaves. Five feet high in the center, the hut is entered by a round portal of three feet at one end. The floor is strewn with carpets and blankets. The lower coverings of the hut I visited were raised and tied to admit light and air. A few poles partitioned the very back of the hut, and it was stacked floor to ceiling with carpets and blankets. A few kitchen implements were in view, as well as a tin chest perhaps four feet in length, perhaps holding clothes. Nothing more. To sleep, people spread bedrolls out on the soft floor. Cooking is done outside over an open fire, and a few more cooking utensils were tied to the roofs of some of the huts. I've seen drawings of wood and hide huts from prehistoric archaeological sites in different parts of the world. This enclosure can't have been much different.

The settlement pattern is also standard. First, the area has to be one with sufficient grass for the animals, and a proximate well. Proximate can be several kilometers. If possible, the nomads seek a bowl or declivity in the topography to provide shelter from the wind. One or two extended families plant four to six huts together in a rough circle. There may be up to a dozen such encampments, associated with each other, spread over a kilometer or two.

Based on what I was served, the food is also rather simple and heavily weighted toward what can be produced in the ferrick itself. The hospitality offering is bouille, the milk beverage laced with millet and sugar that I have described before. This is also breakfast. The main meal will have milk and cheese in various forms, meat sauce, and perhaps chicken. The items from town include the millet or sorghum, which are made into boule, sugar, and tea. There may also be macaroni with cheese and meat. The only fruits we were served were dates and the pudgy, tasteless Kanem bananas from the *ouadis* [wadis]. The only vegetables were potatoes and dried tomato powder in the sauce. What I can't say is how much this offering would be scaled back from a special occasion to everyday fare.

The migration patterns of the nomads seem to be of two types. There are those nomads, in the areas where grass is more reliable, who stay mostly within the same zone. They will move from site to site, but not leave their district of the Kanem. In the second group are the ones who practice true transhumance. During the rains and shortly afterward, they are in the north. As the grass dries and disappears, they will trek hundreds of kilometers south, turning north again when the rains approach or begin. Both types of nomads will stay in a single location for several months during and after the rains. Their movements thereafter will depend on the grass and time in place may vary from a couple of weeks to a couple of months. At the first encampment, both groups will usually practice a little agriculture as well, a few rows of millet or sorghum to limit what they will need to buy from town.

We arrived at the first ferrick late, nearly 8:00 p.m., having gotten lost as dusk fell and having to drive from village to village seeking directions for a couple of hours. I was grumpy because we'd had a light afternoon lounging in an ouadi with Achta's friends, and could easily have left an hour early and avoided getting lost. We were given a typically warm welcome, with children singing and doing demonstration marching, and all the notables from the dozen surrounding ferricks there to greet us. We were shown into a two-room school made of sekko that would be our lodging. Emerging, I was further dismayed to see a goat on the fringes of all this—of course they would kill a goat to feed us, and by tradition we had to see it live before they slaughtered it, so the skinning and cooking would take hours. Still, the lingering evening proved to be the highlight of the trip.

After a small interim meal, most wanted to warm themselves by the campfire. Most of the children were still there, watching us from beside the school, but eventually one of the adults shooed them off. The women had gone into the school, and I now found myself by the fire with several of the men from our party. A fascinating discussion of nomad problems ensued. Comments bounced back and forth in French and Arabic, with hit-and-miss translation. Moubaschar made his usual point that the nomads weren't poor, but had to be convinced to market some of their cattle to tap their wealth and improve their lives. How did I think they could be persuaded? I, of course, had no better idea than he, but suggested demonstrations from where herders did sell their cattle, and perhaps prizes at local fairs to reward quality with extra high prices. And education, especially girls' education: How could you organize a continuous curriculum for children who migrated several times during the school year and didn't know where they would be going next and whether a school was there? Could we help mobile schools with some sort of English instruction? Could we assign Peace Corps volunteers to be nomadic with the herders and teach English? And the problems of health, especially for women who suffered miscarriages: Could we assist with a program like one Moubaschar had seen in Sudan to teach midwives better practices and, in turn, to get them to teach other midwives? What about talented women who were doing well in school? How could the nomads be persuaded to let them finish their education rather than marrying at fourteen or fifteen, and how could they develop a repertoire of acceptable careers for these women—as midwives, teachers, etc.?

The discussion wound on and on until midnight, when at last the goat was served. I was impressed by the emphasis on the problems of women among this group of men who by reputation don't think much of women. Perhaps it was Achta's influence, or perhaps they value their womenfolk more than we have been led to believe.

By the end, I had a very good picture of the nomads' priorities for development: water for animals and people, health care for both animals and people, and finally education. A pretty basic list.

On our third afternoon we arrived at Mellah II village. It was an hour's drive northeast of Mao through a rolling terrain of sandy soils held down by a light cover of dry, strawlike grass. A mile outside of town we were suddenly surrounded by several riders brandishing swords and whips. We followed and in a moment ground to a halt before the welcoming party—again the mass of children, and two groups of male and female notables as well. Here were many more men mounted on camels and horses, including the village chief. We alit to greet them all, and after handshakes and the children's song, I was given a horse to mount and ride the remaining mile into town. It wasn't too bad, considering I hadn't been on a horse in ten years or more.

Mellah II turned out to be a delightful village: clean, square compounds with typical Kanem houses within. These are one-story, from mud brick and stucco with the particular soft, chalky hue of the soil from the infertile ouadi bottoms where the raw material, i.e., dirt, is quarried. The oblong houses measure perhaps twenty by twelve feet and typically have a blue door in the center of the long wall, with one small, high window on each side of it, giving an anthropomorphic look. The doors and windows almost always face west, avoiding the bright morning sunlight but catching the last, low evening rays. We slept in these structures in both Mao and Mellah. The walls are thick, and they stay cool all day, at least in this season when temperatures don't go above ninety degrees. Julie was able to wander the streets and get inside a couple of the houses that were actually people's residences. They had a single room and were furnished with canopy beds, one for parents and one for all of the kids. Like the guesthouses, the floors were thick with layered carpets and mats. The homes of the more wealthy had an armoire, and the walls were covered floor to ceiling with large tin plates of the type food is served on. The simpler homes had only the beds. Stacks of folded cloth and a few other food utensils completed the furnishings. It was almost like a sedentary version of the nomads' huts.

Later in the afternoon, we met with two village associations—actually, with representatives from this and several surrounding villages. Even here, where we were told no foreigners had come in years, the presentation of woes was automatically the order of the day. First the men and then the women made their points. Human health, animal health, reforestation, poor soil, dearth of teachers, miscarriages, lack of water for animals and potable water for people. Only Mellah II had a potable well. One man deplored the need for a mosque, and another deplored the depredations of insects and birds upon the crops. The women echoed the men, with one citing the need for microcredit to encourage small commerce. These were well-organized groups with careful spokespersons, and they didn't beat around the bush but stated their needs clearly. And their needs weren't that different from those of the nomads.

The last day gave me a real sense of the isolation of these folks. Departing at 6:00 a.m., we drove three hours further north to another nomad encampment, and then all the way back to N'Djamena, for a total of sixteen hours on bumpy dirt tracks. I bemoaned the association's poor organization of the schedule for this final stint. But I also noticed something else about the group and its leaders. They are organizing the countryside. Achta and Moubaschar sat up late in Mellah talking with the men who had attended the meeting, noting names and launching another local constituent association. These guys are going to be not only an interest group but a political force as well.

Best regards,

Ambassador Chris

4

Politics

This book is intended as anything but a political and economic commentary on Chad during my years there. But no ambassador can be expected to forgo some comments on his conclusions in this arena. My summary thoughts stem from my overall experience. Because the letters are anecdotal, there is not always a specific correspondence with the comments in this introduction to chapter 4. Those grouped in this chapter, however, come closest to demonstrating the rationale behind my analysis.

Democracy

After a year or so in Chad, I was taken aback and amused during Washington consultations with an assistant secretary of state who seemed to think that, with enough effort, a functioning multiparty democracy could be implanted in countries like Chad in the near term, perhaps five to ten years. This ignores our own experience: It took 200 years, until the enforcement of the Civil Rights Act of 1964, before we had true democracy in the United States. Chad is supposed to leapfrog and do this in a decade? It can't, of course. For one thing, there is no financial base to support a nationwide opposition party to contest the government party. I certainly believe and hope they can do it faster than we did, but we're still talking probably decades. "Getting Off on the Wrong Foot" is one of the more analytical letters, which explores my conclusions about the prospects for democracy in a country like Chad. It challenges rather directly what was then the prevailing view in our foreign policy, i.e., that a flourishing multiparty democracy could be created within a decade or so.

Rebellion

Throughout the letters are references, sometimes cryptic, to Chad's festering rebellion. It was always simmering, sometimes of more and sometimes of less importance. The time that the country has been without an armed opposition since 1975 is to be measured in months, not years. Yet no one seems to want to break up the country. There is a nascent nationalism. That, by itself, is encouraging. The rebellions will likely fade if and when the country starts having good elections. "Waiting for the Other Shoe to Drop" describes the penumbra of rebellion over Chad throughout my tour. "Africa Wars" gives a more analytic treatment whose point of departure is the academic work of visiting speaker Dr. William Foltz.

The Hand of Government

For lack of means, the hand of government is fairly light in the countryside. It relies heavily on relationships with local authorities—traditional rulers and chefs de cantons—to govern. So people locally do have a good bit to say about their own governance. By way of contrast, when things get out of hand and the central authorities must intervene, it is often an overreaction, occasionally violent and bloody. This conclusion comes largely from my rural travels described earlier, but it deserves repeating along with the other political points.

The Regime

My comments about Chad's government and its leadership are, of course, personal and not official. And my judgment is, again not surprisingly, highly mixed. I find it admirable that President Déby brought relative peace and stability to the country after decades of nearly constant civil war, and that his tactics to prevent war's recurrence have been largely peaceful rather than violent. I am critical of continued corruption, and impatient with the lack of even modest infusion of real authority into Chad's democratic institutional trappings. You will see this in this chapter, and there are hints of it in others throughout the book. "Election Day" explores some of the manipulation by the Déby regime in order to retain power, and "The Changing of the Guard or Not" is illustrative of the regime's reluctance to experiment with even limited real democracy. "A State Dinner" describes both my amusement and boredom in attending such events and allows you to read through the lines about the residual cult of the "Big Man" in African politics.

Associations

One of the most encouraging things I observed is the propensity of Chadians in all parts of the country to form local associations, often for accomplishing very specific social or economic development goals or providing services, like garbage collection, that we would view as government responsibilities. In time, this kind of grassroots organization will be a boon to the country's political development. Again, the best evidence for this conclusion comes from my travels in the countryside. But if democracy is ever to grow in Chad, these local associations may well be the roots.

The letters make only limited mention of Chad's democratic opposition, this despite my routine of meeting with half a dozen of its leaders every six months and reporting to Washington on their views and activities. My distinct admiration for two or three of them notwithstanding, I recognized them as regionally or tribally based. There was not the wherewithal economically in the country to support a genuine national party in opposition to the government party.

A State Dinner in Chad

March 8, 2000

Nothing in Chad is ever set in stone.

The invitation read (in French): "On the occasion of the Conference of Heads of State of the Community of Sahelean and Saharan States, His Excellency Idriss Déby, President of the Republic, asks you to participate in a reception on Friday, February 4, 2000, at 8:30 p.m., in the gardens of the Presidential Palace."

The conference program, enclosed with the invitation, referred to a dinner at this time, no venue given. The day after the invitation came (i.e., the evening before the day of the event), we got a call alerting us that the venue might change.

But in the meantime, you're probably wondering what the Community of Sahelean and Saharan States (Cen-Sad) is. It seems to be a loose association of northern and central African countries of undetermined purpose. It is Libyan (i.e., Gaddafi) driven and financed. Stretching from Senegal in the west to Somalia in the east, it has all the correct, nebulous goals with respect to economic development, African unity, and mutually respectful security. For Gaddafi, of course, it is a mechanism for promoting his credentials as a pan-African leader, now that he has been snubbed as a pan-Arabic leader by the Middle Eastern countries—sort of a fan club for him. Chadian president Déby is kowtowing to Gaddafi a bit these days in return for military help in fighting the rebellion in the north. So Chad was just as pleased as punch to host the community's second annual heads of state meeting right here in beautiful (the words of the representative of the Organization of African Unity) N'Djamena.

In the final analysis, the event was indeed a dinner—and the venue changed to the national assembly building, the Palais du 15 Janvier. This was handy because the opening ceremony of the conference was held there too. I had showed up for the opening a few minutes before the 5:00 p.m. time on the invitation, but was told to go away and come back at 6:30 p.m. That turned out to be the ticket, and by shortly after 7:00 p.m., the conference was officially under way.

And may I digress for a moment to describe the opening ceremony? It is, after all, to be a shorter-than-normal letter this time. The opening was interesting for two things. First was the leadership: On the dais were President Déby, the Guide Gaddafi (it is frowned upon for official Americans refer to him as "president"), the representative of the Organization of African Unity, and the secretary of Cen-Sad. Seemingly no one wanted to assume the role of chairman. Déby seemed reluctant to assert himself, even though he was the host. The secretary would not presume to upstage either president, and Gaddafi was initially respectful of Déby's prerogatives on his home turf. But more and more Gaddafi moved into the breach in Déby's reluctance, and after half an hour was completely in the saddle.

The second interesting thing was the Gambian speech. Each of three new members of Cen-Sad was given the opportunity to make a statement of accession. While those of Senegal and the other were platitudinous and predictable, the Gambian president's was remarkable. It was completely retro—something I might have expected from a Marxist sympathizer during the height of the Cold War. He began by enumerating the long list of imported *isms* that African countries have accepted from abroad. He began with colonialism, continued through independence, democracy, the free market economy, and ended up with globalism. It gave him no pause to include colonialism and independence as birds of a feather. But his point was that in each case, the African countries had accepted these *isms* with no understanding of what they were, or any effort to question their validity in the African context. His subtext was that, therefore, outsiders were completely responsible for the contemporary problems of this continent—all in all, a commentary of 10 percent truth and 90 percent fictitious ideology, just the sort of demagoguery certain African leaders have used for two generations to obscure useful debate.

Since the opening ran until close to 9:00 p.m., I was relieved to hear that the dinner would follow immediately afterward in a different part of the same building. So I moseyed on over, chatting up my Algerian and Nigerian counterparts en route.

The banquet hall was a large room with two-story-high ceilings and architectural touches that betray the building's origins as a gift from the mainland Chinese (Chad has since recognized Taiwan instead, in return for several roads, a bridge, and major development projects in agriculture and education). At one end of the room was a modestly elevated head table set for nine or ten. The main floor was covered with about sixteen long tables in two tiers, each seating up to thirty people. There appeared to be two buffet lines, each having a drink stand adjacent to it.

We seemed to be waiting for something. The heads of state perhaps? In the meantime, the staff brought bottled water and bread. I was seated with the minister of justice on my left, another lesser known minister on my right, and the Algerian ambassador across. A significant sampling of the 400-plus seats were untaken. I wanted to joke to one of the ministers that it was like being in jail: We were being given only water to drink and bread to eat, and we couldn't leave. But I contained my effort at wit; I thought the attempt at humor might cause offense.

It turned out indeed to be the heads of state who were holding things up. After a good hour they showed up, fought their way through a crowd of photographers who came out of nowhere, and filed up to the head table. One was missing: the Sudanese. After about ten minutes more he showed up as well, and finally—closing in now on 10:30 p.m.—we seemed ready to get the show on the road.

At a sign from President Déby, the head table rose and descended to the nearby buffet table and were helped by the four or five attendants behind it. Simultaneously, to an invisible signal, the mass of people packing the second tier of tables behind me stampeded the other buffet table across the room. The presidents, meanwhile, retreated. Gaddafi, I noticed, carried back no plate, but later someone brought one to him. Had it been pre-tasted as a security precaution?

Then it was our turn. All of us from the first tier of tables descended on the buffet line that the presidents had just left. I'd supposed we'd have been called table by table, but no such luck. It made the wedding scene in *The Graduate* (or was it *Goodbye Columbus*?) look like a family picnic. As nearly 200 people jostled their way around the twenty-foot-long table, what you got depended on where you stood. Then the plates ran out. Someone appeared with more—salad size. Ultimately, I ended up with a little hunk of camel and a few spoons of the couscous with which the beast had been stuffed for roasting. Not bad. The camel tasted like beef, only tougher, and the couscous was delicious if overly salty. Besides, in view of the paucity of the serving, I could eat again at home.

As I munched I noticed the security measures undertaken to protect the head table—mainly, I supposed, Gaddafi. Between us and them had emerged a solid line of motley security guards strung across the end of the room. I say motley because of their irregular, disheveled garb. There were one or two Chadians in fatigues with Kalashnikovs swung over their shoulders. The other dozen were Libyans in street dress. Some wore shirts or sweatshirts with jeans. Some were in the gray polo shirt and chinos that matched numerous others around the room.

Actual consumption of food took a relatively brief period of time in proportion to the overall length of the festivities; i.e., the presidents and everyone else were finishing up before 11:00 p.m. At about this time, I saw waiters bring a huge green and white cake (Libya's colors—also those of Nigeria, which wasn't represented here), followed by more waiters with trays of coffee cups. Suddenly, however, the presidents rose and quickly retired. We rose too, first in respect, and then to mob the narrow exit and find our cars. We were free, and it was only 11:15 p.m.!

The last wrinkle of the evening was the departure. By the time we reached the front steps of the palais, Presidents Déby and Gaddafi were long gone. But there was a wait while the other heads of state embarked ceremonially. In each case, a Volvo stretch limo sped forward, stopped, and backed up to the steps for the dignitary to enter. Meanwhile, two or three vehicles had pulled in front of the Volvo and two or three more were waiting to follow. In this way each president or head of delegation went away with his own little motorcade. Then the prime minister left, then the commander in chief of the army, etc. As the first mass of "civilian" vehicles pulled up, I spied my ever-alert driver, Chaibo, in my car on the far side of the column. I threaded my way through the vehicles in a most unambassadorial way, jumped in, and off we went. So quick was Chaibo with his shortcuts that, near to the embassy and my residence, we had to stop at a checkpoint for the last of the presidential motorcades to speed by us from the oncoming direction. We were home by 11:45 p.m., not too bad since I'd been led to fear 1:00 a.m. or worse.

Ambassador Chris

March 8, 2000
P.S.

My novel, over a year in the works, is now finished. Would any among you who have become the natural audience for my literary endeavors like to read a draft? I will welcome some quasi-sympathetic constructive criticism. If you'd like to begin receiving the book in fifty-page installments, drop me a line or an e-mail (goldthwaitce@yahoo.com). A couple of you will not escape no matter how hard you try. My goal is to begin circulating the draft in search of a publisher during the summer.

Waiting for the Other Shoe to Drop—Perhaps

March 26, 2000

African time. Those of us who have lived on the mother continent often joke about it, for here things move slower. Time is measured not in minutes and hours, but in days, weeks, and months. I remember a party I went to back in Lagos. It was called for 8:00 p.m.; I went at 9:00 p.m. to be on the safe side, only to find that the hostess (one of our embassy's foreign service nationals, or FSNs) was still out shopping; she came back around 9:30 p.m., and it was 10:00 p.m. before the next guest—also American—arrived. For us Americans this is particularly frustrating. We live by the clock not just at work, like the Germans, but also at home. We measure our self-worth by how busy we are, our overtime, and how much our work encroaches upon our private lives, or as a last resort, how tightly we organize our private activities and social life. What do you mean that this might not get done today, that we might not get news of that until tomorrow?

It sure ain't like that over here. Progress is slow, if at all. The issue of time is not how to cram everything into it, but rather how to fill it at all. Work? In Chad's real economy, underemployment is such that no one has enough to do to constructively fill an eight-hour day. (Admittedly, the women stay a lot busier than the men.) So work devolves into a social activity. There is a time for toiling in the fields, and a time for idling with one's wares in the market, selling a little today and a bit tomorrow, gossiping leisurely all the while with the other vendors in adjacent stalls. And the attitude carries over into the government offices, where the pace picks up only a little, and where dearth of financial resources to invest in programs to accomplish anything reinforces the attitude that all can await its own good time.

Here in Chad, time relapses from the man-imposed rigor of the schedule and "to do" list to the natural cycle of the day and the year.

Just over two weeks ago, the news from the Tibesti on Radio France International, the French equivalent of Voice of America, quoted the Paris spokesperson of the rebels, who said that the government had launched a major offensive and been beaten back with huge losses (huge by Chadian standards—200 killed and as many wounded). After a few days, the government here issued a terse statement acknowledging some fighting, but saying that its forces in the north had the situation in hand—a juxtaposition guaranteed to stimulate both the N'Djamena rumor mill and the opposition press. They, of course, had, respectively, time and columns to fill. The opposition press was jubilant, writing openly in ways that suggested it was only a matter of time before the government would crumble before the momentum of the rebellion in the north and the opposition here in the capital. The president could only contemplate defeat or resignation, etc., etc.

At the end of that week, in the course of Saturday, I learned that the French ambassador had been declared persona non grata. (The press sympathetic to the government later allowed that he had raised eyebrows for a variety of reasons, most recently fanning rumors favorable to the rebellion.) By the time that evening that I had cohosted a dinner—where the French ambassador showed—and had moved on to a private party, the expat community was clearly on edge. The news created the apprehension that a change of regime and perhaps several days of disorder in the capital were imminent. At the SIL church service the following morning, Luke G., who led the service, began with a summary of the news of the fighting and the French ambassador's expulsion, asking that we pray for peace in this country that has known at least thirty years of civil war in its forty of existence. Poised we were for the other shoe to drop. The embassy wrote its cables, the community made its contingency plans. We held a "town hall" meeting for our small American community, chiefly to dampen rumormongering and speculation.

Nearly two weeks have passed. Nothing much has happened. There has been no new fighting in the north. The president returned from the north and was given wide publicity on government TV and radio as he attended Eid services at the Grand Mosque and received Moslem dignitaries. Every day brings its reports and rumors, some alarming and some not. But nothing much has happened. If there are great developments in the wind, they are coming on African time. I am reminded that in Africa, as in China, patience is everything—the supreme virtue.

And it is for me a frustration in the true American sense. My colleagues and I have all these ideas about things we can do here, mainly in development assistance, and, ultimately, things that might advance our policy objectives in areas like democratization. But with everyone who would hear my pleas for resources also hearing the reports on French radio that things are increasingly grave here, the timing isn't right for me to make my pitch. What to do? How to invest *my* hours that I'd hoped to spend developing and selling development initiatives to the folks back home?

On the economic front, where the salient issue is petroleum development, we are also watching and waiting. Last summer, I understood that by the time I got here the project would be signed, World Bank loans voted, and Esso and its partners ready to break ground. It hadn't happened by the time I arrived, because additional concerns about the impact on the environment and local population needed to be addressed. Then, in early November, the private partners aside from Esso withdrew. Since then Esso has been trying to reconstitute the consortium. One new partner has signed. Chevron seemed poised to take the remaining share. They visited here, and I thought they were all ready to sign on. That was a month ago. Now I hear that this weekend all the companies are sending their representatives back to Chad, that Chevron is finally satisfied and ready to go. The end at last of the saga? We'll see. And even then, the World Bank board still has to vote on its loans. If it doesn't come together soon, the consortium won't be able to order equipment to start work in the next dry season, and everything will slip another year. Ah, well. When I show frustration, Les or someone else reminds me that this project has been talked about since the late 1960s, shortly after Chad's independence. Everyone agrees that it *will* go forward—someday.

My expat friends outside the embassy are calmer now. The rumors flow much faster than life itself in the capital. I make my official calls. But nothing seems to be happening. There is enough concern still to distract folks from what they should be doing, but there is nothing new on the military or political front to bring things closer to resolution. African time triumphant.

So life goes on in N'Djamena. After all, only a fraction of its population is politically attuned, and even less in the other towns. There is a strike right now at the abattoir for the city over whether the newly imposed value-added tax should apply to meat. That is affecting life here more than the politics and rebellion, since there is no red meat in the market and this is a meat-eating people. The traffic in the street is the same. There are fewer soldiers in town since more have been sent north, but the traffic police still stop cars to check for documents and extract a small dash from those drivers whose are irregular. There have been a couple of burglaries of expat homes, but that too is business as usual. Will the other shoe drop at all?

Death goes on as well. A couple of mornings ago, Alphonse M., one of my household employees, didn't show at 6:50 a.m. to make my breakfast. I did for myself, and a little after 7:00 a.m., Obert M., the butler, arrived earlier than usual for him. Alphonse, he allowed, was at the hospital. His daughter was near death. She had been severely injured in a traffic accident a month earlier—one leg and an arm badly mangled. Now, Obert indicated, she would die. He had just been with them and it was inevitable.

Shocked, I asked Obert to keep me informed if he heard anything from Alphonse. I didn't ask why no one had informed me earlier. Only half an hour later, Alphonse was there, asking to see me. His daughter had died. I offered what condolence I could. There had in fact been a misunderstanding. He had told me of the accident earlier, but I hadn't understood that it was his daughter who had been involved, both his and my French being imperfect. He went on. Could I lend him CFA 60,000 (a little less than $100), and arrange for an embassy truck to take the body from the hospital to his house? My African experience with rip-offs notwithstanding, I agreed on the spot. Alphonse said he would let Obert know of the details of the funeral, wake, etc.

At lunch Obert told me that the daughter still lived. She had *repris vie*, or resumed life. But the outlook was still dismal. It was doubtful she would survive. My cook, who served dinner in the evening, knew nothing more. In the morning Obert told me the young woman had expired about the time I was eating my evening meal.

In the course of the day, I determined that the one thing I could do to support Alphonse in his loss was to show up at the wake at his house after the funeral. Les confirmed this for me. Here the custom is to organize the burial immediately, and to be at home for callers for two or three days after the death of the family member. With a two-hour delay (African time), the funeral itself took place at 3:00 p.m., and our FSN grapevine told me by a little before 5:00 p.m. that the family was back at their house in the southern part of the city. So off I went.

Turning off the main road that leads south from the embassy, and up an unpaved side street, we entered Chagoua, the southernmost *quartier* of the city. Alphonse's house was about three blocks in from the artery. Nearing it, I saw an agglomeration of people sitting on a hodgepodge of benches and chairs on the side of the street opposite from what the driver told me was Alphonse's house. About forty people were assembled, I would guess, all men.

I alit and approached Alphonse. He rose, as did most of those around him. He took my hand and I hugged him—too demonstrative, I later concluded, but perhaps excusable for an expat. Those around him rose as well; some approached me, and I shook hands with them. Alphonse motioned to me to sit immediately to his right, the place of honor. A gentleman who had been there quickly scuttled over to make room for me. He introduced himself—the newly named minister of health, three days on the job. A citizen of Alphonse's village, he would of course be here for the wake. He spoke proudly in English, being a former instructor of our language at the university.

The placidity of the occasion was what struck me most. I felt relaxed. I didn't need to do or say anything, but only abide a while somberly. Sporadically, I spoke with Alphonse on my left or with the minister on my right. But there was no expectation. Some of the guests were silent, sitting for a quarter of an hour without uttering a word. Others spoke among themselves, even joked and smiled, not unlike a wake back home. Obert was there, and Ozias, our motor pool dispatcher. I felt that by simply sitting there for a suitable length of time, I would somehow contribute something. Les had said fifteen or twenty minutes, but my gut told me I needed to stay longer. But it was all so relaxed that I didn't mind.

To pass the time, I looked at the street life. For N'Djamena, it was a middle-class neighborhood. Most buildings were mud-brick adobe, one or two stuccoed. The compounds seemed to be thirty-by forty-foot rectangles with little courtyards behind a gate, the rest of the space occupied by the dwelling. A vendor passed, carrying a few shirts and other garments on hangers. Goats played and foraged in the piles of debris and garbage a few feet from us. One kept picking determinedly at the stalks of a tree branch, ignoring the leaves on the twigs. A little girl of eight or nine ran up to the gutter the goat had just deserted, pulled up her dress and down her panties, squatted for barely a minute, and ran off pulling the panties up in route. Alphonse told me that behind the wall to my left was the local elementary school. He indicated that one of his children still attended. I said that there were many people here; he agreed with a sweeping gesture toward the group of men around us, and said the women were across the street in the compound with his wife. Women passed with babies on their backs and loads on their heads. Pairs or trios of young men went by as well, some wheeling bikes. There were no cars, but an occasional motorbike trundled past. Some men were working to string an electricity connection from a power pole to the house adjoining Alphonse's, seemingly the only one in the block to be so blessed. The temperature was not unpleasant, and a slight breeze stirred the leaves of the neem tree in front of me. Dusk began to fall.

I sat for a good forty-five minutes. I spoke a word or two sporadically with the minister, and what he said confirmed for me that Alphonse was Christian, which I'd assumed from the locale. His and Alphonse's people were from the same southern village, where they had been educated by Christian missionaries, some of them American. Not a word about the struggle in the north, a thousand klicks from N'Djamena and even further from these folks' homeland in the south. Finally, after the departure of some of those who'd been there when I arrived, I arose to make my farewells. I did no more this time than shake Alphonse's hand with both of mine and could tell from his sad eyes and sagging lips that he appreciated my coming. In the rearview mirror I saw that the minister had arisen in my wake to depart as well; he'd shown me the respect of awaiting my own going.

N'Djamena, we hear, has had so many funerals of late—unnecessary ones due to the fighting in the north. Here, the froth of speculative rumor and opposition journalism and government statements yields to the pain that I saw in Alphonse's face: that of parents who bury their children.

Whither Chad? Does a denouement loom that will end the year-and-a-half-old rebellion in the north? Decisively, one way or the other? Can one side or the other muster the strength to defeat the other? Or will African time win? By which I mean a military stalemate in the north, a period of continued political tension, but a point at which people eventually realize that no change of government is imminent and gradually begin to return to the business at hand. I'm placing no bets. As much as we Americans yearn for activity and closure and certainty, we must remind ourselves that we are in Africa, after all.

Best regards,

Ambassador Chris

Africa Wars

May 20, 2000

Chances are that if you've seen Africa in the headlines lately, it had to do with fighting: The breakdown of the peace accord in Sierra Leone. The outbreak of war between Ethiopia and Eritrea. The violent and bloody farm occupations in Zimbabwe. And the perpetual chaos in the Congo. Even here in remote Chad, as I've mentioned in earlier letters, we have a growing rebellion in the north. All in all, by my count, about half of the countries on the continent are in armed conflict, involved in foreign military interventions, suffering internal rebellions or serious civil strife. What explains such a high propensity to try to settle conflict through violence? How to understand it, let alone try to do something about it, as valiant US and UN policymakers attempt?

Many more experienced minds than mine have tried to develop some basis for comprehension. Two weeks ago we were visited by Dr. William Foltz, a Yale professor and one of the preeminent students of conflict in Africa. I listened to one of his lectures. He cited a number of factors, focusing on the transition from the era of coups d'états in the early years after independence to today's much bloodier fighting in civil war and similar violence. He cited the availability of weapons and the control of salable resources by governments and heads of state, which finance the purchase of more weapons. He noted the accumulation of enormous populations of irredentist refugees beyond the borders of their own states. He pointed to the increased sophistication of national armies, and the deteriorating economies of the countries they inhabit. Even the end of the Cold War has played a role, Dr. Foltz posited, since Russian and American interest provided a certain discipline to the regimes they supported. All true, but does this describe the causes of conflict, or only why it is more violent today than before?

Over these past several weeks I've been reading a novel by a Chadian writer, Ali Abdel-Rhamane Haggar, entitled *Le mendiant de l'espoir*, or *The Beggar of Hope*. Haggar is a Chadian blue blood, related to the sultan of the tribe that controls the government. He is in prison—a white-collar prison, of course—because when he was put in charge of one of the country's leading parastatal enterprises, ostensibly he wasn't cooperative enough (in milking it). His book describes his experiences as a student in the old Soviet Union. From that vantage point he looks back and describes the root divisions between Chadians at home, even as they cling to each other abroad: tribalism and corruption. Haggar, then, adds another dimension to the problem, but still doesn't describe its full range.

After eight months here, I can hardly claim to provide a better answer than these folks. But what is clear to me is that the problem is more complex. During Foltz's lecture, I jotted down some of the things that he didn't mention: ethnicity, a tradition of fighting, the fact that people have very little to lose, corruption, lack of results from government's actions, lack of experience with and faith in democratic institutions. Some of these things came up in the questioning after his lecture, and some repeat Haggar's points.

As much in an effort to clarify my own understanding of conflict in Africa and in Chad as to pretend that I can explain it to you, this Chadletter tries to take a look at the culture of violence here. It's focus is Chad and the reasons for the rebellion in this country, although I suspect that lots of the points are generalizeable. The analysis I offer isn't a tidy academic product; in trying to organize my thoughts and points, I can't avoid overlap and duplication. But below I try to categorize the factors conducive to violence under things that divide the country, the influence of history, lack of alternatives for resolving conflict, and what I call the low cost of starting over. So here goes.

In an earlier letter I referred obliquely to Chad's nascent sense of nationhood. While there isn't much that unites Chadians, no one seems to want to dismember the country. Political dialogue is in terms of what is or isn't good for Chad, not some subunit. But beneath the surface, the myriad divisions in the country are clear: If a journalist writes about "Chad," you can still predict his or her slant by ethnicity, region, or something similar. So to begin with, it is important to understand what divides Chadians.

Perhaps ethnicity is the starting point. Like most African nations, Chad is a hodgepodge of ethnic groups confined or split by artificial, colonially created borders. If language is the measure, some 120 are spoken by 200 ethnic groups among 7.5 million people. So language itself is a division between these groups—French and Arabic, the *lingua franca,* are both imports, even if several of Chad's northern ethnic groups consider themselves "Arabs." Against the background of a precolonial environment in which there was little central authority, localized ethnic affinities and even village affinities loom large in terms of what people here believe ties them to one another. (Alphonse wasn't so impressed that the minister came to his daughter's wake, because they are from the same village and it is expected; he was impressed that I came, because I'm not.)

Another overlay of divisions involves the north/south, Muslim/ Christian, and herder/farmer dichotomies. I group these together because people who identify themselves as northerners tend to be Muslim and pastoralists, in contrast to farming people who have been settled in the south for generations and are mainly Christian, with some animists. But the picture has become much more complex because in the drought years of the eighties, many northerners moved south to settle permanently among the local population. And, of course, all groups have urbanized some. Transhumance during the dry season complicates things—pastoralists drive their herds south toward residual grass and water as it becomes hotter and dryer in the north. A week ago, the local papers described how the herders had burned a village not far from N'Djamena after migrating herders and the local farmers had quarreled. The southern *jachère* system also invites trouble with the migrants: letting land lie fallow for a couple of years invites the herders to graze their cattle on it, even if technically it belongs to another village or family. The fact that northerners replaced southerners as the dominant governmental elite some twenty years ago creates an additional tension. And religion—amid general tolerance, tensions arise when either Christians or Muslims are too aggressive in proselytizing or try to extend their moral codes into the realm of law.

Even the political parties divide people. They are fragmented, mainly locally or ethnically based. Aside from the ruling party there is no truly national party. The opposition, hateful of the government as it is, remains too internally suspicious to field a united front against the governing party.

So perhaps you begin to see how much divides people here. With this much baggage, it is even more surprising that there are not separatist movements. Perhaps it is the poverty and isolation of Chad that deters regions from thinking that they could possibly be better off as separate states.

History has also played a role in encouraging, or at least legitimizing, violence as a road to political change. My purpose in these next few paragraphs is not to relate Chad's history, but only to enumerate the incidents of violence, showing how much the use of force has been a part of politics here. To begin, you have to go back before colonization and at a minimum point to slave raiding by northerners and Sahelean Arabs of the more densely inhabited southern regions. And the French experience was pernicious, beginning with the conquest largely by black African *tireurs* from West Africa under a handful of French officers. These troops cut a swath of blood and scorched earth across the continent, eventually meeting up with the Lamy forces to effect the occupation of the N'Djamena region. This instilled a mistrust not only of the white colonialists but also of unknown Africans. And violence marked the early decades of French rule, when the French forcibly resettled most of the southern population and introduced cotton production.

But perhaps the colonial overlay—and afterward, the Cold War—had a more subtle impact as well. In an archaeology magazine I read, I stumbled across a statement characterizing our era as a "time of increased and increasing focus on national, ethnic, racial, and religious identities." So perhaps along with everything else, the West's focus on all of the divisions I've cited has inadvertently legitimized the African focus on them—and impeded the development of a sense of nationhood.

The postindependence era has been, if anything, even worse. Chad achieved independence on August 11, 1960. François Tombalbaye, a southerner, became president and quickly became dictatorial. In September 1963, Muslims rioted in N'Djamena and Am Timan. By late 1964, Tombalbaye had jailed most opposition politicians, and by 1965, a full-scale insurgency by northerners (the FROLINAT, or Front de Libération Nationale du Tchad) was under way. The French helped to quell the uprising temporarily in 1968, but by the early 1970s it had flared up again. By 1973, Tombalbaye had begun to jail suspect military officers even as Libya occupied the Aouzou Strip along Chad's northern border. Tombalbaye, ever more desperate, resorted to an often forceful "southernization" policy for the government, and in 1975 he was killed in a military coup. Thus passed Chad's first fifteen years of independence.

General Malloum, another southerner, became president. The FROLINAT soon resumed its opposition under Hissène Habré, and by 1978 the group had gained control of much of the north. This time Habré had the help from the French. During 1979, two additional armed opposition groups emerged, the FAN (Forces Armées du Nord) and the FAT (Forces Armées Tchadiennes). The FROLINAT took power under one general Goukouni, but the fighting with the FAN and FAT continued, and Goukouni was increasingly undermined by his erstwhile ally Habré. In 1980 Libya intervened to support Goukouni, and Habré was defeated. But when the Libyans withdrew in 1981, it didn't take Habré long to renew the fighting, OAU (Organisation of African Unity) peacekeepers notwithstanding. In 1982 Habré took N'Djamena and the presidency. Now the situation was reversed, with Habré, a northerner, in control from N'Djamena southward and Goukouni in the north, and a French interdiction line drawn between them along the sixteenth parallel, just north of N'Djamena. As Habré tried to consolidate his support in 1984, an insurrection developed in the south. He put it down bloodily, losing much of his popularity in the process, but by the end of 1985 he had restored control. By this time, France and the United States had both come around to supporting Habré, in opposition to Libya. Sporadic fighting with the Libyans broke out in the north in 1987, but most Chadian northerners were now behind Habré. In 1989 Habré uncovered a plot by one of his key generals, Idriss Déby, to overthrow the government; Déby fled to Sudan. Tensions with the Libyans arose again, even as Habré introduced a new constitution and was elected to a seven-year term as president. Habré turned increasingly to bloody repression to maintain his rule, actions for which he is today on trial. The indictment against him claims he was responsible for 40,000 deaths, many through indescribable torture.

In 1990 Déby invaded from Sudan and, after initially being repulsed, found his way to N'Djamena clear, as the unpopular Habré's forces simply melted away in front of him. Habré fled, taking a plane full of gold and hard currency with him to Senegal, where he's been reposing ever since. Déby announced preparations for a new constitution and transition period, but even in 1991 he had to put down a coup and repulse an invasion by forces sympathetic to Habré. In February 1992, there was an unsuccessful coup attempt, and by May rebellion was brewing again north of Lake Chad. Another coup attempt failed in June, and there were strikes with some violence and heavy repression in July and again in October. Coup attempts were made in January and October 1993, but overall things were beginning to calm down.

It was only in 1994, I would say, that Chad's civil war actually ended, after twenty-seven years. After an International Court of Justice ruling that year, Libya returned the Aouzou Strip to Chad. Déby put in place a new constitution and held elections in 1996. Then came 1998, which saw both a brief, quickly repressed outburst of rebellion in the south, and in October the beginning of the current rebellion in the Tibesti. Although by no means a certainty, Chad again faces the danger of relapsing into civil war or experiencing yet another violent change of government. In forty years of independence, Chad has seen barely a dozen of peace.

Let me turn now to the conditions that encourage a resort to force of arms. Let's begin with the most basic of conditions, poverty: It is abject and there is little hope of escape, so naturally, people hear the appeal of radical change. Lack of communications is another factor. Without a road system or scheduled air service, with only a handful of phone lines (only six crosscountry conversations can be carried on simultaneously), there is little central control over what happens in the countryside. When things get to the point where the government must mobilize and intervene, it is most likely done with overreaction. The light hand of the government cuts other ways as well: Leaving authority to traditional leaders, so-called chefs de cantons, may invite corruption. And most certainly the paucity of government services is evident and invites resentment.

I mentioned at the outset Foltz's point about the huge numbers of weapons floating around. Chad suffers from this as well, with arms as available as in our own country, or more so. Moreover, there is a tradition of violence as a means of resolving conflict, especially among the northerners.

Against these factors one must in fairness weigh the exhaustion of this people after a generation and a half of bloodshed. Especially in the south and in N'Djamena, people are tired of the fighting and the conflict. Overwhelmingly, they want peace, and they want to get on with their lives. But it takes only a disgruntled few to perpetuate the conflict.

Another important factor is the lack of alternatives, or at least mistrust of them. Every government of Chad has suffered from a certain level of corruption and the tendency for the tribe or group in control to use the opportunity to steal enough to prosper when they lose power. This has resulted in the general nonperformance of government; people see no results from its action on the problems that afflict them. Health clinics and schools are built only when outside aid is available, etc. Political parties are equally weak and are nearly all regionally or ethnically based—only the ruling party is truly national. Yet for all the reasons that divide the country, the opposition parties eschew coalitions that would give them a real chance to contest for power.

All of Chad's democratic institutions are new, untried, and unempowered. Even if it wished to, the leadership would not have the money to make the judiciary and the national assembly work effectively. The experience with elections has not inspired confidence. A by-election held last fall in Koumra was so obviously fraudulent that the Constitutional Council, despite the heavy influence of the government, threw out the results and required a rerun. Many questions linger about the presidential and legislative elections back in 1996 that put the current leadership in office.

All this means that the opposition has no confidence in the institutions through which it is supposed to be able to express itself, first verbally and, ultimately, to the point of winning power with the ballot. The peaceful opposition chooses to use the free press as its chosen vehicle for expression (Chad does have one of the freest presses in Africa). It spends little effort in trying to make the other institutions work. There is no confidence in the electoral process, the ability of the parliament or the courts to check and balance the executive, etc. Those who are totally frustrated take to the *maquis* instead.

And there are vague, unquantifiable factors. For Western observers, it is painful to see this country forever going back to the drawing board and starting over with a new government, a new national reconciliation process, a new constitution, and a transition period of several years into a new titularly democratic process. But in fact this costs very little in the eyes of many Chadians. Most people have very little of a material nature to lose, for they are too poor: The villager must replace his straw or mud-brick hut every few seasons in any event. And, as indicated above, there is little emotional or intellectual investment in the new institutions and processes that, over a generation perhaps, could bring some semblance of a democratic process where an opposition could effectively express itself.

We cannot forget, either, that in many parts of the country—mainly, but not only, in the north—we are dealing with the residue of a warrior culture. Violence is not simply a means for conflict resolution, but a certain exercise of force and use of arms is expected of young men. Relatedly, I'll bet that lots of the rebels in Togoïmi's bands are there simply out of boredom, seeking adventure. For with no jobs and no prospects of earning enough to start a family, the appeal of the *maquis* must be very great for lots of adventurous youth.

So where does that leave Chad? With an active rebellion in the Tibesti of the far northwest and an inactive "gang of fourteen," political leaders of various persuasions who are holding up in Cotonou in self-imposed exile. They are vocal, but are having only a modest impact on developments here. And folks here in N'Djamena wonder if they should ignore all this and try to move forward, or if they should pause and await, in African time, the unfolding of events.

Must Chad (or Africa) resign itself to a further cycle of seemingly interminable civil strife and violent changes of government? I can't say. But what is clear is that the vast majority of the people don't want this. We see it even in the statements of the virulently antigovernment opposition press. And that, despite all the depressing backsliding, at least is something.

Regards,

Ambassador Chris

Election Day

May 20, 2001

Dear Friends,

This letter is about Chad's second presidential campaign, which culminates today in the first round of voting. If no candidate scores a majority victory, there will be a run-off on July 1.

To give you some frame of reference as I tell the tale of this campaign, let me term it Shakespearean, first, because any good election has an element of drama, but more because in this election, the interplay of appearance and reality, that favorite theme of the Elizabethan bard, is so critical. We won't ever know the true result, who really won or lost. One could deepen the analogy with comparisons between the stage of development of Chad as a state and nation with that of sixteenth-century England, but that would digress from the main theme.

The campaign officially began April 20, a month before the poll, but its roots go back at least a year, and some would say five years, to the first election held in 1996. My last letter ["Africa Wars"] noted some of the steps leading up to these elections. Suffice it to say that several things cast shadows over the procedures as they emerged: an independent electoral commission (Commission Electorale Nationale Indépendante, or CENI) dominated by the regime, with no representation of civil society; delays in organizing that pushed the legislative elections back a year to 2002; and delays in starting the electoral census, i.e., the process of registering voters.

The census, indeed, seemed particularly egregious. Ultimately, it resulted in 4.6 million voters in a population everyone believed to be around eight million—implying either that the country suddenly had two million more citizens, or an age distribution absurd for a developing country with a high birthrate. The chairman of the ruling political party told me that Chad's only modern census in 1993 had dramatically undercounted people, especially in the northern desert and the Sahelian zone. An analysis published by the Chadian specialists who conducted the national census in 1993 suggested that, after extrapolating for population growth, the progovernment north was overregistered by a good half million souls, and the south underregistered by a couple of hundred thousand (some of whom, in fairness, seem to have later been added in). So already, at its outset, the campaign, was overhung by a certain air of unreality (read bias).

The six opposition candidates had huffed and puffed just prior to the registration deadline for candidacy, most demanding postponement of the elections until the census could be redone. Some threatened a boycott. Delay was, of course, a pipe dream, and the candidates one by one filed their papers. I interviewed them all, asking why they'd decided to run. Some, despite the deck stacked against them, simply refused to give the incumbent president a walk; one or two thought him so unpopular that there was a chance of defeating him.

I was just a little surprised that all the opposition candidates, and the president's party chief, so easily found time for me. The campaign seemed to kick off in slow motion; was it shell shock already on the part of the opposition at the odds they faced?

You deserve some sense of my own feelings in these early days. Having seen no improvement in the legislative conditions for the elections [see "The Roller Coaster" in the next chapter], having seen the travesty of the electoral census and heard the other complaints of the opposition candidates, I was inwardly angry. I set to the side a long cable that made the case for more bilateral aid for Chad; under these circumstances I couldn't in good faith argue for it. At about this time, I met with the president's senior civilian adviser as well, to talk about questions that we were examining before deciding to provide support to the elections process. While wanting ever so much to get involved, we remained mere observers, waiting to see if there was any way our tiny resources might actually improve the process and its transparency.

***

The campaign itself seemed subdued by American standards. There seemed to be three major activities: grassroots campaigning, *les meetings*, and tours in the countryside. Among the grassroots efforts, there seems to have been a good bit of *porte-à-porte*, door-to-door campaigning, at least in N'Djamena neighborhoods. But the major effort was kiosks, set up and manned day and evening. Here the *militants*, or party partisans, held court, offering food, drink, conversation, and campaign materials to the neighborhood residents who happened by. To me, this seems an ideal campaign tactic for Chadian conditions. It exploits the concept of African time—so many in the *quartiers* have time heavy on their hands. This offers them something concrete to do, a meal, and by engaging them it suggests to the unemployed or underemployed that they themselves have value—even if only at election time, someone wants them for something.

The ruling party with a $10 million war chest—enormous by Chadian standards—could do more kiosk work than all the other parties combined, and their stands were evident all over N'Djamena. But does that translate into votes, or is it mere appearance? Candidate Kamougué, a southerner and president of the National Assembly, says of President Déby and the people, "They'll eat his boule but vote for me!" A missionary youth I know tells me all his Chadian soccer-playing friends have been hired to man one of the Déby booths. But they hate him; those old enough to vote will all vote for someone else. So what is the reality beneath the surface? We have only anecdotes and hearsay; there is no independent gauge of public opinion in the country.

And the media coverage: Each candidate gets to make a three-minute statement on the public radio each evening. These, of course, are routine, repetitive, and dull. The news coverage itself is heavily weighted towards the incumbent president. The formula is for one or two of the earlier stories in the half-hour evening news to focus on some campaign activity of one or another of the opposition candidates, but for six or eight stories to cover the ruling party's activities. This conveys at one time the impression of much greater support for and activism by Déby and his folks, and also the notion that ultimately only what he does is truly newsworthy.

Early in the campaign the "independent" media commission laid down strict limitations on the private radio stations.

These I protested to the president himself. One radio station ran afoul of the rules and was threatened with closure, but in an amazing confirmation of Chad's freedom of the press, it negotiated a shaky compromise and has managed to continue its offensive election coverage right along.

One of the disappointing things in my conversations with the MPS (ruling party) chief and opposition candidates alike was the degree to which the dialogue focused on process rather than issues. The opposition candidates all wanted to emphasize the uneven playing field on which they contested this election; the clever MPS chief anticipated these complaints, for example, in demeaning the 1993 census for undercounting nomads and northerners who had seasonally gone south. But under prodding, a few issues surfaced: peace (i.e., ending the rebellion), the rule of law, ending corruption, and renegotiating cooperation agreements with donors that infringed on Chad's sovereignty.

But most of the campaigns were not focused on issues. Déby's is a case in point. It was what I'd call a momentum campaign. Every night there were announcements of new endorsements by leaders of tiny splinter parties, new regional endorsements, and defections by supporters of other parties. It reminded me a little of a tactic we used when I worked in an American presidential campaign as a college student: We plastered campaign stickers and posters all over the campus to create what our leader called a "Humphrey condition," that is, the illusion of broad support. So here, similarly, reports on Déby's campaign rallies (*les meetings*), always highlighted that this or that opinion leader urged a massive vote to put Déby in on the first ballot. It was a clever approach in its way, however much the repeated, vapid news stories made me want to gag. It suggested broad support, especially when leaders of particular ethnic groups or communities made their appeals. Even for nonsupporters it created the expectation of a first-round victory. So there was little on issues. And equally little from the other candidates. Only candidate Kebzabo's critique of the government for having conceded to the World Bank too much control over Chad's future oil revenues, and candidate Yorongar's call for a federalist state, had much play.

With my Western perspective, I found Déby's campaign particularly disappointing in this regard. Why? He has a decent record despite the government's faults, and in a fair, Western-style campaign, he'd have an excellent chance to build a coalition for reelection. First and foremost, he's kept this country more or less at peace for ten years, not a mean accomplishment in anyone's book. He's established the institutions for a democracy, weak and unempowered as they may be. And he's brought the oil project to reality after thirty years of false starts. The shame of it is that he and his circle didn't have the courage to throw the dice, risk alternance, debate the issues, and seek reelection on a level playing field. I think they would have won, enhancing their legitimacy and advancing true democracy in Chad. But perhaps I'm fooling myself about how well prepared the people here are to vote on the basis of substantive as opposed to communal factors. We'll never know. Here again the tension—the interplay—of appearance and reality, and the fear of losing power.

The last half of the campaign was livelier, but before turning to it, let me explain our ultimate decision not to provide any American support for the flawed process unfolding before us. I explained both to the foreign minister and to the other donors, and to a few political leaders privately, that in our eyes there were just too many questions about the integrity of the process. We did explore a last possibility: financing international observation of voting at foreign polling places. This was a sensitive area because it was widely believed that ballot stuffing at some 300 polling places in Sudan in 1996 had boosted the MPS vote considerably. A key reform in the electoral code had now limited voting to "the seats of Chadian diplomatic missions," i.e., embassies and consulates. This implied to us perhaps two dozen polling places in the handful of countries that are home to about 90 percent of the Chadians abroad—Sudan, Libya, Saudi Arabia, etc. We could handle this with our minuscule budget. But to make a long story short, the CENI told us that "seat" would be broadly interpreted even if not entirely in sync with the electoral code. There would still be up to 130 polling places in

Sudan—multiple stations in the embassy and consulate buildings, but also in other locations around the cities that housed these missions. This was another little fudge in favor of the incumbent candidate, whose ethnic group spills over into Sudan. The electoral code had given the appearance of real reform on this point, but in the implementation, it wasn't to be. We decided not to be a party to it.

If we were damping down, the rhetoric was getting shriller. Opposition candidates denounced hooliganism by supporters of the government party—vandalism of their local headquarters, stoning of their supporters, etc. The MPS made similar charges in return. The First Lady's car had been stoned during a drive through one of the southern neighborhoods of N'Djamena. Who to believe? Both? And the opposition candidates began to talk about what would ensue if the MPS stole the election: demonstrations, civil disobedience, riots. There were thinly veiled references to arms. Would it come to that? One candidate began to make predictions about his own first-round victory. He and the president couldn't both be right, especially in a field with five other candidates. Would outrage by the losing side rouse the Chadians from their political passivity, their revulsion of mass violence after the long history of civil war?

In these final weeks, I found myself inwardly rooting for the opposition, not because I think any one of its candidates is particularly more qualified than the incumbent president—I don't know that they are. But I love to see underdogs triumph over great odds, especially in the face of a manipulated process. I would view the need for a runoff as a step forward for democracy here. And not all the news was so bad. The six opposition candidates signed and announced a pact under which they would share the burden of election-day observation, and all agree to support whichever among them might face Déby in a runoff. I saw here a maturation in the opposition's thinking, some small growth in the democratic process. All would not be in vain, even if the result of the election were to turn out to have been fixed from the first.

An interesting sidebar concerned the role of the donors (i.e., aid donors to Chad) that were supporting the election. These were the United Nations Development Programme, France, and the European Union, with lesser contributions from Taiwan, Canada, and

Japan. One, and then another, opposition candidate leveled charges that the UNDP resident representative (sort of the ambassador from the United Nations to Chad), who was coordinating donor support, was conspiring to fix the election for the president by manipulating the computer programs for voting rolls and vote tabulation. It is well known that the gentleman is a great friend of the president, and the statistical specialists he brought in to do the computer work were from his native Ivory Coast. Were these charges all smoke being blown by a now desperate opposition, or was there some ember of truth beneath?

So here it is, election day. The questions are more plentiful than the answers. This is especially the case for us, since, not being contributors, we were cut out of the loop during the final, chaotic days of logistic preparations. For news, I finally visited my friend, the French ambassador, on Friday, and yes, things were falling into place by hook or crook, as expected. With only a few hitches, things were ready by this morning for the vote.

Who will win? There are absolutely no independent or reliable opinion polls or other gauges of national opinion, so we have no idea of the relative strength of the candidates. It's a good bet the president will come in first, and the most radical of the opposition candidates, Yorongar, seems to be building up steam for a second-place showing. The real question is whether President Déby will be forced into a runoff. To further confound things, the minister of the interior issued a decree yesterday proscribing the private media from providing partial results before the CENI releases full provisional returns, which it must do by June 3. Will the results be real, especially if they convey a first-round victory for the incumbent president? A margin of a percentage point or two over 50 would be doubtful, well within the margin of expected fraud. A margin of 10 percent would be more believable. But we'll never know the truth.

Will there be calm or violence when results are announced? Can't say. I just spent an hour driving around the city, watching the polling. Absolute calm. Moderate lines at the two dozen or so polling places I passed, but everyone waiting peacefully in African time for their turn. Why rush or shove when the waiting itself, chatting among your neighbors, is diversion? But is this calm itself deceptive with respect to what will occur when the results are announced?

So perhaps this election illustrates more than anything else the tension between appearance and reality in these nascent African democracies. The institutions are there, created with reverential care. But how to explain the accumulation of biases in favor of the ruling party and its incumbent candidate, which make the conclusion seem foregone? And the opposition, is it increasingly politic and sophisticated, as its compromises suggest, or is it ready to resort to crude, violent behavior, as its threats imply? What of the civility I observed in the people as I drove around—deeply felt, or a veneer ready to fall off if shaken by anger over faked results? Just how much has democracy been institutionalized here? How long before the essence will distill behind the forms? And what is fact and what fiction, ghostwritten by an incumbent power still too fearful to let itself be voted out of office? Shakespeare, I believe, would find African politics a field just as fertile as the lives and courts of the English kings for dramatic exploration.

Best regards,

Ambassador Chris

The Changing of the Guard—or Not

September 2, 2001

Big changes? In August, when Chad, like its French model, slips into a humid, hazy rainy season of vacations and inactivity? It certainly seems to be the case, however: In my embassy, two-thirds of the American staff has turned over. In the expat community beyond, we've seen almost as much rotation, including at the all-important French base, Épervier; and on the Chadian side, the inauguration of the president for a second term and the appointment of a new government.

In the Embassy

If I were a doctor, I would diagnose my embassy with Heraclitus syndrome. All is in flux, too much. Between May and October 2001, some two-thirds of the American staff will have turned over. The DCM and I remain; Ace and Les, our locally engaged Americans, stay on; a couple of others who've arrived within the last year will stay as well. But our admin and security officers, my secretary, our communicators, the consul/reporting officer, numerous marines— these are all turning over.

The disorder is epidemic in Foreign Service hardship posts. There is a strong genetic predisposition to the illness, since service regulations dictate two-year assignments here for all but the ambassador and DCM (these are three years everywhere). Inevitably, the accidents of timing of the individual rotations accumulate to override the neat, 50 percent a year norm, and create episodes of turnover fever such as we've suffered here this summer. Smaller posts, with only a dozen or two Americans, are especially susceptible (Chad, with twenty-five Washington-assigned Americans, is a largish small post). Recently, as the overall attractiveness of a Foreign Service career has declined, the service has been less willing to force assignments upon people, resulting in long gaps in filling slots in places like Chad.

The dysfunctions of the Heraclitus disorder are clear enough. There is little consistency in job performance at all but the senior level in the embassy. There is little institutional memory among the Americans. The successful achievement of mission goals depends more and more on locally engaged employees, who lack the perspective and attitudes, and sometimes the loyalties, of the Americans. And then there is the variation in applying regulations and policy as people rotate. It all serves to keep the embassy a little off balance and out of touch. The absurd extreme was reached earlier this summer when for a month, I, the ambassador, was the only Washington-assigned employee still here to do reporting and analysis.

But what looks like a genetic dysfunction wouldn't persist if it didn't also work to preserve the organism. For most Americans, even Foreign Service people, two years in a post like N'Djamena is a long time. There are the physical hardships: The power goes out and you have to endure the roar of the generator; if you don't boil and filter your water yourself and dust off the daily film of dust, you must endure the presence of a servant in your house to do it for you. Shopping is harder and Western foods rare and expensive. But the real hardship isn't these little inconveniences. It's the lack of accustomed diversions. No movies, fewer restaurants, only a couple of TV stations, no museums or parks on our scale, and lack of access to recreational outlets we'd consider automatic at home. That, and the small size of the anglophone community, is what begins to grind after two years. Time and again, I've seen people with what I consider to be the right, healthy attitude sour as the end of their second year comes round and they begin to count the days until departure.

The Heraclitus syndrome also implies an emotional burden for those left behind. We've barely gotten acquainted with folks, both in their work ways and socially, before they move off. In my case, it is all attenuated by the distance of being ambassador. But there are colleagues and families of whom I've genuinely become fond. Will I see them again after they've moved on? On the whole, I count myself and the embassy fortunate, because this time at least, the replacement folk seem uniformly optimistic, adventurous of attitude, and anxious to jump into their work. This is a rare blessing for an ambassador. But the sense of loss of friends, and their accumulated expertise, persists.

So the advantages of flux seem pale, like Plato's shadows, in comparison with continuity—his forms, perhaps. On one level, we continue to do our duty, deliver our démarches, and so on. But on another, we are constantly relearning the history and customs of this country. Our interpretation of events here suffers, our reactions are less on point. So as I find myself, after merely two years, among the most experienced of embassy officers, I admit the shallowness of my footing, the superficiality of my analysis. Always, it seems, we are dealing in trade-offs.

Among Other Expats

Many other expats are coming and going as well, of course. The French ambassador the other day complained of a turnover like my own. Even among the missionaries, who often stay in-country for decades, there is change. They take sabbaticals, so that several whom I met when I first came have been away for six months or a year, and are now returning. And some of those I've gotten to know best are now heading off.

Among the expats, it was perhaps the turnover ceremony for the commandant at the French base, Épervier, that told me the most about change and continuity in this country, for it incorporated a heady bit of colonial legacy. Here, on African soil, the ceremony was replete with European symbolism: The parity of the French flag with Chad's, the playing of *La Marseillaise*. The assembly of all the French troops in a square around the end of the airfield and their inspection, with tight salutes by the new and old commanding officers. Their formalistic comments, the awarding of medals, and the symbolic exchange of positions of the outgoing and incoming commandants. And watching all this while were the *anciens combatants*, the Chadians who fought in World Wars I and II under the French flag (they counted barely a dozen this time, about half the number at an Armistice Day assembly I attended two years ago, only weeks after my arrival).

In an odd way, the ceremony seemed to sum up the European, or Western, presence here since independence. We are never here permanently, but still exert an influence all out of proportion to our numbers and commitment. It matters when we come and go, as much perhaps for the leadership expected of us as for whatever skills we bring to share. Yes, the country's dependency has persisted, even if now not only on the former colonial power, France, but on multilateral organizations—the European Union as the other large bilateral donor, and the IMF and World Bank.

Is this dependency, the failure to break entirely from the colonial mode that I saw at Épervier, a disorder as well? I think it is more like an addiction, with its highs and crashes, for the country cannot do without the infusions of money and assurance from these outsiders. So it tolerates the residue of colonial symbolism as it does the advice of the aid-giving institutions. There is a deep ambivalence here—Chad is dependent and resentful, but not at all sure it can go it alone, absent either the foreign money or the advice. Nor is going cold turkey appealing to the leadership of developing countries, which still finds ways to benefit personally from the aid relationship. The broader political elite shares this ambivalence when the donors make access to supply, i.e., money, so easy when so many of the good jobs depend on it.

And in the Country Beyond

I've described the embassy's disorder as a change too constant. It prevents the development of depth of analysis and relationships that would help promote American objectives here, but it ensures renewal. And vis-à-vis the big donors, there is an almost narcotic dependency that persists forty years after independence. With respect to internal political change, Chad suffers schizophrenia. The presidential election and, perhaps even more, the recent inauguration are symptomatic.

It was clearer and clearer as the election unfolded that the powers that be would not risk real change, i.e., loss of control. But now they want to create the illusion that change had in fact been possible. This they need for legitimacy, especially in the eyes of Western donors. So the inauguration activities displayed an odd combination of both the inertia and centralized control typical of African politics, and elaborate, dissonant demonstrations that a rotation in power, alternance, had in fact been a possibility and that the election result had been fair and legitimizing.

In this regard, it was very important for the regime that seven other African heads of state, as well as senior Taiwanese and French delegations, came for the inauguration. Their arrival launched the festivities. To ensure the correct dignity and symbolism, the diplomatic corps was called out to the airport to meet the arriving presidents at about 3:30 p.m., August 7, the day before the great event. We spent four hours going back and forth from the stuffy, unairconditioned VIP lounge to the sweltering tarmac, where we and all the government were herded into formation ten minutes before each presidential jet landed. Only the assembled women dancers were more miserable, not being allowed off the shimmering pavement, and having to force enthusiastic shimmying and *youlous*—throat yodels—for each arrival. And a telling bunch they were: Bongo of Gabon, Patassé of Centrafrique, Bechir of Sudan, Obiang of Equatorial Guinea. The presence of Nigeria's Obasanjo and Mali's Konaré leavened the bread at least a little. Each would deplane, be met by President Déby, and proceed to a review stand to hear his and the Chadian national anthems played more or less in key by the Chadian military band. Then the presidents and entourage would proceed the entire length of our formation—several hundred feet—shaking hands with all our multitude.

The inauguration the next day was straightforward. Its prelude was the usual elaborate two-hour arrival ceremony; it finally began an hour and a half late. This meant that even though I came late, there was plenty of time to greet folks and chat with the other diplomats. The Saudi chargé, always sensitive to such matters, complained because the Esso delegation was seated in front of us. But I for one couldn't fault the Chadians for this little breach of protocol—they know where their bread is buttered. When the heads of state and official delegations finally arrived, I saw that my French colleague was among them. His principal from metropolitan France hadn't shown up, and it being of enormous importance for the Chadians to display at least one Western face among the attending dignitaries, he had been pressed into service as a surrogate.

Surprisingly, the first order of business was a recitation of the entire decision of the Constitutional Court with respect to the election results. This was the decision whereby they'd thrown out one-third of the votes originally tabulated by the Independent Election Commission, but still given Déby 62 percent. So here we were reminded of the complete fairness and absolute legitimacy of the election and its winner. But if any Western mind was swayed by this, what came next must surely have voided the positive impression: The Supreme Court justice who would administer the oath of office to the reelected president launched into a fifteen-minute speech that could only be termed a panegyric to President Déby, citing all his first-term accomplishments, describing his glorious and triumphant reelection campaign, and barely mentioning the challenges that still remain to bring this poorest of poor countries into the millennium. However, to his credit, President Déby did list all the right challenges before him in his inaugural address. He cited failures like the lack of progress in rural development, and spoke eloquently of the need for national unity and peace. Only when he plainly warned the absent opposition against expecting any role in his administration did he descend from the mountain-top for just a moment. And when we broke from the hall and drove home at noontime, interspersed among the traditional mounted warriors were genuinely enthusiastic crowds. All along the route the local people had turned out to watch the dignitaries speed by in their cars. It was the biggest celebration I've yet seen in N'Djamena.

If anyone had been tempted to think that the regime had indeed risked change, the impression left by the ceremony disabused one of the notion. The gut appeal of continuity, stability, and big-chief politics quickly reasserted itself. The strongest conclusion I carried away was that big-man politics remains alive and well in Africa. Its roots are deep, seen in the chief s stool as a subject in traditional wood carving. The French may have inadvertently reinforced this: Their experience with the Fourth and Third Republics, and perhaps glorious memories of the Sun King and Napoleon, led them to create a strong presidency only a few years before the independence of the African colonies. They have a similar term, *le fauteuil,* or arm-chair, for their own presidency as well.

At the inauguration, the imagery was explicit. After the Supreme Court and all the other functionaries had been seated on stage in their narrow, high-backed chairs, the curtain parted and President Déby's chair was carried out: First came an oriental carpet to cushion the chair, then a coffee table with a Kleenex box and a fake-flower bouquet, and finally the chaise itself—an armchair in the gold leaf of Turkish Baroque. Déby entered and reclined in the only nonutilitarian chair in the hall. If this and the speech of the Supreme Court justice had already smacked a bit too much of personality cult, the next event cemented the impression: Immediately after his swearing-in, Déby was awarded the insignia of a Grand Master of the National Order—a huge, fake gold necklace and medal that weighed down his neck for the remainder of the morning. The opposition press's later caricature was damning.

***

There was just one more self-indulgence, or act of arrogance, that I'll relate. That evening at the state dinner, all the guests other than the official party were required to arrive an hour in advance, 6:30 p.m., for an 8:00 p.m. event. And then we waited and waited, one, and two hours beyond the specified starting time. At 9:30 p.m., the Nigerian ambassador and his wife, seated next to me, excused themselves simultaneously to use the restroom. I suspected they were going to sneak off home. In a trice they were back. "We couldn't leave! They're all there—out on the steps—listening to music and watching the dancers!" The presidential party was, indeed, on the premises, but had paused, while all 500 guests waited in the dining hall, to see an impromptu folklore presentation that continued on another hour. Finally, at 10:30 p.m., the dignitaries entered and the event kicked off, two and a half hours late—four hours after we'd been told to arrive!

I digress, but you should know that I penned a note of protest to the foreign minister the next day. President Déby had drawn cheers in his inaugural speech when he said that no one, not even himself, was above the law. The same, I wrote, was true of courtesy. Someone in the Ministry of Foreign Affairs must have agreed, for to my chagrin the letter was leaked and published by the opposition press a couple of weeks later. The foreign minister, when I met him, agreed with my points in principle, but scolded me just a tad for having put it all in writing. Another opposition paper picked the letter up and editorialized that my comments showed how the government really wasn't serious about running the country in a mature fashion. And I had a visit by the leader of a splinter opposition party, specifically to thank me for having put in writing the frustration that so many Chadians feel with their rulers.

So the government of Chad (GOC) wants to keep tight control of things. Where is the dysfunction in that? It arises because Chad still has an armed opposition. If the GOC won't allow an opportunity for democratic expression and change, Chad will sooner or later revert to type—there'll be more rebellion, perhaps even someday a violent change in regime. Already since the election, the armed opposition has begun to tinker. There were a handful of people moving through the south back in early August. In July, a band of malcontents—we don't know who exactly—attacked Fada, where I'd visited in January, held it for twenty-four hours, and fled before the arrival of government reinforcements. Today something seems to be happening in the lake area, with rebels on the islands near Nigeria. All of these incidents seem traceable to one or another self-exiled political leader and his local adherents, someone who has given up on the prospects of peaceful change, or continues in the egoistic, warlord mentality. None of the incidents seems serious in and of itself, but together they show the ill effects of too rigid a politics, too slow an admission of the real possibility of peaceful change. If arteriosclerosis sets in and the veins of change become too rigid, the regime could well suffer a heart attack. The schizophrenia of the mindset ultimately results in disease of the body politic. The first visible symptom could be the donors withholding their doses of money medicine—all of us make aid contingent one way or another on political as well as economic good behavior, i.e., progress on the road to democracy. The EU at least has very stringent conditionalities, which the recent election peccadilloes would seem to have violated.

So Where Next?

Do you get the impression that change here tends to extremes that, because too quick or too slow, bring sickness upon the social organisms? I'll dare to generalize: Rapid, visible change in Africa is superficial. It occurs only in the appendages, like my embassy. The appearance of major change in Chad itself only obscures the deep continuities, be it continuing dependency on foreigners or big-man politics.

This is hard for Americans to grasp and accept. We want to see change at our own twenty-first-century pace. We expect measurable progress within the span of one of our own administrations. We forget our own long history—democracy in America (initially republicanism more than democracy) was planted in far richer soil, but took very nearly two centuries to come to full bloom, with the enforcement of the Civil Rights Act of 1964 at the end of the 1970s.

Democratic values are being planted in foreign soil in much of

Africa, albeit with the welcome—at least verbally—of a significant sector of the educated population. They will take root only very slowly, and the fruit of free and fair elections may, as with African cocoa and coffee, emerge only after the plant is years in the ground. In the meantime, indigenous institutions like chieftaincy remain the natural referents of most people outside the small, Westernized elite. The best metaphor of change here is perhaps the *anciens combatants* described above, who have wizened and died out over decades, and threaten now to expire altogether. In the void of the old institutions as they weaken, the more modern can take hold, but slowly.

So should we not give our African friends a little slack if, in a country like Chad, they haven't managed the full journey in the dozen years since the country came out of civil war? We need to appreciate the complex of diseases that arise from too rapid or too little change. Perhaps the best, after all, is to insist on honest dialogue, and small but concrete steps toward economic and political transparency to tackle the disorders of dependency and schizophrenia. But if the patient himself doesn't seek the cure, there is little we can do.

Already these more contemplative thoughts adumbrate where I want to go next with these Chad letters, working their cycle through to completion. Over two years now I've written for you about nearly all parts of the country, its great events and many of its customs and institutions. There may not be many more letters that relate these sorts of experience, although I can see that the next will deal with how we have dealt with the terrorist attacks from this remote vantage. In coming months, the Chad letters will shift into a terminal phase of three or four, focused on my overall evaluation of my experience here—a coda.

Best regards,

Ambassador Chris

P.S.

Some things here never change. Chad is a hardship. Take August 23, for example. Early in the morning there was a break in one of our water mains—the embassy compound was without water for two to three hours. Then we learned that all of our specialized communications with the States had died—the problem might take up to two weeks to fix, forcing us to rely on unreliable international phone lines for cables and phone calls. (This is the third time this has happened this year, but this one looks like the most serious interruption, the others having been fixed in a day or two.) Then, around lunchtime, the city power went off and our generator wouldn't turn on—it was a couple of hours before that could be fixed, so everywhere but the main chancery was dark. At this point, I went to my house to send a couple of official messages over the Chadian Internet over international lines—and, wouldn't you know? Chadnet was down! By the time I got back, Paul, my DCM, was back from a lunch with the French chargé, who reported that Air France had canceled another of its flights this coming Sunday. All this in a single day! Yes, Chad is at the very end of a very long supply line, and that hasn't changed at all.

Getting Off on the Wrong Foot

January 6, 2002

Dear Friends,

We've been promoting democracy in Africa, first rhetorically and for a dozen years seriously, for nearly half a century. And we've done it all wrong, because we've ignored our own experience. In evaluating the outlook for Chad's political development, I want to start with this theoretical point, move on to prospects for what I'll call political maturation (resolution of political conflict by nonviolent means and development of a sense of nationhood), and then back to the possibility of democracy. Why a wrap-up letter on politics and democracy? Well, political analysis is one of the key things ambassadors do, of course, and promoting democratization is a critical element of US Africa policy. Besides, having made the choices it has, Chad can progress only on parallel tracks of politics and economics, and I share the view that ultimately, as I'll discuss below, such progress must lead to something approximating democracy.

Since my last letter stressed the value differences between Chad and the West, it may seem odd for me to start this one by saying that efforts to promote democracy in Africa have failed because the West has failed to apply its own experience. In fact, the consistency is perfect.

What I mean is that, as the West began to prepare Africa for independence in the 1950s and 1960s, the democratic model it applied was that of perfected twentieth-century practice, forgetting that our own eighteenth-century point of departure was a very different world, one much more traditional and much closer in its values to the shame or honor culture of Africa described in my last letter ["Dueling Values" in chapter 6].

The fatal flaw, which even today we don't want to recognize, was the effort to impose all of the (alien) institutions full blown, universal suffrage included, on societies that were politically immature with respect to their ability to accept them, just as the United States was in 1789. Don't take this as some reactionary or racist conclusion that Africa can't govern itself or isn't capable of democracy, or that we're better because we're further ahead. What I mean is that the politically active people have to understand good government and democracy, and really want it, before it will happen. Read on.

When the US Constitution went into effect in 1789, neither the United States nor Britain were democracies. The US became a republic with relatively narrow political participation, and Britain was still imposing constitutional limits of a republican nature on its monarchy. The political history of both countries in the nineteenth and twentieth centuries was one of gradual, crisis-driven expansion of the franchise and other rights beyond the small elite that enjoyed them at the end of the eighteenth century. The same was more or less the case on the European continent where, for example, in Switzerland, women got the right to vote only in the 1970s, after most African women had it! In America, the final step wasn't taken until the enforcement of the Civil Rights Act of 1964—a full two centuries after the Declaration of Independence first averred that "all men are created equal." In those heady federalist days, many of the kind of group loyalties I see in Chad were still strong in the United States—state and region, class, national origin, even religion (it is true that the conditions for their quick erosion were also present).

But for the postcolonial countries (not just in Africa), we and their tiny Western-educated leadership thought it could all be imposed overnight. Perhaps it was due to our own euphoria in having finally placed the keystones of democracy in place in our own countries during those two decades after World War II. We believed that the few political elites, after experimenting with the forms of democracy for barely a dozen years, could really make them take root in soil much poorer than even New England's rocky loam was in 1776. The sad truth is that even today democracy and good government are meaningless concepts to 80 percent of the people in developing countries that remain confined to a world of mud huts and subsistence farming. For them, "government" is the village chief and the occasional incursion of military or senior re-gional officials demanding their exactions. Still too narrow a base? Lovely hindsight: Would these countries be better off today if the effort had been to establish and gradually expand a republican ar-rangement based on indigenous institutions, rather than to plant a foreign, universal democracy?

So countries like Chad have wallowed (or worse, fought) through forty years of independence trying to instill institutions for which only a tiny minority have had any commitment or understanding. However well-intentioned or even idealistic some of the liberating colonialists and first free African leaders may have been, the ex-periment failed. Tribalism, coups, personality cults, authoritarian-ism, civil war, and worse ensued. Decades have been lost, and these countries remain riven by particularistic interests.

I happen to believe that democracy should still be the ultimate goal for Chad and its neighbors, because only democratic processes can referee the internal conflicts with enough fairness and trans-parency to hold the country together over the long haul. But you

don't get there before the local people, or at least the great majority of those politically active, become convinced of this. And for
that, especially in the wake of recent history, they have to trust each
other, at least up to a point. There has to be what I am calling political maturity—a willingness to solve conflicts by something other
than violence, and some sense of nationhood. Ironically, for this,
the countries like Chad that have seen the most turmoil and violence may have a leg up—after thirty years of on-and-off civil war,
no one here wants to see another episode of major fighting.

Political maturation won't gel overnight, but in Chad today I
see three positive signs. First, as I've noted before, freedom of press
and speech is deeply rooted. The last time a journalist was arbi-
trarily arrested and seriously threatened was just before I arrived,
about three years ago. During the presidential campaign last year,
one of the private radio stations defied the government's restric-
tions and pretty well succeeded in giving the editorialized coverage
it wanted to. The government initially allowed freedom of the press
because in the early 1990s it didn't matter—the press's public was
so small and already die-hard opposition. But now, especially with
private radio stations opening up, the audience is growing. I think
it is too late for the government to slam shut the door. Between the
press and the Internet, talk and information seem ascendant.

The discrediting of violence proceeds as well. This was clear
in June 2001, right after the presidential election results were announced. The government behaved repressively, nipping in the
bud the only public protest that might have blossomed into widespread, violent disorders, and twice arrested all the opposition candidates and held them for several hours. On its part, the opposition didn't push things. In contrast to, say, the Ivory Coast, where
postelection fighting cost hundreds of lives, here a sole opposition
party worker was killed. And that worker was given a peaceful,,
and public, martyr's burial. It is also true that in the two and a
half years I've been here the government has successfully defused
several minor armed uprisings in different parts of the country. In
part, this was because the local people wouldn't support them. Just
in the past few days, the leaders of the rebellion have dropped their
demand for President Déby's resignation as a precondition for negotiations; as I write, a Chadian government delegation is meeting

with them in Tripoli. Another group of "politico-military" exiles based in Paris just came here, saying that after the events of 9/11, they feared being identified with terrorism, and they want to open talks with the government.

All this is, of course, very fragile. There will be break offs and recriminations, and of course there will be Libyan meddling. But I think there's a trend here.

But nationhood? The first sign, which I commented on in an early letter, was that no one among the opposition is secessionist. No one wants to hive off pieces of Chad. To a degree, this is a negative positive. After forty years of fighting and quarreling with each other, Chadians prefer they devil they know to the one (in Sudan or Libya or Nigeria) they don't know. Slowly, the concept of being a Chadian is growing, even if it doesn't yet outweigh loyalty to clan or tribe or region.

I hope against hope that the points above aren't just my inveterate optimism secreting its deceptive miasma before my eyes. But I think not. After all the country has suffered, I would hate to see it fall off the bandwagon of political civility; at least some of its political elite, which actually suffered through all the years of bloodshed, must feel likewise. And certainly, the international ethos pushes in this direction too.

The question of real democracy is harder, yet without it political maturity won't endure very long. Ultimately it comes down to the willingness of a leader, or his support group, to risk the loss of power voluntarily. Of that, you can count the number of cases in Africa on one hand. I diagnosed above the problem I see in previous attempts to establish democracy, and I identified what I believe is a critical precondition. Now I'm out of answers. But I do have a couple of thoughts about how a country might work toward it.

Democracy comes from the middle, not the top, and it may look different in Africa than it does back home. To take the first phrase first, we've seen that the effort to impose democratic institutions full blown from above has failed on this continent over and over again. And it is a truism that the staunchest base for democracy is a substantial middle class. I recognize, of course, that there is not such a thing in Chad, but there may be other middle elements of support for fair and transparent processes.

With these points in mind, let me hark back to the group loyalties discussed in my last letter, as I describe something that I saw years ago in Nigeria. There were three governments during the four years I was there, a civilian regime and two military regimes brought in by coups. But beneath the surface it seemed to me that there was a great continuity. Ministers played musical chairs—they moved on, replaced by cousins and in-laws and neighbors. Always it seemed, there was a certain rough balance of Yourabas and Hausas, a couple of Ibos, people from business and the families of traditional rulers, and a few retired generals. There was a republican aspect to this, based on an underlying consensus about how things should be run and who needed to benefit, that required the representation of key groups and constituencies. This was hardly democracy, but it was a rough form of power sharing, or at least power balancing. It broke down only two coups after I had left, under Abacha, when he and his cronies got carried away by absolute greed and power hunger. And, of course, eventually they got thrown out and Obasanjo's civilian regime has been striving valiantly ever since to put things back together again.

I wonder if there isn't a clue here about how honor and shame societies can take the first step toward democracy. The sitting ruler and his tribe or support group will rarely risk being voted out of office. But they may recognize that some sort of inclusion of certain groups and their representatives will enhance stability and perhaps make them more secure in office. Initially, this is likely to take place beneath the facade of democratic institutions, or within the executive branch where power is concentrated. What has to happen is for this kind of representation to become gradually inclusive of all of the politically attuned groups in society, and for it to last long enough for a grudging sort of trust to grow up between these groups. Only then is there a chance that "process institutions," i.e., the surface organs of democracy, may acquire some utility in the eyes of the rulers and gradually take on real authority. Ultimately, the institutions can institutionalize the rough sharing of power that is going on beneath the surface.

To a degree, President Déby and his ruling MPS party have followed a policy of political representation here in Chad. First, the MPS is the only really national party in the country, and it strives to include at least a few supporters from hostile regions. The other parties are all regional, ethnic, or individual in focus. After the first elections in 1996, the MPS formed a coalition with the four largest opposition parties in the National Assembly and introduced what it called "consensual and participatory democracy," a sort of grand coalition government. It generated a degree of consensus on major items until it broke down just before the presidential elections a year ago. Even with small rebel bands, the government has preferred reconciliation to persecution, buying them off with positions, perquisites, or plain cash. It costs money, but saves blood. This isn't yet the substructure I saw in Nigeria, with the strength to survive five changes of government before it fell apart. But it may be a start.

As I write this, the government is really performing above itself: It just concluded initial talks with the Paris exiles, and it has a delegation in Tripoli talking with the rebels and another in Benin talking with the coterie of exiles there. The prime minister is engaging the democratic opposition, and the foreign minister is trying to manage relations with the Central African Republic to avoid a strengthening of Libyan influence there. You have to admire these guys for trying. You have to wish them luck. And you have to hope that they will realize that the key to success is some real power sharing in the interest of long-term stability and the regime's endurance. The easiest approach will be inclusion of the key groups and ethnicities in the governing equation. But the government will have to go beyond representation to power sharing, or it won't last.

Another tactic, perhaps better for donors than trying to insist on perfect elections, is to try to strengthen the institutions outside the executive branch of government that have a chance at becoming real centers of authority or power. I've mentioned the press already. The other obvious candidates are the National Assembly and Judiciary. The courts especially can be helpful in creating a sense of due process in resolving social conflict, giving people a place of appeal outside and above their own family or clan. This could over time lead to trust in and commitment to the broader institutions of society. It is important that these institutions be ready so that the ruling elites will begin to find them useful when the day comes.

Last, let me describe a recent conference here that was designed to produce a new law on transhumance and thereby resolve festering farmer–herder conflicts. I'm proud to say that we funded it, and I'll begin with a descriptive quote from an opposition paper. "For a week 150 people, coming from six ministerial departments, nongovernmental organizations, human rights organizations, associations of traditional chiefs, farmers and herders groups, closed themselves up in an austere and isolated hostel in the quiet market town of Darda. ... Under the guidance of the National Mediator they will try to put into place new measures to manage transhumance and nomadism in Chad, in place of Law No. 4 of October 31, 1959, rendered obsolete by the evolution of events." To me this sounds like grassroots democracy in action. Draw together all the players and stakeholders, lock them up for a week, and expect a compromise solution everyone can live with. In this case, it will be a new law that, if reasonably well implemented, should save dozens of lives each year. (And, to give credit where it is due, all thanks to Les, who convinced me that we really needed to finance the project.) In this case, it worked because it was a problem everyone realized needed solving, and it didn't deal directly with the sensitivities of authority or emoluments. But, nonetheless, it shows what can be done.

As I look back over what I've written I'm less skeptical about the prospects for stability and democracy of some form in Chad and elsewhere in Africa. To the Western policy and aid officials, I would address several cautions. Accept that it will take a lot longer than you thought, generations perhaps, though certainly not as long as it did us. Realize that it can come only when the political elite wants it and develops a genuine attachment to it. Recognize that it may not take the form that we are familiar with any more than, say, the selection process of the British prime minister looks like the election of the American president.

To summarize, I'd say that the first system that we would recognize as "democratic" in Chad will combine a surface appearance of legitimacy and democratic institutions (which is largely present today) with some imperfect transparency, supplemented by a less public sharing of representation and limited power with key groups and constituencies within the country. Only time will then deepen the trust among the various groups and yield more devotion to national, and less to particularistic, interests. Only later will the formal institutions of democracy be infused with real authority and will the rulers risk alternance in fully free and fair elections. The institutions, and the values of the people behind them, will come to look more like our own. The model may be close at hand: Mexico, where power rotated within the PRI (Partido Revolucionario Institucional) for generations before an opposition party won the presidency.

In this discussion, you will have noted, I have concentrated on the rulers and those with whom the rulers may find it interesting to share power, not the broader groups like the middle class that traditionally support democratic development. To the degree that the latter groups develop in Chad and become influential enough to demand inclusion, democratic institutions may become real a little more quickly. This is something to return to, perhaps, after the next letter on economic development.

To the foreign proponents of political development and democracy, I say be confident in the outcome, not impatient at the pace. There are still ways we can help, a theme I'll come back to in my last letter on being an ambassador and on how we relate to the Chadians. But for now, let me close with the thought that our help will always be more effective if it recognizes that the real impetus must come from within, not by imposing an alien model full blown, as we tried to in the 1960s and more recently.

Best regards,

Ambassador Chris

P.S.
January 13, 2002

When I wrote this letter a week ago, I didn't realize the degree to which peace is breaking out here. When I got to the office on Monday morning, I learned the government had signed a peace agreement with the rebels (MDJT, or Mouvement pour la Démocratie et la Justice au Tchad). I spent the week trying to run down all the details, wrapping up with a meeting on Friday with the minister of the interior, who headed Chad's delegation in the Tripoli meetings. As I learned more, two things struck me. First, much of the momentum for the MDJT's new willingness to reconcile seemed to come from the discrediting of violence, mentioned above. The second point is more curious. The minister raised with the soi-disant democratic MDJT the prospect of their participation in upcoming legislative elections. But they had little interest, focusing almost entirely on the positions they will get within the executive branch as the agreement is implemented. This supports the point I made above, that informal power sharing will come first, and what we call real democracy only later, more slowly, over time.

Summing Up—Again

December 26, 2003

Dear Friends:

It was nearly two years ago that I reflected on my Chadian Experiences ["Being the Ambassador," February 24, 2002], anticipating a departure a few months later. I spoke personally of the contradictions in the role of the ambassador in a country like Chad, and some of the incomparable opportunities I've had here to see life and people at their most fundamental. Rereading those words, I would change little and add only that my fourth year here has permitted me to see more fruit from my labors, for example, the return of the Peace Corps. What was missing from the earlier letter was any thought about Chad's situation as I leave it, and its future direction. We are always ill prepared to predict the future, but with the added maturity of twenty more months, I'll scrawl a few thoughts for you.

From a purely economic viewpoint, the future is now. The oil project has been producing for six months and the first royalty check has been deposited in the offshore holding account. The funds are mostly allocated in the 2004 budget. But even before the revenues arrive per capita income is growing 10 percent annually, solely on the basis of local spending by the consortium. Cell phones and internet connections are booming. New construction is visible all over N'Djamena.

The great lingering question is whether the government of Chad will indeed adhere to the oil revenue management plan and whether the income will benefit the people. I'd say the odds are good, but it's still a crapshoot. With the safeguards that are in place, Chad's experience should be better than the egregious cases such as Nigeria, Equatorial Guinea, or Gabon. But you can't preclude every opportunity for corruption. Ultimately, a lot will depend on the goodwill of the government—whether it will tolerate graft big time or only small time. There, the jury's still out.

All things considered, I'm reasonably optimistic about economic development. The international financial institutions (IFIs) and donors will continue to misallocate their enormous resources, but even so there is some impact. The country has 50 percent more paved roads and 50 percent more doctors today than when I arrived in late 1999. There hasn't been a big shift out of agriculture, even in the oil region, and that is very good. The small formal economy is booming. If even half the oil revenues are well spent, the results could be remarkable.

Turning to political development, I'm less sanguine. It will be a long time before Chad achieves pluralism or democracy; it is a serious fault of Western political development theory to believe this can happen in countries like Chad in a decade or two. Chad's current regime has achieved stability in the wake of thirty years of civil war that ended barely ten years ago. This is impressive, and the danger and fear of a drift back to civil strife gives the regime a great deal of discretion in governance and in dealing with opposition—for the time being. But permanent stability will come only with legitimacy that is based on some degree of power sharing. Over the past year, perhaps feeling less pressure as the rebellion in the north withers and oil money looms, the regime has if anything drawn inward. The tradition of a southern prime minister to balance the northern president has been scrapped; there has been little dialogue at the president's level with the democratic opposition; it seems there will be no electoral reform before the communal elections that are to be held in the spring.

So aren't we, the IFIs, and other donor countries promoting democracy? Well, yes, we are, at least on the surface and around the edges. The UN and IFIs just collaborated on the development of a national strategy of good governance, with input from civil society as well as government. And the United States, for instance, helped to finance a private radio station in the northern city of Faya, giving competition to the government as the only source of news. But I increasingly share the conclusion reached by Paul Theroux in his book *Dark Star Safari*: We can't do it for them, i.e., determine the direction of political and economic development from the outside. We can help a little, but the real impetus must come from within African countries themselves. And that can come only when centers of economic and political power grow up outside of government control, and that takes a long time. Chad has a couple of things going for it, such as the relative weakness of the government apparatus, especially outside N'Djamena and the nascent, oil-driven development of a private sector that isn't totally dependent on government contracting for business. But we're talking about a long, long process, and the immediate future is murky.

Much of what we term "social development" is entwined with economic and political development, but here too I would like to summarize a few parting thoughts. First, there is a growing sense of national identity. Against the backdrop of ethnic tensions, farmer–herder conflict, and all the other divides in this country, this is very important, although it too will take root slowly. Further, most social indicators are going in the right direction, even including things like girls' education, HIV/AIDS incidence, and female genital mutilation. But Chad climbed out of the ranks of the ten worst-off countries in the UN's social indicators ranking only last year, so this too is a long struggle. The most promising factor is that Chadians at the village and neighborhood levels are increasingly conscious that they must do things for themselves—form associations to hire a teacher, build a clinic, put in a well, or whatever. This is an important break from the old colonial mentality of expecting and waiting for the government or donors to provide. Again, there are political repercussions.

To conclude, I feel that as I leave, Chad is on the move. What I've most appreciated in my time here has been the opportunity to view the stark contrasts of this place and the human condition at its most basic, where questions of life, food, shelter, and death dominate. That is changing now. Chadians will be better off, at least a little, but something will also be lost. At a minimum, their lives will become more complicated and integrated with the outside world. I am incredibly fortunate to have been here now, in time still to see this lifestyle—not primitive, but ancient and simple—in one of its last refuges, a condition that, nostalgia aside, must soon be banished from the globe.

Best regards,

Ambassador Chris

5

The Economy and Society

As with politics, I should say something generally about the economy. It is amazingly spotty. At least 80 percent of the people are engaged in subsistence agriculture or herding. Trading, in true African form, enlivens N'Djamena and the other main towns. There is almost no industry. The service sector is weak except for cell phones and security guard services, which have mushroomed since the beginning of the oil project. Oil has indeed changed the economy, but perhaps not to the extent anticipated.

Little need be said about the subsistence sector. You will see it firsthand in the letters. Farmers and herders who raise their own food market perhaps $100 to $200 worth of their surplus production, or sell a couple of animals a year. With this, they buy tea, sugar, and the odd garment. These are people living way below the international poverty standard of $1.25 per day.

Yet the markets of the capital and other towns are vibrant: local food, imported cloth and used clothing, and a huge array of cheap, tawdry stuff from Asia, such as electronics, construction materials, bicycles, and housewares. Once I found Washington State apples being hawked on a street corner in N'Djamena; I of course bought some. Exports of gum arabic and livestock on the hoof were, along with cotton, the main pre-oil earners of foreign exchange.

Basic services—electricity, landline phones, water—are largely in government hands, and they are deplorable. Cell phones arrived during my tenure and quickly outpaced the 20,000 landlines in the country. Within perhaps two years they numbered over 100,000.

The security and trucking industries boomed, thanks to the oil project. The demand for trucking retreated when the project was completed, but the security services continued to grow.

And what about the oil project? It will never employ the mythical tens of thousands optimistically imagined. But it created a few thousand jobs at varying pay grades and stimulated the industries noted above. When I returned briefly to N'Djamena in 2006, I could see the trickle-down effect in construction around the city. I'm proud that one of my initiatives, an agricultural development project to keep farmers in the oil region on the farm, succeeded to the point that the World Bank's International Finance Corporation provided follow-on funding once the Department of Agriculture's food aid money ran out.

The letters in this chapter range widely in topic, but all comment to a degree on Chadian society or the economy. "Is It Hopeless?" discusses the challenges Chad faces in education, in geographic isolation, and in finding an engine of economic growth. "The Adventures of Mr. Chidiac" is the impressive biography of an eccentric indigenous Caucasian, a very tiny segment of society in this part of Africa. In "The Roller Coaster," I apply my favorite metaphor for the wild gyrations of economic and political life in the country. "We Thought We Had All the Answers" begins with the death of one of my household servants, but its real analysis, as the title suggests, expresses my skepticism regarding the Western approach to promoting economic development in a country like Chad. "Present at the Creation" discusses the oil project and its economic and social impact. My rare and highly appreciated opportunities to visit Chadians in their own homes is the focus of "Chadians at Home."

Is It Hopeless?

January 1, 2000

A few days ago I met Gaston. Gaston is from Kélo, a town about 150 miles southwest of N'Djamena. He runs a school, actually a preschool, there. He has named it for Barbara Schell, a former deputy chief of mission at the embassy here who was later killed in

Operation Provide Hope, which aimed to help Kurds in northern Iraq. Before helping Kurds, she tried to help Chadians through, among other things, Gaston's earlier effort to found a school here in N'Djamena. About eight months ago, Gaston relocated the school to Kélo because high costs made it unsupportable in N'Djamena and the need was greater in his native Kélo.

Gaston's school says something about the poverty of the country. He somehow got the physical structure built, and has three classes for three-, four-, and five-year-olds. He collects CFA 50 from each child for each day it comes to school (about eight cents). He has fifty-eight students, but some don't come to school every day because their parents don't have the CFA 50. To make it worthwhile for the kids' families, he feeds the youngsters lunch, although he hopes to eliminate that once the value of the education is more appreciated. So his economics are as follows: In a good month he takes in perhaps CFA 50,000. He has three staff members in addition to himself; one of these is the cook for the lunches. If there is enough money at the end of the month, he pays them CFA 10,000 each ($15). If he forgoes his own salary, that leaves CFA 20,000 for the cost of supplies and other overhead. We gave him CFA 106,000, raised through contributions at a pre-Christmas concert at my residence—peanuts for us, two months' worth of revenue for the school. So there we have it: Parents who can't afford eight cents a day for preschool or daycare, teachers who take home $15 a month, and an effort to somehow run a school for fifty-eight on just over $75 a month. These are the facts of existence in one of the world's five poorest countries.

All of this is by way of introducing my theme for this letter, the inevitable question that occurs after nearly three months here: Does Chad, with all its problems, have any real chance at development or bettering the life of its people? So poverty is the first issue—nothing to invest even in so basic a need as a child's education. But why is the country still so poor, nearly forty years after independence?

It has long been my own belief that the Marxists got things backwards. It isn't just that a country's political system depends on its economic system, but also that economics depends just as much on politics. Chad illustrates my thesis perfectly, as its internal political instability explains so much about its lack of development and poverty. In fairness, you need to begin with the ethnic diversity of the country, which has 128 languages and countless tribes, which are often mutually suspicious. The northerners used to raid into the south and sell their captives into slavery in Egypt and Arabia. The sedentary southerners have long resented the transhumance of the nomadic northerners. The harsh climate and geography of the north have for centuries encouraged a warlike and violent culture dependent on family, clan, and tribal loyalties.

And then came the French. It was they who created the artificial colonial boundaries that lumped together all or part of at least four predecessor states or cultures, plus the politically unorganized regions around them. As I write, I am looking at a column from the September 27, 1999, edition of *Le Monde,* which describes the conquest of Chad by a bloodthirsty French expedition led by two sadistic officers, Voulet and Chanoine, who raced eastward along the Niger River and eventually cross-country, leaving in their wake villages populated only with decapitated bodies. It was black recruits who, under orders of their French officers, did the killing, thus reinforcing the fears and suspicions of one tribe about another. A second mission coming down from Algeria, that of Forreau–Lamy, is generally given the credit for Chad's conquest, however, since Voulet and Chanoine finally succumbed to their own medicine (i.e., they were killed by their own troops) and the remnants of their mission were merged with the one that had come down across the Sahara. But the point remains: This part of Chad's history was marked by bloodthirsty conquest and an uncaring administration, which was one of two in French Africa that always remained under military, not civilian, control. Chad was pacified by the French only with difficulty on the eve of World War I. The main French legacy, aside from an administrative center in Fort Lamy (N'Djamena), was the forcible introduction of cotton production, of which more below. And the French preferred to rule through the more sedentary southerners, maintaining a light hold over the northern half of the vast territory through military posts in Faya-Largeau, Fada, Abé-ché, and Ounianga Kébir.

So is it any wonder that, after independence, the country slowly drifted into incompetent administration, ethnic hostility, corruption, and twenty-five years of civil war, often marked by a north–south divide? Eventually the warlike northerners took prominence, and the current president, Déby, ousted a different northerner, Habré, in late 1990. Déby has had to fight a series of rearguard actions since, allowing us to say that the civil war ended only in the mid-1990s, or to argue that with the reignited rebellion in the north, it never really ended at all.

What does this mean in terms of government? It means that President Déby has from the first trusted only his own kinsmen, and lavished upon them the lion's share of governmental largesse and responsibility. It means that where he has not needed to fight outright, he has sought to co-opt his multifaceted opposition through political patronage or outright bribes. It has meant that a government with meager resources, degenerating early after independence into corruption, has come to be viewed mainly as a patronage system rather than a service provider. Each governing elite, up to the present one, has sought to extract, to rape actually, as much as it can as quickly as it can, knowing that its own hold on power is tenuous and of limited duration. The civil service this has fostered is one that is venal, has limited capacity to render any real services, and spends most resources on salaries and perks, leaving little for program investment.

To make it all worse, we can add the salt of perpetual demobilization. As the Déby regime has sought to disarm four or five groups of the fighting opposition and channel their leadership into a co-opted role of political party opposition, the problem of the groups' armed soldiers has arisen. These soldiers have usually been taken into the army, and then demobilized—often with their weapons still in hand. So the country, in making an honest effort to downsize its military to a reasonable level of 25,000 men or so, has left another 25,000 former fighters roaming armed and unemployed through the countryside or hiding out in N'Djamena, with only petty crime—or not so petty crime—on which to feed themselves. And there is always the lure of going back to the bush when some disgruntled politico raises his sword in opposition to the regime.

The current rebellion in the north is a bit more than just this disgruntlement. Youssouf Togoïmi is given credit for being a man of principle, even of great integrity, by Chadian standards. He is known as a man genuinely desirous of a change in attitude of the administration. But his uprising is sapping the strength of the country: It's diverting all the attention of the government from what should be its business, encouraging those in power to sock away their nest eggs in case they should find themselves out in the cold, and just generally adding to the destabilization of the country.

Does this begin to explain the lack of progress in development since independence? Let us now turn to the country's economic handicaps, which should not be underestimated in their own right.

I hear again and again of Chad's *enclavement*. The term means more than just being landlocked; it connotes a deeper sense of isolation. Chad is both at the center of Africa strategically, and in a backwater economically. Access to the sea is 1,000 kilometers away in the closest direction, through Douala, one of the world's most overtaxed, inefficient, and corrupt ports. The lack of population in-country means that Chadians must look outside for a market, but outside, because of the remote sea, means neighboring African countries with their own poverty and problems. The *enclavement* has so far prevented development of Chad's medium-sized oil deposits—always, other sources have been cheaper to exploit. And the isolation is internal as well as external. This country, one-quarter the size of the lower forty-eight, has no all-weather road system and no scheduled air service among its five major cities. Gaston's Kélo is a half-day drive now, in the dry season, but the last fifty miles beyond the paved road is almost impassable during the rains of July–September.

So what are the economic resources? Well, there is cotton. One-third of the population is directly or indirectly dependent on cotton production. The crop was introduced in the 1920s through massive, forced resettlement of Chad's southern population, because a cash crop grown by accessible people was needed for taxation to cover the costs of administering the colony. A French firm carefully controls the parastatal that has forever managed the provision of inputs, ginning, marketing, and cottonseed processing— Cotontchad. The farmers are paid about half of what farmers in India, Zimbabwe, or South American developing countries get for their lint. What isn't taxed away by the French is hived off by the corrupt Chadian management of Cotontchad, leaving the farmers to take the hindmost. The country's one textile mill with its value added died a decade ago, and Cotontchad runs huge deficits. It will be privatized under the pressure of the IMF and World Bank, but will the marketing of cotton itself be liberalized, giving farmers multiple outlets for their product?

Elsewhere in the economy, too, agricultural production and food processing are the only real developmental possibility, always shadowed by the threat of desertification. The country is unusual in the Sahel for having ample water during the rainy season, but today there is no way to capture that water to extend the growing season. Nor has anything been invested in agricultural processing — the domestic market won't support it, and neighboring markets with big populations, such as Nigeria, have been weak in recent years. What little trade exists is informal or smuggled. And there has been a vicious cycle of no surplus production, no market for selling it, and no profits that can be reinvested.

So does this all help you to understand my question of the outset, is it hopeless? If Chad's history since independence is our standard for judgment, you might well conclude that it is. Without a struggle, the past might well become a self-fulfilling prophecy of the future here.

But I don't buy that it is hopeless. First off, I won't be able to spend three years here if I start with that premise. But beyond my own infernal optimism, there are other things that give me hope. There is, for example, Gaston. Somehow, despite all the baggage, he is still determined to give his school every chance he can. Our assistance may help around the edges, but he is determined to make it self-sustaining. There must be other Chadians out there engaged in similar endeavors. There is the chance of a shot in the arm from oil development, and some groping evolution in the public ethos of what must be done: The Chadians are marvelous at saying what they know we want to hear from them about democracy, development, national reconciliation, etc.; sooner or later they will start to believe some of it themselves.

So no! It isn't hopeless, only incredibly difficult. More difficult than the miracles of development in East Asia. More difficult than the fiscal and economic recovery of the District of Columbia in our own country. More difficult than the challenges facing South Africa or other African lands. But the people here will face the challenge because they have no choice. Is there anything we can do to help them?

Sincerely,

Ambassador Chris

The Adventures of Mr. Chidiac

January 12, 2001

From time to time, we meet a remarkable person. This was my immediate impression of Mr. Chidiac, and I am going to relate his biography to you. You'll find the narrative slightly amazing. But perhaps in the end, you will, like me, see something deeper in his history and current straits than simply the story of a single man.

I met Mr. Chidiac because I'm a stamp collector. It took me nearly a year after arriving here to look at my oldest hobby in the Chadian context. But sometime during last summer, a letter I received from Bob Lamb, president of the American Philatelic Society, got me focused. Bob is a retired ambassador whom I had known in Bonn, where he was administrative counselor in that mammoth embassy. We both specialize in collecting Austrian stamps. Bob asked the embassy's help in sorting out which recent Chadian stamps are authentic—lots of them deal with non-Chadian topics such as Lady Di and the settlement of the American West, and this raises questions of legitimacy. Ace G., our commercial officer, did the legwork, but in the process I began to visit the philatelic sales window at the main post office, and there I became acquainted with the attendant, Mr. Eloua. One Saturday, after I had bought most of the current issues he had for sale, he showed me a stock book of older stamps being sold by a friend. With Mr. Eloua as intermediary, I bought the lot. Mr. Eloua told me his friend had huge quantities of stamps from all over, and he would introduce me.

After a couple of false starts, on Saturday last I went to visit Mr. Eloua's friend and neighbor. What sort of Chadian, I pondered, would be a stamp dealer? We were headed for Moursal, a Christian middle-class (by Chadian standards) neighborhood on the southern side of town. I pictured in my mind's eye an older man, retired, perhaps someone who had had the means to collect earlier in life and was now pressed to liquidate a large collection. Following Mr. Eloua's directions, Chaibo turned off the main road, down a secondary artery, and around a corner. As we turned, we passed the home of a prominent southern politician on the right, and then Mr. Eloua's mud-brick compound on the left. A few doors down we stopped before a blue metal gate leading into Mr. Chidiac's compound. Mr. Eloua banged on the gate and a child came to open it. The youngster allowed that Mr. Chidiac was there, took me by the hand (!) and led the way. In the courtyard we passed a few other children, an adult or two squatting over busy work, and a couple of goats and perhaps a cat. Small adobe structures lined the exterior walls of the compound. Our goal, at the back, was a slightly more substantial structure in white stucco. Mr. Chidiac heard the slight commotion and came out to greet us. He matched my image, save in two details: He was white, and he greeted me in English.

I'll spare you the list of honorifics with which I was received and mention only Mr. Chidiac's quick reference to having once known the American ambassador in Yaoundé and having studied at the American University in Beirut. I'll spare you as well the philatelic details of our discussion, although I ended up buying $20 worth of older Chadian issues. But you won't understand Mr. Chidiac if I don't give some description of his dwelling. Nearing the back of the compound, we had jogged left under a porch, to where he met us. He led us past a woman cooking in the open air on a little foyer. Entering the house at its far left, we passed through a narrow little kitchen with a tiny gas stove against the wall (unused?). Mr. C. led us to the right, into a substantial room that measured perhaps twelve by twenty feet. This made up the majority of the house. To the left as we entered was a little dining table supporting a lamp and a blaring radio; at the far end, against the wall of windows on the right was a cot-like single bed. You couldn't tell if it was disarranged merely by people sitting on it or whether it had been slept in and hastily smoothed rather than fully made. Most of the remainder of the room was taken up by a suite of overstuffed couches and chairs. A coffee table and the seats were overburdened with many boxes and envelopes of stamps and all of the attendant paraphernalia. This interior was clean and airy, with a fairly even concrete floor and white walls and ceiling. At the far end were two more doors (a bathroom and a bedroom?). Mr. Chidiac relapsed into French and, to my great relief, rose and switched off the radio. Through nearly two hours of talking and "stamping," I pieced together his story.

Mr. Chidiac was born in about 1930 in Douala. Of Lebanese parents, he is by nationality a Cameroonian. His parents, traders, had come to Douala in the 1920s and raised their family there. Mr. C. related little of his childhood beyond his description of a tidy house, but it was clear that he considered himself an African, with few ties back to Lebanon.

The first real adventure would seem to have been Mr. Chidiac's first journey out of Africa, to attend the American University in Beirut. In 1945, just as the war was ending, he left Douala with a plane ticket and five pounds sterling, all one could get in hard currency. He flew to Lagos, where he changed planes. To his immense good fortune, he was bumped from his connecting flight to Egypt via Khartoum by VIPs—I say good fortune because the plane crashed, killing all on board. The next flight, two days later, was also overbooked by VIPs, and it also crashed. After the third crash on the route within a week, BOAC shut down the route pending an investigation, leaving Mr. C. stranded in Lagos. He refugeed with a cousin. Eventually, he and forty other stranded passengers were given transit to Port Said in a British troopship. The passage, however, took six weeks because the Atlantic and Mediterranean were, of course, heavily mined. The troopship was preceded by a minesweeper that would work its way along the coast for some distance, signal the troopship to catch up, and the whole process would be repeated. From Port Said, Mr. C. made his way to Cairo, and in a day or two hitchhiked up the coast of Palestine to Beirut. All of this must have been very daunting and exciting for an enterprising and intelligent fifteen-year-old youth on his first major trip away from home.

Mr. C. was a bit hazier in describing his second adventure. He studied at the American University, which was divided into three faculties, with instruction in French, English, and Arabic. Mr. C. took the French curriculum, although he must have studied English copiously to have acquired the proficiency he still retains. But something happened in the time of turmoil surrounding the Jewish immigration and the founding of Israel. The story was fuzzy enough to have hidden some youthful peccadillo. Mr. C. ended up escaping to hide in the foothills outside Beirut with no passport or papers. Did whatever it was have something to do with Mr. C.'s ultimate acceptance of Africa as his homeland, not Lebanon? Did Mr. C. briefly embrace Arabic nationalism? He didn't elaborate, indicating only that after payment of a certain fee to an acquaintance, he obtained documents reading "nationality indeterminate"—not unusual for the chaotic times.

The third, and milder, adventure followed immediately, i.e., during his return to Douala. There had been an opportunity to go to America to study to be a pilot, but somehow that had come to naught. After his few years in Beirut, Mr. C. would return to Cameroon. All went well until he reached Paris, where he learned that Air France had canceled his onward flight to Douala. He was housed in a left bank hotel—I didn't recognize the name—for two days until he could proceed. Now intruded a hint of romance, for there was an attractive young lady in the hotel, en route to New York, whom he found in tears in the lobby. Put up initially by Air France, she had been eight days delayed. Now, told that her flight was imminent, she had been billed, despite Air France's assurances, for her lodging, and she had no money to pay. Mr. C. was at this point perhaps twenty, the perfect age for a Sir Galahad. Empathizing with the damsel's plight—and perhaps foreseeing his own—he stormed the Air France office, bursting in on its director. He shouted and pounded his fist. So eloquent was he that the damsel—having missed now her Air France connection to New York—was placed on the next Pan Am departure. And Mr. Chidiac was boarded on a flight for Douala the next day but one.

There comes now a gap in the biography. I suspect that, like many of us, Mr. Chidiac undertook the adventures of youth with long toil in the workaday humdrum of earning a living. He gave me the odd reference to his real estate activities, but he didn't really describe his life's work in commerce or business.

Apparently these main years of the man's business life included activities in both Cameroon and Chad. Up until Chad's independence in 1960, movement back and forth would have been easy, normal, inviting for a businessman. At one point, Mr. C. opined, he'd sold the US embassy in Yaoundé the grounds upon which the ambassador's residence was constructed. In N'Djamena, in the years before the first civil war ended in 1979, Mr. C. was the managing director of what is still the main hotel, Novotel La Tchadienne. He told of receiving various notables. And perhaps this was when he acquired his N'Djamena real estate. But when the next civil war broke out, he returned to Cameroon. His locus of activity seemed to range from Yaoundé to Koussérie (just across the river from N'Djamena in Cameroon), and he had holdings in both places as well as in N'Djamena.

Here again Mr. C.'s narrative left a couple of decades of gaps about which I'll have to inquire further. What he did before the Novotel, and immediately afterward back in Cameroon, was left undefined, in what was becoming a bit of a pattern.

Jumping now to the present, it seems that Mr. C. returned to N'Djamena sometime between six months and a year ago. His wife is apparently still in Yaoundé, watching out for some assets there. But Mr. C. had been residing in Koussérie, across the river, doing what wasn't exactly clear. Somehow things had become hot. He had been arrested and jailed for some forty-five days. The charges had to do with having fostered smuggling into Chad. Whatever the case, it is a reminder of the fragility of security here, even for expats, without an embassy to watch over them. It seemed that a general falling out with the local Koussérie authorities was the real problem, which at a certain point led Mr. C. to move back across the river to Chad. This too would have been a small adventure, as he described it, quietly mobilizing what resources he could carry once released from jail, and crossing as unobtrusively as he could the border and bridge to N'Djamena. So here he is, filling his days with the quotidian details of running a small household and the interminable work of organizing his stamp collection. And, he finally admitted, at his age he was looking to turn as much of the collection into cash as he could. His children (he mentioned a daughter in Paris) and siblings didn't seem much interested in the collection; cash would be preferred.

It didn't surprise me that Mr. Chidiac talked a lot about the past, about his heyday running the Novotel here in N'Djamena and being a real estate mogul in Yaoundé. He described how he would welcome the leading political figures of the age to lunch at the hotel. He related how he had sold a piece of land to our embassy in Yaoundé and once had even been invited to dine by the American ambassador there.

If you heard this refrain from out of the blue, you might dismiss it as the nostalgia of an old man. But to me it struck a familiar note. It was so like what I hear from a host of Chadian elder statesmen. Take, for example, Colonel Djimé (pronounced like "Jimmy"), whom I'd met at a Veterans' Day reception the French hosted. He called on me a day or two before my visit to Mr. Chidiac, wanting help to get his youngest son to study in the United States. Colonel Djimé had risen to command Chad's Gendarmerie (federal police) in the early days of independence. He had been instrumental in the 1975 coup that toppled President Tombalbaye. He had gone on to serve as Chad's vice-president, and in that capacity he reached the acme of his career, a call on President Carter during a visit to Washington. Being received by me in the embassy decades later restored some faint hint of the glory he had enjoyed on that day in Washington.

Like Mr. Chidiac, the colonel was full of laments about how wrong things had gone in Chad. A few like he, out of an army of former players, remain active on the political scene. Some are respected, but most are of little influence. They are so many because of Chad's frequent changes of government, and most have been forced into retirement or onto the sidelines. But all share a frustration, not just of having been players and lost out but also of having something to contribute still to their country as elder statesmen, yet lacking an avenue to do so. Mr. Chidiac is the exceptional businessman among this host, but he shares with the politicians the fact of having been displaced well within his prime, and having grown old living with the frustration of exclusion from the once familiar inner circle. And do these folks have something to offer? Undoubtedly they do. But how, today, would even an open-eared leadership extract it from the pride, latent agendas, and biases with which the veterans have encapsulated themselves over the years?

Mr. C. symbolized another kind of displaced person as well. It is a role adumbrated by the protagonist in V. S. Naipaul's *A Bend in the River*, and portrayed more vividly in today's headlines by the white farmers of Zimbabwe. Cameroonian in his citizenship, he has lived his life and raised his family there. But now he is no longer welcome. He is the accidental residue of the colonial era, with nowhere else to go. But Mr. C. lacks the option of escaping to England, so he has fled the least distance he could, across the river to Chad. I mentioned this to Anne-Nicole, my Cameroonian French instructor. No, it didn't surprise her—the Lebanese were resented in Cameroon; the current regime didn't think that they invested enough in their adopted homeland. That government wasn't likely to try very hard to differentiate between Mr. C., who perhaps had invested more than a little, and the expatriate white foreigners in general, who hadn't.

In a more fundamental way the hostility toward Mr. C. as a Lebanese isn't a racial issue, but only one tiny part of the larger ethnic tensions that seethe everywhere on this continent, and seem to boil over so often where visible groups of immigrants live and share the economic benefits of an adopted country. The recent (September 2000) rioting in Libya against black African workers left hundreds dead and thousands streaming back to Chad and other countries. Only a day or two ago I read of persecution of longtime Burkinabé residents of Abidjan. Mr. Chidiac's plight may jump out because of his skin color; it may seem more poignant since he must go further in distance and into the past to find an ethnic homeland. But otherwise his circumstances merely demonstrate one of the many dilemmas the people of this continent must solve before they can achieve good governance and development. And don't forget, it is with black Africans that Mr. C. shares his sense of having outlived his times, of being marginalized by his society while still in his prime.

There is one more caveat as well. I've noted the great silences in Mr. C.'s biography, and hinted at a misadventure or two. Chad, Cameroon, and other countries in Africa are not societies where the average man, or even an educated man, can work hard, earn a decent living, and eventually make something of himself and create better opportunities for his children. No, nothing works here without the rules being read a little loosely, without some pushing around the edges. Success reflects various degrees of honesty and acuity. So don't judge me too soft if I fail to probe much into the convenient gaps and shady side of Mr. C.'s narrative—not, at least, until I know him better.

The last chapters of Mr. C.'s biography remain to be written. There may well be one more adventure, for his current situation exudes a sense of disequilibrium. I don't believe Mr. C. is one to simply bide his time in the back of the little compound in Moursal until he expires. Will he make some last flamboyant move typical of his irrepressible soul? Does he await some deus ex machina to again reverse his fortunes? I'll go back in the coming weeks to buy more stamps from him; perhaps I'll find a clue.

And perhaps this brings us ultimately to Mr. Chidiac's philosophy of life, if so exalted a term can be used about a person who has lived so chaotic a life. Just as Mr. C.'s individual troubles blend in my mind into some of the broader issues of this continent, I remember a curious juxtaposition in his comments. Early in our chatting, he remarked that he is a fatalist—that he believes that whatever will be, will be. Then, just as I was leaving, he remarked, "I'm an optimist; you can't survive in Africa without being an optimist!" I can't stop thinking about these two comments, and I can't decide whether they are complementary or contradictory. At home, in America, one might immediately focus on the apparent contradiction; here in Africa, perhaps not. Despite his seventy years, Mr. Chidiac's remarkable African journey is not yet over.

Best regards,

Ambassador Chris

The Roller Coaster

April 15, 2001, Easter Sunday

Dear Friends,

You can't tell what color the sky is this morning; there's a harmattan blowing. Looking up, it's not far off its normal bright blue—
gentler, perhaps, as if some wispy white cloud has interceded to
shelter us in this hottest of Chad's seasons, when daily highs ex-
ceed 110 degrees. But peering toward the horizon, all is a murky,
muddy yellow-brown, rather like how I've imagined the mustard
gas must have billowed over Flanders Fields.

I call it the roller coaster effect. At times, everything here just seems
to be perfect, on track, getting better and better—the sky's the limit.
Then, all of a sudden, having hardly noticed a change in trajecto-
ry, everything is crashing downward, no bottom apparent in the
depths.

A year ago, the country seemed to be embarking on one of its
gravity-defying climbs. The winter, figuratively speaking, had had
its share of storms. There had been serious fighting in the north,
and for just an instant, it had seemed as if the regime was in real
danger. And the oil project had fallen apart with the withdrawal
of two of the partner firms. No one thought it was fatal, but it was
worrisome—especially against the backdrop of rebel momentum.
But ironically, just as April's light mango rains reminded us that
the dry heat would soon succumb to the rainy season, the meta-
phorical clouds seemed to dissipate.

The first good news was that Exxon-Mobil, the remaining firm
in the oil consortium, had found two replacement partners: Petro-
nas, a Malaysian firm, and Chevron. From my standpoint, this was
very good news, since the consortium went from being 40 to 65
percent American. In a stroke, the United States would supplant
France as Chad's largest foreign investor. The country would loom
larger in terms of US interests, and I even had visions of it getting
more attention from the folks back in Washington.

There was a hitch, of course—there still needed to be a World
Bank loan for the project to come together, and that necessitated an

executive board vote. Lobbying was intense, and the United States was the key uncommitted vote. It was inconceivable to me that we would oppose the project—it was such a no-brainer. The quality of the environmental mitigation plan was unprecedented anywhere in the developing world. Chad's oil revenue management law was also groundbreaking—it guaranteed 80 percent of the resources for four key development sectors. And how could we oppose the interest of two of our major corporations opening up Africa to investment, as if to concretize administration policy? But certain environmental groups were dead set against the project in any form, and the Treasury Department seemed to be listening to them. The vote was to be Monday, June 12.

And of course, ultimately, reason prevailed and the United States voted favorably, and the loan was approved. On the Friday before the vote, the wife of the local Exxon-Mobil chief tracked me down at dinner at our diminutive American Club: Her husband had just phoned from Washington, where he awaited the vote; someone from Treasury had given him a nod that all would he well. Over the weekend, I had a call from the local World Bank director, also back in Washington for the vote, who had similarly been given a discrete thumbs-up. But within the US government, word was not passed, and it was I who informed the State Department folks when they opened up on Monday morning. And no, this lack of communication didn't surprise me a bit.

When the official news of the vote reached N'Djamena early Monday evening, the city burst into celebration. It was to a degree organized, but there was genuine feeling in the crowd that gathered at the parade grounds opposite the Presidential Palace. There was spontaneity in the horn-honking motorists who sped around the town. The president walked over to receive the congratulations of the crowd, relaxed and clad in a polo shirt for the evening warmth. The most important economic project in the country's history would go forward.

Against the balmy backdrop of this victory, other economic reforms seemed to be coming together as well. Word came of a second World Bank loan, one under which the country would be one of five pilot participants in an anticorruption project. And Chad, of course, would be an early participant in HIPC (Heavily Indebted

Poor Countries) debt forgiveness. A steering committee with ample representation of civil society was launched at a widely heralded three-day seminar; it began its work of formulating, together with the government, a poverty reduction strategy. On our side, things were falling into place for approval of a monetized food aid initiative to support agricultural development in the oil region, lest Chad go the way of Nigeria and neglect its mother industry. I visited the region and confirmed the interest of Africare, OICI [Opportunities Industrialization Centers International], and World Vision, private voluntary organizations that would execute the project. And then there was the matter of the "bonus," a special $25 million payment made against future tax benefits by the two new members of the oil consortium. In the euphoria of the moment and to universal surprise, the president announced that it, too, would be used according to the provisions of the revenue management law.

The first real rains came in early June, but even so the skies were serene for days at a time between the welcome showers. On the political front, there was ferment and excitement, as on the economic front. Chad was beginning to gear up for its 2001 presidential and legislative elections. The administration and National Assembly were beginning work on the electoral code, a decentralization law that would fix new legislative districts, and a measure to establish an independent electoral commission.

About this time, we had a visit from one Dr. McM., a specialist on elections from SUNY Binghamton. Together, we made the rounds of the political party chiefs, the ruling party and the opposition. Dr. McM., before he left, put together a report that was actually a compendium of additional steps toward electoral transparency that were the consensus desiderata of the opposition.

Meanwhile, the electoral code was taking shape, with critical changes from the 1996 elections that would check ballot stuffing by Chadians abroad and prevent tampering with vote totals between the polling places and the central compilation point in N'Djamena. Upbeat about a real improvement from the 1996 abuses, I decided to share Dr. McM.'s conclusions with the government. I met with the foreign minister and the president's chief of staff. Would I, asked the chief of staff, be willing to see the president to present the same report? Of course I would, and in the early days of July I did. The president was cross and defensive, but he listened. I was comfortable at having been heard at the highest level in the land. I was optimistic that, somewhere in the mix of legislation, there would be another modification or two along the lines Dr. McM. had suggested.

There had been more fighting in the north at the onset of July. But here, too, the news was good. The rebels had finally attacked Bardaï, which everyone had been expecting them to attack and capture. But they couldn't hold it. The government counterattacked within twenty-four hours and retook the town, giving the rebels as good as they got for the first time in this two-year conflict. The government was jubilant.

As July unfolded, the European expats, diplomats, and wealthier, Francophile Chadians began their summer exodus for France or wherever. The skies had remained a little too blue, the rains a little too light. But no one was especially worried, and it was still early. A sunny summer was particularly deceptive for us Northern Hemisphere types. I took leave for three weeks, and left contented. In consultations in Washington, I could give a glowing report on the country's economic prospects and progress toward economic reform. And there was genuine and open debate about how to run the approaching elections; there too I could hope for further changes in the direction of transparency. Eerily, this was all a little like the NASDAQ in that summer of 2000. It seemed things could only go up on this roller coaster. It took your breath away even before your car surmounted what you would later see had been the crest of the highest peak.

"It's a long, long while from May to December, and the days grow short when you reach September," Kurt Weill's tune lilts in the background as I scrawl....

As September rolled around, I'd been back a few weeks from leave. The rains, we noted, hadn't been good, but we wouldn't know if they'd been really bad until we saw whether they'd score a catch-up reprise at the end of the month. But there was already a little something in the air as the rainy season ended—just a touch of that marvelous melancholy that Lotte Lenya throatily belts out when she sings her husband's paean to September. And notwithstanding Chad's divorce from our familiar seasonal cycle, it was nonetheless in late September that we began to sense that our car had passed the peak of the roller coaster's elevation; we didn't yet see that we were plunging into the artificial terror of a seeming free fall.

Sometime in early September, a team from the World Bank and IMF arrived to do its routine evaluation of Chad's progress under its structural adjustment program and related matters. As the team proceeded, it determined that somewhere in July, spending had exploded, tax receipts had evaporated, and the country had gone terribly off track. Military spending on the war in the north was, of course, a big factor. More alarming, the bonus was now half gone. Completely contradicting the president's pledge, it had been spent on road construction, N'Djamena's sanitation, the war effort, and some vague, untraceable items (graft?). In a trice, Chad had gone from "A" to "F," or perhaps, more realistically, from "B+" to "D-," in its structural adjustment and economic transparency scores.

Further, it was more and more clear how bad the rains had been. Agricultural output was down a quarter, perhaps, from the good harvests of the last few years. Tales began to circulate of the traditional reactions to hardship: People migrate, they raid the stores of the insects in anthills, they eat the seed grain set aside for planting for the next year. But over all this hung a cloud of uncertainty as well—there was no consensus on the degree of need early on that would have stimulated an immediate food aid response.

Politically, the omens also dimmed. The government pushed through the electoral legislation with no modifications. This left the opposition with many doubts about fairness. The CENI was dominated by the government and its friends. The decentralization law as enacted had established National Assembly districts of 3,000 to 5,000 residents in the progovernment north, as opposed to 100,000 residents in some southern districts. So it goes.

By early fall, we'd had a tremendous comeuppance on the economic and political fronts. What to do?

Today, six months later, things are glummer still. Our roller coaster car has continued to hurtle downward, leaving us panting and wondering if we'll ever hit bottom. Are we at the trough?

Today, April 2001, I know a few things. The government is positively out of money.

Since its sins were disclosed last September, all new disbursements by the Bank and the Fund have been on hold; they won't resume until May or June, assuming good behavior continues. As a result, the government isn't spending money at all, except for defense and the war up north. In the countryside, salaries are now two to three months in arrears except for those provinces that generate their own income through tariffs.

While we in N'Djamena talk of food aid for drought relief, none has yet hit town. Food is more and more a problem in the countryside. Prices of grain in April are equal to the normal rate just before the new harvest in August. The United States and the European Union have committed food for relief, but I can't tell you when it will actually be in the country or whether it will reach the needy pockets before the rains lock down all transport. At the same time, several epidemics have surfaced in the country—meningitis and measles, to name two. Unfortunately, this is normal for the hottest months of April and May, with hundreds of deaths.

In the north, there has also been more fighting, at Zouar, around Bardaï, and elsewhere. The government hasn't lost, but there have been bloody draws. Can the government, dependent in large part on Zaghawa warrior support, maintain the blockade around the Tibesti that has confined the rebels?

And now the elections. How to characterize them? Many factors tilt the playing field in favor of the ruling party and sitting president, without doubt. The electoral commission was handpicked by the executive. The electoral law allows nomads and overseas residents, both groups heavily sympathetic to the incumbents, four days to vote rather than one—an invitation to multiple voting? The electoral census underregistered antigovernment people in the south and overregistered progovernment people in the north. Private radio stations are permitted to give only cursory coverage, no editorials or debates. And so on and so on. Should we do anything at all to support these elections? If we don't, we have no voice with the government; if we do, we risk supporting a stacked-deck process. The representatives of civil society—human rights groups and labor unions—called a press conference which I attended a couple of weeks ago. They urged civil disobedience to protest the electoral census and talked of strikes and demonstrations. But nothing seems likely to come of it.

Another World Bank visit took place only a day or two ago. Its conclusions were mixed: Despite difficulties such as not paying rural salaries for three months, the country was on track with respect to its structural adjustment plan. And I see lots of clouds in the sky—a harbinger of early, blessed rains? Has the nadir been passed? The roller coaster goes up and it comes down and it rises again. The highs and lows excite and shock us. But ultimately it is our senses that exaggerate. Things here are really more like the harmattan sky, neither bright nor obscure but some hazy mix of both.

Best regards,

Ambassador Chris

We Thought We Had All the Answers, But Guess What?

January 20, 2002

Dear Friends,

It was a slow Friday, December 27, and we were using the Christmas lull in the office to catch up on things. Around 9:30 a.m., the phone rang and the receptionist told me that Obert, the butler, had called from my house. It seemed that Alphonse had fallen from a ladder and been hurt. This puzzled me—why would Alphonse be on a ladder? Mustn't have been high, couldn't have been much. A little later Obert called again, directly. It was Simone who had fallen, on the front porch, and he was badly injured. About that time Marty, our nurse-practitioner, called as well and told me that it was indeed serious and he was taking Simone to the hospital. I rushed out, just in time to catch the group departing. In the back of a shiny blue embassy pickup, Simone was splayed out, barely conscious, Marty on one side and Obert on the other. I wrung Simone's hand, but he didn't react, and the truck drove out the gate. In an hour, the phone rang once again, and Marty told me Simone was dead.

I stumbled numbly through the rest of the day, and the following morning I went to the wake. It was the familiar scene, with nuances. A throng filled the ample yard of Simone's compound. He was a Christian, meaning that women were mixed with the men. Someone escorted me up to the open coffin, where Simone's slight frame was laid out in white, and huge dark glasses disfigured the unrecognizable face. My Simone? Behind the coffin a chorus of churchwomen in identical ample cloth wraps sang and chanted a series of hymns. I was led to a chair across the way, from which I had a good view of things. Senior family were to my right, and I shook their hands. My duty would be to pass a half-hour in dignified presence. Simone's youngest daughter, wearing a sweatshirt inscribed "London City" above a print wrap, moved to the coffin and away, and back and forth among us, distracted in public grief, wailing the while, leaning on a girlfriend for support. The widow was secluded with close women friends. The latrine must have been near, for its odor outbid that of the people around me. A white cat wandered aimlessly in a faint accent of Simone's daughter's movements.

I returned two days later, after the ritual, to visit the family more personally. The clan leader who had guided me before still presided. This time Simone's widow came out to meet me, her arm in a sling from the fall she took when she heard the sad news. There were six children, five girls and a son with birth defects who wasn't around. The guide explained the plight of the family, which didn't own the compound and feared eviction. Two daughters I hadn't seen on Saturday had arrived from the south, Simone's region, and were now present. Some of his children had apparently been educated but didn't have jobs. How would they all survive without a breadwinner? Poorly off despite a reasonably good salary, Simone left behind a family typical of half of N'Djamena's population.

I want to devote most of this letter, as I did in the last one ["Getting Off on the Wrong Foot," chapter 4], dumping on the supposed experts. This time the subject is economic development. My thesis is that while the bilateral and multilateral aid folks think they have the ticket for Chad's development train, they no more do than Chad has a railway. As I develop my argument, I ask you to bear in mind Simone's destitute survivors, and think about whether the development work I discuss offers them any solace or hope for the future.

So let's go back to the top. What's wrong with Chad's development strategy anyway? The country has a finely honed strategy that came out of the Geneva IV roundtable process. The donors, theoretically in partnership with the Chadians, determined four priority sectors for the country back in 1997. These are health, education, infrastructure, and rural development. A "lead donor" has been designated for each, and a detailed sector strategy elaborated. Donor funds are flowing, and Chad has qualified for debt forgiveness as well; oil money will arrive in a couple of years. So what's wrong? Here's a clue: Ask yourself if Simone's family is even aware of these things.

Simone's survivors surely know of the oil project, but most likely little more. Their ignorance may well reflect the fact that Chad's economy is highly fragmented: Stimulating one part of it, usually the minuscule formal sector, doesn't necessarily spill over to the rest. Chad has, in effect, three economies. At the top is the smallest, the formal economy of state enterprises and top-tier companies: banks, some service professionals, and the growing transportation and communications industries. The firms normally have some foreign participation, and I've called on most of their managing directors. A handful of Chadian trading houses make it into this category, even if they hide much of their operations. All in all, we are talking fewer than 100,000 employees.

The gray sector is huge by comparison, even if it includes only 10 percent of the workforce. These are the folks the Bank and the Fund keep prodding the authorities to tax, small firms, some with and some without storefronts, intracity and market merchants, a few better-off street vendors, artisans and skilled workers of all sorts. These people, the bulk of the workers in N'Djamena and in the handful of larger towns, are in the cash economy but outside the tax economy. Or, rather, their "taxes" are the fees and bribes they pay informally to neighborhood and local officials to keep them at bay. Simone straddled the formal and gray sectors. He was paid in cash and we made the social security payments for his retirement, giving his widow a claim to a pittance now that he is gone. But she'll have a hard time collecting, and he most likely paid no other formal taxes.

Beyond and beneath is the subsistence sector. Only a handful of the urban folks at Simone's wake would fall into this category, but a half dozen close relatives who had made the trek from his home village near Mbaibokoum to N'Djamena would. Back in those villages, nearly everyone would. In fact, at least 80 percent of the people in this country, farmers and herders, still live mainly on what they produce, bartering or selling a bit around the edges. In season, they may see $20 to $50 a month in cash, but in most months there is less, if anything at all. The ties to the cash economy depend on proximity to N'Djamena and major towns. A backwoods cotton farmer, such as I saw driving from Zakouma to Sarh, may see cash only twice a year: once when he gets his advance from Cotontchad to purchase inputs, and the pittance more due him at harvest, once he has repaid the advance.

I cannot fail to note that the economy is geographically divided as well. N'Djamena acts as a natural pull for grain and a few other food products, but the poor roads—cut during much of the rainy season—limit internal trade, and nearly all nonfood products you see in the major towns' markets are imported. The divisions are betrayed in how the goods come in. Half or more of the population in N'Djamena and the south look toward Douala. But Abéché and markets as far west as Mongo feature goods that come in largely from Sudan. Faya-Largeau looks north toward Libya, and this oasis town's trade north, east, and west through the desert is more vital than that with N'Djamena.

All of these economic segments meet and have points of contact and exchange. So there were people from each at Simone's wake, despite the overwhelming presence of people from the urban gray sector. These folks are related and close friends with the handful present from the villages (subsistence sector) and the formal economy (the clan spokesman, to judge by his demeanor). But the economic sectors are no more integrated than the people in Simone's compound work together on a daily basis. Do you begin to see why donor efforts that focus largely on the formal sector, and occasionally a little on the subsistence sector, have limited national impact?

The sense of helplessness I saw in Simone's family when I made my second visit to them (and was hit up hard to do something for them) reminded me vividly of what I described to you in my letter "Gaps" [chapter 6] Here was a family of six or eight individuals who had relied entirely on one member, the patriarch, who had edged his way into the formal economy in my employ. A couple of the children had acquired a high school education, but they were girls, i.e., second-class job applicants. I don't know the story with the lone son and his disability, but the key point is that after a step beyond the subsistence or gray economy, there was no way for this family to consolidate the advance for the next generation. I believe even more today than when I wrote a year ago that we have a gap here in the development model. You can do infrastructure from the top down, and that will help. Simone's village relatives could have gotten to N'Djamena in one day rather than two if the paved road ran all the way to Mbaibokoum instead of stopping at Kélo. And grassroots improvements can get people one step above subsistence into artisanal food processing. But ultimately it won't be sustainable if there is no market pull. In fact, even if Chadian officials go along initially with the foreign development gurus and adopt the policies they find so distasteful to ensure transparency and all of that, they'll become frustrated and backslide when no development results. Just as Simone's family will, if they're lucky, drift back into N'Djamena's gray economy and not have to return to the village (subsistence).

So, more specifically, what are the errors of the development specialists? Where do they fail to connect? We can begin with their arrogance, as I noted in my last letter. It deafens them to any suggestions from those most directly affected, the Chadians. But two structural elements make it worse.

First is the use of loan funds to develop nonremunerative activities that ultimately depend on domestic revenues for perpetuation. Huh? Sorry for the Bankspeak. What I mean is that the Bank and the Fund lend Chad money to develop health and education infrastructure, but they ignore the private sector economy that eventually has to yield the taxes to keep these social improvements going and repay the loans that established them in the first place. In Far Eastern countries with a market-driven expansion, this might have made some sense, but in Chad? Already there are more students graduating with a "bacc" than find jobs, and most don't have any specific skills to go with their literary education. Simone's daughters epitomize this, since they have basic education but little chance of getting a job in an office or store to use it. And the more that educated young people go jobless, the greater the chances of instability.

The second element, the other side of the coin really, is the lack of attention by Westerners or the Chadian government to technical or vocational education, skills for employment in the existing private sector. Again, how is the governmental infrastructure of education and health services to be sustained by tax revenues, and how are the loans that established them to be repaid, if there isn't a vibrant private sector? Yet here the donors do absolutely nothing! The Bank and the Fund, in fairness, do work on privatization of various state enterprises, but that hardly addresses the fundamental question. Whence will come economic activity that generates tax revenue to support the superstructure of services established by the donors once those donors leave? Whence will come the jobs to sop up the graduates of improved education? The only priority developmental sector that deals with the guts of jobs and productivity is rural development. It lags all the other three in funding, and has basically gone nowhere.

And to this must be added all the "normal" problems of development—corruption in government, employment, and contracts; leadership favoring personal goals over common goals: rule of law honored in the breach: etc., etc. So where does Simone's family fit in? Perhaps nowhere, and that is the issue. Where's there a decent job for one of them?

So what is the future of Chad in terms of economic development? If the natural forces aren't strong enough to push it, and the donors don't know how, what happens? Will the likes of Simone's family fall further back than the gray economy, back to the subsistence level at the home village?

Let's start by going back to what we know does work. From

the top down, we know that infrastructure—roads and communications—will yield enormous benefits. Example: Although overall
Chad is rarely food deficit, the surplus in areas of good growing
conditions can't move to deficit areas until well after the rainy season, because until the roads dry out, they are impassable and regions of surplus and deficit can't be determined. Similarly, from
the bottom up, we know that grassroots microprojects yield good
returns. That might help Simone's relatives back in the village. But
we are left with a vast middle with no direction—the families like
Simone's, in which some breadwinner made one step forward but
has nowhere to put down his second foot, and subsistence farmers who've increased their productivity but aren't yet commercial
farmers.

As with politics, I see some pointers, if no obvious solutions.
First there is the oil project, and Chad, I feel sure, has much more
oil than people think. Already the formal economy is benefiting.
When I ask my business friends how things are now, they say,
"*Ca bouge un peu*"—it's moving a little. Six months ago they were
complaining about the project's lack of impact. The first effect in
N'Djamena is superficial—rising real estate prices, improvements
in hotels, and more restaurants, more imported goods in the little
Western stores. But between N'Djamena and the oil region itself,
5,000 more people are now being paid cash wages. And in both
places the trickle-down effect operates, magnified as Chadian companies receive subcontracts. But we all know that the oil industry is
extractive, that its impact will be limited, and that the real benefits
of petroleum will come only if the government's revenues are well
invested.

I can also identify industries where Chad could produce if there
were a market. These are mostly agricultural, and the prospects for
value added come from food and agricultural processing—fruits
and vegetables, meat and leather, perhaps poultry production and
wheat milling. Ultimately, the same holds for cotton spinning and
weaving, if energy costs can be reduced. Finding an outlet for whatever might be produced or processed depends heavily on regional
integration, however, for the natural market is Nigeria. Today that
market is depressed, as well as distanced by poor roads and difficult border crossings.

Last, I see excellent prospects in Chad for ecological or adventure tourism. You've read my descriptions of the sights. I can envision a healthy week or ten-day tour, especially if the Tibesti opens up. The circuit would include the Zakouma Game Park, Lake Chad, the Guéra, Abéché and Ouara, the Ennedi and Tibesti for the scenery and rock art, and perhaps Lake Léré, all in addition to a day in N'Djamena. Fans of the Sahara could add the salt lakes at Ounianga Kébir. There are people (like me) who do this today, working through one or two hand-holding travel agents in town. What's lacking is the transportation and lodging infrastructure to make it viable on a larger scale.

And how would all this help? It would begin to stimulate economic activity in that vast, empty middle zone. It might mean 20,000 to 30,000 more service and manufacturing jobs in N'Djamena and a few other locations. It wouldn't solve the problem, but it would be a start: As many as 200,000 family members might benefit. One of Simone's six offspring might be lucky enough to get a job.

But just as important, the development "specialists" need to admit what they don't know (in fairness, they usually do when we talk privately). Then, by talking more with the Chadians, they just might come up with some middle-gap solutions. If so, they need to be willing to risk some money to experiment and see what really works, and not endlessly study everything to death.

Somewhere here I need to say a word about globalization. Do you suppose Simone's daughters have any idea what it is all about? They will have heard the word on the radio, and the youngest may have left the lycée recently enough to have some notion of it. The others? Doubtful, and that's the problem here. Even the most educated, who do recognize that it has some effect, don't fathom how it touches Chad or understand its workings. They know intellectually that everything is interrelated today, but only the country's 1,500 Internet users and the 5,000 employees of Esso have any firsthand experience with globalization. Opinion, naturally, is reserved, if not downright skeptical. The influence of the French media, which snidely equates globalization with evil American domination, doesn't help. So no one here really sees how globalization will bring Chad the benefits that faster communications and freer trade are supposed to confer. And if globalization brings into question Chad's few trade preferences with France and Europe? That adds more concern. And no, it will bring no obvious boon to Simone's daughters for a long time to come. So Chadians remain ambivalent.

Fundamentally, my conclusion here, as in the last letter, is that the foreign experts have only a fraction of the answer. The model that they (we) so fondly espouse doesn't really serve here. To a degree, we're goofing things up more and delaying development by pretending it does apply. We know only how to start and how to help around the edges. I don't know what it is, but I suspect the real answer must be found and developed by the Chadians themselves, just as with politics. And perhaps it won't be a sterling, crystal-clear model, but muddling, plodding through the mire of Chad's rainy season toward something that gradually takes form as the clouds lighten and the bottomlands dry. We must continue to help some, but more as true partners in the adventure of finding the solution, not as didactic teachers of what doesn't work here. Ultimately, we can't do it for them, nor should we. I can subsidize Simone's family, as I plan to, for a few months with a handout, but in six months, I'm out of here. Then they must find their own way.

Best regards,

Ambassador Chris

Present at the Creation

May 19, 2002

Dear Friends,

There are times in life when all the calculation and inner analysis you can do can't provide absolute confidence about a course of action you are about to take. You make a decision and plunge ahead. For me, buying my house on Porter Street with some creative financing was such a decision. For some, I suppose even marriage falls into this category.

After my first trip to Chad's oil region in nearly a year, I'm convinced that countries face these kinds of choices too. The petroleum project is remaking the southern part of this land in ways that could not have been anticipated in advance by the so-called decisionmakers.

To start, I should give you a little background about the enormous $3.5 billion project and its components. It is the largest single private-sector investment in sub-Saharan Africa's history. Its development consortium is owned 40 percent by Exxon-Mobil, whose Esso subsidiary is the development partner; 35 percent by Malaysia's Petronas; and 25 percent by Chevron. The pipeline is separately incorporated, and the Chadian and Cameroonian governments own shares in addition to the consortium. The first major component is the 1,000-kilometer pipeline from Kribi, on the Cameroonian coast, to Kome, the center of the oilfields in southern Chad. A road of hardened laterite runs roughly parallel. The oil wells spread through a region of several hundred square kilometers around Kome. Sixty are under development; eventually there will be over 300. At the heart is "Kome 5," a huge complex where oil from surrounding wells is collected, purified, and sent by a huge pumping station flowing down the pipeline. Here also are a camp for hundreds of workers and an enormous power plant, driven by gas from the oil fields, to give electricity to all the project's operations. Add to this the growing Kome Base Camp, an airfield, several other construction camps, the pipeline/road route to the Cameroonian border, and a matrix of roads and oil pads in the oil fields around Kome. This country looks nothing like what I saw when I first visited it nearly three years ago.

During two-plus days in the region, I saw that the construction is somewhere around a third complete. The trunk road is nearly finished, with the last sixty to eighty kilometers scheduled to be done by July 1. The pipeline is 20 percent complete, working inland from the coast. All the secondary roads are finished in the oil zone. Kome-5 is moving ahead full blast, also perhaps 20 percent complete. The wells are being drilled at the rate of three or four a month. A dozen have been drilled and capped since December, and the initial sixty will be finished by mid-2003. Esso recently made a major design change: Instead of developing and paving a three-kilometer airstrip in Kome, they will use N'Djamena's airport for the entry of their heaviest air cargo, and truck it down south. This means they'll have to improve about 330 kilometers out of the existing 550 kilometers of road from N'Djamena to Moundou and east to Doba. I observed that the work, decided only in April, was already under way at breakneck speed.

It is hard for me to convey to you the visual impact of the transition that is beginning to occur. For you, not having seen the sleepy villages before, it would all still appear very meager and undeveloped. Perhaps the road construction conveys it best. All the way from N'Djamena south to Baiboukoum and the border, and then from Bam west to Kome, up to Doba and back to Moundou, road construction is under way or just completed. There are hundreds of trucks, dump trucks, earth-moving CATS and graders, and countless smaller vehicles. Strung out along the roads are thousands of Chadian workers in their Day-Glo orange and yellow uniforms—a nice change, to my mind, from the military uniforms in which you all too often see young African men. The new or improved roads themselves are smooth, with tidy deep gutters to drain the rains. Add the busy network of feeder roads and oil pads. Kome-5 is now a vast, level plain, whereas a year ago the area was rolling bush; its new flatness is interrupted by huge concrete cisterns, temporary dwellings by the hundred, and the skeleton of the future pumping station. It is by far the largest single complex in the country. The traffic along the roads is voluminous, whereas a couple of years earlier only a handful of vehicles would pass in a day. The last morning we drove through Bebedja, heading back to N'Djamena: The town that a year before had been a motionless overgrown village, with folks dozing under shade trees, was now a hive of bustling commercial activity.

Statistics tell the tale as well. The power plant at Kome-5 will produce some 120 megawatts—several times the existing capacity of the country, rated at 20, but rarely producing half that. The roadwork I've described involves constructing or improving just over 500 kilometers in a ten-month period; by contrast, under Chad's infrastructure development priority, the European Union, Taiwan, and Chad together manage to pave roughly 75 kilometers per year and improve from 100 to 200 kilometers of laterite road annually. The bridge to carry pipeline and road across the Mbere River at the Cameroonian border was built in less than a year; the longer but much simpler new Chari River bridge in N'Djamena has dragged out for three years, and Esso will probably have to finish it in order to move gear south. What greater proof could you want of the private sector's greater efficiency in executing these nuts-and-bolts activities? And fiscal numbers numb as well: The $3.5 billion value of the project dwarfs the country's annual gross national product of $1.5 billion to 1.75 billion.

As we rolled along the smooth, new road towards Baiboukoum, I mused over how to convey to you the impact of what I was seeing. I tried as well to put myself inside the head of one of the villagers who would see my car as part of an incredible transformation of his world.

I can only start to give a little of the sense of life and change that must strike a villager between Bam and Baiboukoum. Before, one day was much like another: a few hours of field toil in the morning, hot afternoons snoozing and chatting in the shade of a tree, an early evening meal, and an early retreat to bed. Once a week is market day, but otherwise change is seasonal, rhythmic. Catherine, who was on this trip as well, observed that life is easier here than in the north, the greener land less reticent, more yielding. Until now the village has been largely self-contained. It sends out cotton once a year, and occasionally a little surplus grain or produce. Then for a month or two there is cash to "import" sugar or other nonnative foodstuffs, and perhaps some bolts of cloth. The old potholed road saw a trickle of cars each day and perhaps a couple of long-haul trucks to Bangui. The officials and community leaders I spoke with in Baiboukoum were frustrated, feeling isolated and abandoned by the government.

So what has changed in the village we see today? First, the road is high and even now, and has a drainage channel on either side with concrete panels to bridge the gutters. Some of the sons of the village have gone to work for the contractor—grueling days under the harsh sun, but paying sums like FCFA 60,000 to 80,000 per month, which a family here sees maybe only during two or three months of the year at harvest time. Moneyed now, these workers — and the ones from outside — want something to spend it on. First, there is food: A cottage industry is growing up, with women portaging boule and other dishes to the work site at mealtimes. There may be dietary changes too, since the workers will want meat and heavy carbs to help them through their toil. And already I see little stands springing up in the villages selling soft drinks, cigarettes, and sundries. In the evening there will be beer and women.

The stream of vehicles is also new. The Toyota 4x4s are constant. The work trucks move back and forth. Everything is slow, since Esso enforces strict limits — sixty kilometers per hour, forty in villages, only twenty near schools. And truck convoys: Once a day, a file of fifteen to twenty trucks comes in from the railhead at Ngaoundéré in Cameroon. Later, when the road is officially finished, these may come twice or thrice a day for several months. And the white expats: Before, they might have been sighted here a few times a year; now they are out on the road every day, inspecting and directing the work, along with types never seen here before — Asians from the subcontinent and Southeast Asia.

The Esso folks have come through and consulted the village elders and people and, where productive trees or fields were disturbed, paid compensation. Esso gave people their choice: cash or the equivalent in farm implements, replacement plants, etc. Most took cash, and the nongovernmental organizations are lambasting Esso because it didn't force payment in kind or at least require recipients to attend lessons on how to spend money responsibly; many recipients have drunk their compensation. In a few spots, where existing public buildings were too close to a work site, Esso or its contractors have done more — a beautiful new school near the Mbere Bridge replaced a hovel.

My guess is that with all these physical changes, my villager feels a loss of control, or perhaps a change of control, for if formerly his success depended on beneficent natural forces, it now depends on these strange men. Esso's consultation may help him to understand the specific impact of the work, and the compensation is welcome. But I'd posit that the ultimate goals of the project still seem fabulous for him. How can Chad's black tar be so valuable that, pumped all the way to the coast and shipped on to Europe or America, it warrants all this effort? Is the end result, electricity or gasoline, so important when the villager has lived without either all his life? With the ends so nebulous, the benefits as of yet meager, our dazed villager must be wondering if it is worth all the disturbance in traditional rhythms, disturbance in which he had no choice.

Looking ahead, the pros and cons may be more distinct. The village may hope for more teachers, its own dispensary, better houses for job holders, more commerce. It may suffer from inflation in food prices and a higher incidence of HIV/AIDS. Most important, it will not prosper if it abandons agriculture because of the lure of the few oil jobs. And if this is the impact near Bam, how many times multiplied will it be in Kome, in the heart of the oil fields? The villager is being wrenched from traditional into quasi-modern thought patterns, and in return he gets mildly positive material benefits. But the change is inevitable, and the consortium a benevolent vector.

If the villager along the road to Baiboukoum feels modestly rewarded for his disorientation, in Kome the impact is maximized. The disorientation probably isn't much greater, but the positives add up—more employment, more demand for local production, more money coming into the local economy, etc. Better roads, and before long cell phones. And all this before the government starts investing the money from the oil revenues. Success with that, indeed, will be telling.

Have I told you before about Chad's landmark revenue management scheme? Under a law passed prior to the final World Bank blessing (read loan approval) for the project, revenues are divided up by formula. Some 10 percent off the top goes into a Swiss bank account, to be held for the benefit of future generations when the oil runs dry. Of the remainder, the government gets 10 percent for general budget support, the oil region itself gets 10 percent, and the remaining 70 percent is to be invested in Chad's four priority development sectors (health, education, rural development, and infrastructure). A nine-person committee watchdogs this, with five government and four civil society members. The World Bank and IMF oversee things as well. If it works, this will be a world precedent of incredibly progressive stature. I'm hopeful but taking no bets.

Another thing that struck me was just how much control the government has ceded to Esso over what happens in the south, almost a loss of sovereignty! Perhaps unwittingly—for who could have imagined the impact of the change? But to its credit, the Chadian government bit the bullet and hasn't looked back. Today, in four of the most populous of Chad's twenty-eight *departements,* Esso calls the shots on security (it suggests routes and accompanies military and paramilitary patrols), communication (it controls the roads and has its own satellite radio network reaching to N'Djamena), and, of course, economic development (Esso's social payments dwarf those of government and donors). Esso coordinates every step of the way with central and local authorities, but insists on what it needs; Esso rules the south. When I see this and think of what control freaks African rulers are, the voluntary relinquishment of authority by the Déby regime boggles my mind.

So whither? What lies ahead for oil in Chad? This trip made me feel very much like I have been present at the creation of a new order whose development and ultimate ramifications I cannot foresee. I mentioned above that you wouldn't notice much, but that for Chadians in the village, yea, for me, the visual change alone is dramatic. In a year or eighteen months, when the camps are complete and the first wells are pumping, the face of the country will have changed even more—it will be like the transplanted Texas oil town John Updike imagined in *The Coup,* the novel he wrote about a thinly disguised Chad back in the 1970s. But the Esso folks I spoke with see no relaxation in the activity once the Kome fields begin to pump. There is more oil to the north and east, and other consortia are exploring further afield. One Texas oilman hinted to me that the country sits atop a sea of oil as vast as Lake Chad once was. Where will it end?

Some of the possibilities are intriguing. I learned, for example, that the project's own power source is to be gas, not heavy, polluting crude. Is there gas enough for local power generation outside the project? Or, even using the crude, of which Chad owns 12.5 percent, could a minirefinery be built? Does that open the prospect of cheap domestic electricity in southern Chad? Perhaps in Sarh, to run the mothballed textile plant? To make the sugar plant cost-effective? Or to build a canning and juice plant for mangoes and citrus? Where will oil have taken this country in ten years' time?

But come back to earth, Chris. Remember you are in the Chad of today, where predictions of the future are always risky. Two slightly bizarre episodes riveted me back to the peculiar reality here.

En route back to N'Djamena, we stopped to stretch our legs just south of Kélo. And there, by chance, I found a single wild iris blooming not far from the road. The classic spiked leaves pushed two or three inches out of the ground; resting atop them, a single bloom unfurled its unmistakable trefoil of billowy white fronds. I know not if this is a native here, or some seed escaped from a European import miles away. But it is a reminder that always in Chad, nature too introduces the unexpected. For most Chadians—farmers and herders—rain, not oil, remains the critical liquid.

Ten days after coming home, I heard an odd story from an expatriate friend while dining with him and his family. They run N'Djamena's only good, three-star hotel, among other things. A few nights before, the president had shown up at the hotel in the early evening, accompanied only by his chauffeur, and stayed the night. Bizarre, it underscored for me the traditional streak in the government here. What was it that made the president eschew the dwellings of his four wives, as well as his palace, and instead seek to sleep anonymously at the hotel owned by a business friend? Not fear, if he came only with his driver. But the story makes me sympathize with this tribesman turned political father of his country, who, like me, occasionally flees his duties into anonymity for a few brief hours of repose.

All of which leads us to a final question. Can Chad handle the changes being thrust upon it without once more breaking apart into warring factions? To some degree, this is rhetorical, for the country has no choice, and, today at least, no one wants to tear it apart or forgo the coming era of (modest) oil wealth. But how will it adjust? The donors' involvement has done more to prepare Chad to adjust to mineral wealth than has been the case anywhere else. But, that said, the strong holdover of traditional ways and values will inevitably clash with modern introductions. There will be strains and compromises, and we can't yet know the outcome. I am leaving Chad at a time when the country is truly being re-created. It has my best hopes and wishes that what it becomes will be an improvement over other oil countries. Chad's leaders have my congratulations for their courage in moving confidently into the unknown.

Best regards,

Ambassador Chris

P.S.

This Chad letter has been woefully long in coming, in part because of the hectic pace of work, and in part because I took a two-week vacation in late June, visiting Kenya and Tanzania (I heartily recommend that to you). There is likely to be at least one more major trip, and therefore one more letter. I'm planning a ten-day to two-week foray into the north, including a desert crossing from Fada to Faya-Largeau, probably in mid-September. Yes, September—I've been asked to stay on a few months longer because of delays in my successor's confirmation process. I'm now looking at late October, but have been told to refrain from fixing any dates, so I imagine that could slip as well.

Chadians at Home

September 27, 2003

I don't get invited to many Chadian homes. It isn't surprising since most live in hovels, and these people, rightfully proud, don't want to show the American ambassador how meanly they live. But occasionally I see a poorer household when I visit a tradesman in the *quartier*. And I've had several invitations to the homes of the wealthy. This letter is about those extremes.

Some weeks ago the daily newspaper ran an article about a carpenter who carves wooden pens by hand. It sounded interesting—a unique souvenir or small gift item, and a chance to support a local artisan. Two of our FSNs tracked down the locale—a compound on the main road south, opposite "Le Building," N'Djamena's only ten-story structure, and I went there on a Saturday.

The compound was typical, similar to what I'd seen in Bardaï and around N'Djamena three or four times before. I entered through an archway in the mud-brick outer wall between two commercial stalls—one a shop, the other a bar. I stepped over a tiny rill that brought milky wastewater out of the compound toward a deep gutter a foot in front of the wall. The odor was of human waste and decay.

Inside, the overwhelming impression was of brown-gray. The sandy floor, mud-brick walls of permanent structures, and straw of temporary shelters were all the same hue. Everything seemed to be eroding because it's the rainy season. The compound was oblong, perhaps forty-feet wide and sixty-feet deep. To the right and before me, I had the impression of a series of mud-brick rooms, but I couldn't see them clearly because of the intrusion of huts of sekko, or straw, that were built out into the open space. After a few minutes a woman emerged from the monochrome and directed me to my left, where I found the carpenter under one of the sekko shelters. We chatted and I ordered a sample pen.

On a subsequent visit I was disappointed—the adults were all away and there were only a few children in the compound, none of whom seemed to understand French. I took the opportunity to look more closely around the compound, but there was little I'd missed. In the center was a sorghum patch with perhaps a dozen healthy stocks, its green relieving the brown. A boy of five or six was dutifully watering it by peeing into it. I looked again at the carpenter's workshop—a primitive lathe and a couple of tables were evident, the other tools all stowed away.

And the pens? The samples were crude, carved in a soft wood with jejune slogans like "Je t'aime." I asked the carpenter to do new ones, replacing the words with panels in the colors of the Chadian flag, and I ordered ten, at $5.00 apiece. The carpenter, catching on, did some with both the Chadian and American flag—there's hope!

Let me go to the opposite extreme and describe three dinners with prominent Chadians, moving from the most to the least Westernized.

M. S. is a prominent businessman, certainly wealthy by Chadian standards, who has recently become honorary consul for Turkey. Perhaps the dinner he invited me to was designed to confirm that status—the other guests were the French ambassador and his wife, the IMF resident representative (a woman, my "date"), and the chief UN representative in Chad and his wife. Together we might be said to represent the top echelon of Chad's small diplomatic corps.

The house was in a central neighborhood off a main street. The homes of the wealthy seem intermixed with others in all but the poorest neighborhoods. Entering, the living room was what I've seen in the homes of other prominent Chadians. A very long rectangle, it was lined with overstuffed chairs and couches along all sides of the perimeter, save one. An end table here and there and a sole étagère broke the monotony of the leather seats. The placement left a huge open area in the middle, a gulf across which conversation in Western fashion was impossible. I was reminded that when Chadians visit each other presence is more important than what is said. They will sit, gossip idly with neighbors to their left and right, but never feel compelled to keep a conversation going. There are long periods of unembarrassed silence that drive type A Westerners up the wall.

With effort, we chatted Western style on light topics, although it was clearly a business dinner. The host's wife was present and participated with relaxed poise. After an hour we adjourned to the dining room. It was tiny by comparison with the huge parlor. The table set for eight pushed its chairs so close to the wall that, when we were seated, the servants had a hard time moving behind us to serve. This too is a local architectural twist: Had the guests been Chadians, the dining room would have served only to house a buffet table, and everyone would have taken their plates back to the living room to eat on their laps seated either in the perimeter chairs or on the carpeted floor in the middle.

The meal itself was vaguely Western. A delicious, spicy soup as the starter was the tastiest dish of the evening. A main course of fish in a sauce with rice followed, then salad, and, last, a dessert. Afterward we retreated to the living room for coffee, and it wasn't long before the French ambassador, claiming an early morning the next day, rose and cleared the way for all the guests to leave *ensemble*. Even if the conversation had been rather dull and predictable, I felt the warmth of my host's hospitality throughout the evening, and the gracious concession of his wife's presence and attentiveness.

Through our visits back and forth during my jaunts to Washington and his longer stays in N'Djamena, the Chadian ambassador to Washington, Ahmat Hassaballah Soubiane, has become a good contact and almost a friend. He spends time here because he remains very much a player in Chadian politics. Of course, I invited him for lunch a couple of times when he spent three months here recently on business of the ruling party, and he reciprocated by hosting a dinner for me at the home of a relation who is also a prominent businessman. He encouraged me to bring different folks from the embassy, but only Nelson, the incoming Peace Corps director, could make it.

This was in May, the height of the hot, dry season, and while the house this time was in the Western quarter, the arrangements were traditional. The event was held outdoors, beginning at 7:00 p.m., when the temperatures had begun to drop below 100 degrees and the slightest of breezes had sprung up. Arriving, we were led to an open area spread with carpets in front of the house itself. A line of tables was strung further back, awaiting food, and to one side was a little line of chairs, just in case the Westerners needed them. But Nelson and I quickly kicked off our shoes and squatted on the pillows that lined the edges of the carpet. The ambassador and our actual host, M. A., had met us as we descended from the car and escorted us back.

The other Chadian guests were less timely, and filtered in over the next forty-five minutes. There were the mayor of N'Djamena, a couple of other well-known businessmen, and some relatives. It was a largely "Arab" group—"Arabs" being the third or fourth largest ethnic group in the country. After most of the guests had gathered, M. A.'s wife and daughter made an appearance, sitting and chatting briefly with us men, and then retreating.

Our cocktails were bottled water and *karkanji*, a delicious local fruit punch made from hibiscus flowers, lightly sugared and with a hint of ginger to give it a bite. There were the traditional dates and groundnuts (peanuts) to snack on. Sprawling and sitting on the carpet, the dozen guests were closer than at the home of M. S., but the conversation still broke down into three or four segments. Mine, with the principal hosts, was more substantive: politics a little, commercial relations between Chad and America, the desire to strengthen these ties, and M. A.'s interest in obtaining information about growing alfalfa on an American scale on his farms. Nelson was a big hit because the return of the Peace Corps is so widely welcomed.

Shortly after the stragglers arrived, servants began to lade the tables with covered dishes. In due course, I was invited to lead the guests through the buffet. Flatbread and rice and donutlike beignets, the staples, were there. Also there were a stew with chicken and potatoes, beef brochettes, and a huge roast fish. The salad was garnished with tomatoes and avocados. We returned with our plates to the carpets and resumed our squatting position to eat. Eventually as dessert, there was *bouillie*, a milk-based liquid thickened with saturated grains of wheat or rice, served warm in a bowl. Tea followed.

The ambassador let perhaps twenty minutes elapse after all the eating was done and the dishes had been borne away. He then arose and thanked the guests for coming, mainly myself. He noted the latening hour, but underscored the importance of this relaxed sharing of a meal among friends. And then there were the hospitality gifts—for Nelson, an embroidered tablecloth, local work. For me, a gorgeous, flowing *boubou*, or northern robe. It was a lovely, light green pastel, just the color of local lemons, and heavily embroidered as well. I made short remarks of thanks, seconding the ambassador's characterization of the evening as one of friendship that strengthened our national relations.

Before I tell you about the third evening, I have to introduce Nassir to you. He is a businessman of Mauritian origin, short and slightly spreading, fortyish. He's been in Chad nearly ten years. He typifies the kind of expatriate that oils the economy in developing countries. He knows Western business practices and has international connections, but understands equally well how things work in developing countries. He can do things that General Motors can't, and acts as a bridge between the local and the world economy. He's been successful here. His bread-and-butter business is N'Djamena's third-best hotel, Hotel Sahel, which in the time I've been here has grown from one compound with a dozen rooms to five compounds scattered around the expat and business neighborhoods, with fifty single rooms and perhaps a dozen apartments. One of his more spectacular ventures is the Zamzam Mineral Water plant here in town. Somehow he managed to marry Libyan financing with sourcing the equipment in the United States. He does a little import business—used clothing from the United States, light machinery from India (which named him honorary consul). His current irons in the fire include two more water plants, a juice factory, a cement factory, and a detergent factory. At a minimum, one of the water plants will be a go. It's the Nassirs who develop real, going enterprises in countries like Chad, and it doesn't bother me that I can't ask too directly about some of the things that are necessary to make it happen.

But I mention Nassir here because he invited me to the third event, a wedding. Not his, but that of Jean, a young Frenchman who is trying to develop a computer business here. Through Nassir, Jean became acquainted with a prominent Chadian businessman, a brother of a former prime minister, and became enamored of his very Westernized and beautiful daughter. I had met Jean several times chez Nassir. Now Nassir called and asked if I would join the wedding party, for local custom calls for the groom to call, with a group of relations and friends, upon the bride's family for a betrothal ceremony before the wedding. I jumped at the chance.

Our arrival at the bride's home was precisely timed. We had gathered at Nassir's, and got a phone call telling us when the bride's menfolk were ready to receive us. We piled into three or four cars and were there within a few minutes, the event kicking off only five minutes behind the promised 7:00 p.m. Somehow Chaibo eased my enormous Suburban into the dirt street to discharge us before the compound.

A male family member waited at the gate to lead us to the house. Two little girls scattered flower petals from tiny baskets before our feet as we proceeded. The women of the extended family were gathered off to our left in the yard. Immediately upon our entry, they burst into song and throat-yodeling, some shaking tambourines and beating little drums. But we were led directly into the house with no opportunity to acknowledge the women.

Entering, I noted the typical large, oblong living room of a well-to-do Chadian. All four sides were lined with armchairs and sofas, broken only by the odd table or étagère and a few doors. All thirty or forty of the seats were occupied, and the overflow of the bride's relatives were seated on the carpets in the rear third of the open area in the middle of the room. It was clearly expected that the groom's party would squat on the carpets at the front of the room, looking up at the half-dozen senior hosts who occupied the chairs.

We entered and greeted the seniors in protocol order—Nassir first as surrogate father, me next, and the others. The bride's father was in the center chair. Among his business ventures is supplying the South African satellite TV feed, to which the embassy subscribes. To his right was the president of the Supreme Court, whom of course I knew, and to his left, the grandfather and a couple of other senior male relatives. The president was surprised to see me but greeted me warmly. After shaking hands with the front row, we quickly settled onto the carpet, me refusing the chair that was offered.

Nassir, as senior groomsman, spoke to formally request the hand of the bride for Jean. He presented a dowry in an ornamental box—several gold coins and banknotes totaling FCFA two million, or about $3,000. The father acknowledged the offer and asked a *marabout* to offer a prayer. Several chanted prayers followed, hands first palm up, then palm down. I bowed my head in respect but glanced surreptitiously around. Most eyes were closed, reverently. Then, in all of ten or fifteen minutes, the formalities were over.

We were quickly invited to proceed to dinner. Sharing a meal would further solidify the alliance of families just agreed to by the fathers of bride and groom. The small dining room had been turned into a buffet with dishes typical of an upper class Chadian spread. The pièce de résistance was a six-foot-long capitaine (fish), broiled and stuffed. There was roast chicken, boule and sauce, lettuce and tomato salad, stewed vegetable dishes, samosas, and more. I heaped the delicacies onto one of the small plates and returned to the living room, this time agreeing to take one of the chairs to the left of the seniors.

The women outside had been carrying on all this time, and I heard their noise as I ate, returned for the dessert of fruit and Western wedding cake and pastries. Then rather suddenly everything was over. Nassir and our hosts rose, spoke briefly, shook hands, and we were on our way out.

As we filed out, we encountered a concession to Western expectations—we would be allowed to greet the bride and senior women en route to the cars. I gave my congratulations and passed to the bride-to-be a card enclosing a modest sum of money, FCFA 30,000, or $50, I'd been warned to bring. I then greeted one of the president's wives, whom I recognized; the bride's mother; Nassir's wife, Farah; and others. Within an hour and a half, all was over, Jean in absentia was betrothed, and we were headed back to Nassir and Farah's. The next day, Farah told me, there would be a similar event for the women.

What I haven't told you is how a middle-class Chadian lives—say, one of our embassy employees or a salary worker for one of the banks or a foreign aid agency. I haven't seen much, but from what some have told me I can infer a few things. Chaibo, my driver, lives in a mud-brick compound I saw on the occasion of his daughter's death. But he has since acquired a battery-operated TV, and he recently let drop that he has a second compound in another part of town (for the second wife I know he has?). Anne-Nicole, my French tutor who also teaches at the American School, has more—her compound may be partly stuccoed like the old Lebanese man's, and she has an electric connection, a small refrigerator, and a little generator for power when the city power goes out. But for a good picture of this middle zone, you'd get a better description from one of our newly arrived Peace Corps volunteers in six months than from me.

A couple of things do strike me, however. For one thing, the country is so poor that you don't have the extremes of wealth and poverty I observed in Nigeria. The homes of the wealthy here are very middle class by American standards. Only once have I been inside an owner-occupied Chadian home fancier than my own in Washington—the owner wanted to rent it to us as a new ambassador's residence. This leads me to observe that, according to a calculation someone at the embassy did shortly before I arrived, there are only a dozen or two families in the country that are wealthier than I or other leading expats such as the head of Esso, and most of their assets are in France. And here? The wealthy live in an odd mixture of traditional and Western. My glimpses of both the rich and poor are exotic in their way, and given their rarity, they reinforce that odd feeling I have sometimes of being a voyeur as I try to observe and study things here.

Regards,

Ambassador Chris

6

Contrasts: Internal, and Chad versus America

This final chapter focuses on what was for me the most fascinating aspect of my life in Chad: the razor-sharp contrasts in the lives of the people here, and those between Chad and America. Is it the information overload in the West that dulls our senses to the differences between rich and poor, healthy and sick? In Chad, all is starker: It's a hard life for the rural family living in a straw or mud-brick hut with a cash income of $100 to $200 a year; the same is true for the polio victims on tricycles in N'Djamena, hawking the sugar they're allowed to bring in from the Cameroons.

How to contrast N'Djamena and its dirt streets with the already rich American capital that underwent a remarkable revitalization of its own during my years away, thereby becoming even richer? The difference was sharp enough at the outset, but when I moved back home, Washington looked to me like it had streets of gold. "A Trip from Heaven" is an early description of the material contrasts between the two countries, not always coming out in America's favor. My last letter, "The Sparrows Are Fat," was written after my return to Washington and deals mainly with the new lenses through which I viewed my own city after nearly four and a half years in Chad.

The contrasts that struck me were countless: within Chad, between the polished elites and the illiterate poor in their mud hovels; between the very modest development spending on what we know works at the grassroots and massive funding at the macro level, which never seems to generate the intended return. The second letter I wrote after six weeks in-country, "Of Mud-Brick Huts and Polished French," shows how this struck me immediately. "Gaps" describes some of the challenges Chad faces and the lack of a suitable development model to tackle them.

Not all of the contrasts are physical, of course. More fundamentally, there is the clash of values that I explore in "Dueling Values." "Chad and America" explores not only the differences between our countries but also what we have in common, especially the human connections individuals have forged between the two countries. Similarly, "The Events from Afar," whose topic is 9/11, displays the strength of this human connection in the Chadian reaction.

What makes these contrasts, especially those between the two countries, such a recurrent and entrancing theme for me? I can't fully explain it. But a lot of it goes to what I learned during nearly four-and-a-half years as ambassador to this country and its stalwart people. Chad taught me much about life that I would never have learned sitting at home in America, where even the sparrows are fat.

Of Mud-Brick Huts and Polished French

November 11, 1999

It is ironic that a country located only a few hundred miles from the cradle of mankind—or perhaps even containing that cradle—should be one of the most backward, at least according to the UNDP Index of Human Development.

Did you know that the cradle may have been right here in Chad? Last Saturday I went to La Source, one of N'Djamena's two recognized bookstores, and the little pamphlet was right there: *Tchad: Berceau de l'humanité?* I thumbed through it. It is probably the only book published so far in 1999 right here in Chad. It describes the preliminary results of Chadian-French (mainly French) archaeological expeditions, beginning back in 1995 with the discovery of an australopithecine mandible in the desert about 300 miles north of here. The find was important because it was the first of this hominid to be found west of the Great Rift Valley, demonstrating that these prehumans roamed a wider range of savanna than had been recognized. The booklet, which of course I bought and immediately read, goes further in claiming that this 3.5 million-year-old fossil is the earliest *Australopithecus* on record, raising the possibility, yep, that Chad and not Kenya or Tanzania is the fount of man! So, of course, when the French team comes back for its spring campaign, I will have to go up and visit their dig. My colleague Les knows one of the French archaeologists who lives permanently in Chad (Les, roughly my age, has been here since Peace Corps days, employed in one way or another by the US government, and either directly or through his Chadian wife, he knows everyone who is anyone in Chad—this is possible in a country of 7.5 million in which the influential number only a few thousand). Today I went to see the mandible—read on!

But Chad's backwardness is visible everywhere. Let me start with the mud-brick huts. Last Sunday some of us took the embassy boat out on the river and spent about three hours chugging slowly up and down looking for hippopotamuses. We saw some, four adults and a baby, but that was secondary to what struck me about the mud-brick huts we saw in the riverside villages. These are the same structures that the men of early civilizations built along the banks of the Nile and the Tigris and the Euphrates. They are of adobe brick. The brick is just moistened earth with a bit of straw to give it some consistency. We see the brick being made alongside the huts as we drive through villages on the outskirts of town. The structures built of the bricks are single-story, with few windows. Doorways are always into a little receiving room, with another doorway beyond into a courtyard, the two doorways staggered so that passersby have no view of the courtyard where, presumably, lots of household activity, including that of the women, takes place. The roofs are supported by poles. Some roofs are straw mats, some of an adobe stucco supported by mats. In town, one finds the same architecture, but the roofs tend to be tin, held down against the wind by concrete blocks or big stones. Some of the brickwork is left exposed. Sometimes there is a layer of adobe stucco coating it, and occasionally this stucco is incised with simple designs (nothing as ornate as I recall from Kano or Katsina in northern Nigeria).

Today, for the first time, I had the feeling that I may actually be able to put together for you, when all of you come out here, the sort of day-long city tour I developed for Bonn and Cologne in Germany and for Lagos. I began the morning at the French air base for a commemoration of the armistice. Like most ceremonial events, it dragged a tad at first. But it got interesting when one of the French officers gave a ten-sentence history of World War I from the French perspective. The German ambassador who was next to me got SO MAD, and said to me in German—"Those French didn't win World War I or World War II—you Americans did!" After the ceremony we went to lay a wreath at the Christian cemetery, and there was the grave of General Lamy, founder of the city through his death, his grave a candidate for first stop on my tour.

Later in the morning I was treated to a tour of the National Museum, a mile or so down the road from the embassy. It is a modest affair, only four little exhibition rooms with tawdry displays. Much of the collection disappeared during the two-plus decades of civil war and strife. The assistant director took us around. She had been to the United States three years ago under a USIS program. She was so proud of her meager, carefully tended rooms, and honored that an American ambassador wanted to see them. The highlight of the collection for me was, of course, the mandible. The French Cooperation Agency had financed one of the four rooms, devoted to the findings from the desert digs. There is a replica of "Chad man," another early hominid found back in 1961 in the same general region, and an interesting display on the progression of the dental development of protoelephants. The other three rooms cover ethnology, history, and handicrafts. The handicraft room doubles as the admission and sales center. Modest indeed, but worth a stop on my tour. I hope I can think of something that we can do for the museum.

Returning to the old, the Assistant Director noted that there are thirteen or fourteen sites of archaeological interest in the N'Djamena region. But they are slowly being despoiled by lack of protection. People move into them and squat there for a year or two, growing their sorghum and building their huts. When the hut erodes and the soil wears out, they move on and in a year or two someone else comes along. There used to be fences and watchmen. But that too perished in the civil war, along with the means to pay for such.

One thing that probably won't make the cut on my tour is the airport. You'll see it coming in anyway. It reminds me a little of the first airport I really got to know as a child, that in Sacramento, California, when it had all of three gates. I remember having a great Caesar salad in the restaurant in Sacramento; there's no restaurant at the N'Djamena airport. I don't think this one has more, if indeed it has any, identifiable gates as opposed to general access onto the tarmac. It is a decaying structure that is manned by staff only when the half dozen or so flights during the week are expected. And the service is unpredictable. One of our temporary-duty personnel missed his flight out the other day because it left three hours early—unheard of in Africa. Well, it turned out that the pilot decided not to go on to Bangui, Centrafrique, this time, and then got tired of waiting around in N'Djamena and just left. But what really impresses is the planes on the skirts of the runway—DC-3s and DC-7s! The defunct internal airline owns one of them, but it can't fly because it is minus an engine. That's why they can't sell it to cover their deficit and go quietly out of business. Some friend of the World Bank director here made her son a wooden model of the Chadair plane, which is hanging in her living room, complete with the hollow engine cone.

As I stared at these huts, their monotony broken by the colorful, newly washed garments drying on poles in front of them, it struck me that this is the way the bulk of mankind has lived for thousands of years. This is what the traders saw first of Ur or Thebes as they poled their boats up to the edge of the city. They would pass through blocks and blocks of this dusty brown agglomeration before reaching the open squares and impressive multistoried structures for which we remember those early urban centers.

One other thing, and then I'll stop slinging mud. The dwellings and shops are all in a state of constant decay and repair. It seems that after a few rainy seasons, the structures literally melt away and need rebuilding. The preferred method seems to be one wall per season, for when I drive through town I often see a building with a single wall pulled down, the roof drooping above, and piles of new brick amid the ruins of the old.

And what of the new and sophisticated side of things here? Well, there seems to be just about every means of telecommunications available or on the way. Embassy phone service is good. We have a tie-line to Washington, DC, and Uncle Sam even lets us use it for limited personal calls in the off hours (but only to 202 and 800 area codes). Chad is on the Internet through Tchadnet. It took a month of trial and error, and the best minds of the local post and telecommunications (P&T) office as well as the embassy communications staff, but my American laptop is now hooked up and in Internet communications over Tchadnet. The P&T is gradually being privatized, and a Western firm—30 percent US owned, I'll have you know—has just gotten the contract to develop cellular service here. Satellite phones are also available. A few days ago I was handed an Iridium phone for my use. It's just like back in the States—more technology than this poor mind can ever learn to deal with. And yes, we have CNN at home, along with nine Arabic TV stations, TV Chad, and three French stations.

N'Djamena itself is a new city. It was founded in 1900 by the French on the site of a fishing village on the Chari River. But in its bare century, it has come to look run down, as only a poverty-stricken city in a developing country can. Start with the fact that 90 percent of the buildings are of the mud-brick style described so laboriously above. Add the dearth of paved streets, arid climate, lack of money or skills for maintenance, torrential downpours and flooding during the rainy season, and on and on.

You will remember from my first letter that I said my first impression of N'Djamena was that there's nothing here. Of course, with a month now to have looked around and explored a little, I'm noticing the life beneath the rather squalid veneer. The other day I rode through the real downtown. This isn't the five-block modern zone that looks like a town from an old Western movie. It is the old market area around the Great Mosque. The Great Mosque is brand new, a gift from the Saudis, along with the Islamic high school adjacent to it. In pale pink stucco, it is an impressive structure. And the shops around it look like a real African market district: tiny, narrow shops jam-packed with goods hanging right up to the rafters, a variety of goods and colors to distract anyone from the dusty mud streets and tin walls and roofs of the booths. And, of course, in the administrative district, I'm gradually getting behind the high compound walls and seeing the more modern structures and gardens they mask.

The Chadians themselves seem so sophisticated! When I go to meet with a minister or a parliamentary leader, I am awed by their polished French. These are educated people who have well-thought-out views about the myriad problems of their country. But articulate as the Chadians are, I fear that my German colleague may again be correct—there isn't much depth behind the literacy, he cautions. The problems are easy enough to identify, rock-hard to solve. And the Chadians, he tells me, have acquired an attitude of dependency, i.e., looking to donor countries and international organizations to provide the solutions. And money. Perhaps he is right. But these guys are impressive interlocutors. I'll withhold judgment a bit longer.

Another impressive feature is the complete freedom of speech and press. There *is* a dramatic democratic dialogue on major events affecting the country. While I'll reserve detailed commentary on this for another letter, it merits mention as one of those things that is striking here. As President Déby told me yesterday when he called me in to an unscheduled conference, with respect to freedom of expression, Chad is far and away ahead of most African countries. In this, at least, he's right.

Perhaps I've been able to convey what I mean when I speak of the ancient and the modern. It is a country where it seems that nothing has changed since at least the 1950s, if not earlier, but where there is a thin overcoat—atop the mud brick—of a sophisticated and intelligent society that at least recognizes its own shortcomings.

I've waxed on far beyond what I meant to for this theme, so let me stop. Personally, I continue to find my way. My tennis is getting back in shape just a little. My sea freight should be here next week.

Best regards,

Ambassador Chris

Chad and America

April 19, 2000

A week or two ago Chad was mentioned prominently in a front-page article in the *Washington Post* and a few days later in an editorial. Why? What do Chad and the United States have to do with one another that is so important, and what are American interests in Chad? It's a fair question for an ambassador who has now been here six months.

The *Post* references, of course, were to the oil project I've mentioned before. Specifically, the article anticipated and the editorial commented upon protests in Washington against the World Bank and International Monetary Fund on account of, among other things, loans for "a pipeline through the rain forest in Chad." Never mind that there is no rain forest anywhere in Chad. But the oil project will be partly financed with a World Bank loan, and it is the largest US interest in Chad.

The oil project is, in fact, the only major US direct investment in Chad. After the reformulation of the private-sector development consortium—one of the two big-ticket news items since my arrival here, the other being the rebellion in the north—US companies have a two-thirds interest in the project, Exxon-Mobil, 40 percent, and Chevron, 25 percent. After endless delays, a vote in favor of a World Bank loan next month should be the last piece to this puzzle, and the $3.5 billion project should be ready for construction to start.

From Chad's standpoint, this is critical. The foreign investment in the project is estimated at $3.5 billion, versus Chad's GNP of under $2 billion. Over the twenty-five-year span of anticipated oil revenues, the project will supply Chad with nearly $3.5 billion in income, nearly doubling the government's annual budget. So from Chad's perspective, the project and, by extension, American participation are paramount.

From the US perspective, this means a lot less, of course: a nice profit point for two of our big companies, but in the bigger picture of things, small change.

Why were the protesters so concerned? First, the staunchest environmentalists among them oppose any oil project anywhere in the world. But in Chad's particular case, there is a complex overlay of north-south, Muslim-Christian, and government-opposition tensions that complicates the legitimate environmental, revenue use, and land compensation issues. It is much too complicated to explain with precision, but let me try a nutshell approach. Chad's government is northern/Muslim dominated, but the oil is in the Christian south. Organized civil society here is a largely southern phenomenon allied with the political opposition. With some justification, these folks lack confidence in the government's commitment to appropriate revenue use (as opposed to Swiss bank accounts), including the investment of some of the money to benefit the people of the production region. Add the elements of the "evil" World Bank's loan and an IMF stabilization program. You get a perfect crosshatch of legitimate domestic concerns by Chadians and the phobias of the rabid opponents of globalization. So blind are the latter, well-intentioned folk that they fail to see that the involvement of the international institutions is absolutely vital to avoid corruption, and that without this project they condemn Chadians to the continued poverty and lack of reform they claim to oppose. Well, I'll stop since I'm beginning to sound equally rabid, but you get an idea of how complex this largest American interest in Chad has become. Nothing in life is ever simple, especially in Africa.

So what does Chad mean in the overall picture of US foreign policy interests? Although Chad itself is not a focus of US foreign policy, it remains a good illustration of what we are trying to accomplish with our Africa policy. The United States has diplomatic relations with about 170 countries, of which over 50 are in Africa. Here we have three major policy objectives: (1) promotion of democratic governance—our ideology; (2) bringing Africa into the mainstream of the world economy (what better means could you find than the oil project in Chad?); and (3) countering terrorism and other transnational threats to Americans and their interests.

Location, location, location! Washingtonians among you will recognize the term from dinner table real-estate chatter. Chad has a tertiary geographic importance as well, in that it is proximate to two countries that we don't like very much—Libya and Sudan. That may change but for the moment it gives us here the additional role of watchdogs.

So how does Chad fit into these three major policy goals? The economic point needs the least explanation. What better example of drawing remotest Africa into the world economy could be found than our oil project in the Chad *enclavé*? You'd think the US government would trip over its heels rushing to support the project, but we aren't. Because of more fundamental problems with the World Bank, US support for the loan to Chad is by no means a foregone conclusion, no matter how much the project is in American interests both economically and from a foreign-policy perspective. Such are the arcane workings of the Washington policy process.

And democracy. Here Chad is like most of Africa, but more so. If democracy can grow in soil as inhospitable as Chad's, there is indeed hope for it everywhere. I happen to agree very strongly that promoting democracy should be a major policy goal on this continent. In these hopelessly diverse and divided countries I see no ultimate hope for stability and progress without a functioning pluralism to instill enough confidence for the opposition to be willing to use democratic processes to contest for power. Leaders must be willing to risk alternance (i.e., being voted out of office) in the interest of their historical reputations. And here in Chad? The institutions are all there, put in place in response to the prevailing wind from the donor community, upon which the country is utterly dependent. But are they real? No, not yet. These organs are weak and unimpowered. It will be a generation or more before they find their feet and begin to exert themselves, if a violent change of government doesn't intervene and take everything back to square one. Democracy, yes, but it will take decades to emerge, not the six or a dozen years hoped for by some of our DC policy wonks.

What a struggle it is for Chadians as well as sympathetic well-wishers to build an enduring structure that defies the history of centuries of indigenous slave raiding, mercilessly exploitative French colonialism, and thirty years of civil war.

Combating terrorism? It seems almost like an afterthought against the pathos of Chad's struggle for nationhood. But it's a threat we must take seriously after Nairobi and Dar es Salaam. Chad isn't a likely venue or avenue, but there's always a chance of violence when it borders Libya and Sudan, both sympathetic to those hostile to the United States. So here we watch carefully and, thank goodness, we have very good cooperation from the Chad-ians.

After all this US perspective, what are Chad's interests in our relationship? Much simpler. No grand policy objectives. They want attention and money. A little more recognition from the world's superpower. And a return by the United States to its rightful place among the donors. Since we closed our AID and Peace Corps oper-ations here some years ago, we've gone from providing $10 million to $15 million in aid annually to only $2 million to $4 million. Only this pittance, in one of the ten poorest countries of the world. So the Chadians ask why we don't like them anymore—despite their hesi-tating steps toward the democracy we exhort. (Already through the USDA food aid programs I used to manage, I've ensured that we'll do a little more. But will it be sustainable?)

So you see that there are no vital US interests at stake in Chad. But there is the oil project and the promotion of good governance and stability—not a whole lot different from our situation in many African countries.

From this abstract realm of national interests and systemic objec-tives, let me try to descend a little. Let me turn to the geographical similarities and trade relations of our two countries—perhaps the best backdrop for moving eventually to the human relationships.

To begin with, both the United States and Chad are huge, espe-cially when one factors in Chad's population of 7.5 million in an area one-sixth the size of the lower forty-eight. Like the United States, Chad has enormous climatic and geographical diversity, which I've described in earlier letters. The mountains of the north here are like Bryce Canyon, the drainage of the Chari-Logone system a minia-ture Mississippi, at least during the rainy season. And, amazingly, the population speaks over 120 different languages. So diversity in environment and people is the keynote of any comparison of Chad and America. What Chad lacks is a metropolis. N'Djamena does it in the numbers—10 percent of the country's population—but it resembles an overgrown village much more than a medium-sized American city.

Turning to trade, the numbers are infinitesimal but the prod-ucts are critical. Mostly, it comes down to food and Coca-Cola.

US exports include two big-ticket items: expertise and food aid. The expertise is in the form of demining training. Thanks to my predecessor's efforts, we obtained significant funding to train and equip an indigenous Chadian demining team, which will begin clearing mines in the north around Faya-Largeau next month. Our effort has spanned three years and can be valued in the millions of dollars.

Food aid: My forte. At present the largest US export to Chad is food aid flour, some 3,000–4,000 tons annually, monetized, with the proceeds devoted to agricultural development projects by Africare, a respected US private voluntary organization. Suffice it to say that there will be more due to my efforts.

But Chad's largest export to the US is fascinating: gum arabic. Never heard of it? It is a secretion of the ubiquitous acacia tree—like amber, a sap. It is used in tiny quantities as an emulsifier in a multitude of products—Coca-Cola, cosmetics, pharmaceuticals. After Sudan, Chad is the largest supplier to the United States, perhaps 5,000 tons worth $15 million annually. So I'm making the rounds of the principal exporters, those that ship to Europe as well as to the United States. Most US imports come from shaky Sudan, so there's an interest in diversifying origins.

But to really understand what these exports mean in human terms, you need to get out of the statistics and office meetings. After a half-hour discussion, Ali Annadif (younger brother of the foreign minister) invited me to visit his "*dépôts.*" En route he reminded me that he ships about 2,000 tons annually to the United States, about half of our imports from Chad. He had already described how his agents buy the gum arabic in small quantities from peasants or local merchants in the Sahelian zone and send it in big bags to N'Djamena a few tons at a time throughout the December–March harvest period.

The car pulled up before a nondescript adobe structure in this *quartier* toward the northern end of town. A number of men of varying ages, mostly in northern garb, lounged under a sort of arcade that lined what turned out to be the front wall of the dépôt. Several rose and one or two jumped forward to escort their *patron,* i.e., Annidif. We threaded our way through a gate and were inside the dépôt.

Annadif had already proudly explained that his factory (look up the seventeenth-century meaning of the term) employed 200 women seasonally, making him one of the largest employers of women in N'Djamena. UNICEF had complimented his efforts. And before us we saw them squatting in little groups of six or seven on big polypropylene bags and cloths spread on the ground. They were beneath *hangars*, like in the market—cloth sunshades strung across rickety crooked stakes (acacia wood?) at a height of about six feet. The work of each team of women was to sort the raw gum into three categories: (1) first quality—clear, icelike in uniform globules about half an inch to an inch in diameter; (2) second quality—similarly clear, but bigger or smaller in size; and (3) discolored, mainly orangish, or that gum with trash adhering that couldn't be easily extracted. Qualities one ($1,500 per ton) and two ($800 per ton) will go to the United States, Europe, or the Far East; quality three will remain in Chad for local use. Interestingly, Annadif sends his product overland to Nigeria and out through Lagos rather than exporting through Douala, as is more common.

The dépôt was basically a large courtyard, perhaps 100 square feet, with a hundred or so women in the open area and sheds lining the walls. The outer walls were adobe, the roofs tin, and the inner walls of the sheds were like a chain-link fence with lockable gates. We turned toward the sheds. Along one wall they were all filled with big, rough bags of gum straight from the bush. Along another were the tidier fifty-kilogram bags of sorted, export-ready gum, the bags labeled "Product of Chad "in both French and English. In the corner we saw a scale and a simple stitching machine. The factory employs about thirty men in addition to the women, mainly as porters—they lug, load, weigh, stitch, and stack the bags of gum after the women have sorted it. Dismissing for a moment the European cotton, beer, and cigarette enterprises down in Moundou, this was the closest thing to an industrial enterprise I've yet seen in Chad. And most of it goes into your Coca-Cola. And a tiny portion of the secretly constituted Coke syrup eventually comes back to the bottling plant up in Farcha. The real circular linkage of Chad and America!

But perhaps the most profound link of Chad and America is in human terms. Today I was visited by a delegation of representatives of the Sara people here in N'Djamena. They wanted to officially express to me their condolences over the death of Dr. Seymour, an American, and the Albert Schweitzer of Chad. He was the founder and chief doctor at the Baptist hospital in Koumra in southern Chad, where the Sara come from. Dr. Seymour, like his father Pastor Seymour, devoted his life to serving this people, and the Sara consider him to be one of the great men of their community, so esteemed that the N'Djamena descendants of the Sara felt it incumbent upon themselves to visit the American ambassador to share their grief. The chief of the community made an opening statement explaining the contribution of the Seymour family (which continues—Dr. Seymour's son and daughter, both physicians in the United States, return to spend the entire month of February each year working in the hospital in Koumra). After the chief spoke, each of the five other visitors made brief additions to his words. The body language and pauses between their comments imparted an aura not unlike that I felt at the wake for Alphonse's daughter. It was moving. I said some predictable words about how these human relationships were the real heart of the relations between our two countries. And this is true. People like the Seymours, much more than I and the other diplomats at the embassy, represent America to this struggling, but oh-so-dignified, Chadian people.

It is true that there are few Americans in Chad—a couple of hundred, not more. But many of them become extremely devoted to the place and, like the Seymours, form deep relationships with Chadians. A surprising portion have been here fifteen or twenty years or more. There is Ellen B., the Esso sociologist, who has been in and out since her Peace Corps days here in the 1970s. There are Les and Ace at the embassy, and one or two others out there whom I haven't met yet who came with the Peace Corps and married and stayed. And some of our missionaries: Some rotate in and out on tours like us at the embassy. But the Hodges have been here nearly thirty years. And the Ortmans up in Bardaï, and others over in Abéché, and Louise D. in Bol, and others who have been here one, two, even three decades. Those that leave are also often lifelong fans: viz., my predecessor a few times removed, Ambassador Bogosian, who raves over the place for hours whenever the opportunity presents itself.

What on earth would make an American forgo the comforts and luxuries of our lifestyle to live out here in the boonies? For some of us, it's a good career step. But for those spending a decade, a generation, or more? What dedication. Even for those like our missionaries and Peace Corps types, there is work to be done back home in the ghettos and slums (relatively speaking) of our own cities. So why devote a life to Chad?

Perhaps by the time I leave I'll have a better understanding, but let me hazard a guess. There is something about the hardship that is intrinsically appealing. The missionaries and the dedicated (as opposed to merely adventurous) Peace Corps types are seeking a trial of sorts. Hardship in lifestyle has an innate appeal of its own in how it tests you and in the satisfaction of getting things done in spite of it. Moreover, there is something about life here that is more elemental. We see it, even from our sheltered havens. Take, for example, my driver Chaibo who was out for several days suffering from typhoid fever and a bout of malaria at the same time. Or the tiny baby (seven pounds at three months) one of the missionaries brought to the club, hoping to adopt: The mother died in childbirth and the sixteen-year-old father's family is reluctant to yield custody, preferring the child's quiet starvation to the shame of its out-of-wedlock survival. Life and death aren't subtle here—they slap you in the face.

This is at least part of the incredible, ironic appeal of Africa. Does it explain why some choose to remain, and remain in awe of the place? And it is they, the Seymours and Les and the others, who become the essence of the relationship of Chad and America.

However close the personal relationships, there remains, of course, a vast gulf between Chad and the United States, and it will last for as long into the future as I can see or imagine. I don't just mean the distance. To express it, I cannot do better than to relate a story told at last Sunday's American Church service. Richard, who led the service, is both a preacher and a doctor.

Richard had spent the afternoon before the service with close friends at a funeral at the Muslim cemetery out beyond Farcha. The deceased was a baby boy, eight days old. It had seemed to be a healthy baby, and at six days Richard had attended the naming ceremony. Only thereafter did it become clear that the baby had antenatal tetanus. Denise, our health practitioner, was there and explained to me after the service that this meant the baby had been born with tetanus, contracted from its mother. In great frustration, Richard had gone with the father to both of N'Djamena's hospitals: Neither would admit the infant, having not the antidote for the poison. And nowhere else, scour the pharmacies of the town as they did, could Richard and father find it. So, inevitably, the baby died two days after its naming ceremony.

This then is the ultimate gulf that divides Chad from America, for this could hardly happen in America, in even our poorest ghetto neighborhoods.

How to communicate across such a divide? We at the embassy work on the abstract level, promoting the oil project and whatnot. Important as that is, it doesn't communicate across the gulf. Richard succeeds better, for he went with the baby's father from hospital to hospital, pharmacy to pharmacy, in the futile tragic search. Acts communicate more across this gulf than ideas and words, and become the deepest relationship of Chad and America.

Yours truly,

Ambassador Chris

A Trip from Heaven

August 12, 2000

R&R. Rest and Recuperation. Never during any of my overseas assignments has it been such. Rather, R&R is a whirlwind during which one tries to conduct the maximum of professional and personal business, and see the greatest number of family members and friends, in the shortest amount of time. But after ten months in N'Djamena, I decided that it was time for my first R&R, and scheduled it for the July—August time frame when rains and the expat exodus make things, in theory, the slowest here. My timing was constrained on both ends, making it difficult to allow the full length of time (four to five weeks) one normally does for R&R. There was a one-day course I wanted to take in Washington on July 25, and I needed to be at my third stop, New York, by August 3 to see god-children before their vacation departure. Thus, these parameters confined my R&R to between two and three weeks only.

When I travel, I always think of trains. Train travel is a mar-vel—you move faster than "traditional" means allow, but not so fast that you lose a sense of orderly progression. There is a pas-sage of time before you reach your destination that allows sufficient mental preparation for the new surroundings. In air travel between continents, the same end is achieved when the trip is broken by a layover of several hours in the business class lounge of an interme-diate airport—in my case, Paris. Never mind that my 11:50 p.m. flight, which would have allowed something resembling a night's sleep airborne, was delayed until 3:00 a.m. If the grogginess was increased, the layover was shortened to a comfortable handful of hours. But why, oh why, did my travel office schedule me for a United connection at the other terminal of the miserable Charles de Gaulle Airport, when a Delta flight left half an hour sooner from the terminal I flew into? It was my good fortune to encounter my colleague, our ambassador to the Central African Republic, on the same flight from N'Djamena to Paris (it originates in Bangui), and he was on the Delta flight.

But everything worked, more or less, after I lugged my luggage to Charles de Gaulle 1 and got aboard the United flight. It departed on time, reached Washington on time, and allowed me to reach my hotel in the late afternoon. Hotel? Nearly all the Washington recipi-ents of this letter generously offered lodging, but I chose a hotel to avoid a choice among you and for proximity to the State Depart-ment, where I would spend the business days of my week in the city.

After ten months outside it, my immediate reaction to the United States was that it is green and golden. After ten months in the Sa-hel, the Dulles Access Road was a verdant parkway of lush, relaxing plant life, even in summer. And one sensed the renowned prosper-ity of the United States immediately, not only from the construction cranes and myriad office buildings in Northern Virginia but also from the well-kept vehicles and general tidiness along the roads. The United States TIDY? But so it seems after N'Djamena. So pardon, if you will, a chauvinistic word: America has the right degree of cleanliness and order, more than the underdeveloped world, and a definite sense of propriety, but not so much that you feel the sterility of northern Europe with every blade of grass combed into place. We are too big for that.

I don't know how to describe the incredible prosperity of America—the golden surface I saw—without being trite. Was it the new buildings going up? The cleanliness of the streets and sidewalks? The small number of homeless people begging? The general air of confidence and satisfaction in the people I spoke with? Or perhaps the real estate prices I checked, being the owner of property in the District of Columbia? Everything seemed fresh, alive, and comfortable, with an air that cost didn't matter because expenses were surmountable.

One can see his own country for what it is only after an absence—time in other lands where he has some comprehension of what life is like there, too. Tourism doesn't do it. In a few weeks floating on the surface of a foreign nation's façade, too often you see the image it wants to project to outsiders. Even those of us there diplomatically see only a little deeper into the country—but it is these images we depart from when we look at our own land again when we go home. Such was my preparation for the glittering United States.

So let me jump in. The best and worst of the America I visited this summer is its prosperity, a two-edged sword.

Is it possible that America today is even more prosperous than it was a year ago when I left it? How can I describe the visual, non-visceral aspect of the wealth that struck me as I strode its streets? Was it the tidiness, contrasting with the shabby Washington I remembered of a decade ago? Or was it the purposefulness and confidence of the people who walked vigorously by me? Such a pace and activity, even in August! The construction along the Dulles access road, echoed in town, where practically an entire city block had been leveled and excavated a block from my hotel? The restaurants and stores were full, no one hesitating to buy. And dinner for two, my first night back, cost half what I pay one of my household staff here for a month's wage. The *feeling* of this prosperity, where everyone seems to have everything they want, is overwhelming. Even the handful of street people I saw (fewer now than before, with the park across from the State Department depopulated) looked fit in comparison with their ragged N'Djamena brethren.

But this is a negative as well. In the parental house and in those of friends, I saw the mentality of unlimited affluence. One buys what one wants, what one thinks one should have, and the cost is secondary. One has no budget, and any surplus is a residual. Massive spending on home renovations? Hundreds for the weekly groceries? The new SUV? Fine wines and cognacs to accompany the steak and salmon? No thought to eating out rather than in, for it is all the same. Clothing doesn't even enter in. It is an incidental, especially in these days of casual business attire. It wasn't the specific expenses that bothered me, but the unconscious attitude. The assumption that every demand should be met, the money would come somehow, and the devil take the hindmost. But perhaps I'm only jealous, seeing that my own federal salary is capped at a fraction of that of my private-sector friends. But even this sum places me among the two dozen or so wealthiest people in Chad! And that's it—that's what bothers me about the tremendous American prosperity—the lack of a point of reference to let people know just how fortunate and affluent they are. I'm a crusty old conservative capitalist, but I can't help but ask you, do you know how the other half (or 95 percent outside the United States) live?

And there's one thing more. All that money and the conveniences it buys fail to deliver one thing: some relief from the eternal rat race of bourgeois life in America. The endless competition of work and family life. The business trip versus household errands versus quality time with the children. From that quandary, it seems, no amount of wealth buys relief. If anything, the responsibility of more material possessions intensifies the pressure.

But nonetheless America is heaven for me after ten months in Chad. Why? Well, first of all, there was a newspaper outside the door of my hotel room every morning—an actual physical thing that gave me news of events deemed important, advertising, stock prices, and all the rest, without having to log on from 5,000 miles away.

And then there's the walk to wherever I'm going. My first full day in Washington was a Sunday, and I'd reserved it for museums. So I walked from Foggy Bottom to the National Mall, arriving just as the Smithsonian was opening. That day I must have walked six or seven miles, more perhaps than in a month here in N'Djamena.

Ah! The museums! What a thrill! First, the Viking exhibit at Natural History. Then on through the sculpture garden to reach the National Gallery, with exhibits on models of Baroque architecture, Gerrit Dou, the Impressionists at Argenteuil, not to mention a peek at my favorite Mannerist and Baroque masters. Then up to the Phillips for a look at Ben Shahn's photos of New York, whetting my appetite for the days I would spend there. You cannot imagine the pleasure I felt in strolling through the cool, quiet rooms, staring at the images carefully composed to evoke some deeper sense of being.

What more impressed me? The variety. Whether in restaurants or stores, the wealth of goods and choices presented. Wal-Mart, which I got to down in Florida, is a paradise of choice, not to mention the department stores in Washington or the specialty shops there and in New York and Greenwich. How to choose among a hundred dishes on a menu? How to confine myself to my precomposed shopping list for the things I needed and would mail back to myself in Chad?

But the marvel of America is also what we do not have: no pesky servants at every turn. Instead, I have a room of my own, undisturbed whether in the hotel or the house of my parents or friends. No one hanging about, needing to know if you want lunch or dinner served, and at what hour. The freedom to move around in scant dress and come or go without alerting staff or driver. Freedom! Anonymity! Independence! Doing for yourself!

But nothing is cast in black and white. What are the inconveniences of being in America? Perhaps the most obvious is the need to carry a wallet—and to spend. Again the materialism. In Chad, I rarely bother with more than a single identification card, the embassy's, and a few dollars in CFA, the local currency, in my pocket. I'm recognized wherever I go, and I rarely need more than a few dollars in the course of a day or a week. It is a pleasure to do without. But does this seem to contradict the joy of nonrecognition I triumphed above? Of course, but such is life.

***

In fact, my time in the United States was rushed. The first days in Washington were devoted to business, consultations on a series of issues important to my work in Chad. Then I spent a week with the parents in Florida, interrupted by two day trips to see old Lagos friends and my godmother. And I needed to shop. Then came a few days in the New York area—more visiting with Lagos friends and a chance to spend some time with the families of my godchildren. Even crusty old bachelors care for posterity, and nothing would replace the chance to see these kids of various ages from two families, by happy coincidence resident within a mile of each other in Greenwich. The friends? Oh, yes, my time in Washington incorporated a very dear evening with the closest among you (largely the recipients there of these letters) that I could not have done without.

If the United States is a profane image of heaven, one must leave it and come back to reality. So after barely two weeks, not of R&R but of hectic work and visiting, I returned. For whatever unknown reasons, the embassy had booked my return from New York via Washington, but I found occasion to change that and flew out from JFK on a Monday evening. I'd arranged business meetings in Paris for the Tuesday, and felt more tired than normal in dragging through them—undoubtedly the effects of early weekend mornings in New York with the children, which I wouldn't have exchanged for anything. Or perhaps the problem was the lack of breakfast on the flight—business class notwithstanding, the Delta staff forgot me, and when I asked, too late, responded in a surly tone that I should have reminded them sooner (I guess United was better after all). It took a second night of flying to reach N'Djamena.

My flight arrived more or less on time, around 4:00 a.m. I could sense immediately that the season had changed. It was now the rains. When I'd left, they were threatening, late by a few weeks. Now from the humidity and the puddles on the tarmac, I could see that they were here. My car was there, as expected, and I was driven right home. By the time I'd checked out the house, changed clothes, and set the alarm for morning, the expediter arrived with my baggage. I was able to pull out one or two items before retiring for another few hours of sleep.

The following morning, entering the office at around 9:30 a.m., I found all in order. The DCM noted that little had happened in my brief absence, save for the exchange of one or two people in the summer rotation. I would find all as I might have expected.

Coming back from one's first US trip in an overseas assignment inevitably poses metaphysical questions. Where's home, for instance? Is "home" with friends and loved ones that one has just left back in the United States, or is it here with the routine responsibilities of daily life? In earlier assignments abroad, I didn't feel this question—in Lagos, for example, it was clear that home was there; I had close friendships, my house there was the first I'd ever had to myself, and I'd transported what little I owned into it. Now my friends and family are in the United States, not here. For however much I like the individuals I work with, there is a distance. I am Mr. Ambassador, not Chris. And here, the house is possessed by servants more than me. In contrast to my single Lagos housekeeper, who kept discreetly to the first floor, here I find myself in a goldfish bowl with servants, guards, and gardeners peering ever in. I am a transient, with most of the goods I value in storage in Washington. When coming back to Lagos, there was never a question: It was my place, where I belonged. But an ambassador, I find, is always a little aloof. By definition he is the representative, the embodiment of a distant place that is always his first frame of reference. Always a little out of place, or perhaps more accurately, between two places.

But feel no sorrow, for what speaks is not self-pity but mere melancholy, contemplative and sort of nineteenth century. I relate it because it is part of the experience.

Perhaps it is just as well that I was involuntarily launched directly back into the life of an ambassador. The week of my return coincided with the visit of our Air Force plane, which comes twice yearly. So in my first three days here, there were two day trips by air, with Chad's national day squeezed in between.

The first of these was at my own request—to Sarh, where I wanted to see the defunct textile factory. One of my back-burner goals is to explore whether there might be some interest in investment by a US company, taking advantage of the new Africa Growth and

Opportunity Act to export the resulting printed fabrics back to the United States. And so I spent a day in Sarh. First I paid the necessary duty call on the préfet, who was recovering from a three-week bout of malaria. Then I made a stop at a local private voluntary organization that helps microenterprises. (I'm more and more convinced that these are the most successful aid projects in very underdeveloped countries, and I wanted to hear of the local experience.) After that, I went to the idle meat-packing plant and on to the spinning mill. It proved to be an integrated operation; raw cotton going in and printed bolts of cloth going out. Too bad that it had been idle for the last decade. There had been a half-hearted attempt to restart it a couple of years ago, and with government subsidies, earlier in 2000 there had been a run to produce cloth designed to commemorate the century of both Sarh and N'Djamena (I was given a bolt). I was also given a paper describing the enterprise, indirectly soliciting foreign investment. The visit helped me understand some of the obvious reasons for the enterprise's failure—paying the state monopoly the world market price for cotton, when the farmers get barely a quarter of it. Will I find a US investor willing to look at this kind of risk? Perhaps, if sympathy for Africa also plays a little role.

The following day, a Friday, was Chad's fortieth anniversary of its independence from France. It was a national holiday, although I had both a morning and an afternoon event in commemoration. The morning event was essentially a military parade, organized not unlike the ceremony for the opening of the new market. I arrived with the rest of the diplomatic corps about forty-five minutes before the president. It was a chance to greet them all after my brief absence. There were representatives of some sixteen military units in place, across from and on either side of the reviewing stand in which we were seated. Again we were just to the right of the president's seat, much closer than would be the case for diplomats in America. My eyes ranged up and down the ranks opposite me. Soldiers slouched as they waited—many squatting or sprawling on the ground. Officials arrived. At some point a sergeant major blew a whistle, calling the troops to attention. They all formed up. The prime minister arrived with three cars, then the president with thirteen, including the Ford Crown Victoria I'd seen before. The sergeant major presented the troops, the president said a few words, and the units all trooped off into the nearby military camp, only to reemerge in march formation and parade by us once again. I hadn't seen the goose step since some World War II movies I watched as a kid, but here it was, crisply performed. And then it was all over as quickly as it had begun.

The highlight of my first week back, however, was the trip back up to Faya. This was to be the kick-off of Chad's demining program, the actual fieldwork of clearing mines (which it wasn't quite, in fact). We arrived at the airport at 8:00 a.m.—myself, the minister of economic cooperation who oversees Chad's demining office, the representative of the United Nations, and the Italian consul. Others came as well, and after a brief scrap over whom there was no room for, we left.

Arriving in Faya, we were met by a brand new préfet, a southerner, very enthusiastic and energetic. We proceeded to the demining center, where there was a brief ceremony with both the minister and yours truly giving remarks. His were prepared, mine off the cuff. And then to the minefields. We went south of the town, to where the main road had been blocked by mines for some fifteen years, causing all traffic to go out through the desert before coming into the town, a sixty-five-mile detour, a full day or more for the camel caravans. I thought we were blowing the first mines in what would be the ongoing effort to clear this field. But no, I learned from one of the international organization people there, this was only a demonstration. The mines we would blow had been placed for us, for show! Elsewhere this would have maddened me, but this is Africa, and I swallowed my rage—even the demonstration was progress, and brought us closer to real operations. I heard here and there some of the reasons for another three-week delay before real operations would begin: the doctor for the deminers had walked off the job, for example, because an obscure Chadian government regulation kept him from drawing danger pay for the operation. But we blew mines, we did. The minister blew the first—a small antipersonnel mine. And I blew the second—a larger collection of old stockpiled mines that were captured from Libya some twenty years ago. And in two to three weeks, the actual fieldwork of demining should be under way.

Someone had arranged for a video of the day in Faya. The

minister kindly sent me a copy. It is revealing to see ourselves as others see us! Or, perhaps, to see ourselves from several angles. If, on the one hand, the film shows me an ambassador, speaking publicly and moving around doing beneficial things for this country and the US relationship with it, it also tells me little dirty secrets like how much I've aged since coming here to Chad. When I alit from the plane just under a year ago, I felt that I was trim and vigorous, thirty-five despite my fifty years. And in this video I see the difference: the hair grayer than in the morning mirror where I still detect the blond; the extra ten pounds I would have avoided, and the stumbling in sand I would have navigated soundly, if only I'd found a way to keep my jogging up. All this, not to mention the stuttering in my presentation in French! And the film itself? Yes, it shows us blowing up the mines, my friend the minister and myself. The film is neatly spliced to put the best foot forward. But I can report it back only when it is real—when it is not a demonstration, but the real beginning of demining in an actual mine field! I hope that will happen later this month. And myself? Well , there will be a time when I again have more control of diet and exercise.

So how is it to be back?

In an earlier letter I referred to a book set in the Sarh area, entitled *Roots of Heaven.* I haven't yet read the book, so I don't know the full meaning of its title. But in at least two ways I can say that my equation of America with heaven in this letter has its roots in my experience here in Chad. First, I think I now appreciate America's magnificent achievement more than you or anyone could, without the experience of living in a land of abject poverty and political and social vulnerability.

The second factor is harder to capture. Here maybe Chad has the edge through its slower lifestyle, one in which much is immutable, family is always first, and time languishes, waiting to be filled rather than crammed with empty activity and therefore lost just the same. There is a serenity to life here that I saw to be scarce among you back there, though a little commoner for the recipients of these letters than among the general population, but scarce in comparison with Chad nonetheless. This is the missing element of heaven in America, which, again, I could not appreciate without my time here.

So how is it to be back? To have been to heaven and to return to its roots here in this poverty-stricken backwater of central Africa? The United States and Chad are worlds apart. Perhaps there is no valid way to make a comparison, try as I have in this letter. What makes sense here simply doesn't there. Yet without knowing something of both worlds, there is no way to truly appreciate either.

Regards,

Ambassador Chris

Gaps

November 26, 2000

Everywhere I look in this country I see gaps. Not just little holes of the Hans Brinker variety, but big yawning abysses. They are physical: the distance between the high, broad banks of the river and the tiny trickle of water that runs through it in the dry season. And they are social: between Chad's refined leading businessman, Mr. Doudou, with his polished French and his tailored suits, and the coarse soldier from the bush whose pay is $27 a month when he gets it. But it isn't these obvious gaps that I want to tell you about, but something more subtle: the gap, for example, in our development model for a country like Chad, or the gap between the country's institutional structure and the reality of how things happen, or between the large presence the United States projects here and the little we really do.

The gap that bothers me the most is in our development model for a country as poor and isolated as Chad. We know what works at the grassroots to help farmers or herders take the first small step beyond subsistence, and that is important because these people comprise perhaps 80 percent of the population. And we can identify a handful of critical big-ticket infrastructure needs such as paved, all-weather roads or reliable supplies of water or power. But this leaves a huge void before the country achieves sustainable economic growth, and we don't know how to bridge it.

At the most rudimentary level, what works is our self-help program. We provide grants, usually under $5,000, to local organizations that undertake a development project. They contribute at least a quarter of the cost, in cash or in kind. This year we spread $90,000 over seventeen projects: a plant nursery to support reforestation; an orchard of mango, nut, and citrus trees; a gas-powered rice mill for a village farmers' co-op; support for a women's sewing co-op; support for a women's group making mango and guava jam (it's good—they sent a sample that I'm currently enjoying on my morning toast). These projects are marvelous, and they generate incredible goodwill for the United States as well. But they are limited, taking people only a step or two beyond subsistence. They are confined to the artisanal level, limited by what the poor local market will absorb.

At the other end we have infrastructure. Even before leaving the United States, I had determined in my own mind that Chad's greatest "macro" development need was a good, paved, all-weather road system. A year here and a couple of thousand miles of overland travel have only confirmed my belief. And thankfully, under the rubric of "infrastructure," one of the country's four priority developmental sectors, the roads are improving. The European Union is the lead donor here, and the United States isn't contributing a dime. In my year here, paved road has increased nearly 50 percent, from about 300 to 450 miles (this in a country one-sixth the size of the lower forty-eight). But I digress—it is obvious that a few big-ticket things like roads, water, and electricity generation are critical needs.

But what comes in between? Where is the stimulus for enough economic activity to continue growth beyond the artisan scale, to provide enough revenue through taxation to maintain the roads and buy the fuel for the power plants, and so on? I don't know. Nor does anyone who has been working in the development community these past fifty years. Chad's problem can be summarized by paraphrasing the old parable: You can give a man a fish, or better, you can teach a man to fish; but if he can't sell some of the fish he catches, he'll remain stuck at the subsistence level. More bluntly, were Chad to develop its natural resources, which are mainly agricultural, it would have no market for what it might produce.

The shame of it all is that the development agencies are flush with money that can't be remuneratively invested in development here because we haven't found the right model. If we were to scour the country each year for quality self-help projects, we could expand that program manyfold, but would still only absorb a few million dollars a year—single digits. The infrastructure development is more costly, but still only makes sense up to a certain level because there is no base of economic activity that can be taxed to produce funds for maintenance. I had wondered since arriving here why there was no job-producing, economic growth–producing element in the country's priority development programs, and now I understand why. No one knows what would work. It's a big gap.

So what do the development agencies do? Sadly, they feel they must spend what they can't invest remuneratively. They compensate for the lack of a development model by endless analytical studies of economic sectors and problems. These documents form a comforting repetitive circle, renewed every few years, confirming that at least we know what the problems are even if we don't know the solutions. The conclusions are glittering generalities of theoretical guidance, but very thin on local specifics. Further comfort is drawn from the fact that studies are produced by blue-ribbon expat consultants, no expense spared, so we know those studies must be quality work even if they fail to tell us what to do to achieve economic growth.

The other thing the development folks do is equally sad. Since they don't know how to solve the problem, they spend years building their own infrastructure and delay tackling the problem. This, even more than the studies, does a very good job of eating up millions of development dollars. The beauty of this is that for anyone who knows the situation here, need for infrastructure is a very believable prerequisite, at least up to a point. And the infrastructure development is neatly quantifiable and measurable for the bean counters. But sooner or later the chickens come home to roost, and people like the US Congress ask what's being done to solve the underlying problem through all this spending. And by that time the impatient Congress will often jump on the lack of results to cut funds or terminate projects that just might be on the verge of producing.

Another thing the development agencies do is shift their focus from "hard" to "soft" activities. USAID has perfected this art. Rather than spend money on things like road construction or agricultural development projects, today it focuses its attention on democratization, capacity building, environmental awareness, and the like. By stepping away from the hard-core development problems for which we lack a model, USAID gains a whole host of process measures to demonstrate its effectiveness—the number of people contacted through such and such an activity, numbers of people trained in x-y-z, support provided to a legislature or union or vocal nongovernmental organization. And of course, sooner or later, the clock runs out on this sort of thing as well. Eventually the congressional committee wants accountability and results. It increases its scrutiny over time as it sees no obvious reduction in third-world poverty.

To summarize, the gap in development model leads to consequences that are not just ineffective but positively pernicious. Available resources and guilt feelings force the dispensing of resources beyond what can be fruitfully absorbed. The waste becomes obvious to all those outside the development circle. Scrutiny becomes more micromanaging, and the development folks become even less prone to experiment and spend even more on studies and audits to justify their activity. Development spending gets a bad name with groups such as our Congress, stifling micromanagement is introduced, and budgets get cut.

All right. I've drawn a rather far-reaching conclusion from a simple fundamental point: There's a gap in our developmental model. But I hope you'll agree that there's an element of truth here and a certain logic to my argument.

Another vast gap in Chad is what I call the "good governance gap." Like the gap in development theory, it has many facets. I could talk about the gap between policy objectives and administrative capacity. I could go on ad infinitum about the budget shortfall, the void between receipts and expenditures that began to open up in July and August and which is currently giving the IMF fits. But instead I think I'll relate the story of two recent events that display this gap more poignantly.

First, the arrest and illegal detention of two members of the embassy's locally hired guard force illustrates perfectly the chasm between laws and institutions on the one hand, and how things really work, on the other.

On a Friday morning a month or so ago, my regional security officer informed me that two days earlier, two of our local guards had been arrested and were being held at the gendarmerie without being charged. The origins of the incident reached back several days to the wee hours of a morning when the pair noticed an intoxicated loiterer with a mean stare outside an embassy residence. He responded hostilely when confronted, and the guards fetched a gendarme to arrest him and transport him to jail in a vehicle we provided. Cooperative at first, the man resisted leaving the car and was roughed up a bit before being confined to a cell. Our people didn't touch him, but only watched. Three or four days later the suspect, who turned out to be high on glue, was released and a couple of days thereafter died of injuries apparently received during incarceration.

This immediately became a big problem for the gendarmes, because the young victim was a Zaghawa, i.e., of the president's own tribe. The Zaghawa are desert people, untouchable, and rumor has it are responsible for much of the crime around town. It was then that the gendarmes, seeking cover, arrested our own two men, trying to pass off responsibility for the murder and the blood price.

When informed, I was alarmed for several reasons. First, our folks were being held unjustly on specious suspicion, i.e., that they were responsible for the beatings that led to the suspect's death. Second, due process had not been observed, as Chadian law requires that charges be filed within forty-eight hours or the suspects be released. Last, I was concerned that the arrests would have a devastating impact on the morale and work of the rest of our local guard force. I determined to elevate the matter immediately and set up a meeting for the following morning, Saturday, with the minister of the interior, who has jurisdiction over the gendarmes.

The minister is no slouch and saw immediately that the issue needed to be resolved to our satisfaction. He would phone the gendarmerie and set the matter right. And phone he did. In the afternoon, the regional security officer reported to me that he'd met with the chief of the gendarmerie. It was clear that due process hadn't been followed, and our folks should be released immediately. But the chief advised us to be patient. These were Zaghawa and, even if unimportant Zaghawa, had a certain influence. If the case were handled wrong, the family of the victim could make trouble down the road and the matter would draw out. A meeting with the family was set for Monday, when it would be explained to them that the government had taken some investigative action, but that it was unlikely that the wealthy Americans could be forced to cough up the blood price.

We decided to take the chief's advice. The RSO went off to visit our two men, taking food and water, since rations aren't the norm in Chadian jails. On Monday, our folks were formally charged, as they should have been the previous Thursday, and we set the embassy lawyer to preparing a brief to establish their innocence. Angry as we were that our employees were still held, we were advised to show continued patience. On Wednesday, a formal hearing was finally held with the state prosecutor, who determined that the charges didn't hold water, and our folks were released. I met with them, thanked them for their service and loyalty, and tried to explain that we'd gotten them out of the clink as expeditiously as we could. And, true to the counsel of our Chadian contacts, the affair ended there; the family of the deceased has been unable to trouble us further.

So there you have the strange interplay of the formal institutions of a democracy that protects individual rights, with the informal channels of power through which things really happen. Justice was done, but it was very messy, with only very rough conformity to process, and lots of irregularity around the edges. Moreover, an informal power imperative had to be placated along the way. Do you think the result would have been the same if the case hadn't involved the American embassy, and I hadn't intervened personally with the minister? What gaps there are in the form and substance of justice here!

The second story I want to tell you demonstrates another aspect of the good governance gap, the distance between intentions and actions. Earlier in the summer, in the euphoria of the World Bank vote endorsing the loan to finance the petroleum project, the government announced that a $25 million bonus payment had been received from Petronas and Chevron, the two new firms joining the reconstituted oil consortium. In actuality, it was an up-front payment against later tax benefits. In a mood of confidence and transparency, the government announced that the windfall would be spent in accordance with the Revenue Management Law—a landmark law that ensures petroleum income will be invested in Chad's priority development sectors. Great!

That was June, and now is now. By early October, word had leaked out that half the bonus had been spent, even though the College of Revenue Management, a committee to oversee expenditures, hadn't even been constituted. Major problem! The World Bank was outraged! The IMF was outraged! The US Treasury was outraged! I met with the minister of finance and officials of the presidency to convey the US concerns.

In the past few days the government of Chad, or GOC, has made public the rationale they gave me privately for spending the money: There were military spending needs to ensure the security of the country, which is prerequisite to development—i.e., fighting the rebellion in the north. There were outlays for ensuring electric power in the capital—escalating fuel costs and repairs for generators, inescapable exigencies.

So here you have a good example of the gap between fine intentions and the press of reality. Shit happens here. Things aren't neat and tidy. But even if I can be a little sympathetic toward the spending imperatives, I must insist on process. In point of fact, this is yet another blow to an already shaky confidence in the government's commitment to transparency and good governance. The GOC should have come to the donors up front to discuss the needs, and not simply spent the money it had pledged to preserve for developmental priorities. Here, as it is so often, the distance between stated intent and eventual practice is enormous.

I think these two incidents tell you more about the good governance gap than any statistics on capacity building and the like. This is the blood, sweat, and tears of life and work here.

So far I've blamed gaps on those nebulous developmental agencies and the GOC. Now I must home in on the gap that I find most frustrating personally as I try to do my work here: the gap between US presence and policy objectives on the one hand, and what we are willing to actually invest here on the other. You need to understand that two beliefs lie behind my comments. First, that US policy objectives in Chad will best be advanced by sustained economic development. And second, that the Chadians listen most to the foreign partners who invest the most in pursuit of that economic development.

By Chadian standards, the American embassy in N'Djamena is a grand presence. Only the French is bigger. With our local guard force included, we are among the dozen or so largest employers in the country. My residence is among the three or four grandest in the town, never mind that only the vast living room and swimming pool elevate it above my private house in Washington. I can't calculate with precision the cost of our presence here because it is split among several local and Washington accounts, but I reckon it to be nearly $5 million annually.

And for what? To maintain a presence, a voice, for what we actually invest in pursuing our policy objectives is barely half of what we invest in presence. Our aid has declined from some $9 million in fiscal year 1997 to only $3 million in FY 2000. It will blip up in FY 2001, but only because I've tapped my old food aid programs at the Department of Agriculture for commodities that we will monetize to raise funds for investment in agricultural development.

I don't believe that this gap between what we spend on presence, and what we're willing to invest in policy is unique to Chad. It reflects a broader failing of our Africa policy that invests tens of millions in a handful of favored countries. Perhaps $100 million a year is swallowed up in Nigeria or South Africa; what leverage could I achieve with an additional $2–$3 million here, invested as I judged best?

This gap is hardly invisible to the Chadians, either government or private folk. Why can't USAID and, especially, the Peace Corps come back? I'm asked constantly. Through bluff and bravado, I almost lie in saying that this reflects tight budgets at home, not disregard for Chad, that we remain the largest donor through multilateral organizations, etc. But the gap between presence and performance can only be partly hidden by my fancy words.

There is a comparative aspect here as well. In bilateral aid we are a smaller force than the French, the European Union, Taiwanese, and Libyans, and perhaps also the Germans, Swiss, and Saudis. How does that reflect on the world's greatest economic power when I go in to ask the Chadians, say, to support our point of view on some UN issue?

So you see that our aid, or lack there of, creates a number of additional gaps. And I haven't even mentioned the disconnect between our private sector investment, i.e., the $3.5 billion petroleum project, and our official aid. Or the gap between what we were when we had USAID and the Peace Corps here, and what we are today. So, as I try to explain all that to the Chadians, do you wonder why I'm not having fun yet?

Since I have never believed that criticism without prescription is responsible, let me give you at least a few thoughts about what to do. Of course, my advice is worth what you pay for it.

With respect to development, I don't have any answer as to a better model. But it seems to me that the development agencies should step back. They can invest in what obviously works—the micro projects at the local level, basic infrastructure like roads. And perhaps invest too in a few major sectors, such as reforestation and power generation and building schools, clinics, and wells, where results are measurable. Beyond that, they shouldn't feel compelled to spend their money. If they want to spend more, they should recognize that developing health clinics and schools will create a demand for sustaining resources over time—countries like Chad will be hard-pressed to fund these institutions over time. Development agencies should be willing to foot their ongoing, as well as start-up, costs.

With respect to the good governance gap, I can only exhort the international organizations to keep doing what they are doing. Pressure the government to adhere to best standards. My favorite metaphor for events here is a roller coaster. For a while, things are on an upswing: The World Bank votes for the pipeline loan; the government commits to use the bonus according to the Revenue Management Law; and when the rebels attack at Bardaï, they are repulsed (even while capturing lots of equipment) in what is at least a half-success for the government. But then we're over the top and plunging into an abyss of mismanagement and questionable government measures: Government spending is out of control, contracts have been issued without due process, and half the bonus has been spent. With enough pressure by the Bank and the IMF, the headlong dive is broken, and we begin, slower now, the ascent toward some new goal. But how irregular and up-and-down the course!

And what of ourselves and our lack of attention to countries like Chad? I propose a 20 percent solution. We should invest at least 20 percent of our African aid resources in the half of countries that, like Chad, get almost nothing today. But, for this 20 percent to be effective, I would ask that it be allocated as advised by the ambassador and team in country, not according to preconceived USAID programs. In Chad, this would mean a severalfold increase for our self-help activities, modest participation in the country's infrastructure development, and money for building the institutions of civil society. Ideally, we would see the Peace Corps back in some capacity. If we could go from $3 million annually back to $6–$7 million, and if the embassy could design the spending plan, the impact would be enormous.

Even as I conclude this epistle, a crisis has gripped the country, illustrating yet another gap. In the heart of the Sahelian zone, some forty miles northwest of the town of Ati, lies a well. Its possession has been contested for years by two closely related tribes of Arab herders, and four years ago the local authorities closed the well, unable to resolve the dispute. A week ago the local préfet, for reasons either of great stupidity or venality, gave the well to one of the two tribes. The result was a small war that left eighty dead. President Déby, who was at a donors' conference in Geneva, rushed home and on to Ati, and personally intervened to stop the bloodshed. One of his aides who accompanied him told us that the battle was downright medieval, with mounted bands of warriors charging each other, shooting muskets and brandishing swords and locally forged lances.

The president's journey is a perfect metaphor for this gap between the modern and traditional. On Wednesday, he is in a contemporary conference room in *gutbürgerlich* Geneva, negotiating concessions in transparency and good governance against commitments of donor funding. The coffee service is punctual, the atmosphere refined and polite, if just a trifle unreal. Then a hurried flight through the black night, a change to a light aircraft capable of landing at Ati's airstrip, and last of all an overland ride through forty miles of bush — this last stage taking nearly half as long as the Geneva to N'Djamena leg of three thousand miles. So on Thursday afternoon, Déby is seated in the brush in a mud-brick hut, or perhaps beneath the shelter of a sort of tent made of the portable straw mats the nomads carry. He is playing the centuries-old role of a traditional ruler, mediating between the two unruly tribes, restoring the status quo ante bellum as best he can. He closes the well because the animosities are too sharp to permit its sharing, and doles out enough largess to each side to console them for their losses.

As I contemplate this particular gap between modernity and tradition, I contrast it in my mind with the good governance gap. Certainly the government is wrong to have spent the bonus money as it did and it needs to make amends. But I can't escape a certain sympathy for Déby and his henchmen in their need to respond as well to the imperatives of the moment. Having kept the peace in this country, more or less, for ten years is not an inconsiderable accomplishment. Our view of what should happen here is often a little too tidy and too impatient. Not all the ups and downs of the roller coaster are the fault of the leadership — only some of them.

Will you indulge me in dragging this out just a few words more? It is only to say that I hope I've been able to convey to you some sense of the fascination of these gaps and contrasts. They are what makes life here interesting and challenging. Without them N'Djamena would be very dull indeed.

Best regards,

Ambassador Chris

"The Events" from Afar

October 6, 2001

It is 4:30 p.m. on a Saturday afternoon. I've come home from a boisterous farewell cookout for an embassy couple and am seated on the porch overlooking my pool. The water is motionless. The shadows have fallen, giving the air a hint of coolness after the humid midday heat. The only sounds are African sounds—birds calling in various voices from the trees, the women in the squatters' camp beyond my rear wall pounding grain in their mortars—the most peaceful moment of the week, before the flurry of activity brought on by dusk.

Yesterday at this very moment I was at the National Assembly, attending its formal opening ceremony for the fall term. The Assembly president, who had been among the opposition presidential candidates, was just back from some months of medical leave in Paris. To my surprise, as he opened the parliament, his first words were to ask for a moment of silence in honor of the terrorist victims of New York, Washington, and Pennsylvania. We stood. Here, too, despite the languid afternoon, the world has changed.

You've no need for another dissertation of lament about the terrorist attack. My words will be of interest only if I can offer a new perspective about reactions from the vantage of this poor, isolated, developing country. That I will try to give.

To begin at the beginning, it was midafternoon when someone called my office to report that a plane had crashed into the World Trade Center. Hmm. "How big a plane?" I asked. Well, not a small plane, but maybe not big either. A little later, another call: A second plane had hit the WTC. I decided to head over to the American Club across the compound, where we get CNN, and perhaps I could see what was happening.

A dozen or so folks, embassy employees and missionaries, were present, glued to the TV. I walked in and sat behind them. There were the images of the smoke billowing up from the first wounded tower and, over and over again, the second kamikaze plane crashing into the second tower in a sudden burst of orange flame. It seemed too close, too slow motion to be real. More like a horror flick. As we sat riveted to the TV, we heard the reports that a third plane had hit the Pentagon, and that a fourth aircraft was missing—perhaps hijacked over western Pennsylvania. Then we saw the twin towers crumble before our eyes, and we heard that there were a car bomb and a fire at the State Department. Blow followed blow, and I struggled to put each into perspective, to tell myself that even the WTC didn't affect the vital core of America. Yet I couldn't stop reeling and wondering how much further it would go.

I guess that my reaction to all this was much like your own, except that I felt a horrible detachment from these events occurring in the cities dearest to me, a helplessness imposed by distance. I felt every inch in these long miles, and was suddenly more homesick than I have been since coming here. From my house that evening I dialed and dialed, finally able to reach both families of my New York friends and learn, a little before midnight, that all of you were safe. One friend worked in a damaged building adjacent to the WTC; mercifully, he hadn't been in Manhattan that day.

The sense of unreality, the worry about friends and acquaintances, the fear, the simple horror. Not knowing if it was over, or if more was to come. Those emotions I shared with you. But there was also a great sense of distance, isolation, not knowing the latest developments despite the constant TV coverage. Not being able to get beyond whatever the TV cared to portray. Lack of control over events, yes, we all felt that. But an absolute lack of control over news of them—that, perhaps, was different.

All this time, as I watched, I had a sense of something indefinable yet valuable slipping away with those lives in the WTC and the Pentagon, a sense of shelter, freedom for the individual, and supremacy all rolled together into one. On the way out that evening my DCM, a black American, shared his fears about the potential impact on our recent progress in civil liberties.

The reactions of the Chadians and third-country nationals here were overwhelmingly supportive and a great comfort. On Wednesday, the day after the attack, the president summoned me to receive his personal expression of condolence. With him were the prime minister, minister of foreign affairs, and other senior dignitaries.

On Friday, the prime minister came to sign our condolence book, along with nearly all the senior most officers of the presidency and Foreign Ministry. And so it went. Nearly all the ministers and ambassadors came, and countless others. By the end of the week, running down to our condolence book and back to greet dignitaries, I felt inundated and blessedly distracted by the torrent of expressions of sympathy.

And the letters: They began to flow in as a torrent that is only now abating. Government offices, nongovernment organizations, simple citizens; the stream seemed endless. In all, there were perhaps 200 letters and, in addition, another 200 messages in our condolence book. And the phone calls. All in all, an incredible outpouring of sympathy and support.

Delving beneath the surface, what do the Chadians really think about the disaster, and will they help us with our campaign against terrorism? I believe that their condolences are genuine and that they sincerely feel our hurt. They too are shocked. Death comes more frequently here, but is no less painful. We have also gotten great credit for the restraint of our response, and for the careful distinction our leaders have made between terrorism and Islam. I've seen the grand imam at two or three functions and he has gone out of his way to greet me cordially; after I sent him President Bush's statement from the Washington Islamic Center, he too sent a letter of condolence. We have received ample assurances of help at all levels, and I know that the government here watches carefully for any signs of fundamentalism that would be destabilizing, as in neighboring Nigeria. There has been only a little anti-American preaching in three or four mosques, nothing like the reaction in some neighboring countries. But I do have the sense that this sentiment would grow quickly if military action on our part were anything other than precisely targeted.

We held our own modest commemoration of the events on Friday, September 14, in the form of a noontime minute of silence. The marines raised the flag back to full mast, lowered it again, and at the end of one minute hoisted and lowered it yet again. I said a few words to the crowd, which included nearly every employee in the embassy—very few words, since I believe that the symbolism of such occasions conveys more than I can.

It surprised me just a little that our church community didn't organize a special service the Sunday following the events (it was the "off" Sunday for our biweekly services). Soon I learned that there would be a commemoration the next Sunday—organized not by our little group, but by the Chadian pastors with whom they work. They came in the strength of about a dozen. One took the role of master of ceremonies during the time normally reserved for the sermon. He said a few words himself, and passed the floor back and forth among five or six of his colleagues. They made brief statements, led prayers and chanted unfamiliar hymns, some in English, some in French. It was touching but typical of Chadians that they would want to demonstrate how they shared our grief, and offer what consolation they could.

How did the tragedy affect our little group of Americans, some forty at the embassy and a hundred more in our broader N'Djamena community? Again, probably not much differently than it did you. There were one or two blusterers who immediately started talking war and bombs, but most of us were merely somber and subdued, in shock for several days, with the vivid TV images almost surreal. It is a very quiet sadness, more of a melancholy. Something ethereal is gone that we cannot recapture, like the passing of youth and innocence. What is different here, perhaps, is the extra feeling of helplessness that comes with distance. We cannot go and give blood (the Red Cross won't take it from people who have lived in this part of Africa, anyway). We have less information than you, confined as we are to a single all-news station and the Web. It underscores our separation and isolation. But I repeat myself.

The reach of the attack stretches here as well. Several days after the events I got a call from the Africare office. One of their American employees who works up country in Abéché had finally learned that his brother was among the missing in New York, and he had come down to N'Djamena. Could we help him to get in touch with the authorities? Of course we did. Closer to home, my deputy chief of mission's brother-in-law had been booked on one of the flights but had gotten to the airport too late and missed the plane—thank goodness! Earlier today I was chatting with our public affairs officer, just back from leave. She had visited with a neighbor in

Washington, a removed New Yorker, who had lost five friends at the WTC, three office workers, a fireman, and a police officer.

"Why Do They Hate Us?" This is the title of an excellent article by Peter Ford that appeared in the September 27 issue of the *Christian Science Monitor*, and this was the question in all our minds in the days following the attacks. Does living abroad in a half-Muslim but largely secular country give me any particular insight? Not into the minds of madmen, surely, but perhaps into the ambivalence with which America is viewed around the world. My answer is simpler than Ford's, but perhaps it comes down to the same thing: Abroad, America does not, cannot, live up to its ideal. How could any country, populated by mere mortals?

To begin, let me first distinguish between domestic and foreign affairs. At home we still have lots of warts—racism, child poverty—you can name them. But our path is teleological and progressive. Overall, we have achieved a balance of prosperity and freedom and, in the words of the founders, the pursuit of happiness, that surpasses anything in human history.

Abroad, this breaks apart. First off, the United States looms so large that we are scene stealers on the world stage, especially in recent years: The downfall of communism and the magnificent US economic performance have placed us apart from all other countries. The spread of American mass culture has made us everywhere a visible presence, but not always showing our best face. Reluctant or not, our role verges on hegemony. Against this backdrop, we have a foreign policy that is, perhaps inevitably, dichotomous. On the one hand, we pursue our national interests as any country must. On the other, we propagate as no one else does the ideals of freedom, democracy, and economic liberalism that have made us so successful at home. You'll see immediately that there is a contradiction here.

This bipolar policy leads to two specific problems. First, when we practice realpolitik, we breed disenchantment and even fear. Second, our proselytizing often neglects the fact that, international conventions notwithstanding, many countries or groups of people within them do not share our liberal values. I see this clearly here in Chad where, for example, most people valued order over the quality of democracy in the presidential elections I discussed in an earlier letter.

Our preeminence and the first two problems foster a third. Everyone around the world expects, or at least hopes, that the United States will intervene to solve their own problems. I deal with this daily on the economic front, since I have so few bilateral assistance resources to contribute to Chad's development effort. It is my biggest frustration, and I'm always on the defensive explaining why we don't have the Peace Corps or USAID here. We get blamed when we fail to intervene and people know we could help if we wanted to.

Turning from economics to politics, it's really a case of damned if you do and damned if you don't. The Chadian opposition would have loved it if we had intervened to force fair elections. But the risks are tremendous. We become even bigger targets of frustration when we do intervene in ways that some people find offensive. This is so especially in countries that, like Chad or Pakistan, are deeply divided within themselves and where our intervention seems to favor one set of unshared values over another, or where our immediate national interests lead us to support a regime that doesn't share our ideal values. Add to this the healthy dose of hubris with which we have proselytized those values, unable to hide our pride in our political and economic triumph. Can you begin to understand why those who share neither our values nor our success resent us, or worse, see our idealistic talk as mere hypocritical veneer for proactive hegemony?

It is probably inevitable that some will hate us. We can't be all things to all people, and our preeminence makes us a natural target. But pride and failure to be up front about the inconsistency in our bipolar policy has made it worse. We have quite literally been blinded by our own success, unable to see ourselves as others see us. In the Middle East specifically, we have been unable to see that our policy has been hopelessly one-sided in favor of Israel and against the Palestinians.

To summarize, our magnificence has set us up as the target of resentment of those who are dissatisfied with their lot, anywhere in the world. Our own human contradictions, pride, and lack of sensitivity have allowed this resentment to be galvanized into hatred for us, innocent as we may be.

Is it premature or Pollyannaish to try to find some positive results from this great tragedy? The hope that Americans may have
a better understanding of Islam, which, after all, is a major faith in
our own country now? A more evenhanded policy in the Middle
East, more conducive to a final settlement and peace? And, perhaps most important, a healthy recognition that even the superb
United States must accept some limits, a check on the hubris that
had threatened to carry us away these past few years.

The attacks have changed our daily lives in N'Djamena only a
little. In the office there are many little taskings that have resulted.
We're also keeping in closer touch with Chadian authorities to learn
quickly of any suspicious activity that might develop. The most immediate impact was that after about ten days, Air France belatedly
informed us that they were holding all of our unclassified diplomatic pouches and would not transport any unaccompanied baggage to the United States. So, in effect, we had no outgoing mail for
roughly three weeks, until we could negotiate a much costlier arrangement with DHL. But more than anything else is the automatic
tendency to think of everything as either before or after *les evene-
ments*, "the events," as people here are coming to call the attacks. I
still remember vividly how I heard of President Kennedy's shooting and death. I am sure that the same will be true of September 11.

Best regards,

Ambassador Chris

Dueling Values

December 30, 2001

Dear Friends,

I think the best way to begin the three or four wrap-up
installments to these Chadletters is to start with the conflict between
Western (European and North American) and Chadian values. This
draws together a few strands from earlier letters, and will serve
as a platform for speculating about Chad's future—or at least its

political and economic future. I want to be delicate, avoiding both cultural chauvinism and an extreme relativism that says all cultures are equally (im)perfect in all ways and for all purposes. You be the judge of whether I succeed in that!

The morning of December 6, about 8:00 a.m., the general services officer (GSO) called my office and reported that Chaibo's wife had given birth to a stillborn baby. (My first thought was "Small wonder"; it was the woman's eleventh delivery. Days later I finally got the correct details from Chaibo: It was his eldest daughter in her first childbirth, and both she and the baby had perished; Chaibo of course knew this at the time.) Chaibo had my schedule and knew he was supposed to take me on several calls outside the embassy; he refused to go home, thinking that his first duty was to me and my convenience. I went down to the lobby and there he was, arguing with the GSO over his radio, about whether he should go or stay. I drew him out the front door where fewer people could overhear. Taking him by the arm, I told him how sorry I was about his misfortune, and said, "Je voudrais que vous soigniez pour la famille aujourd'hui!"—I wanted him to spend the day caring for his family. He was clearly shaken both by his loss and the moral dilemma between duty to employer and duty to family. I couldn't tell which shook him more. I took his hand, pumping it vigorously in mine. He looked down, muttered a few incomprehensible words and turned to go. It was clear that he had had no intention of leaving without my own direct assurance that it was okay. The backup driver, already on the spot, also pumped Chaibo's hand in sympathy, and Chaibo hurried off.

    A similar if less dramatic case had occurred exactly a week earlier with Dogo, my cook. It was a Thursday and I was giving a farewell dinner for the departing UNICEF resident representative (the equivalent of an ambassador from an international organization). When I checked in the kitchen an hour before the guests were due, Dogo assured me all was ready, and pointed to a couple of medical receipts in the little spot where the staff always leave them for me. Sheepishly, he explained that his wife (undoubtedly the second one, for whom I'd refused a loan last spring to finance the wedding), had delivered a baby girl that morning. Both were healthy, he assured me in response to my question. The receipts totaled about $25 (life, you will recall, is cheap in Chad). I plunked down the money, but at this point I was in a moral dilemma. I couldn't dismiss Dogo— he'd given me no warning, and my eight guests were due in now only forty-five minutes! Later, after the guests had come and gone with full, contented tummies, I asked Dogo if he wanted the next day off to spend with mother and child. No, he said, that wasn't necessary. But a week and a day later the naming ceremony would be held; that day he'd like off. Wouldn't any American man have prepared weeks in advance to depart quickly when the baby's birth was imminent? And insist on being present for the event? But here children are less rare than good jobs, and at a deeper cultural level, birthing is women's work; the men take credit only for the results, and then mainly if it is a boy.

These incidents are, respectively, shocking and amusing. But the exercise of some traditional values can shake the very foundations of the state. Take *dia*, which means both revenge and blood money in Chadian Arabic. This fall a prominent case drew lots of attention, including the president's.

Understand that nearly two years ago, a local customs official from the president's Bidiyat tribe was accosted by a Zaghawa military officer and accused of pocketing the duties he collected. The Zaghawa are closely related to the Bidiyat and closely aligned with them as the chief supporters (and beneficiaries) of the regime. But here the two individuals fought, with the result that the Zaghawa killed the Bidiyat. Revenge killing led to revenge killing with escalating fierceness and frequency, and by last September the two tribes most critical to the president's power were at war. Some reports told that the Zaghawa sultan, the gentleman whom I'd called upon on my way to Fada, had actually declared war against the Bidiyat. President Déby had to act. Three ministers and the commander-in-chief of the army spent most of November in the northeast trying to resolve the conflict. Meanwhile, a couple of dozen soldiers were killed in skirmishes. In the end the government paid *dia* of FCFA 300,000,000 ($420,000) plus 400 camels (worth perhaps an additional $100,000). Presumably, this was divided among the offended families on both sides of the quarrel. So, after a blood feud that makes the Hatfields and McCoys look like boy scouts, the stability of the regime was restored!

One lingering question: Just where, in the neat little table of receipts and disbursements provided by the IMF and World Bank for
purposes of budget transparency, do you enter this expenditure?

The list of divergent values goes on and on, so I'll mention only
one more in which the conflict in Western and local viewpoints is
particularly acute: child labor. On Saturdays, as like as not, I ask
Chaibo to take me down to Charles de Gaulle Street, where the
Western stores are. Always when I disembark, I'm immediately
surrounded by little girls selling peanuts in 500-gram bags. Each
will have a sack in hand, and eight or ten on a tray on her head. The
peanuts cost FCFA 500, about 65 cents, a bag. These kids have the
light work—only a few hours a day in the warm sunlight accosting
expats. I'm guessing they get perhaps FCFA 100 of the revenue from
each bag they sell. So on the rare day when they sell all their dozen
or so bags they may clear a little less than $2.00. They are smiling,
neatly dressed in their Sunday best. They don't look exploited, but
in the West we'd howl, unless it were the once a year ritual of selling Girl Scout cookies. And compare these girls to the little boys in
the countryside who, from eight or ten, take their place herding the
smaller livestock, day in and day out, during many months of the
year. Their toil is genuine and painful. Child labor is pervasive in
Chad. As soon as children become old enough to perform any economically remunerative function, the family expects it of them, and
at each grade level fewer and fewer kids return to school.

To us, this seems wrong because of the exploitation, the harsh
burden on the still fragile children, and the interference with the
education they will need to better themselves. The World Food Program gives commodities (largely American) to families of children
in 800 schools in the country, in effect bribing them to leave the kids
in class by offsetting their lost earnings. But if you were to reproach
the parents of the diminutive vendors or herders, you'd likely hear
a diatribe in return: Of course the children work, it makes the difference between whether the family has more than one meal a day!
Or whether the children have the required school uniform on days
they do attend school, etc., etc. And how do we answer that?

Let's go from the concrete to the abstract. Tradition, poverty, and
probably many other factors result in a world view that is very

different from ours, and you've probably already concluded that it explains many seeming oddities I've related hitherto. Is there a way to systematically understand these differences?

One of our local missionaries, Ruth Lienhard, wrote and published an article that tries to grapple with these value conflicts ("A 'Good Conscience' — Differences between Honor and Justice Orientation," *Missiology: An International Review*, April 2001). Her point of departure was Ruth Benedict's work distinguishing between "shame" and "guilt" cultures. (Benedict was focused on differences between Japanese and American outlooks immediately after World War II.) Guilt cultures like Western Europe or North America have absolute standards of morality that people internalize in a conscience as they grow up. For transgressions, they gain relief through confession, often publicly. In shame cultures, the reference point that matters is membership in a group rather than absolute standards. Bad behavior is wrong only if it becomes public in a way that shames the group. Personal relationships with other group members are critical. Hence, there is no feeling of guilt, no incentive for or relief from a confession, unless you've done something so egregious as to shame the whole group.

Lienhard's research in northern Cameroon and Chad has led her to redefine the critical distinction around here as one between "justice orientation" and "honor orientation." In honor-oriented societies, as in shame societies, honor is shared by the entire group (family, clan, tribe, etc.) rather than being individualistic. Honor is, in effect, performing the behavior that is expected by the group, or what reflects well on the group as a whole. Showing preference to members of one's group, or even shaming those outside the group, can constitute honorable behavior, especially under competitive circumstances, if it makes the group appear superior. This can explain everything from Chaibo's perplexity (his membership in two groups, his family and the embassy community, resulted in conflict), to *dia*, to the lavish hospitality offered to me from everyone I visit anywhere in Chad.

The justice, or guilt, orientation is strongly individualistic. It implies weaker personal relationships, but this generates a great need for internalized behavior rules that in turn result in great conformity in behavior. Hence rules, and the need for equal treatment they imply, become critical measures. This leads to a host of familiar Western norms: being on time, getting one's job done, paying debts, sticking to the facts—all those things we criticize developing countries and their citizens for not doing. The individual focus and clear rules of the game legitimize competition, but lead to guilt when one fails to play by the rules.

Lienhard goes on to discuss transgression and atonement. But for our purposes it suffices to note that in a justice society, guilt arises inwardly, driving the individual toward confession and ultimate atonement in a publicly acceptable fashion. In an honor society, shame will occur only when the transgression becomes public, and then only if the group itself feels shamed. Failure to provide hospitality to a visitor will shame the group; theft of public resources to benefit the group won't. Atonement here comes from the restoration of personal relationships within the group.

This is heavy academic stuff. Lienhard is a scholar with twenty-five years of experience in the field in this region, so I won't pretend to add to her analysis. It is, of course, simplistic in its way and doesn't give all the answers. For one thing, it totally neglects the big, important area of differences in values among the Chadians themselves. (And there are, of course, differences on the justice orientation side, where the Brits and Americans are puritans compared with the continental Europeans, who are always willing to fudge a little.) But it seems to me to make a lot of sense. If you remember that the strength of group memberships dissipates like the rings around a pebble cast in a pond, from family to clan to tribe to religious affiliation and only ultimately to being a Chadian, lots of things fall into place. The difficulty President Déby seems to have in disciplining or forbidding the corruption of his close relatives and supporters is one example. Another is child labor, where the focus is on what the child can contribute to the family rather than, as with us, on what the family can do for the individual development of the child.

In retrospect, two things amaze me. Why did it take me over two years here to focus on something as critical as these value conflicts, and to write to you about it? And why isn't something like the Benedict/Lienhard hypothesis included uppermost in the briefing materials for anyone coming out to Africa?

***

Let's look next at what Chad's honor orientation and the conflict with Western values mean both for Chad's development and for the interplay with Western development agencies. Let's begin by acknowledging that the development model and the universal goals of development are dominated by the Euro-American justice orientation. For better or for worse, this is the world economy and international system of today. Nor would most historians posit that it has triumphed accidentally. Rules, standards, transparency, fair competition, all override group loyalties and personal relationships. If the objective is a polity and economy functioning in the Western manner, there is a long list of ways in which the honor orientation is dysfunctional: (1) The individual has only a weak commitment to nation, to being a Chadian as opposed to being loyal to subgroups. Even the opposition folks who decry tribalism by the regime may only want more for their own group. (2) Both tribal favoritism and corruption (which only mean helping out family or clan) become excusable, even honorable. (3) Commitment to process is weak, be it the ordinary citizen's obedience of the law, respect for commercial practices, devotion to efficient practices in the workplace, or commitment to democratic principles and equal protection under the law. If all these nice Western ideals come into conflict with key personal relationships or group loyalties, well, you can guess the outcome.

It all becomes more complicated when modernization interrupts the calm ripple pattern of decreasing loyalties and poses conflicts between different group memberships. I am reminded of Minister Annadif's choice during the presidential elections between his government position and his political party membership, and of the interplay (conflict, sometimes) between Chad's centrally appointed and locally nominated administrative officials.

Before we Americans jump all over the Chadians, let's review a little history—it helps to try to understand why our Euro-American justice orientation differs from most of the world's. For one thing, Chad didn't share in the 600–700-year process that led to the creation of the nation-state (or the related nationalism, which exploded into the Napoleonic Wars and World Wars I and II). Put more positively, Chad had no experience like the American melting pot, which, along with continental mobility, dissolved all the competing group associations beyond the nuclear family and left only the nation as the focus of loyalty (even Europeans were shocked and impressed by the outpouring of patriotism in the wake of 9/11). At the most basic level, the question for the African, who faces many threats to his or her precarious existence, is "Who can I trust?" The answer, provided by the honor orientation, begins with family and widens, though more weakly, from there. The point struck Chadian novelist Ali Abdel-Rhamane Haggar from the opposite angle: During the student life in Moscow he portrays in *The Beggar of Hope,* all the little group of Chadians were brothers; back in Chad, they were pulled apart in different directions by their tribal, clan, or family loyalties.

So what does this mean? Chad, or any country with an honor/ shame orientation, faces enormous obstacles in achieving development and modernization as defined by today's international norms.

Now let's turn to the interplay of the development specialists with the Chadians. I don't believe either side is fully cognizant of the depth of the value divide, and the resulting dialogue is a recipe for misunderstanding, disillusionment, and disaster. Take Western aid to Africa in general. During the Cold War, it was simple — we wanted to perpetuate a certain kind of aloof, postcolonial control; we wanted the Africans to side with us, not them. The Africans repaid aid with membership in our alliances and intergovernmental associations. The relationship fit nicely into both value systems: Loyalty with reciprocity was the rule that the West demanded be obeyed, and it was also the kind of relationship that the Africans could understand from their honor perspective.

Today everything is more complicated. Western objectives are more amorphous: economic development, democratization, humanitarianism, development of commercial ties, environmental mitigation, combating transnational threats. There is an underlying sense of obligation, whether altruistic or driven by residual guilt for slavery and colonialism, by the West to help with Africa's development. But more dominant is the more and more explicit premise of the justice orientation, that aid will be contingent on a series of good-government reforms that will enhance its efficacy. If the Westerners fail to see or acknowledge that they have fundamentally changed the rules of engagement, the Africans are now bewildered because they don't understand why we are suddenly starting to demand real internal reform instead of just the politically correct rhetoric.

Let me add my own supposition that aid workers are extreme exemplars and proponents of the justice orientation. First, the natural recruitment pool is ultraliberal (in the twentieth-century meaning) do-gooders. Further, many are frustrated in their attempts to turn domestic policy in their own countries in their ideological direction, and are more vociferous in applying their notions in perfecting foreign societies, where they have the leverage of money. (I saw this in spades vis-à-vis Eastern Europe and the former Soviet Union in Washington policy debates in the mid-to-late 1990s. It is also familiar from the socialist domination of European colonial offices in the 1920s and 1930s, resulting in the introduction throughout Africa of parastatals and commodity boards, which remain a curse to this day.)

Whatever the personal views of the aid types, conflicting political pressures today reinforce their rule orientation. On the one hand, there is the imperative to help the poor countries develop at all costs—let's not worry about whether this is driven by guilt, commercial interest, or humanitarianism, or all three. But there is the terrible legacy of past aid misspent, which demands accountability. And in times of tight budgets, legislatures demand that aid dollars be well spent. This means a lot of measurement, analysis, and focus on what can be shown to work. So the transparency demanded by the justice orientation becomes ever more the touchstone for both the bilateral and IFI folks who "do" aid in Africa today. (Never mind that gobs of money are wasted by endlessly studying rather than tackling problems.)

And the mystification of the African leaders only gets deeper and deeper. Africa's political elite has rotated much less than the West's or Asia's, with its upper-echelon membership little changed since the 1960s or 1970s. So many senior officials are old school, with viewpoints formed during the Cold War. Then they supplied a relationship, we paid for it, no questions asked, and all was hunky-dory. I've seen the genuine puzzlement in the face of President Déby and his senior advisers as I try to explain the kinds of reforms that would make it interesting for USAID to come back to Chad, or that would support an exchange of high-level visits to elevate the country's stature.

The dialogue of the deaf that results is a spiral of ever greater frustrations on both sides. A World Bank/IMF mission explains its terms and conditionalities. The government grudgingly accepts, and a loan is disbursed. After a few months, "genuine" imperatives lead the government astray—in Chad it might be the need for munitions to fight the rebellion in the north, or the *dia* payment described above. The IMF team returns, charging violations and betrayal. Mea culpas, more conditionalities, and the process repeats itself. The Bank/Fund folks grow more and more frustrated as more conditionalities fail to be met, and begin to doubt the genuine commitment of the government to structural reform. The government sees the IFIs as more and more intrusive with every new demand and wonders why the foreigners can't see that it must behave as it does. Little changes in the way of good government. Loans are postponed. Then there is a grand conclave to clean up the mess, from which result a few steps toward reform and a few new loans. Then the process degenerates all over again.

Tragically, earlier attitudes and prejudices are reinforced. For the bilateral and IFI folk, largely French or Belgian among the francophones, colonial attitudes of contempt and tutelage are subconsciously reinforced. For the Chadians, the agenda comes across accordingly, as one of control rather than development. They totally miss the message, that for development in today's world, they need to adopt elements of the justice orientation—standards, rules, transparency, etc. Instead, their tendency to get what they can for themselves and their own group(s) is reinforced.

The donors' briefings I've attended after the Bank/Fund missions have conducted their structural review illustrate this perfectly. Chadians are usually not invited. The team leader begins with a summary of conditions at the end of the last review, and particular developments (mainly slippages) in the interim. He or she proceeds to describe the current round of meetings, GOC commitments, and where the team sees the country in its structural adjustment process as it departs, to return in another three to six months. The briefing is purely justice oriented, and its rules and conclusions are unassailable from this vantage point. But the entire tone is didactic and condescending; if I were a Chadian, my blood would boil and I'd walk out.

This letter has grazed a vast pasture. We've looked at behavior that is shocking for Westerners. We've seen a plausible model to explain the cultural and value divide behind it. We've set the stage for a look at Chad's political and economic prospects by speculating about how the prevailing honor orientation (and its differences from the justice orientation) create obstacles to development, according to Western rules, and are a recipe for misunderstanding with Western development officials. I hope that this admittedly academic discussion has also shed some light on the behavior described at the outset of the letter, as well as on many of the fascinating local customs and practices, such as hospitality from the destitute, that I've noted in earlier ones.

And where does that leave us? Chad has chosen (here I believe the rhetoric) to try to modernize, perhaps because it feels it has no choice. But it hasn't yet recognized that this game isn't just rhetorical, as during the Cold War, that it entails real changes in domestic behavior. The country's leaders haven't yet accepted the consequences of a decision they may have made with short-term objectives (more aid) in mind. I think it is fairly self-evident that the value complex shifts to a degree from the honor to the justice orientation as part of the modernization process. But how long will it take? Africa has been trying, and by our measures failing, for over forty years.

Best regards,

Ambassador Chris

The Sparrows Are Fat

Late February 2004

One of the first things I noticed, coming back to Washington, is the difference in the sparrows. In Chad, they're sleek little critters, thin or downright scrawny. Here, they're plump, rotund, hopping heavily among the winter-fallen leaves. Moreover, to deepen the mystery, there are no edible bugs in view here. Not a fly, or an ant, or a spider have I seen in over a month in the city. Looking back during these waning winter days, N'Djamena's balmy weather would be paradise, were it not for the flies. But how do the sparrows in this town get so fat?

Washington in general seems to be living off the fat of the land. Perhaps after Chad's destitution, the impression is inevitable. Or perhaps, over nearly five years, economic boom, minibust and recovery, swelling tax revenues and now deficits, low interest rates and asset appreciation, have all enriched the bourgeoisie of the city I am so fond of. Even bureaucrats are buying second homes.

A symptom: the gourmet supermarket. In both my novel and the Chadletters I raved about what you can find in an African market. Nonetheless, I found my first visit to a Whole Foods Market here overwhelming. There were esoteric items from every corner of the earth. And choice—twenty varieties of apples! But most shocking were the customers. The store was teeming with shoppers, their carts laden with goods at prices that struck me as astronomical. At the checkout counter, for half a dozen items, a buyer lays out a Chadian's monthly income. The market has valet parking, no less!

No, despite the official statistics, it doesn't seem to me that inflation has been dead these years I've been away. I mentioned asset inflation; housing prices in convenient neighborhoods have skyrocketed. Compared with the house I bought in 1992, I'm spending a third more for a third less house in a hot, but distinctly less desirable, neighborhood. And food prices seem sharply higher, especially for beef.

I did get one clue as to why the inflation stats are so low when I went to a Target store in the outer suburbs. In order to live in my new house for a few days before the arrival of furniture from storage and personal effects from Chad, I bought several things: an inflatable camp bed, two sheets and a pillowcase, a blanket, a pillow, a hot pot, a toaster, and a bathroom scale—nine items altogether, and for only $89! That, and cheaper housing in the exurbs, explains why the inflation figures are restrained. But on inspection, seven of the nine items were made in China, one in Brazil and only one in the United States of America. And that brings up the outsourcing issue.... But I digress.

Both of my shopping experiences raised another resettlement issue—complexity. In the Whole Foods Market and Target, the complexity of options was baffling at first, but in the end it didn't matter too much: At the market, whatever you ended up picking was expensive; at Target, it was cheap. But in ordinary and unavoidable chores like filing a travel voucher and arranging phone service, complexity hit me full face. At the State Department, even as an ambassador, I found it advisable to handle the complicated voucher process myself. To file a travel voucher and two temporary-quarters vouchers took about a dozen meetings and over twenty-four hours of work time. Transferring back to the Agriculture Department made me "special" and seemed to create endless special problems. But it isn't just the public sector that is exceptionally challenged. I ran into similar difficulties with Verizon when trying to arrange phone service in the new house before the old owner had vacated. As at State, different people told me contradictory things. On the third try, I got someone who was willing to reconnect the phone the day after the previous owner moved out without me having to do silly things like fax Verizon all of my settlement documents.

Ironically, all the stress I suffer today is from these settling-in problems that everyone must go through, and not from the job where, after fifteen years as chief of mission and USDA's general sales manager, I'm now working in a relaxed sort of in-house consultant capacity.

Washingtonians have always lived under stress and time pressure, but now more than ever. In the Metro, signs have appeared that tell you how many minutes you must wait until your train comes. Downtown there are flashing signs at intersections that tell you how many seconds you have to cross the street before the light changes. Are these symptoms of time pressure, or are they themselves stressors? And how meaningless would it all be to my Chadians, whiling away a scorching afternoon on a mat beneath a shade tree, until the sun dips enough to let them move about without pouring sweat.

There is one area in which, sadly, I find that Washington resembles Chad more now than when I left. Partisanship. In Chad, as I've told you, there is a great divide between the government and the opposition. Reading the opposition press, you'd conclude that the president and government are the devil incarnate. Any kind of exaggeration of small foibles is fair game. Alas, I now find the same lack of restraint and fair play in political discourse in Washington. If the Clintons were bad in this regard, this administration (George W's) is absolutely the worst I've ever seen.

The casualty I mourn here is truth. Politics drives all statements by the administration, Democrats, and interest groups. I find I have no confidence in the honesty or correctness of anything they say. Everything seems driven by the desire to mold opinion. There are ads to this effect everywhere. There are even ads by one interest group trying to discredit another interest group. Dueling posters on the subway! Questions well up in my mind about the statements of organizations and government agencies whose word I would previously have accepted as fact, sacrosanct. Now I feel anchorless, drifting, not being able to rely on anyone's word. Even my aggie friends are not immune from the disease. When I left for Chad, I still believed that they had, overall, a dedication to principle—that free trade would ultimately work to their advantage and enable them to prosper. Now it seems they have become divided and disharmonious, each commodity group wanting only to preserve its own subsidies.

Nastier yet are some steps by this administration that seem to undermine our democracy in the name of partisan advantage. Recess appointments of conservative judges are just the beginning. The Federal Election Commission seems now to be partisan, suppressing anti-Bush ads. There are reports of politicization of scientific research by federal agencies. And the president's behavior itself—giving an interview to selected journalists on background. For what purpose, since they couldn't report it? To flatter them and perhaps dispose them toward favorable coverage during the campaign?

In various agencies around town, my friends are more turned off by this administration than I have ever sensed before. And they are turned more toward their personal goals. There is no more idealism in public service. In my own agency, the only thing that seems to matter is pleasing the under secretary, not good public policy.

So what's good? The cultural life! Today Washington seems to have a program like New York or London. A dozen plays any night. And concerts and shows. Opera, ballet, museums, and dozens of movies. I've been overdosing on this, going out one or two evenings a week.

I've changed as well—for the better? I've bought so little since coming back. Has Chad made me immune from the ad-induced feeling that I need this gadget, book, or clothing item? Or is it only that I'm not yet ensconced in a house? But so far I've felt no pull to buy this or that, and purchased only things I've noted in advance that I need.

To conclude, it seems to me that in the last four to five years, Washington has made a quantum leap, not necessarily upward. It has become an imperial capital rather than capital of the world's greatest democracy. Not merely the capital of the wealthiest and most powerful country on earth, today it is Rome. The Rome of the first century AD, or perhaps the family Buddenbrooks in Thomas Mann's novel, where the seeds of ultimate decay were already active beneath the surface while the greatest achievements are trumpeted. And my sparrows are a pretty good metaphor for the city's well-to-do: pecking here, pecking there, becoming personally fat and wealthy, and gaining short-term partisan advantage, but without much consideration of where the country is going as a whole.

That's pretty heady. But it's nearly spring in Washington. The city is beautiful. The weather has become mild, and I see the plants sending up their leaves and stalks. In a few weeks, tulips and daffodils will run rampant, especially the daffodils that have naturalized, bank upon bank, along Rock Creek Parkway. Nature and art soar to new heights in this town, even as its essential politics are ever more venal and anticivil. Another sharp contrast, just like back in Chad. No, I won't move away in my coming retirement or second career. The dialectic here is too intriguing, and the sparrow's life too comfortable.

Best regards,

Ambassador Chris

Printed in the USA
CPSIA information can be obtained
at www.ICGtesting.com
LVHW091629021123
762913LV00005B/30